Skip·Beat!

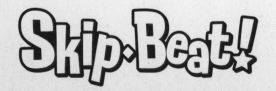

Shojo Beat

Skip·Beat!

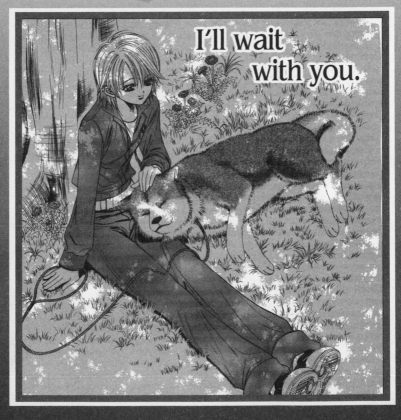

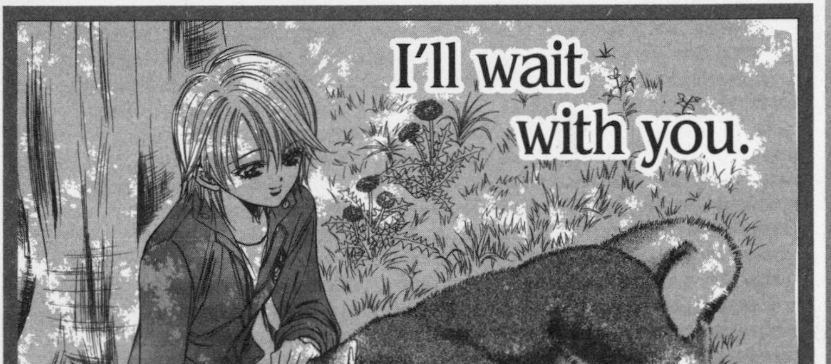
I'll wait
with you.

26

Story & Art by Yoshiki Nakamura

Skip·Beat!

Volume 26

CONTENTS

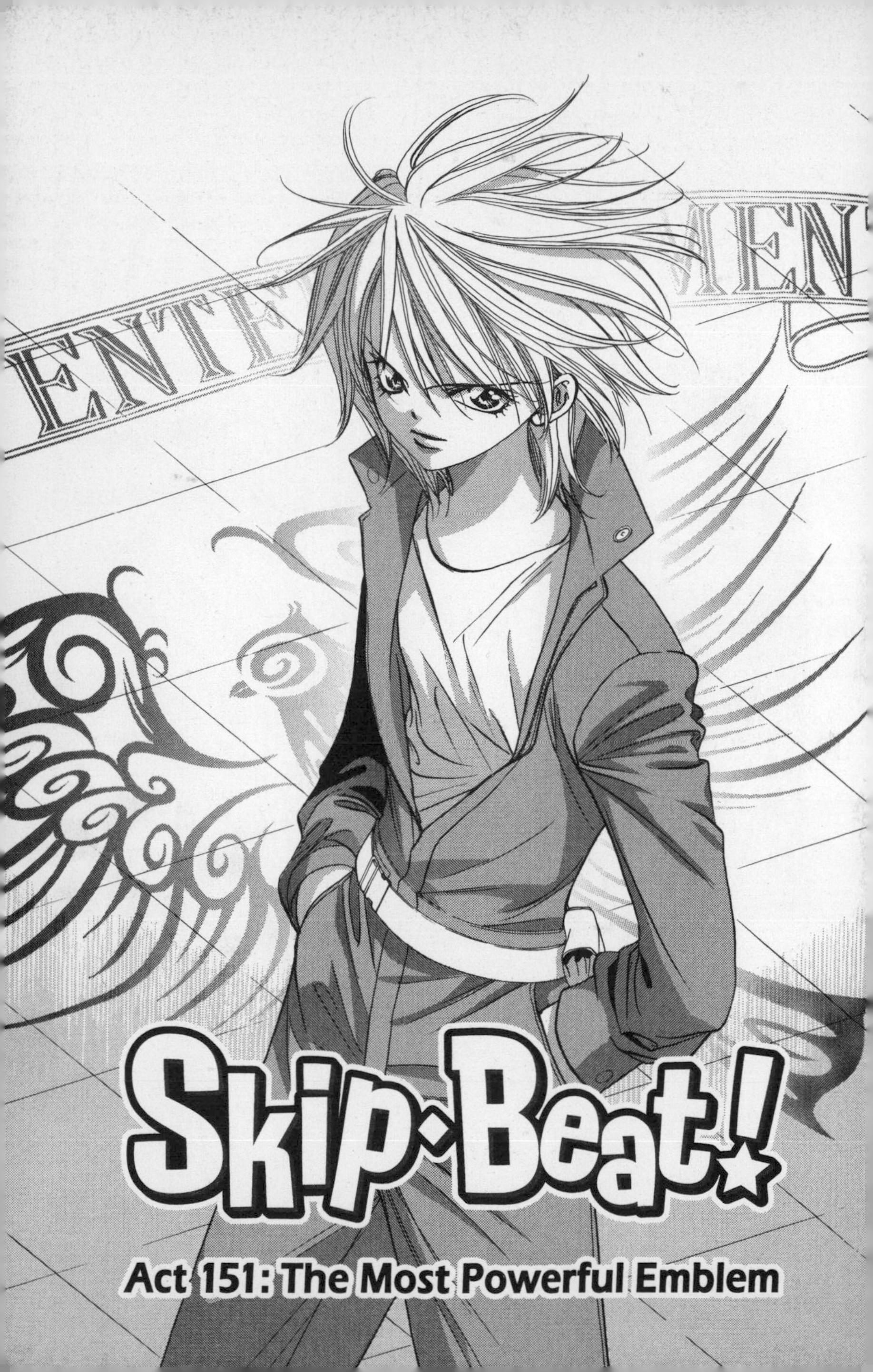
Skip·Beat!
Act 151: The Most Powerful Emblem

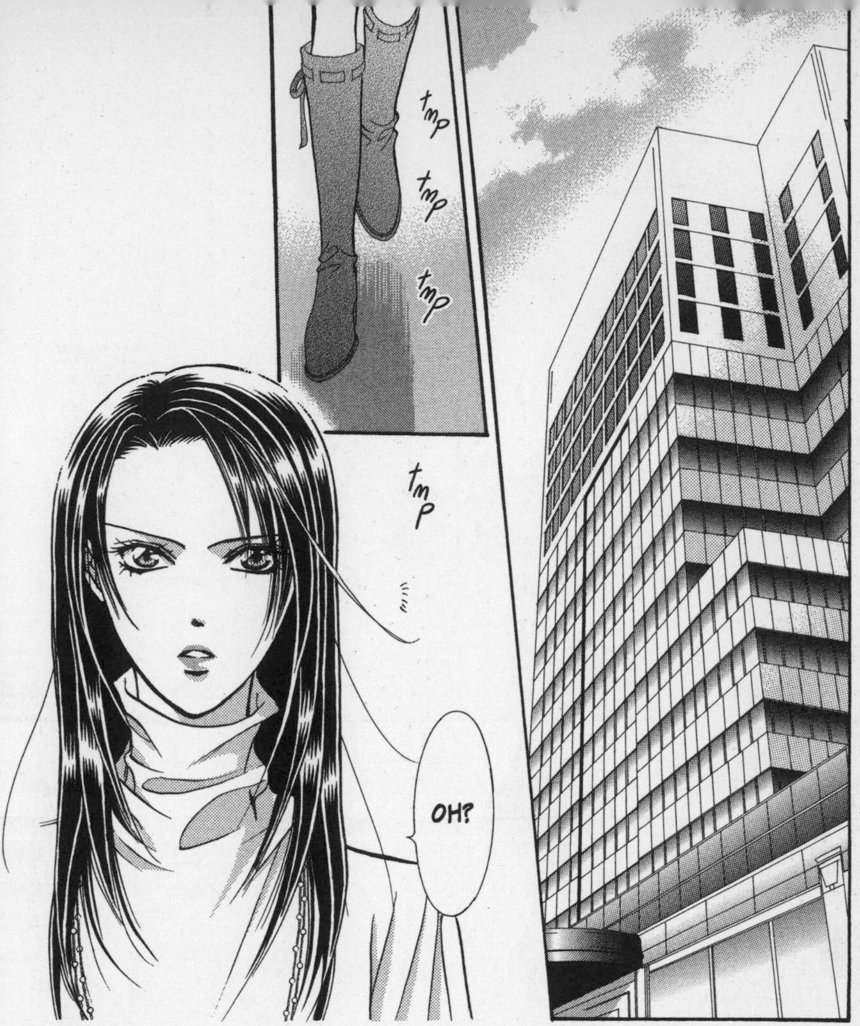
tmp
tmp
tmp
tmp
OH?

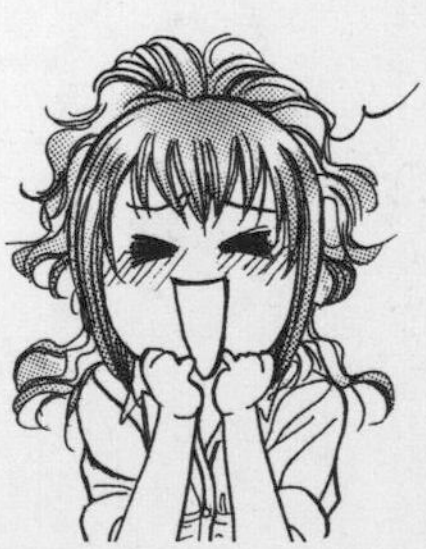

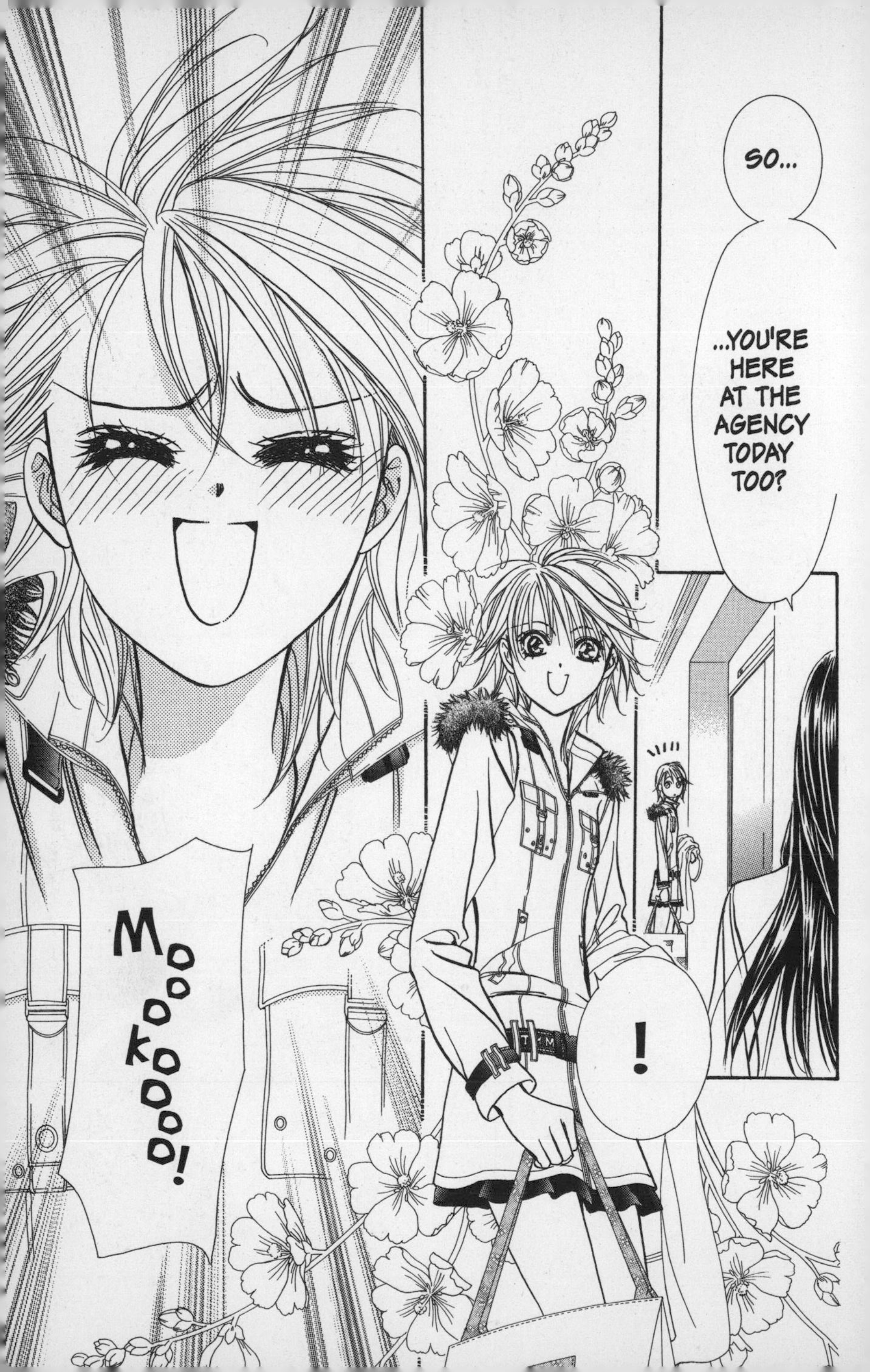
SO...
...YOU'RE HERE AT THE AGENCY TODAY TOO?
!
MOOOKOOOO!

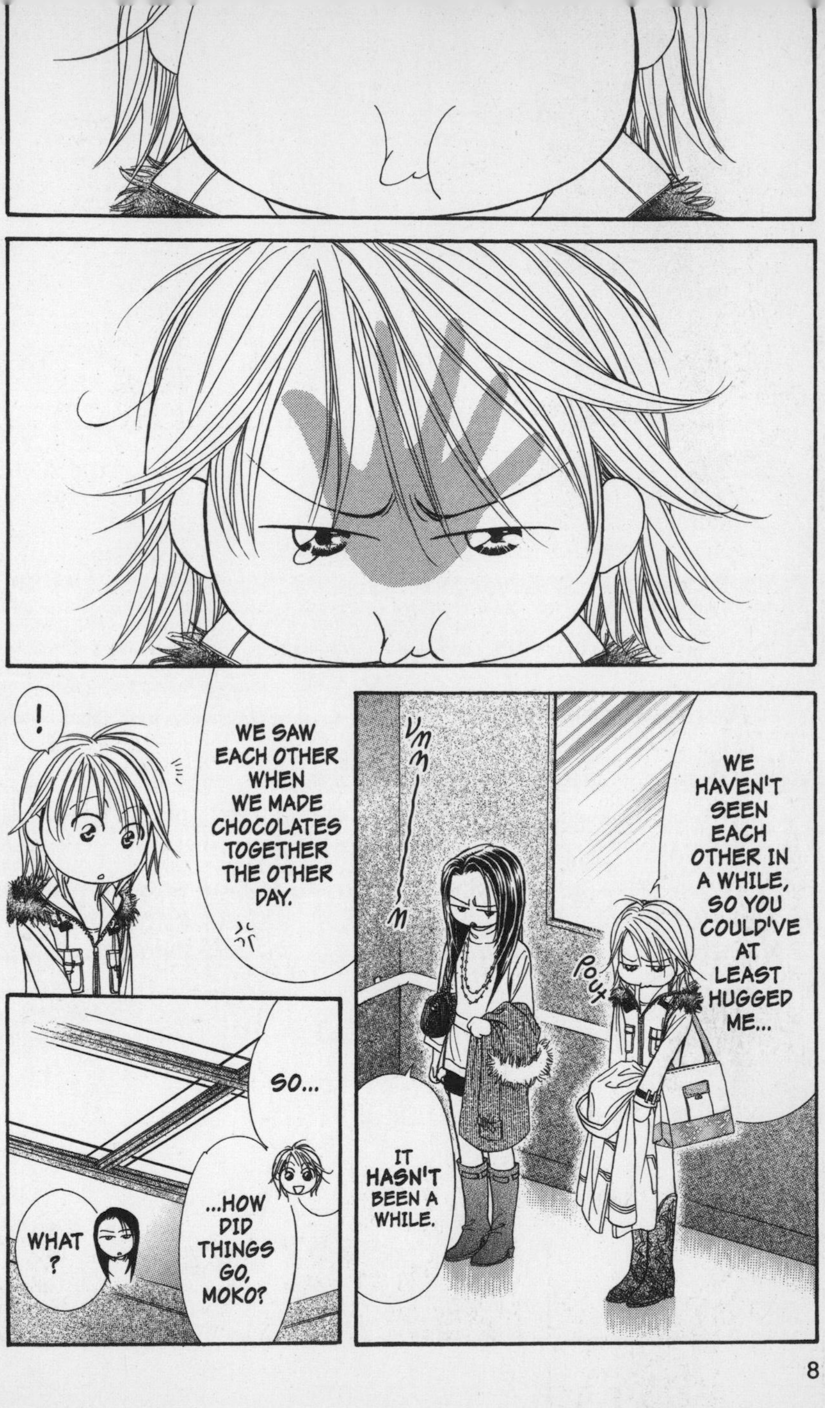
WE HAVEN'T SEEN EACH OTHER IN A WHILE, SO YOU COULD'VE AT LEAST HUGGED ME...
POUT
IT HASN'T BEEN A WHILE.
!
WE SAW EACH OTHER WHEN WE MADE CHOCOLATES TOGETHER THE OTHER DAY.
SO...
...HOW DID THINGS GO, MOKO?
WHAT?

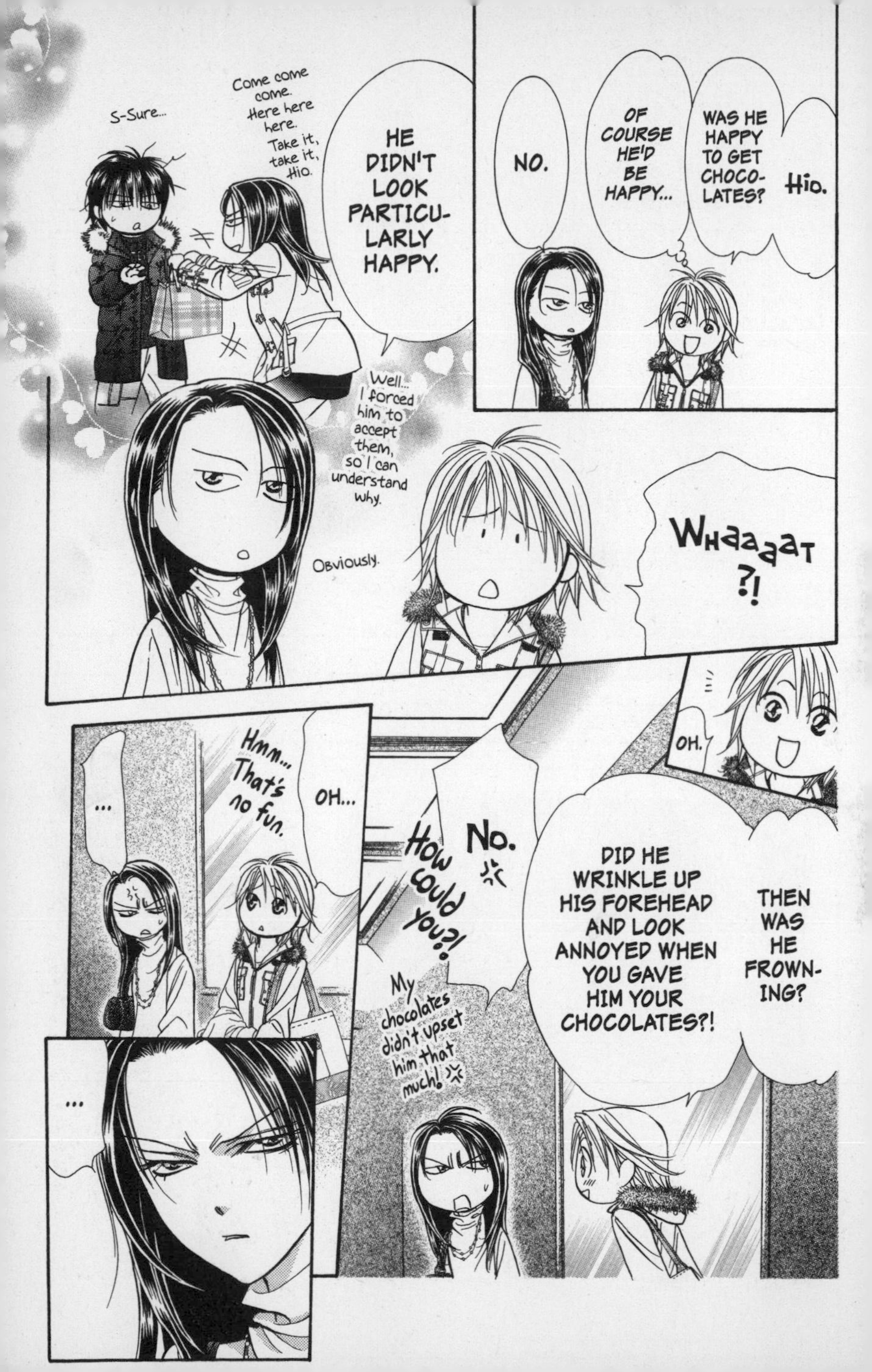
Hio.
WAS HE HAPPY TO GET CHOCOLATES?
OF COURSE HE'D BE HAPPY...
NO.
HE DIDN'T LOOK PARTICULARLY HAPPY.
Come come come. Here here here. Take it, take it, Hio.
S-Sure...
Whaaaaat?!
Well... I forced him to accept them, so I can understand why.
Obviously.
OH.
THEN WAS HE FROWNING?
DID HE WRINKLE UP HIS FOREHEAD AND LOOK ANNOYED WHEN YOU GAVE HIM YOUR CHOCOLATES?!
No.
How could you?!
My chocolates didn't upset him that much!
OH...
Hmm... That's no fun.
...
...

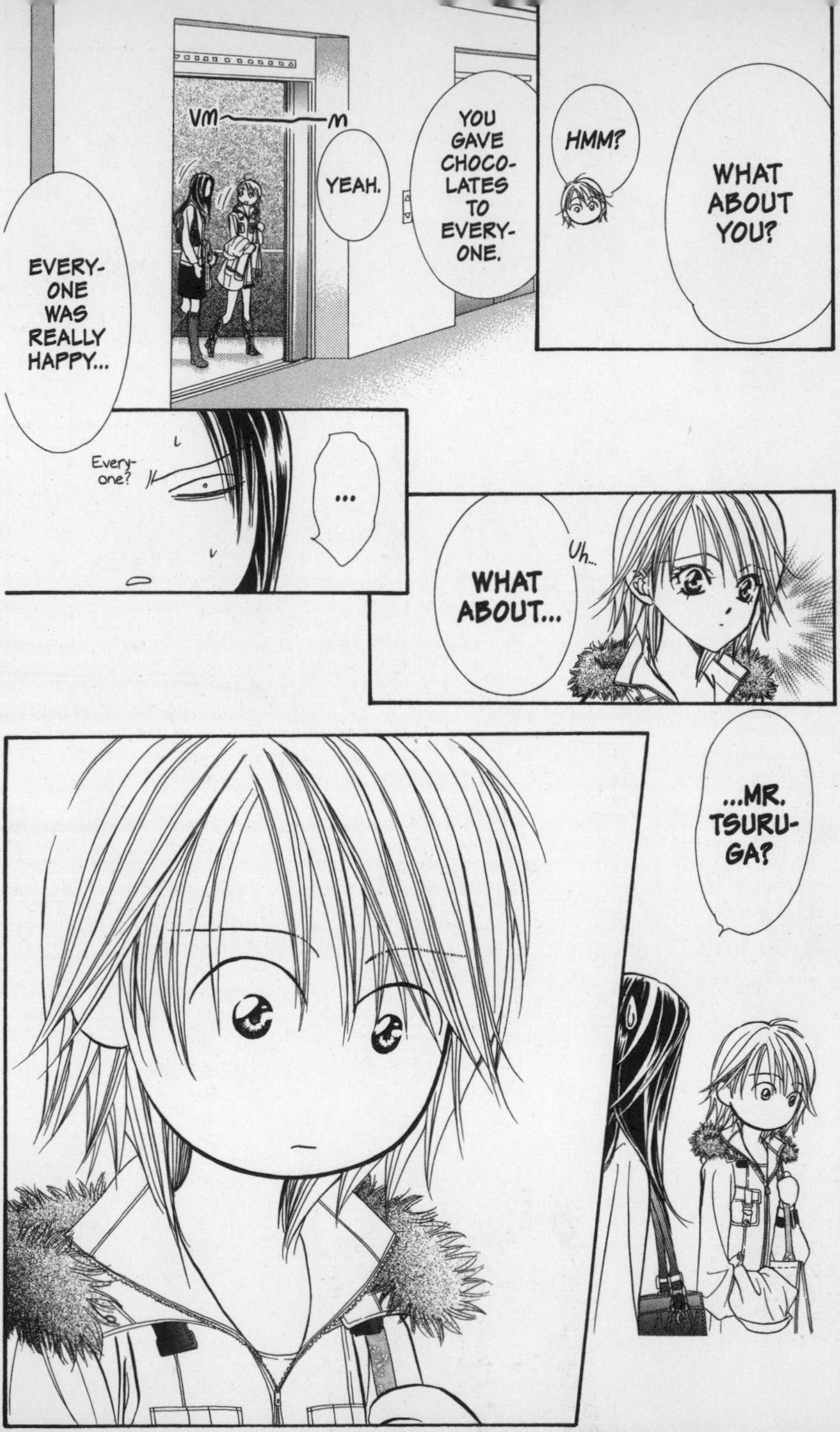
WHAT ABOUT YOU?
HMM?
YOU GAVE CHOCOLATES TO EVERYONE.
YEAH.
VM~~~m
EVERYONE WAS REALLY HAPPY...
...
Everyone?
Uh...
WHAT ABOUT...
...MR. TSURUGA?

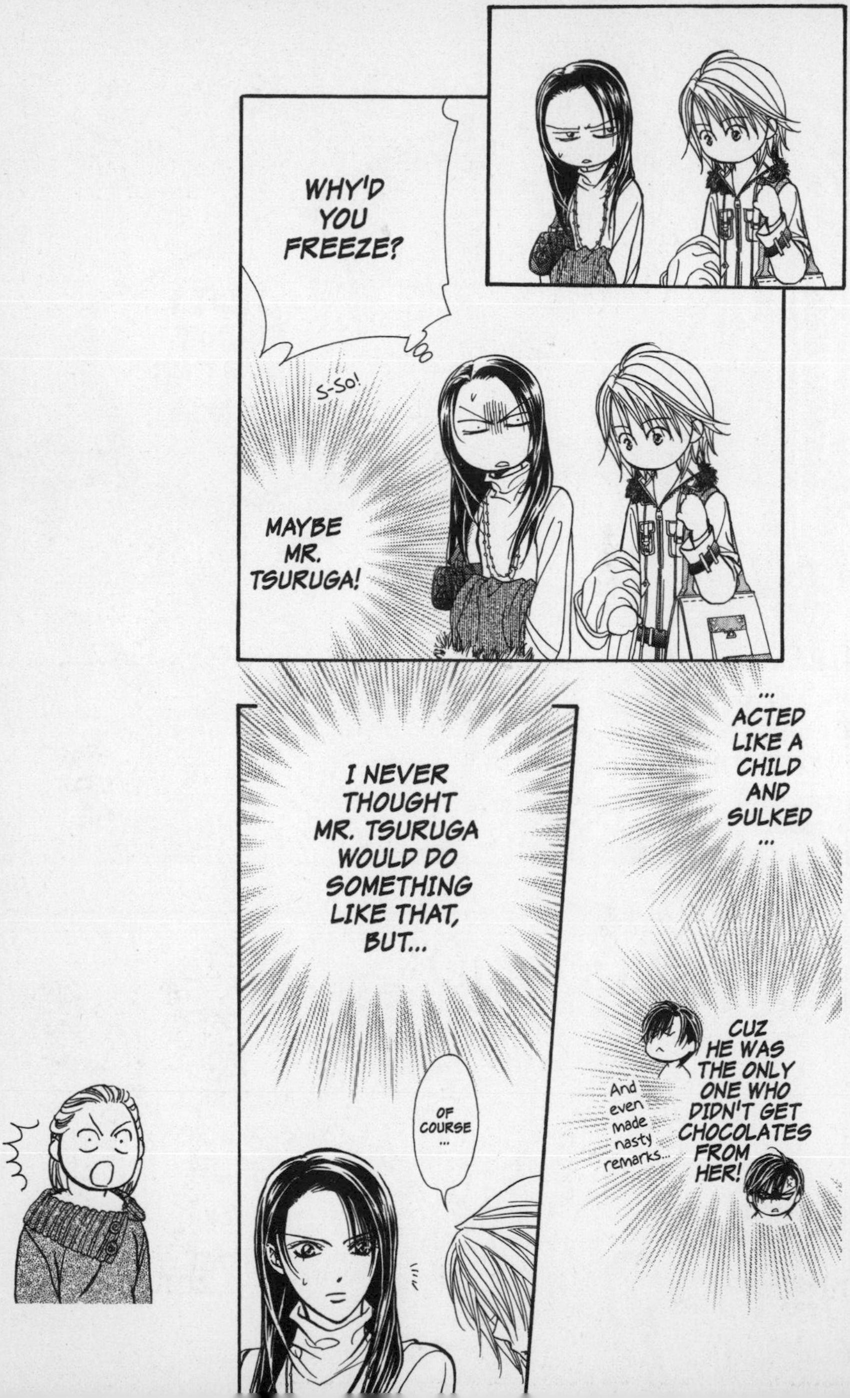
WHY'D YOU FREEZE?
S-So!
MAYBE MR. TSURUGA!
...ACTED LIKE A CHILD AND SULKED...
CUZ HE WAS THE ONLY ONE WHO DIDN'T GET CHOCOLATES FROM HER!
And even made nasty remarks...
I NEVER THOUGHT MR. TSURUGA WOULD DO SOMETHING LIKE THAT, BUT...
OF COURSE...

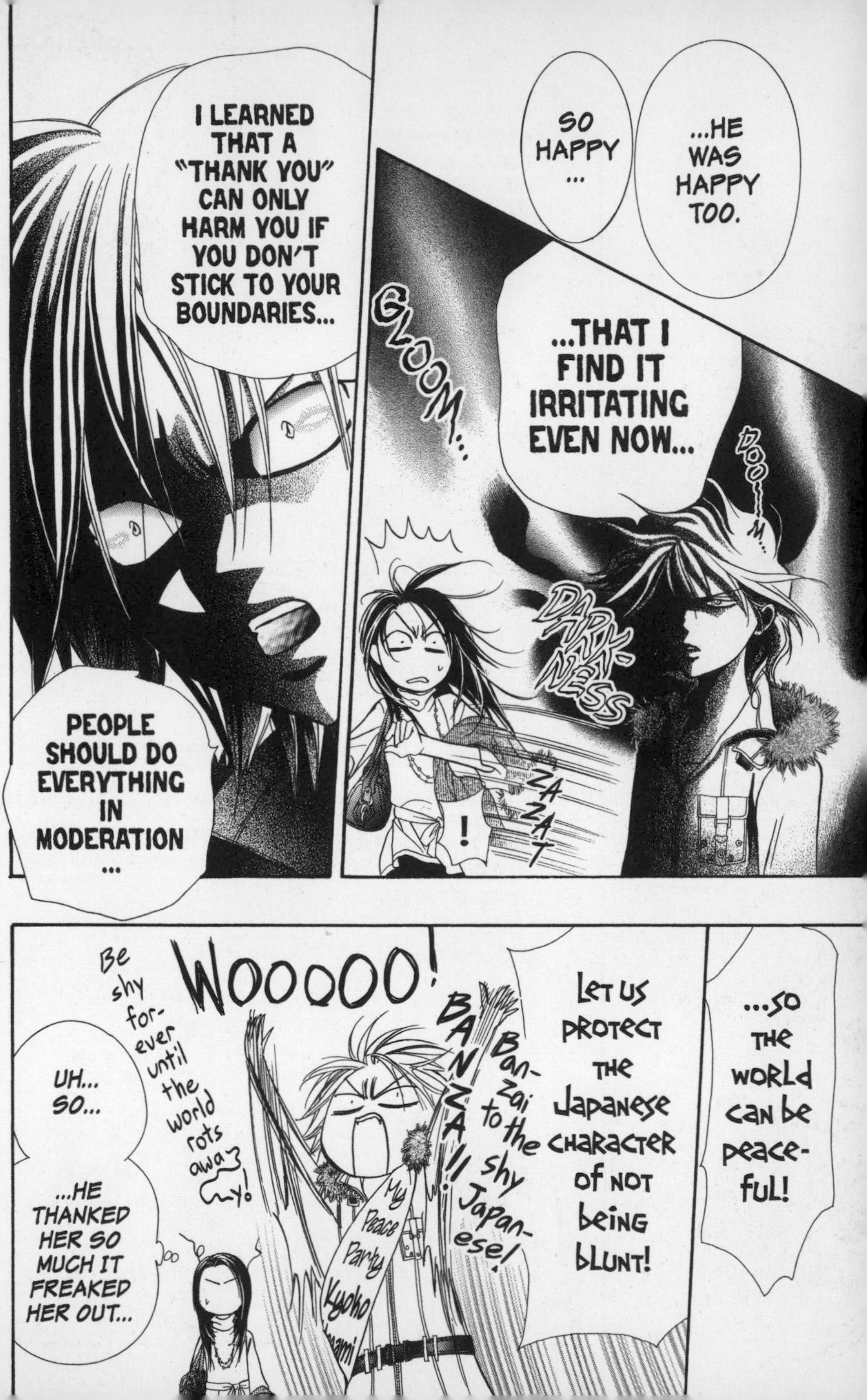
...HE WAS HAPPY TOO.
SO HAPPY...
...THAT I FIND IT IRRITATING EVEN NOW...
GLOOM...
DOOOM...
DARKNESS
ZAZAT
!
I LEARNED THAT A "THANK YOU" CAN ONLY HARM YOU IF YOU DON'T STICK TO YOUR BOUNDARIES...
PEOPLE SHOULD DO EVERYTHING IN MODERATION...
...SO THE WORLD CAN BE PEACE-FUL!
Let us PROTECT THE Japanese CHARACTER OF NOT being blunt!
Ban-zai to the shy Japan-ese!
BANZAI!!
WOOOOO!
My Peace Party Kyoko
Be shy for-ever until the world rots away-y!
UH... SO...
...HE THANKED HER SO MUCH IT FREAKED HER OUT...

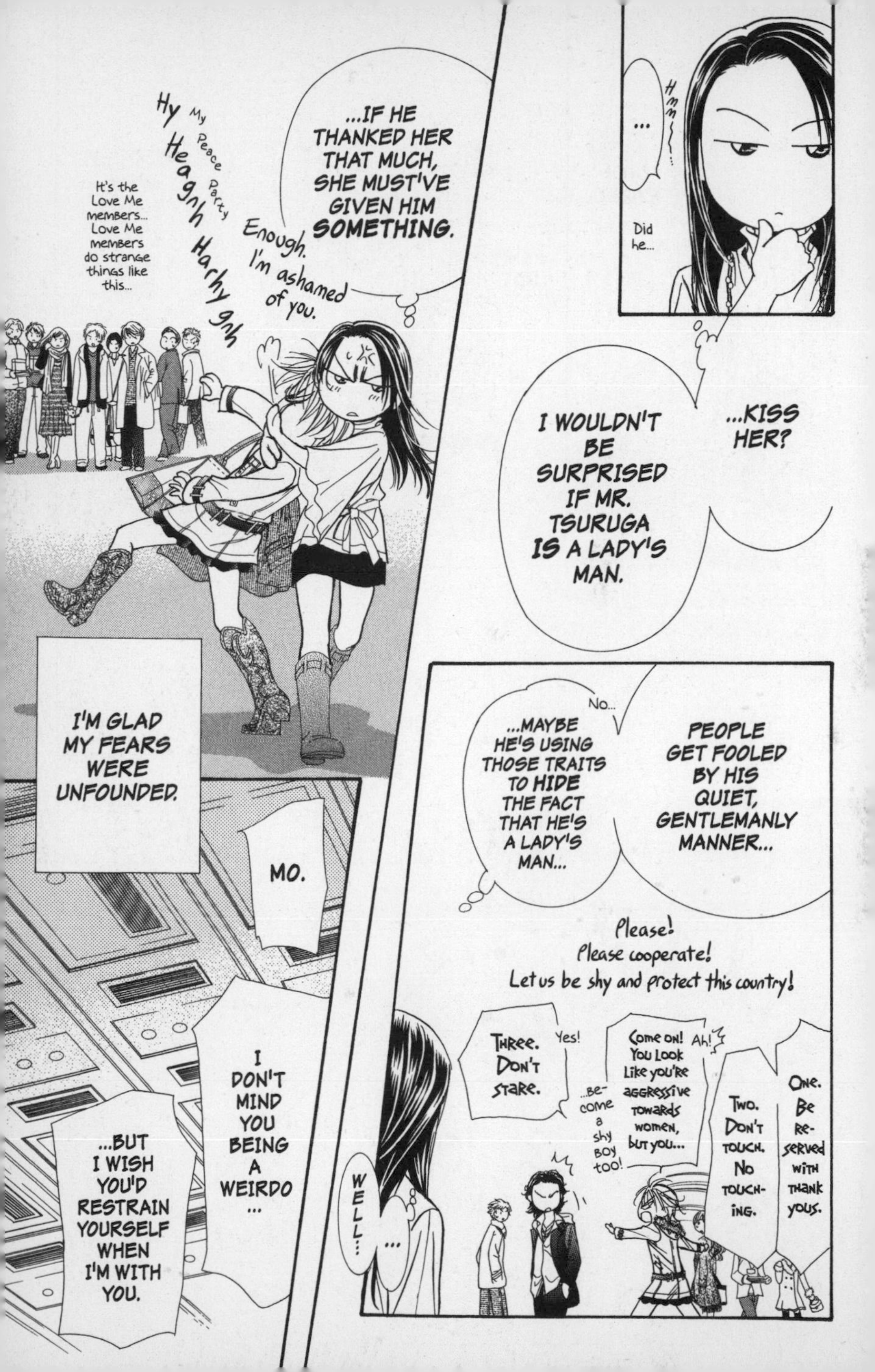
Hmm~~...
...
Did he...
...KISS HER?
I WOULDN'T BE SURPRISED IF MR. TSURUGA IS A LADY'S MAN.
PEOPLE GET FOOLED BY HIS QUIET, GENTLEMANLY MANNER...
No...
...MAYBE HE'S USING THOSE TRAITS TO HIDE THE FACT THAT HE'S A LADY'S MAN...
Please!
Please cooperate!
Let us be shy and protect this country!
One. Be reserved with thank yous.
Two. Don't touch. No touching.
Ah!
Come on! You look like you're aggressive towards women, but you...
...Become a shy boy too!
Yes!
Three. Don't stare.
WELL...
...
...IF HE THANKED HER THAT MUCH, SHE MUST'VE GIVEN HIM SOMETHING.
Enough. I'm ashamed of you.
My Peace Party
Hy Heagnh Harhy gnh
It's the Love Me members... Love Me members do strange things like this...
I'M GLAD MY FEARS WERE UNFOUNDED.
MO.
I DON'T MIND YOU BEING A WEIRDO...
...BUT I WISH YOU'D RESTRAIN YOURSELF WHEN I'M WITH YOU.

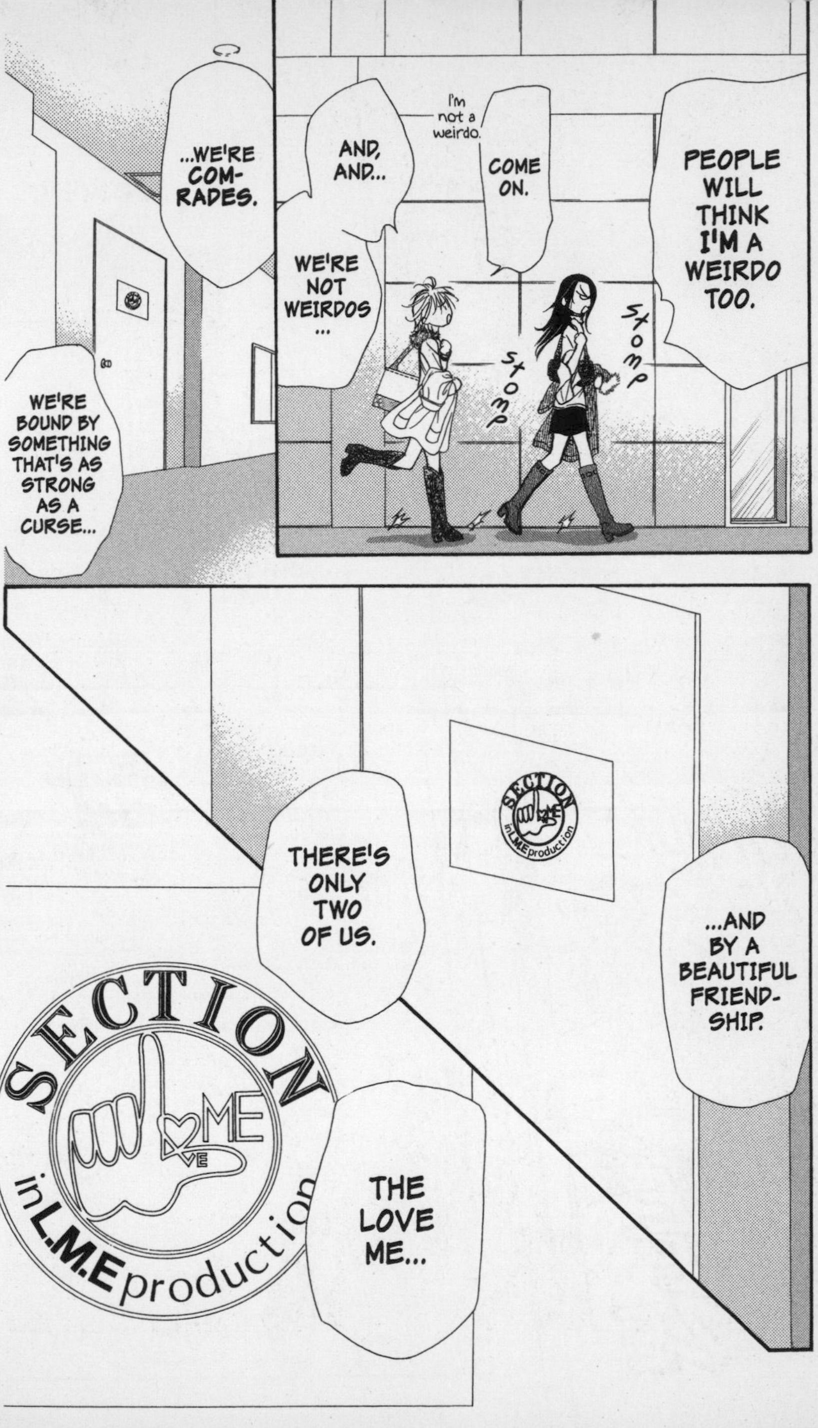
PEOPLE WILL THINK I'M A WEIRDO TOO.
COME ON.
I'm not a weirdo.
AND, AND...
WE'RE NOT WEIRDOS...
STOMP
STOMP
...WE'RE COMRADES.
WE'RE BOUND BY SOMETHING THAT'S AS STRONG AS A CURSE...
...AND BY A BEAUTIFUL FRIENDSHIP.
THERE'S ONLY TWO OF US.
SECTION inL.M.Eproduction
THE LOVE ME...
SECTION LOVE ME inL.M.Eproduction

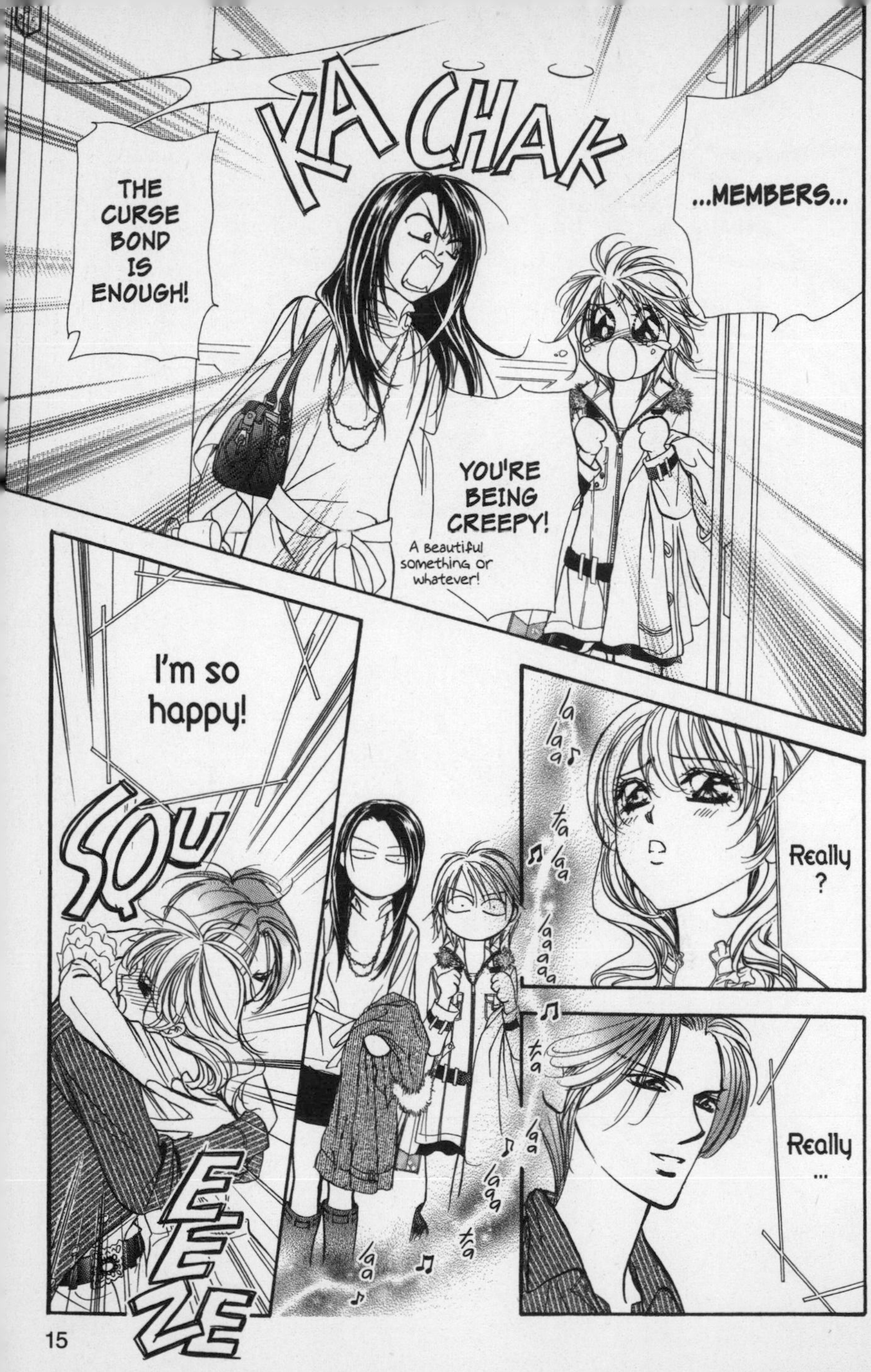
...MEMBERS...
KA CHAK
THE CURSE BOND IS ENOUGH!
YOU'RE BEING CREEPY!
A beautiful something or whatever!
Really ?
Really ...
la laa♪ tra laa laaaaa ♫ tra laa ♪ laaa tra ♫ laa ♪
I'm so happy!
SQUEEZE

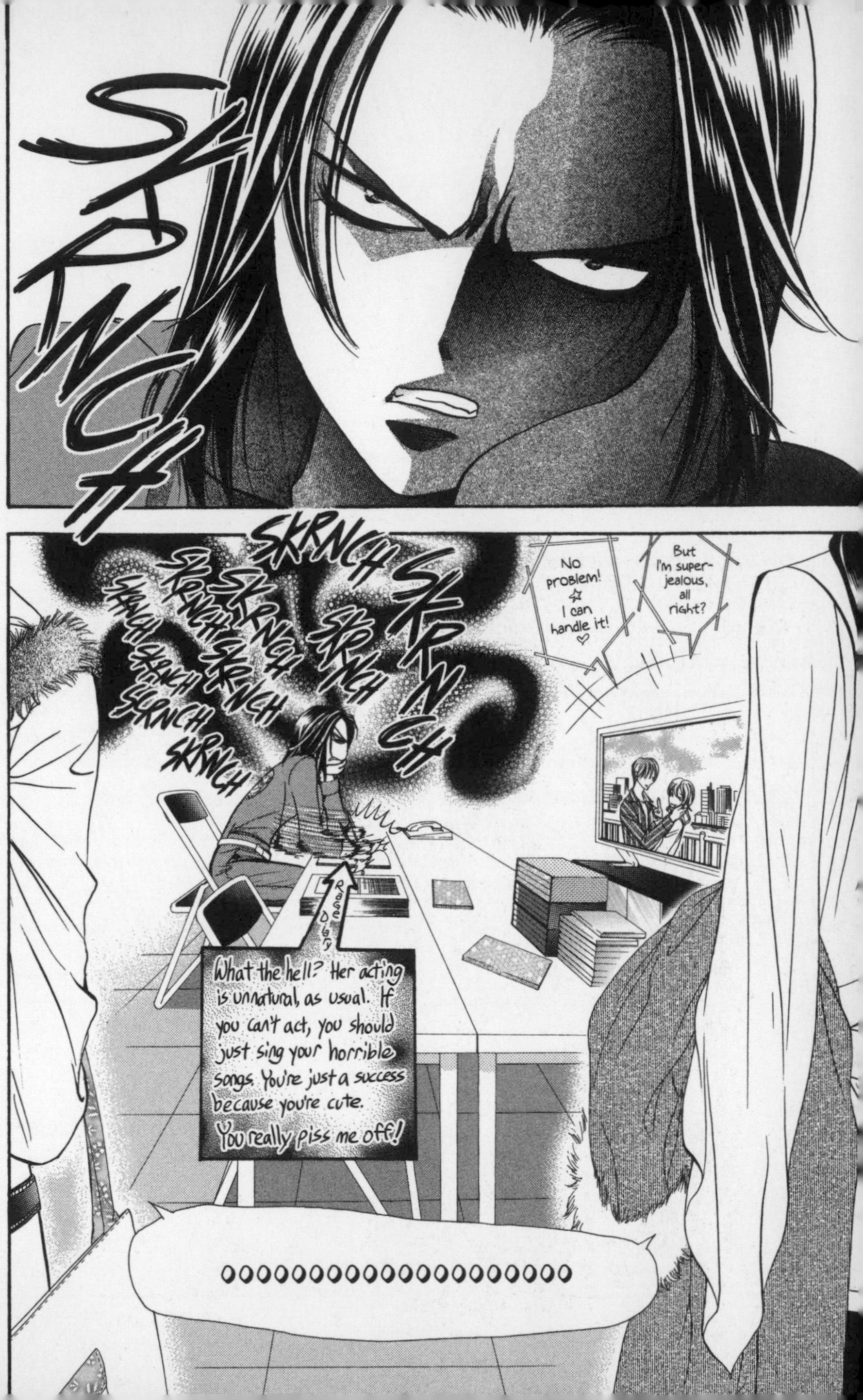
SKRNCH
SKRNCH
SKRNCH
SKRNCH
SKRNCH
SKRNCH
SKRNCH
SKRNCH
SKRNCH
SKRNCH
But I'm super-jealous, all right?
No problem! ☆ I can handle it! ♡
Rage Diary
What the hell? Her acting is unnatural, as usual. If you can't act, you should just sing your horrible songs. You're just a success because you're cute. You really piss me off!
OOOOOOOOOOOOOOOOOOOOOOO

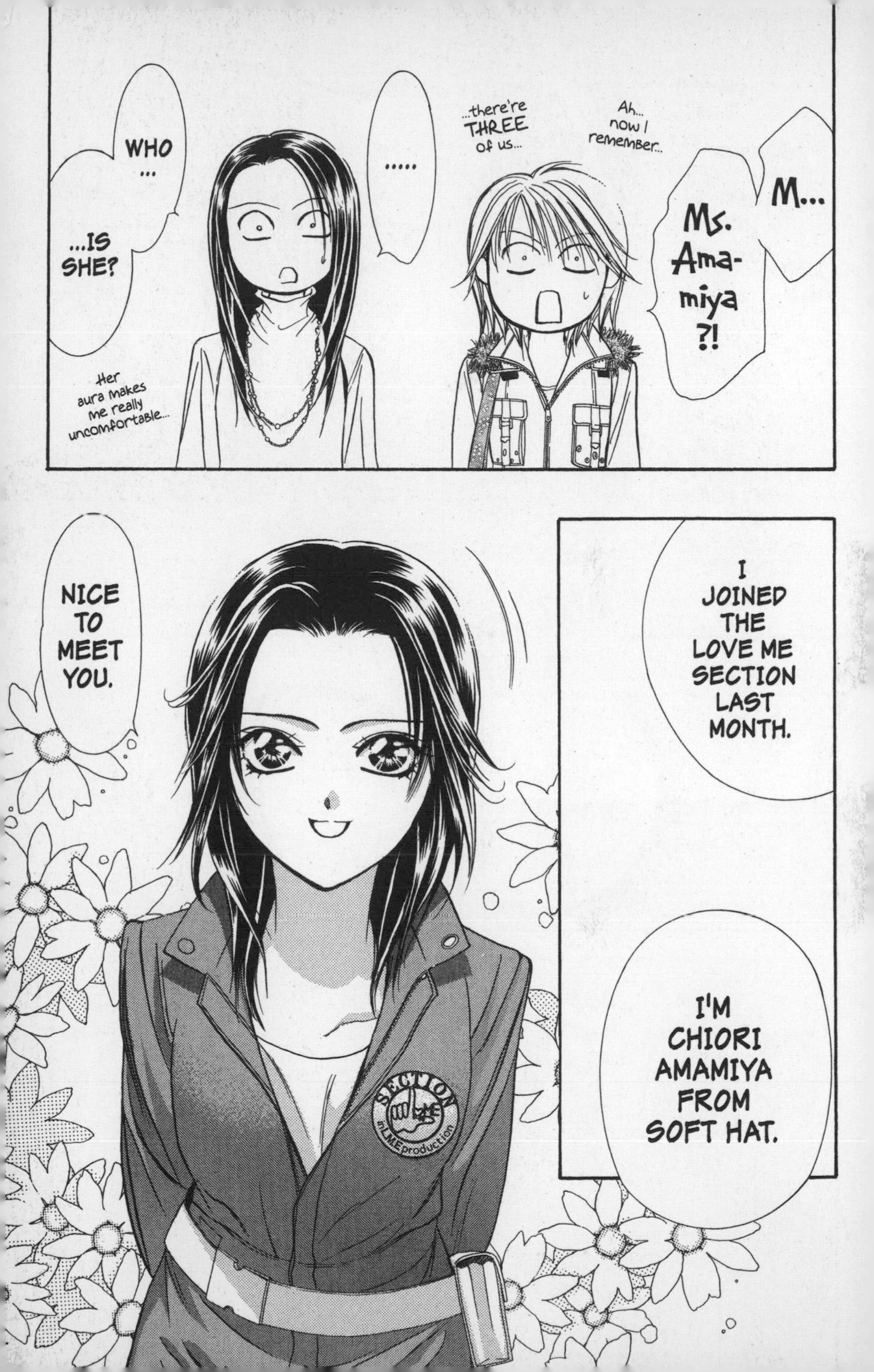
M...
Ms. Amamiya?!
Ah... now I remember...
...there're THREE of us...
.....
WHO ...
...IS SHE?
Her aura makes me really uncomfortable...
I JOINED THE LOVE ME SECTION LAST MONTH.
I'M CHIORI AMAMIYA FROM SOFT HAT.
NICE TO MEET YOU.

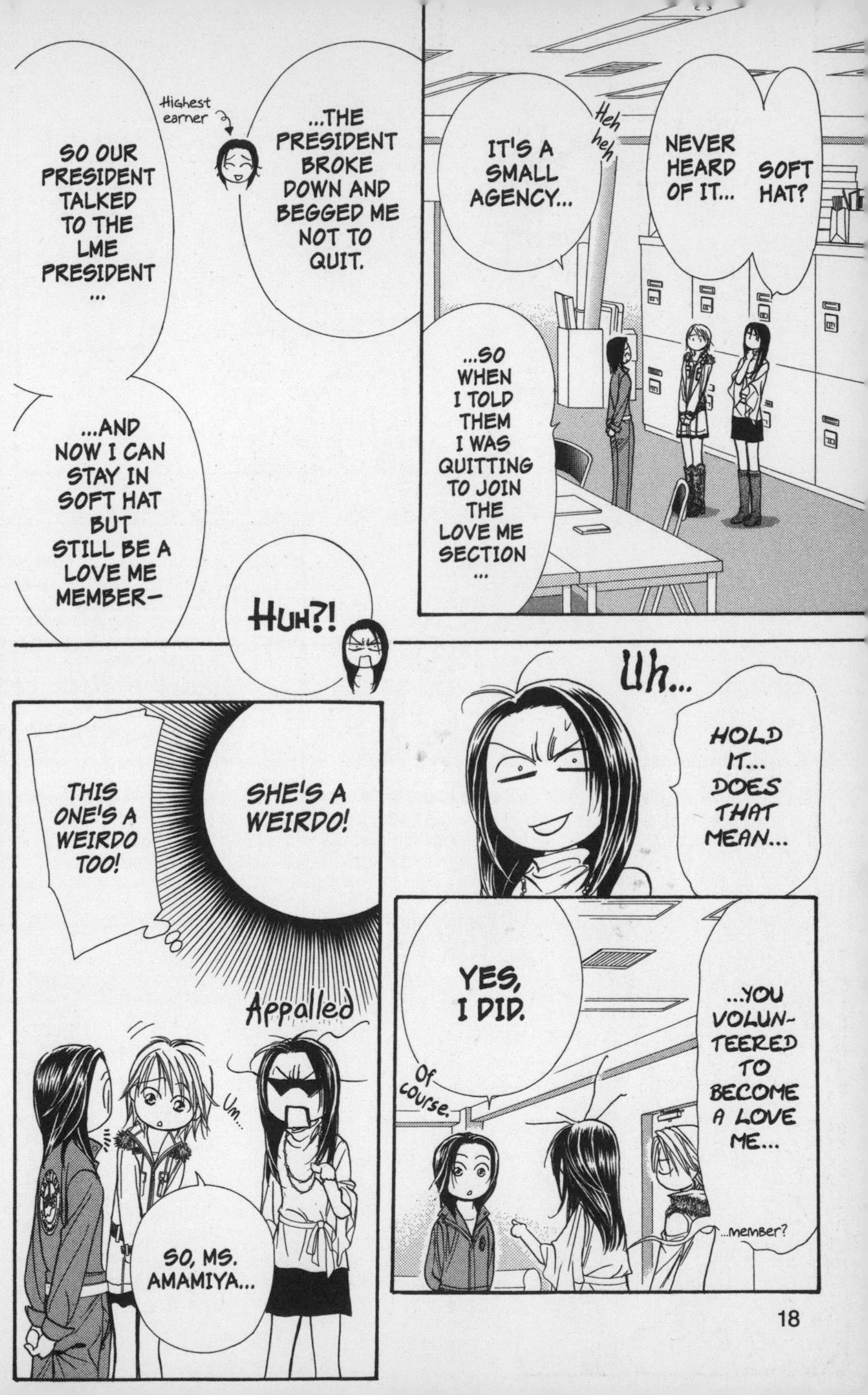
SOFT HAT?
NEVER HEARD OF IT...
Heh heh
IT'S A SMALL AGENCY...
...SO WHEN I TOLD THEM I WAS QUITTING TO JOIN THE LOVE ME SECTION ...
...THE PRESIDENT BROKE DOWN AND BEGGED ME NOT TO QUIT.
Highest earner
SO OUR PRESIDENT TALKED TO THE LME PRESIDENT ...
...AND NOW I CAN STAY IN SOFT HAT BUT STILL BE A LOVE ME MEMBER—
HUH?!
Uh...
HOLD IT... DOES THAT MEAN...
...YOU VOLUNTEERED TO BECOME A LOVE ME...
...member?
YES, I DID.
Of course.
SHE'S A WEIRDO!
THIS ONE'S A WEIRDO TOO!
Appalled
Um...
SO, MS. AMAMIYA...

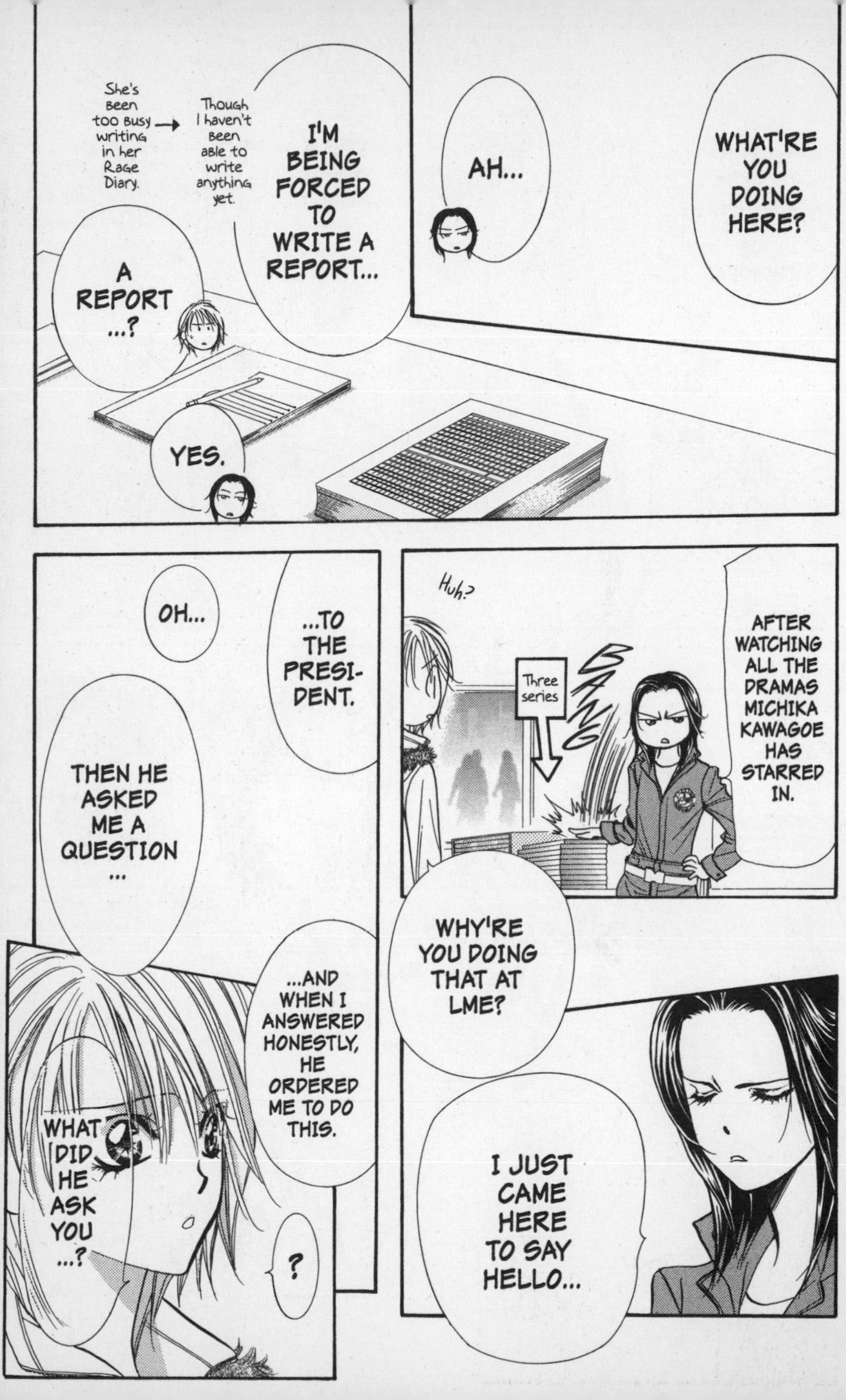
WHAT'RE YOU DOING HERE?
AH...
I'M BEING FORCED TO WRITE A REPORT...
Though I haven't been able to write anything yet.
She's been too busy writing in her Rage Diary.
A REPORT ...?
YES.
AFTER WATCHING ALL THE DRAMAS MICHIKA KAWAGOE HAS STARRED IN.
Three series
BANG
Huh?
WHY'RE YOU DOING THAT AT LME?
I JUST CAME HERE TO SAY HELLO...
...TO THE PRESI-DENT.
OH...
THEN HE ASKED ME A QUESTION ...
...AND WHEN I ANSWERED HONESTLY, HE ORDERED ME TO DO THIS.
?
WHAT DID HE ASK YOU ...?

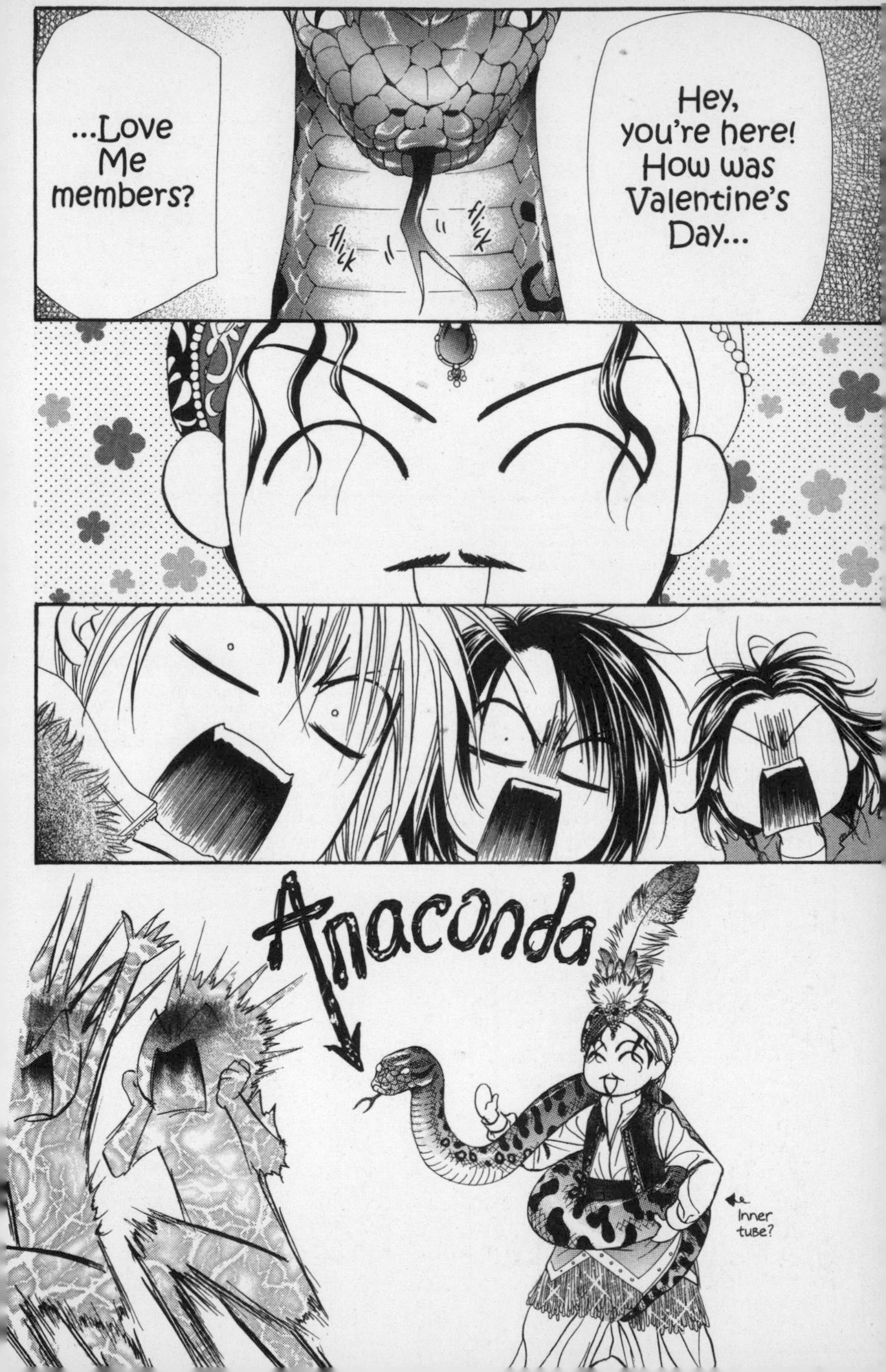
Hey, you're here! How was Valentine's Day...
...Love Me members?
flick
flick
Anaconda
Inner tube?

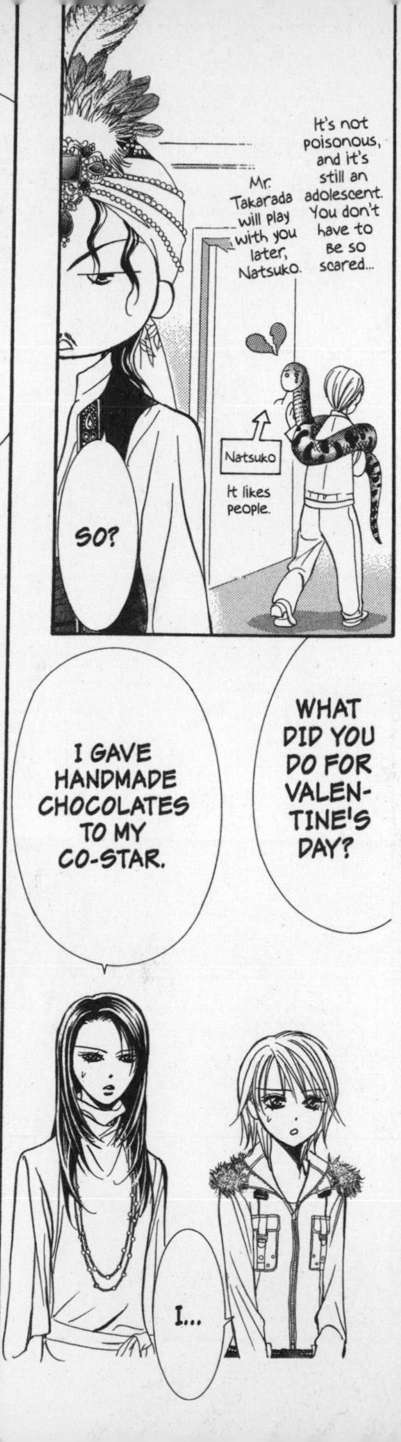
It's not poisonous, and it's still an adolescent. You don't have to be so scared...
Mr. Takarada will play with you later, Natsuko.
Natsuko
It likes people.
SO?
WHAT DID YOU DO FOR VALEN-TINE'S DAY?
I GAVE HANDMADE CHOCOLATES TO MY CO-STAR.
I...

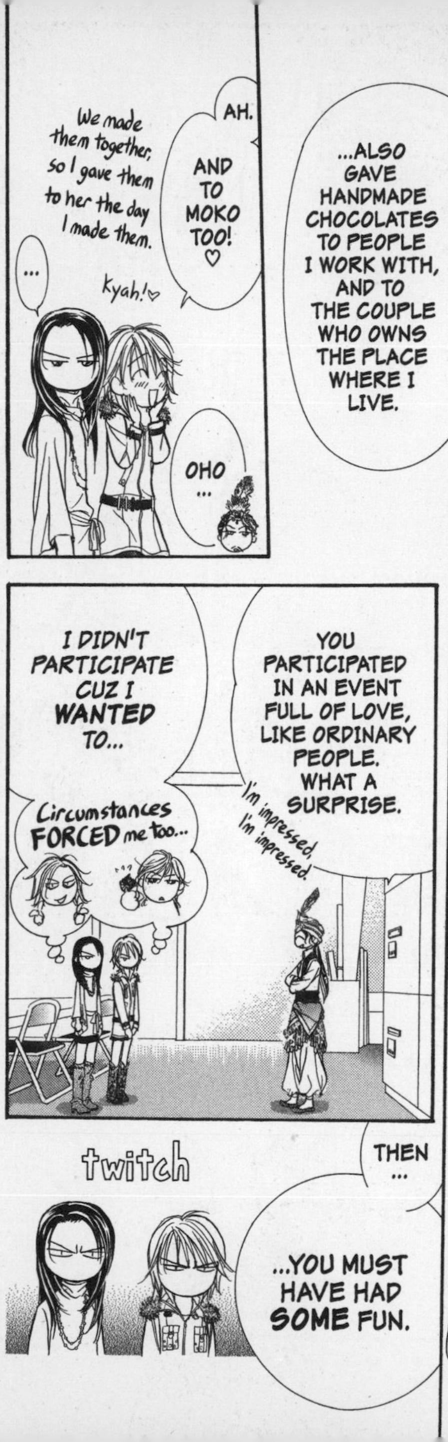
...ALSO GAVE HANDMADE CHOCOLATES TO PEOPLE I WORK WITH, AND TO THE COUPLE WHO OWNS THE PLACE WHERE I LIVE.
AH.
AND TO MOKO TOO! ♡
We made them together, so I gave them to her the day I made them.
...
Kyah!♡
OHO ...
YOU PARTICIPATED IN AN EVENT FULL OF LOVE, LIKE ORDINARY PEOPLE. WHAT A SURPRISE.
I'm impressed, I'm impressed.
I DIDN'T PARTICIPATE CUZ I WANTED TO...
Circumstances FORCED me too...
THEN ...
...YOU MUST HAVE HAD SOME FUN.
twitch

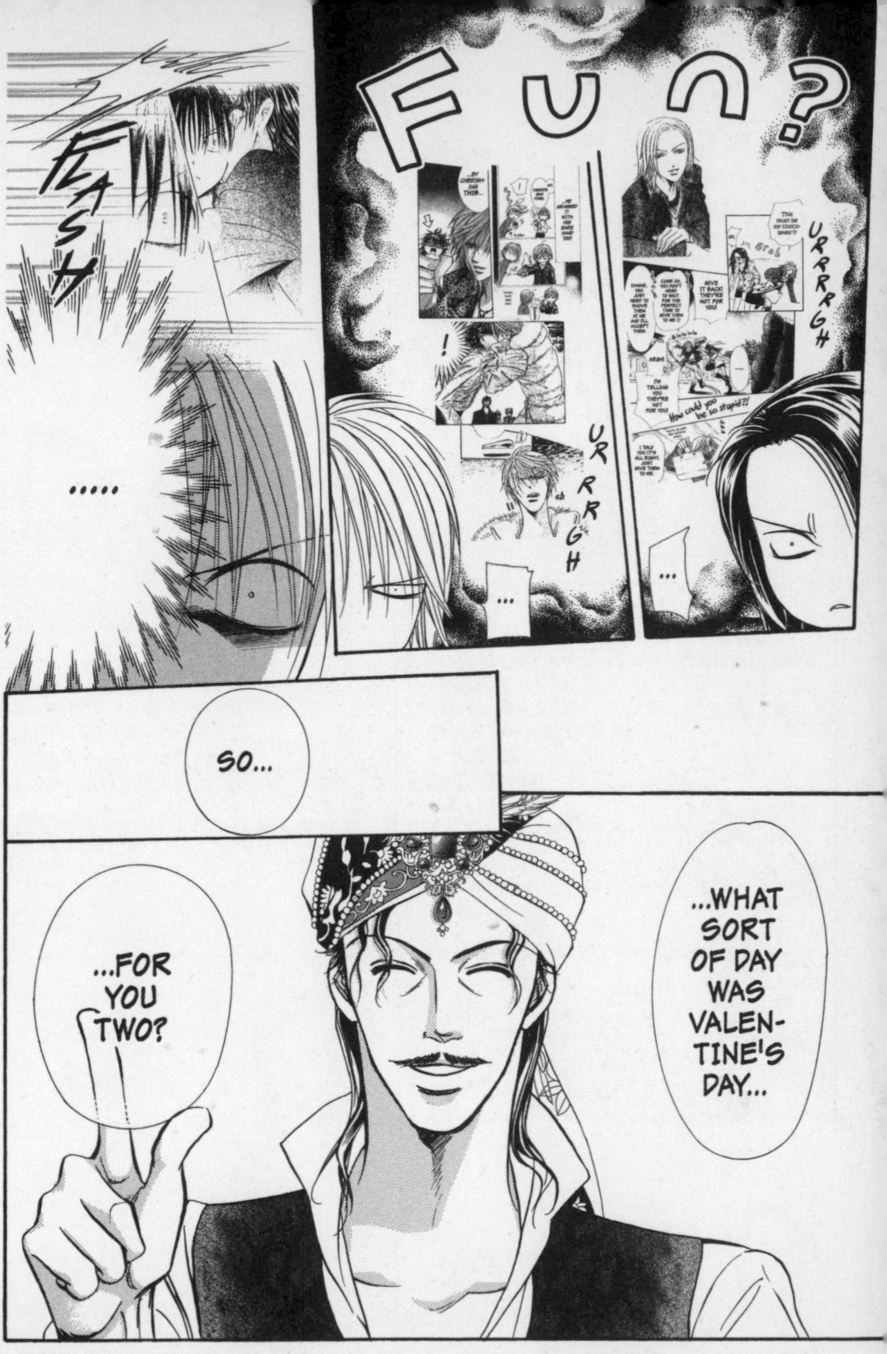
FUN?
This must be my chocolates!♡
grab
GIVE IT BACK! THEY'RE NOT FOR YOU!
COME ON, YOU DON'T NEED TO WAIT FOR THE PERFECT TIME TO GIVE THEM TO ME.♡
KANAE, YOU JUST NEED TO SHOVE THEM AT ME AND I'LL ACCEPT THEM.
ARGH!
I'M TELLING YOU THEY'RE NOT FOR YOU!
How could you be so stupid?!
I TOLD YOU IT'S ALL RIGHT. JUST GIVE THEM TO ME.
URRRRGH
...
...HE GRABBED IT WITH HIS BARE HAND TOO!
!
...BY CHERISHING THIS...
!
URRRGH
...
FLASH
.....
SO...
...WHAT SORT OF DAY WAS VALENTINE'S DAY...
...FOR YOU TWO?

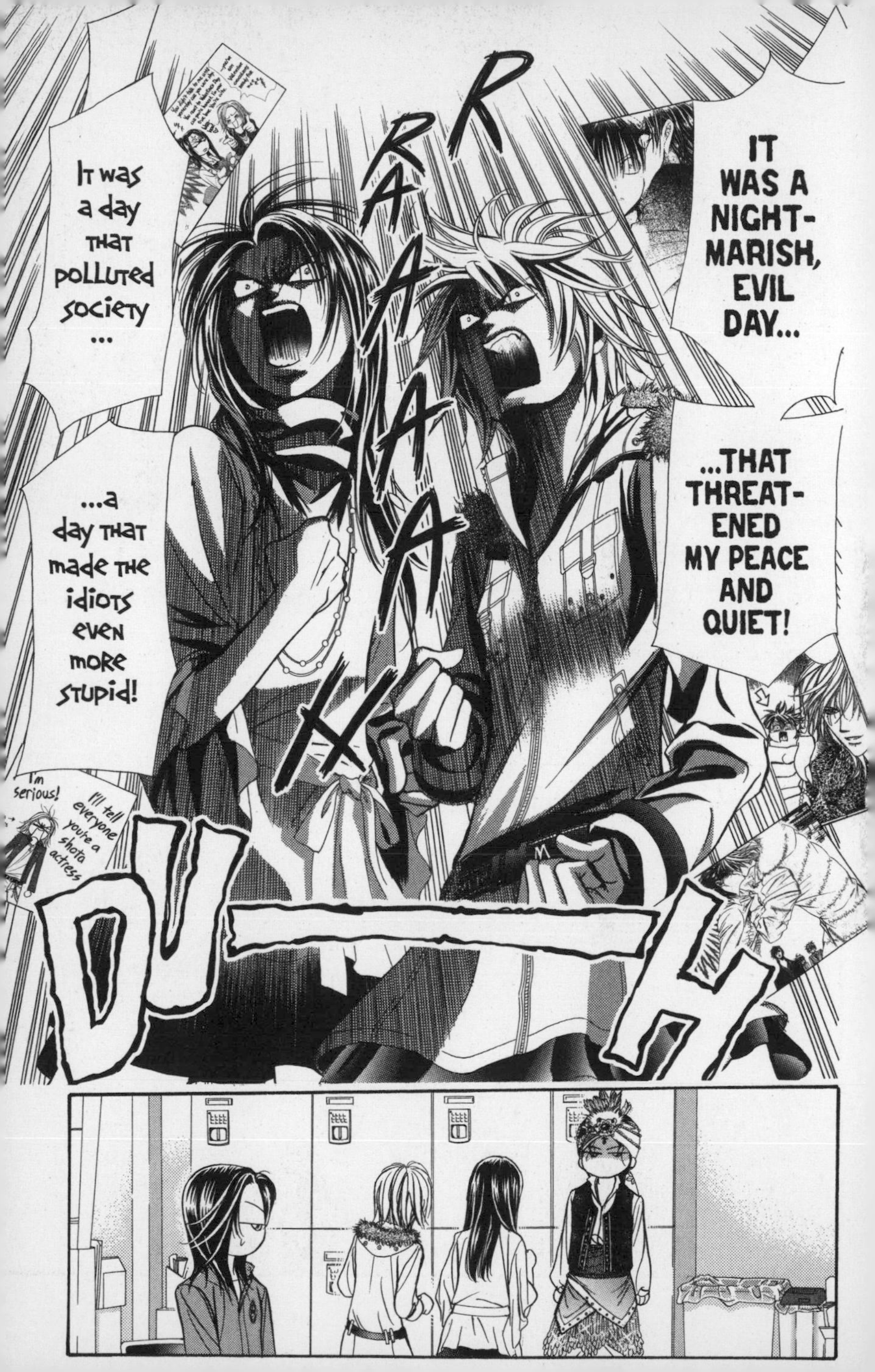

IT WAS A NIGHT-MARISH, EVIL DAY...
...THAT THREAT-ENED MY PEACE AND QUIET!
It was a day that polluted society...
...a day that made the idiots even more stupid!
RRAAAAAH
I'm serious!
I'll tell everyone you're a shota actress
DU—K

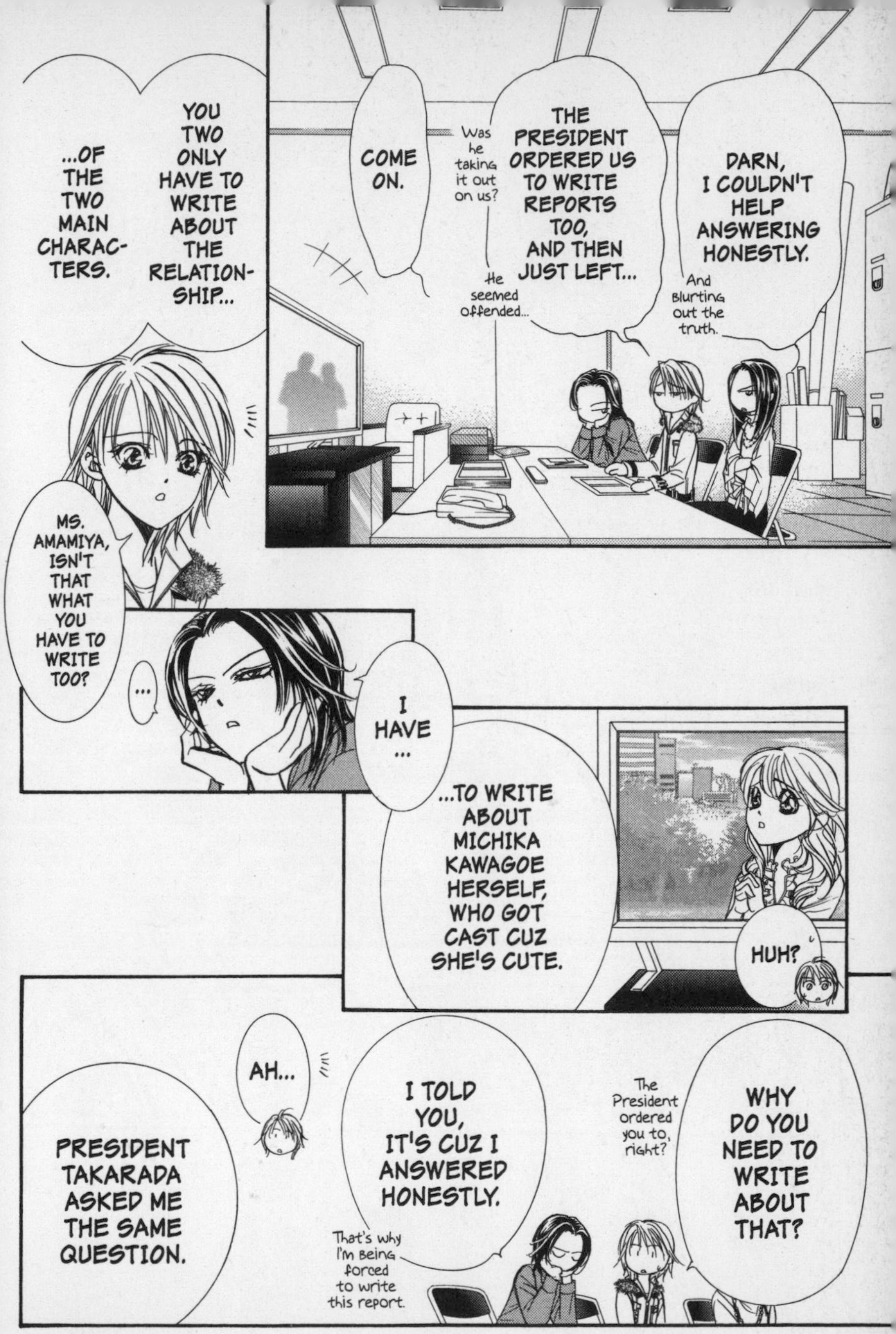
DARN, I COULDN'T HELP ANSWERING HONESTLY.
And blurting out the truth.
THE PRESIDENT ORDERED US TO WRITE REPORTS TOO, AND THEN JUST LEFT...
Was he taking it out on us?
He seemed offended...
COME ON.
YOU TWO ONLY HAVE TO WRITE ABOUT THE RELATIONSHIP...
...OF THE TWO MAIN CHARACTERS.
MS. AMAMIYA, ISN'T THAT WHAT YOU HAVE TO WRITE TOO?
...
I HAVE...
...TO WRITE ABOUT MICHIKA KAWAGOE HERSELF, WHO GOT CAST CUZ SHE'S CUTE.
HUH?
WHY DO YOU NEED TO WRITE ABOUT THAT?
The President ordered you to, right?
I TOLD YOU, IT'S CUZ I ANSWERED HONESTLY.
That's why I'm being forced to write this report.
AH...
PRESIDENT TAKARADA ASKED ME THE SAME QUESTION.

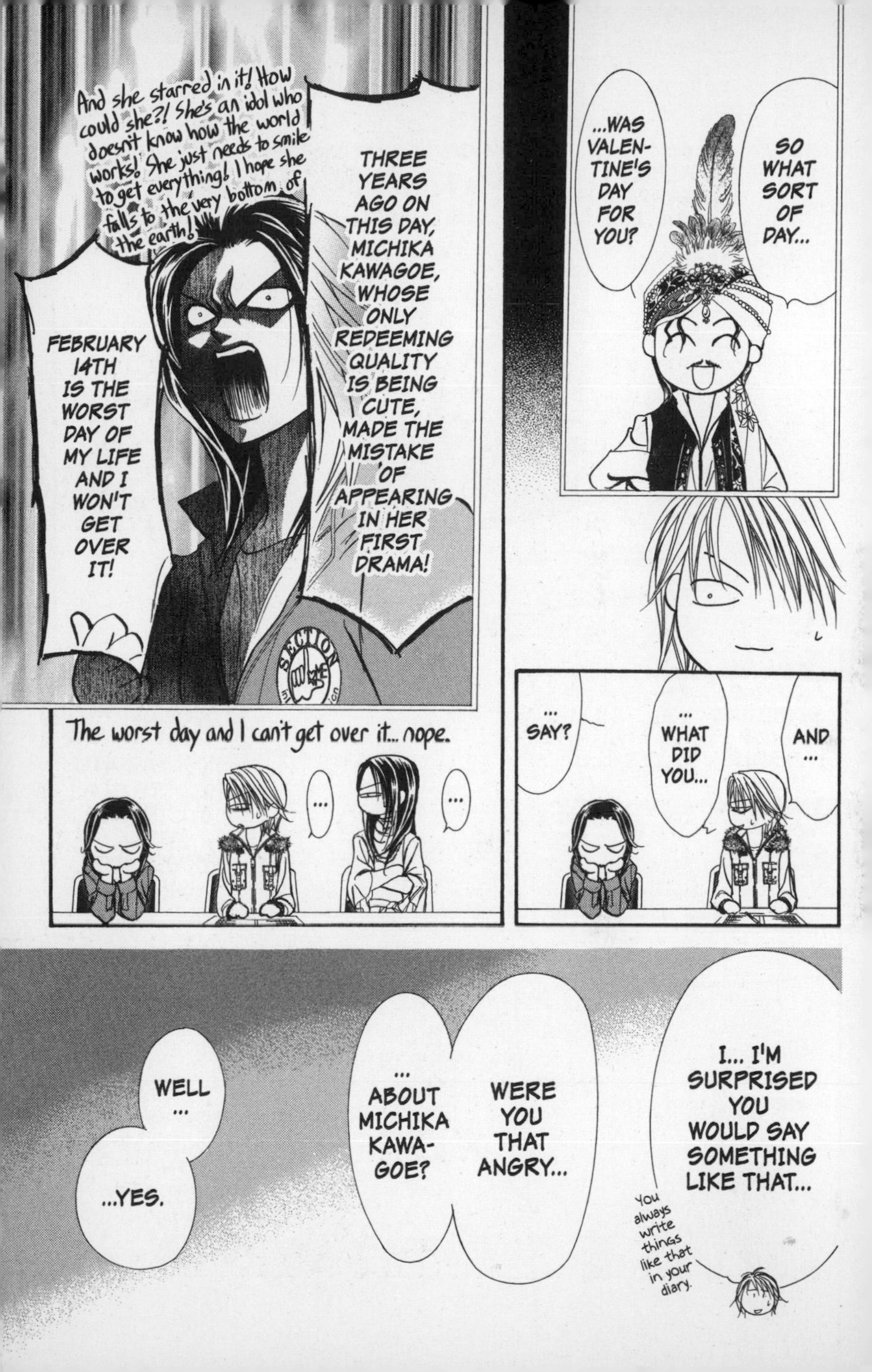
SO WHAT SORT OF DAY...
...WAS VALENTINE'S DAY FOR YOU?
And she starred in it! How could she?! She's an idol who doesn't know how the world works! She just needs to smile to get everything! I hope she falls to the very bottom of the earth!
THREE YEARS AGO ON THIS DAY, MICHIKA KAWAGOE, WHOSE ONLY REDEEMING QUALITY IS BEING CUTE, MADE THE MISTAKE OF APPEARING IN HER FIRST DRAMA!
FEBRUARY 14TH IS THE WORST DAY OF MY LIFE AND I WON'T GET OVER IT!
SECTION
AND...
...WHAT DID YOU...
...SAY?
The worst day and I can't get over it... nope.
...
...
I... I'M SURPRISED YOU WOULD SAY SOMETHING LIKE THAT...
You always write things like that in your diary.
WERE YOU THAT ANGRY...
...ABOUT MICHIKA KAWAGOE?
WELL...
...YES.

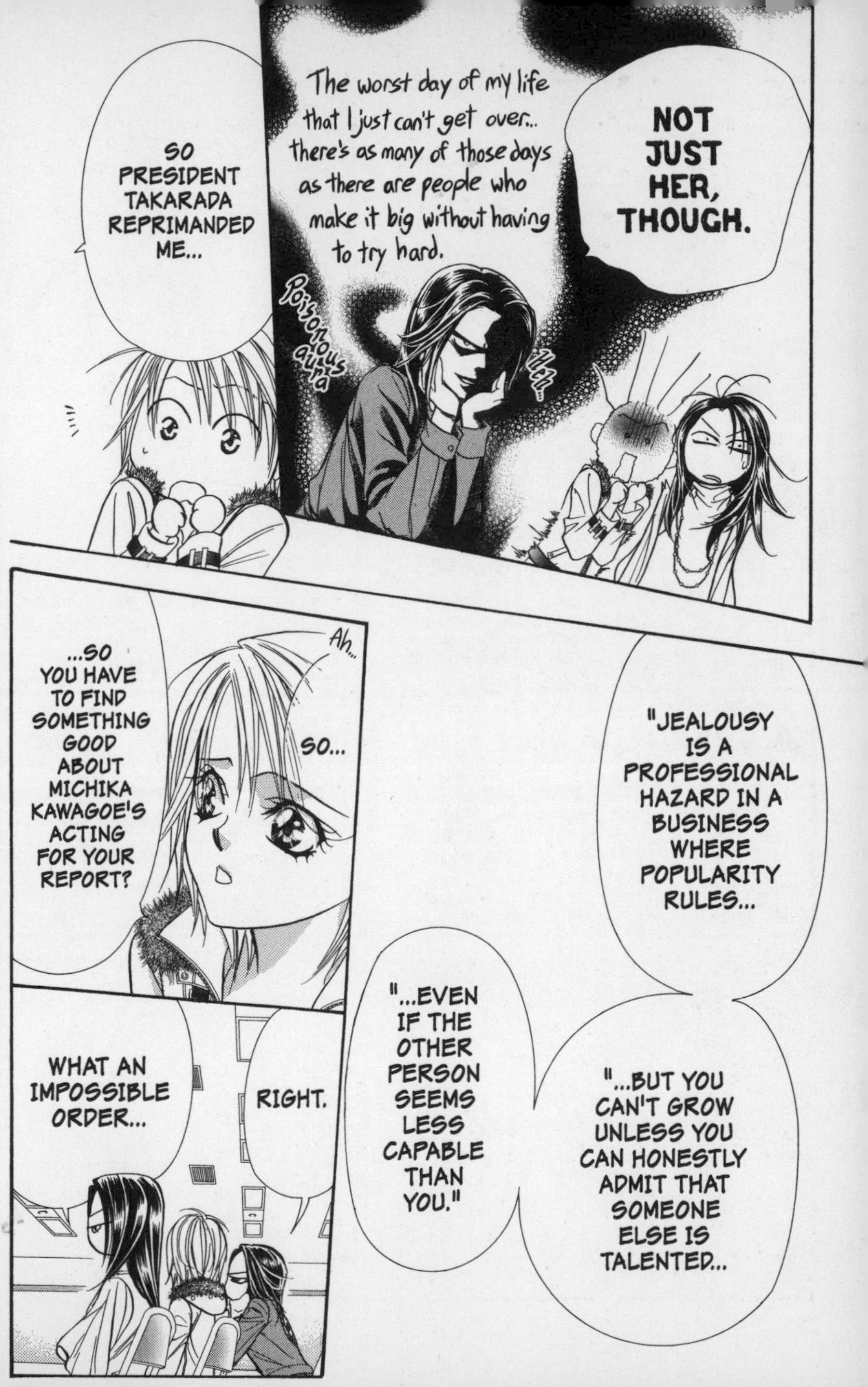
NOT JUST HER, THOUGH.
The worst day of my life that I just can't get over... there's as many of those days as there are people who make it big without having to try hard.
Poisonous aura
Heh...
SO PRESIDENT TAKARADA REPRIMANDED ME...
"JEALOUSY IS A PROFESSIONAL HAZARD IN A BUSINESS WHERE POPULARITY RULES...
"...BUT YOU CAN'T GROW UNLESS YOU CAN HONESTLY ADMIT THAT SOMEONE ELSE IS TALENTED...
"...EVEN IF THE OTHER PERSON SEEMS LESS CAPABLE THAN YOU."
Ah...
SO...
...SO YOU HAVE TO FIND SOMETHING GOOD ABOUT MICHIKA KAWAGOE'S ACTING FOR YOUR REPORT?
RIGHT.
WHAT AN IMPOSSIBLE ORDER...

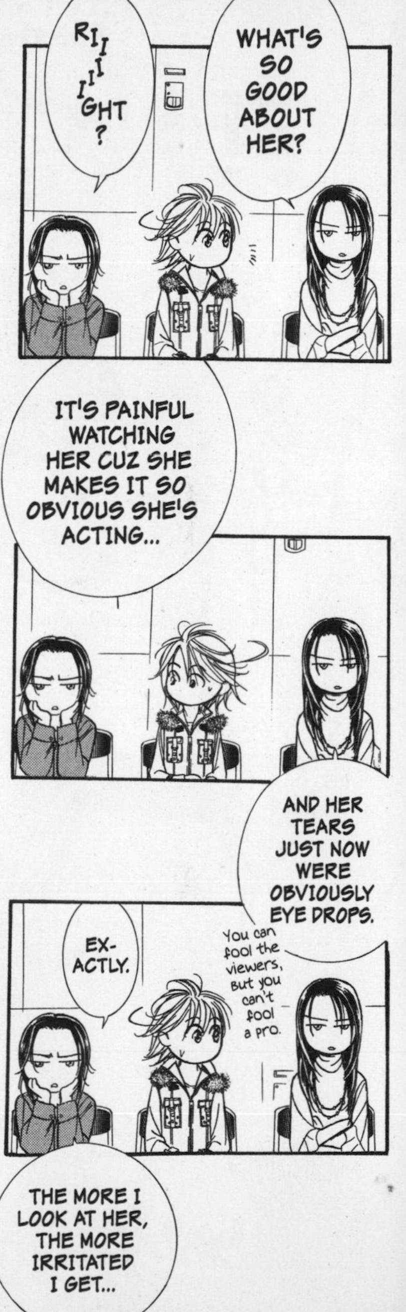
WHAT'S SO GOOD ABOUT HER?
RIIIIIGHT?
IT'S PAINFUL WATCHING HER CUZ SHE MAKES IT SO OBVIOUS SHE'S ACTING...
AND HER TEARS JUST NOW WERE OBVIOUSLY EYE DROPS.
You can fool the viewers, but you can't fool a pro.
EX-ACTLY.
THE MORE I LOOK AT HER, THE MORE IRRITATED I GET...
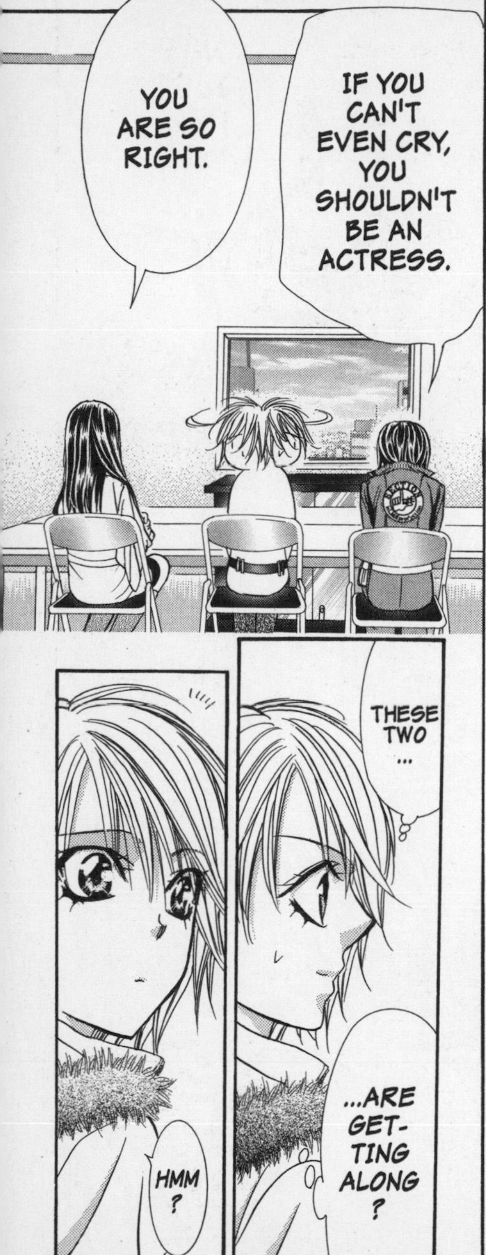
IF YOU CAN'T EVEN CRY, YOU SHOULDN'T BE AN ACTRESS.
YOU ARE SO RIGHT.
THESE TWO...
...ARE GET-TING ALONG?
HMM?

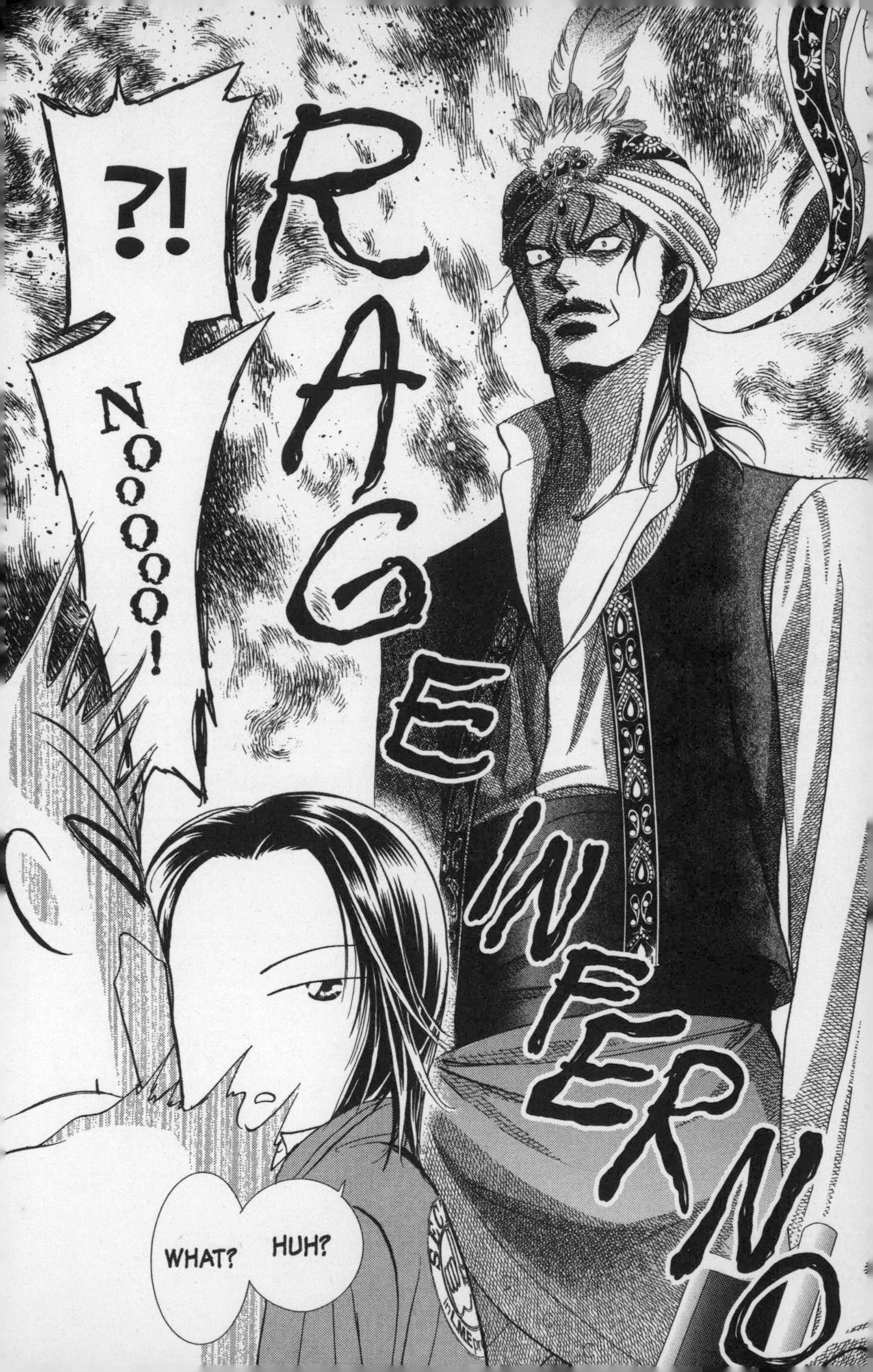
RAGE INFERNO
?!
NOOOOO!
HUH?
WHAT?

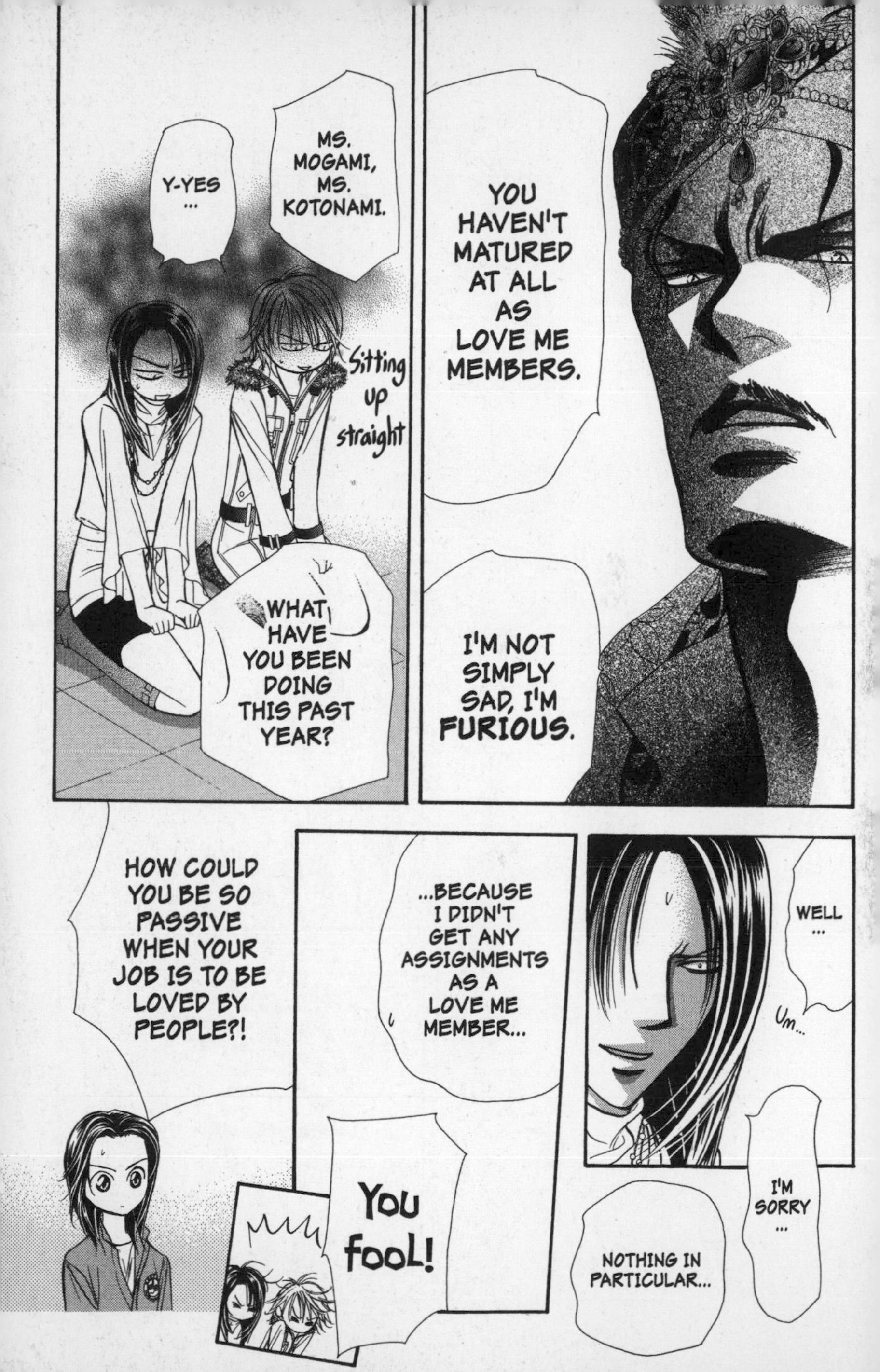
YOU HAVEN'T MATURED AT ALL AS LOVE ME MEMBERS.
I'M NOT SIMPLY SAD, I'M **FURIOUS**.
MS. MOGAMI, MS. KOTONAMI.
Y-YES ...
Sitting up straight
WHAT HAVE YOU BEEN DOING THIS PAST YEAR?
WELL ...
Um...
I'M SORRY ...
NOTHING IN PARTICULAR...
...BECAUSE I DIDN'T GET ANY ASSIGNMENTS AS A LOVE ME MEMBER...
HOW COULD YOU BE SO PASSIVE WHEN YOUR JOB IS TO BE LOVED BY PEOPLE?!
You fool!

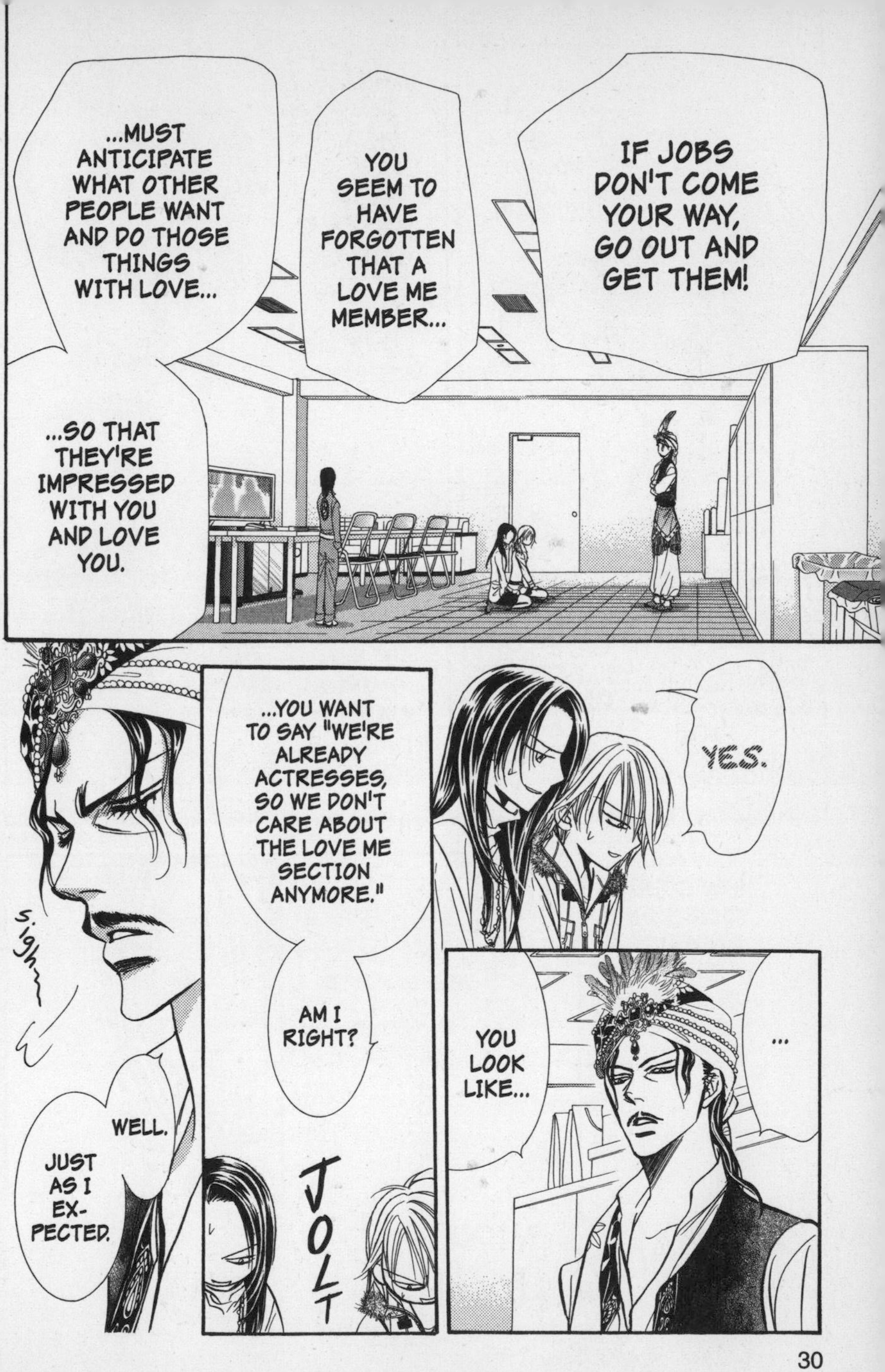
IF JOBS DON'T COME YOUR WAY, GO OUT AND GET THEM!
YOU SEEM TO HAVE FORGOTTEN THAT A LOVE ME MEMBER...
...MUST ANTICIPATE WHAT OTHER PEOPLE WANT AND DO THOSE THINGS WITH LOVE...
...SO THAT THEY'RE IMPRESSED WITH YOU AND LOVE YOU.
YES.
...
YOU LOOK LIKE...
...YOU WANT TO SAY "WE'RE ALREADY ACTRESSES, SO WE DON'T CARE ABOUT THE LOVE ME SECTION ANYMORE."
AM I RIGHT?
JOLT
sigh
WELL.
JUST AS I EXPECTED.

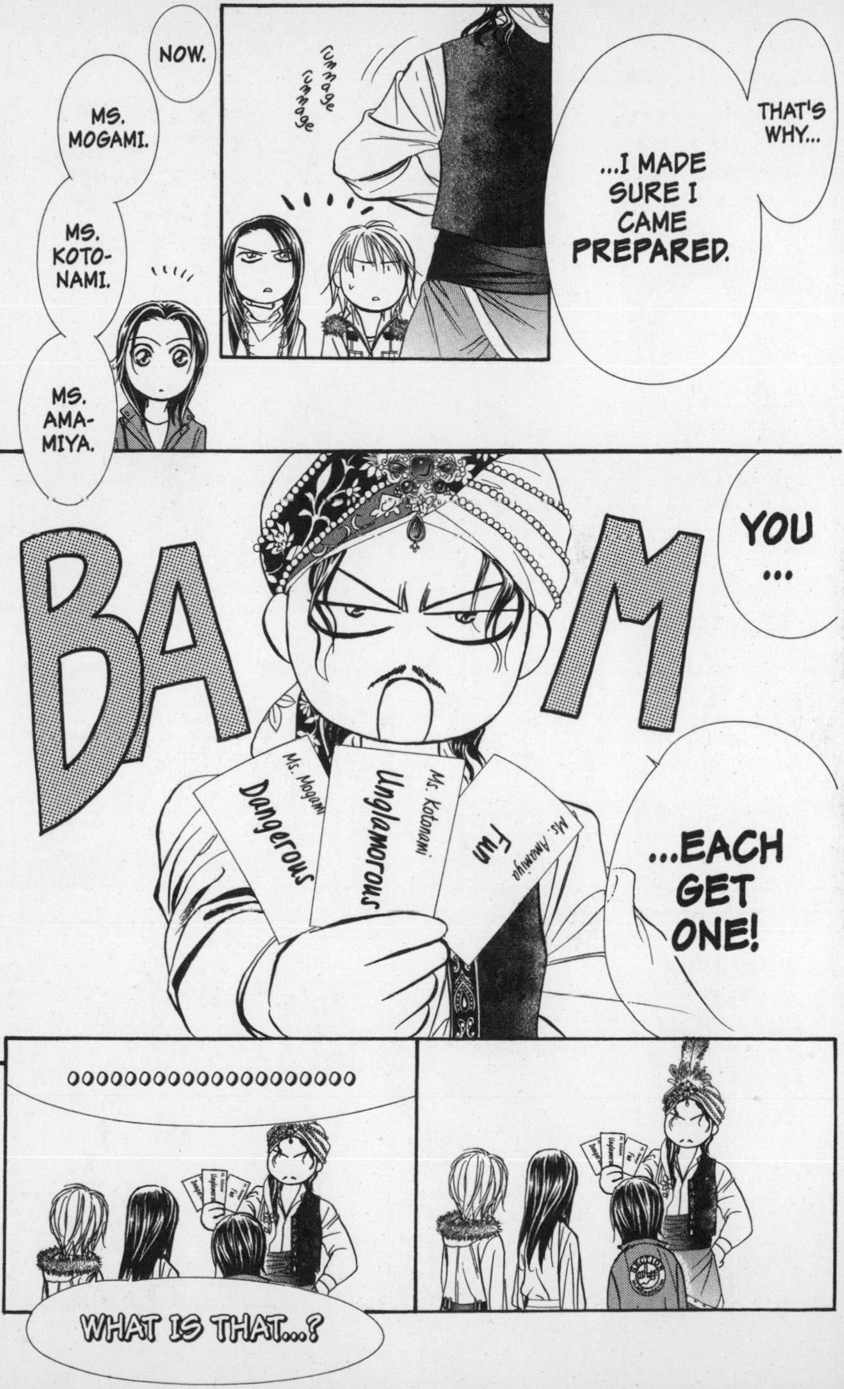
THAT'S WHY...
...I MADE SURE I CAME PREPARED.
rummage rummage
NOW.
MS. MOGAMI.
MS. KOTO-NAMI.
MS. AMA-MIYA.
YOU ...
BAM
Ms. Amamiya Fun
Ms. Kotonami Unglamorous
Ms. Mogami Dangerous
...EACH GET ONE!
OOOOOOOOOOOOOOOOOOOOO
WHAT IS THAT...?

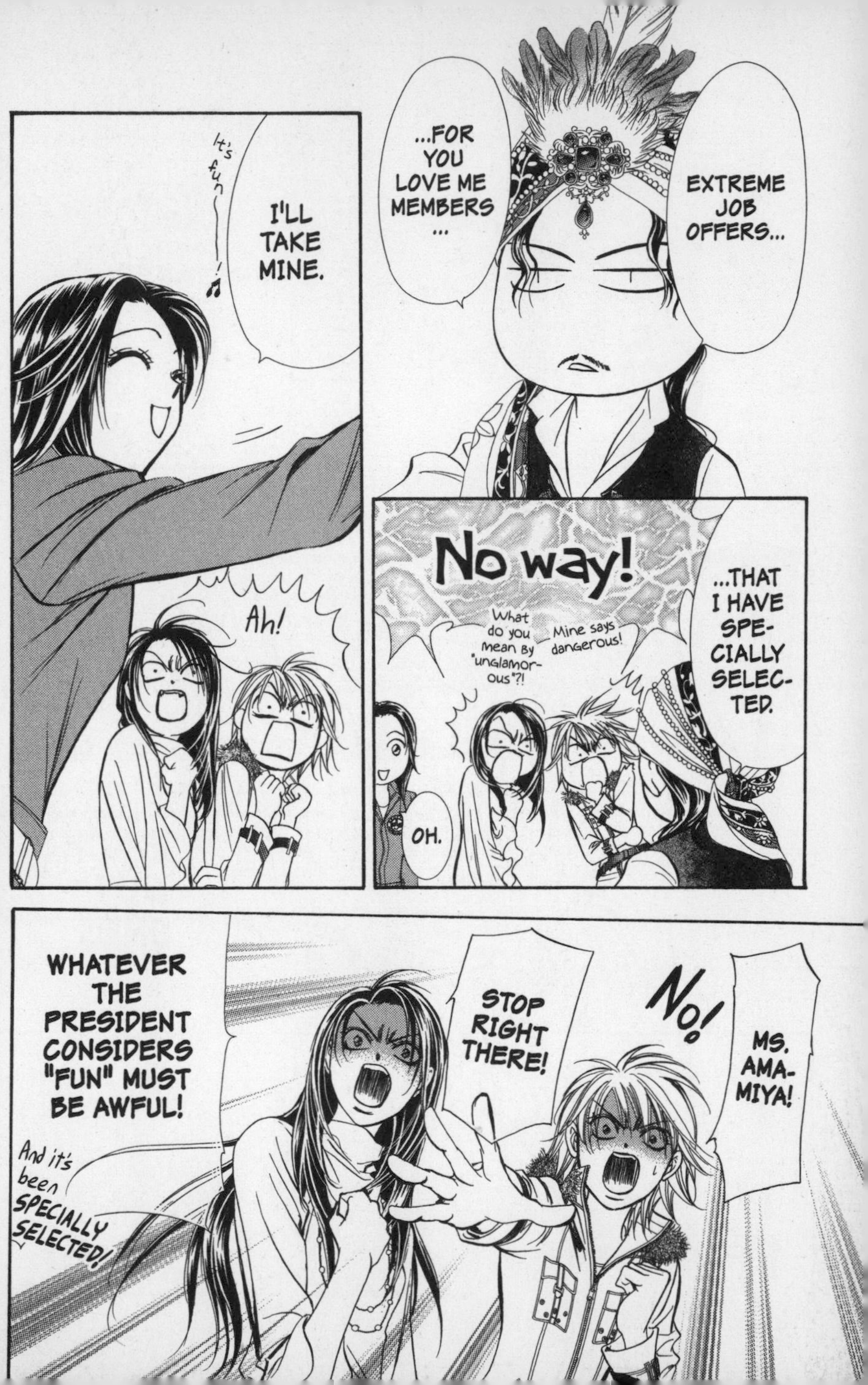
EXTREME JOB OFFERS...
...FOR YOU LOVE ME MEMBERS...
...THAT I HAVE SPE-CIALLY SELEC-TED.
No way!
Mine says dangerous!
What do you mean by "unglamor-ous"?!
OH.
I'LL TAKE MINE.
It's fun~!♪
Ah!
MS. AMA-MIYA!
No!
STOP RIGHT THERE!
WHATEVER THE PRESIDENT CONSIDERS "FUN" MUST BE AWFUL!
And it's been SPECIALLY SELECTED!

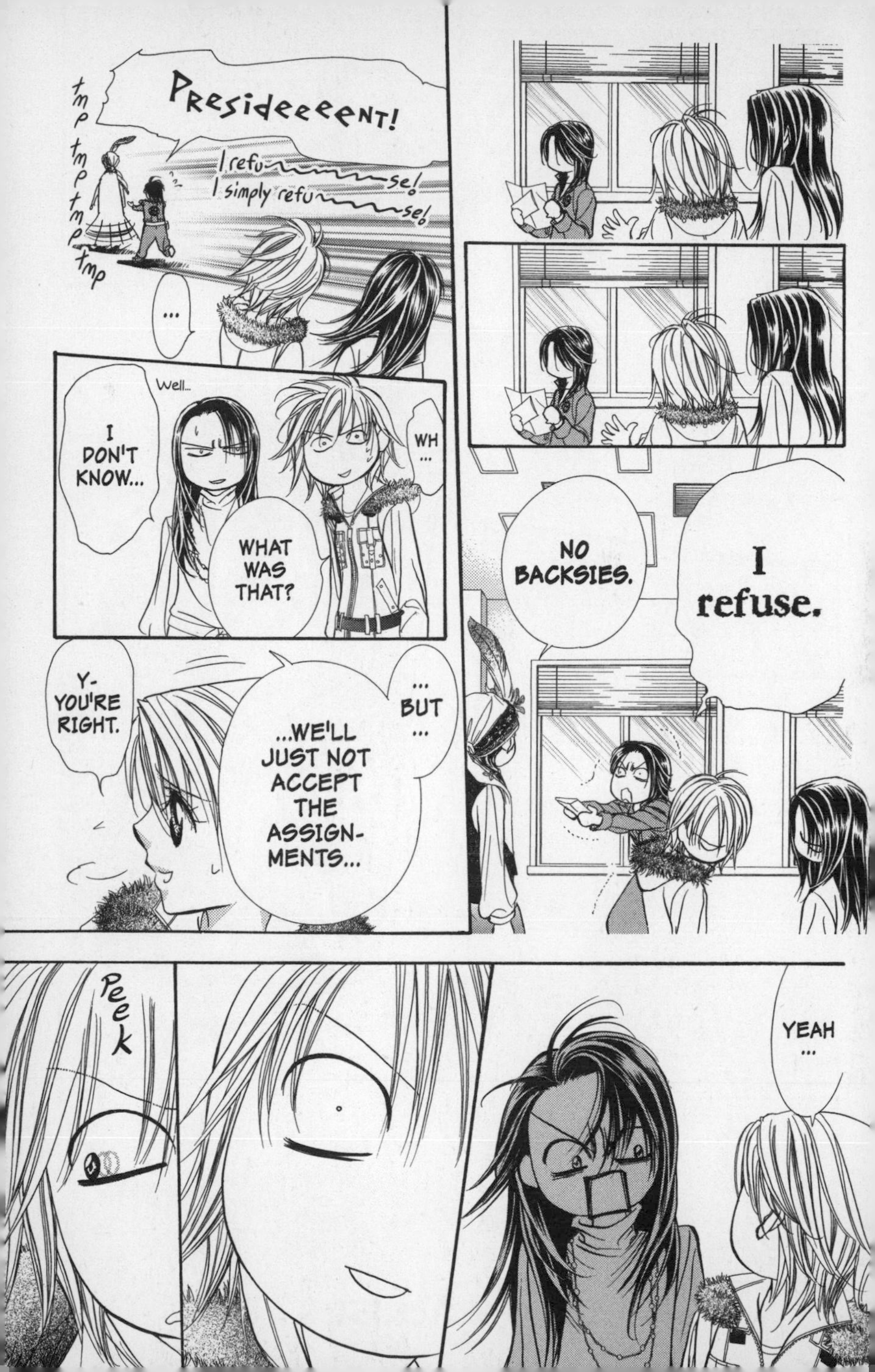
I refuse.
NO BACKSIES.
Presideeeent!
I refu——se! I simply refu——se!
tmp tmp tmp tmp tmp
...
WH...
WHAT WAS THAT?
Well... I DON'T KNOW...
...BUT...
...WE'LL JUST NOT ACCEPT THE ASSIGNMENTS...
Y-YOU'RE RIGHT.
YEAH...
Peek

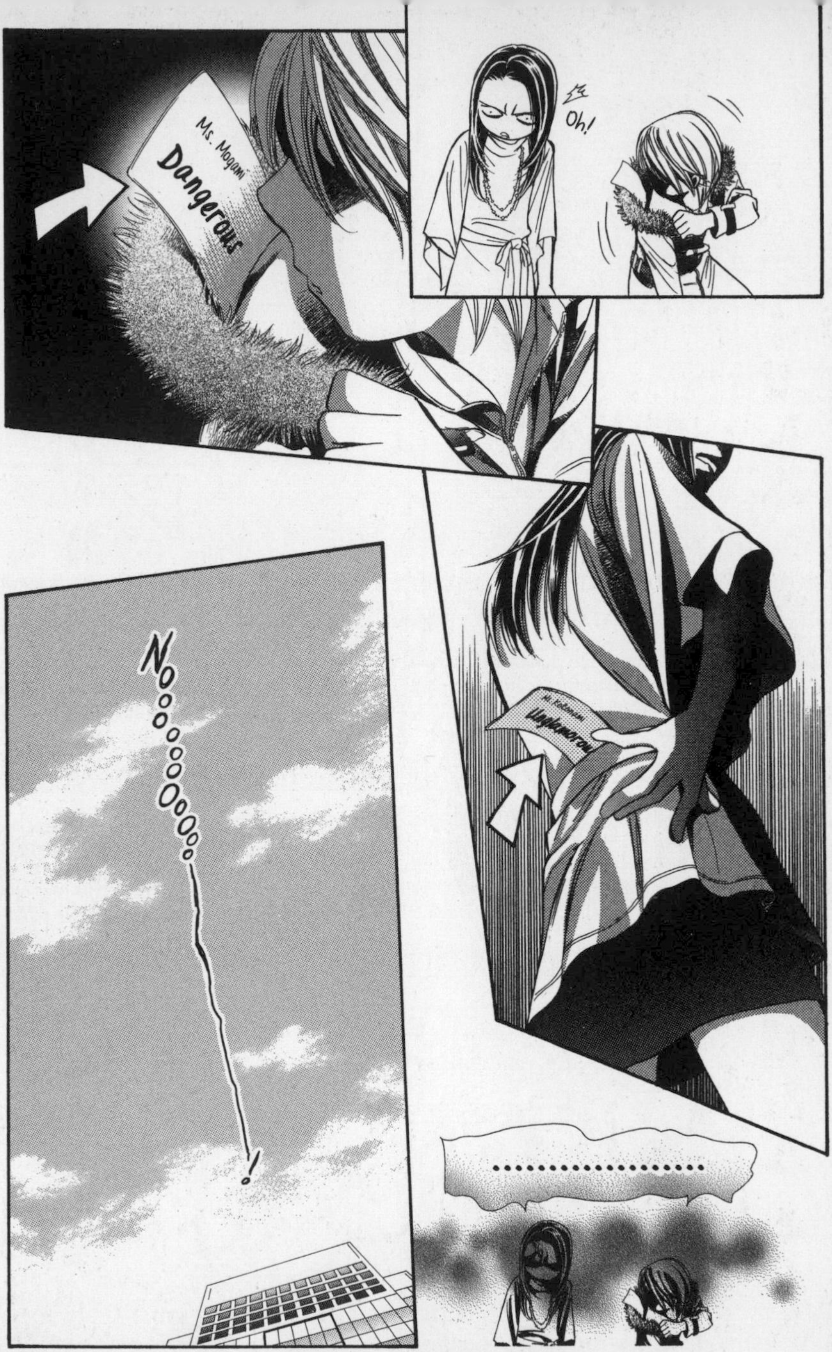
Oh!
Ms. Mogami
Dangerous
....
Noooooooooooo—!

End of Act 151

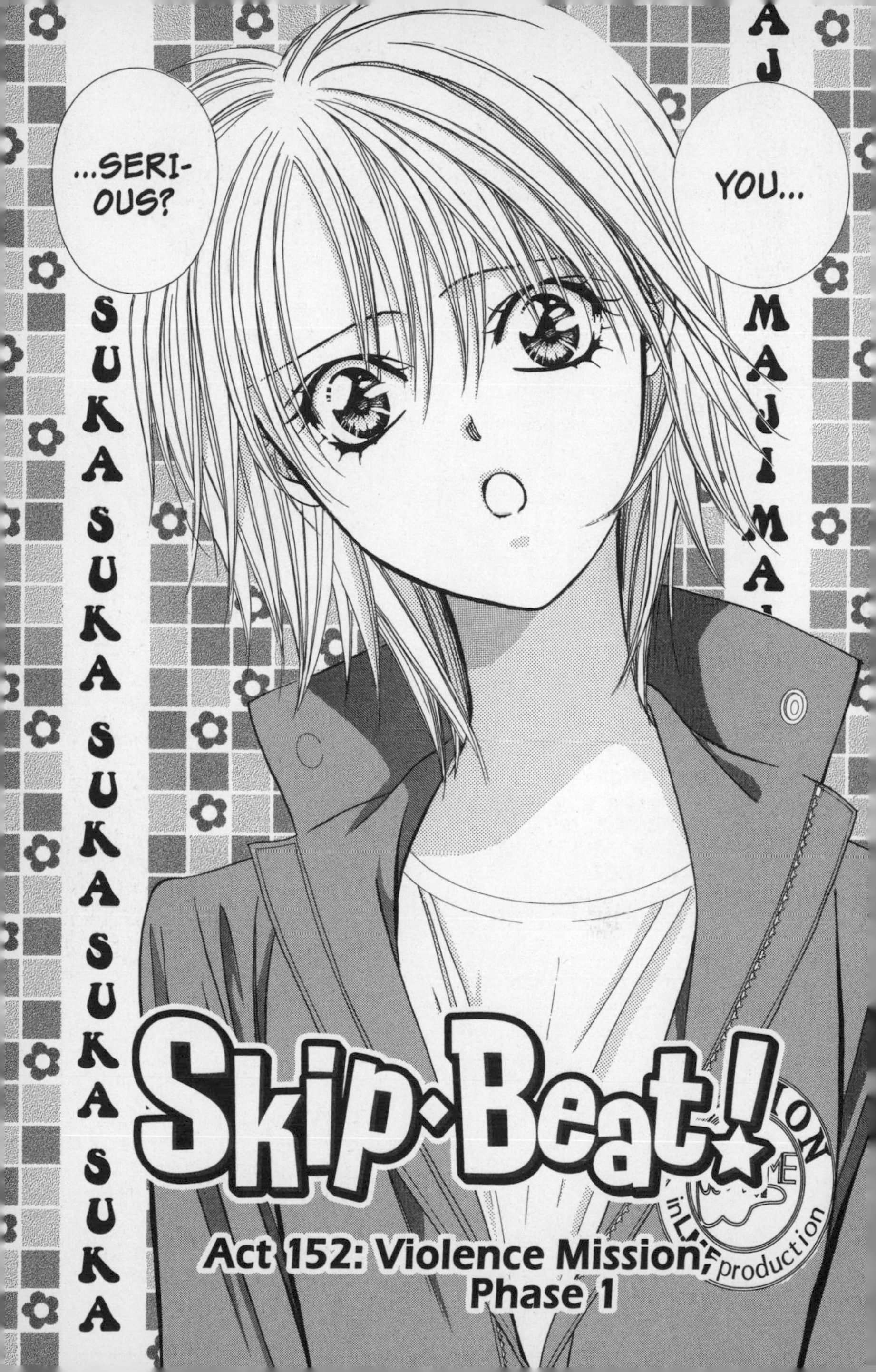
YOU...
AJ MAJIMA
...SERI-OUS?
SUKASUKASUKASUKASUKA
Skip·Beat!
Act 152: Violence Mission, Phase 1

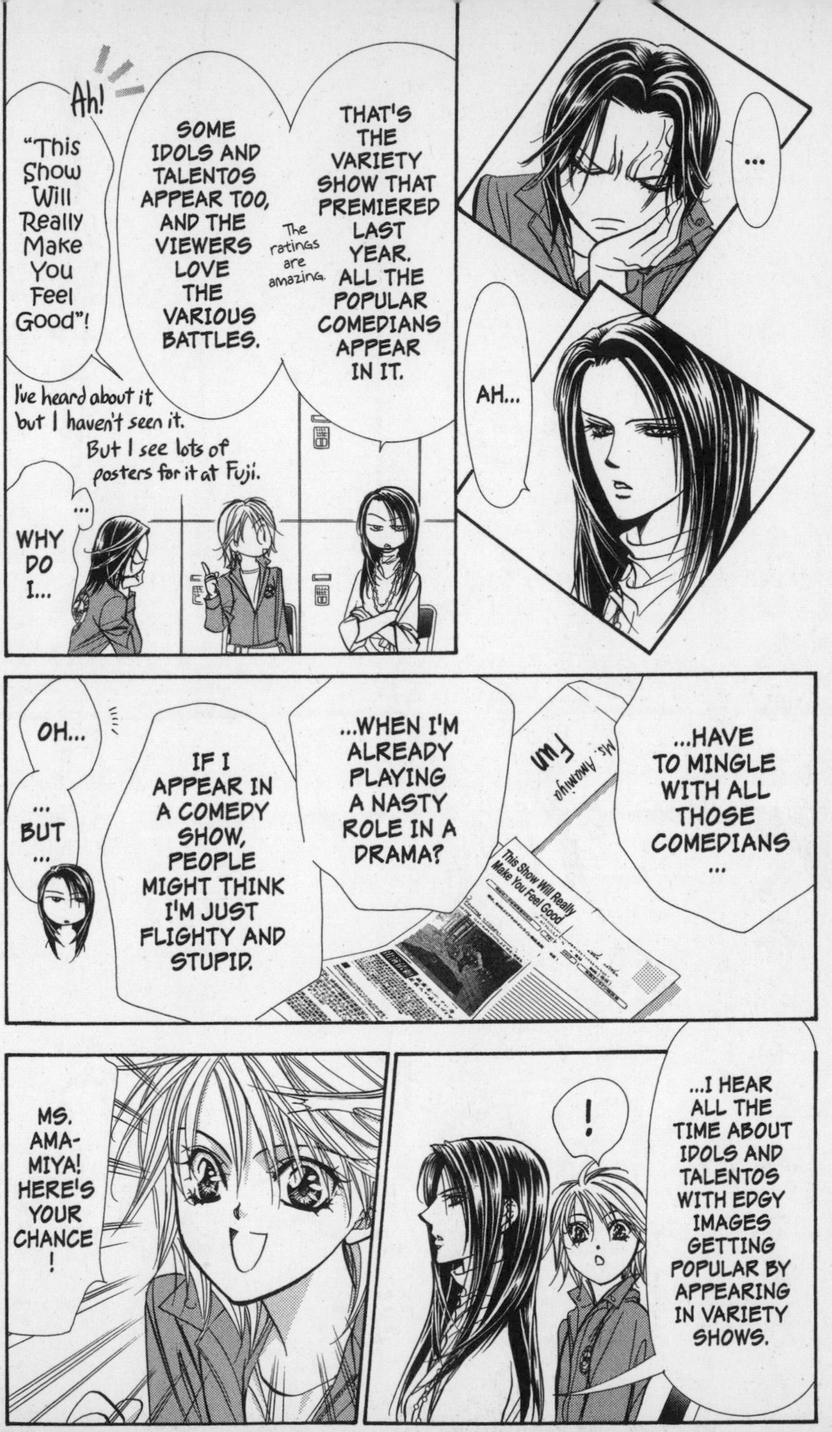
...
AH...
THAT'S THE VARIETY SHOW THAT PREMIERED LAST YEAR. ALL THE POPULAR COMEDIANS APPEAR IN IT.
The ratings are amazing.
SOME IDOLS AND TALENTOS APPEAR TOO, AND THE VIEWERS LOVE THE VARIOUS BATTLES.
Ah!
“This Show Will Really Make You Feel Good”!
I've heard about it, but I haven't seen it.
But I see lots of posters for it at Fuji.
...
WHY DO I...
...HAVE TO MINGLE WITH ALL THOSE COMEDIANS ...
Ms. Amamiya
Fun
This Show Will Really Make You Feel Good
...WHEN I'M ALREADY PLAYING A NASTY ROLE IN A DRAMA?
IF I APPEAR IN A COMEDY SHOW, PEOPLE MIGHT THINK I'M JUST FLIGHTY AND STUPID.
OH...
... BUT ...
...I HEAR ALL THE TIME ABOUT IDOLS AND TALENTOS WITH EDGY IMAGES GETTING POPULAR BY APPEARING IN VARIETY SHOWS.
!
MS. AMA-MIYA! HERE'S YOUR CHANCE !

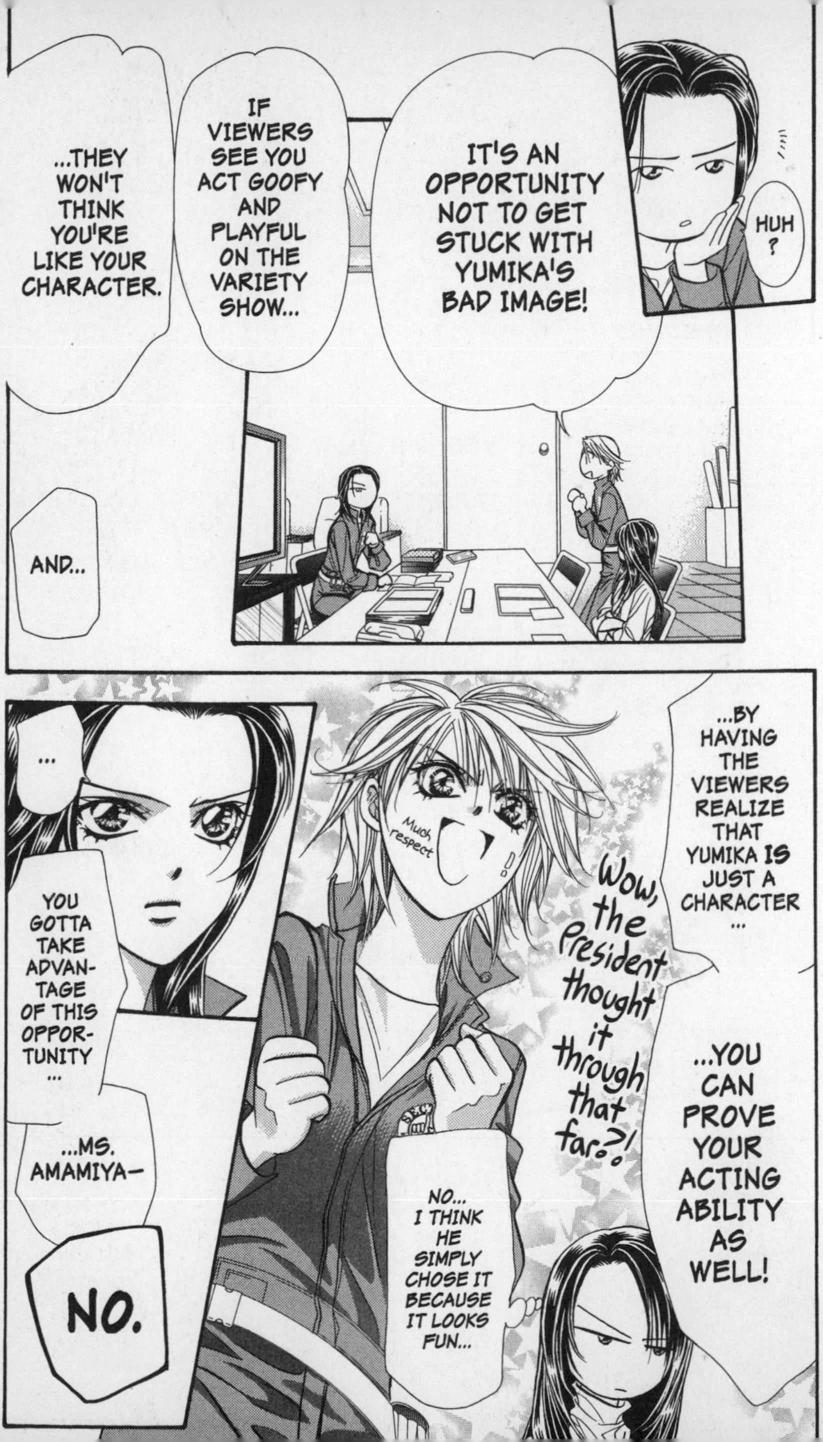
HUH?
IT'S AN OPPORTUNITY NOT TO GET STUCK WITH YUMIKA'S BAD IMAGE!
IF VIEWERS SEE YOU ACT GOOFY AND PLAYFUL ON THE VARIETY SHOW...
...THEY WON'T THINK YOU'RE LIKE YOUR CHARACTER.
AND...
...BY HAVING THE VIEWERS REALIZE THAT YUMIKA IS JUST A CHARACTER...
...YOU CAN PROVE YOUR ACTING ABILITY AS WELL!
Wow, the President thought it through that far?!
Much respect
NO... I THINK HE SIMPLY CHOSE IT BECAUSE IT LOOKS FUN...
...
YOU GOTTA TAKE ADVANTAGE OF THIS OPPORTUNITY...
...MS. AMAMIYA—
NO.

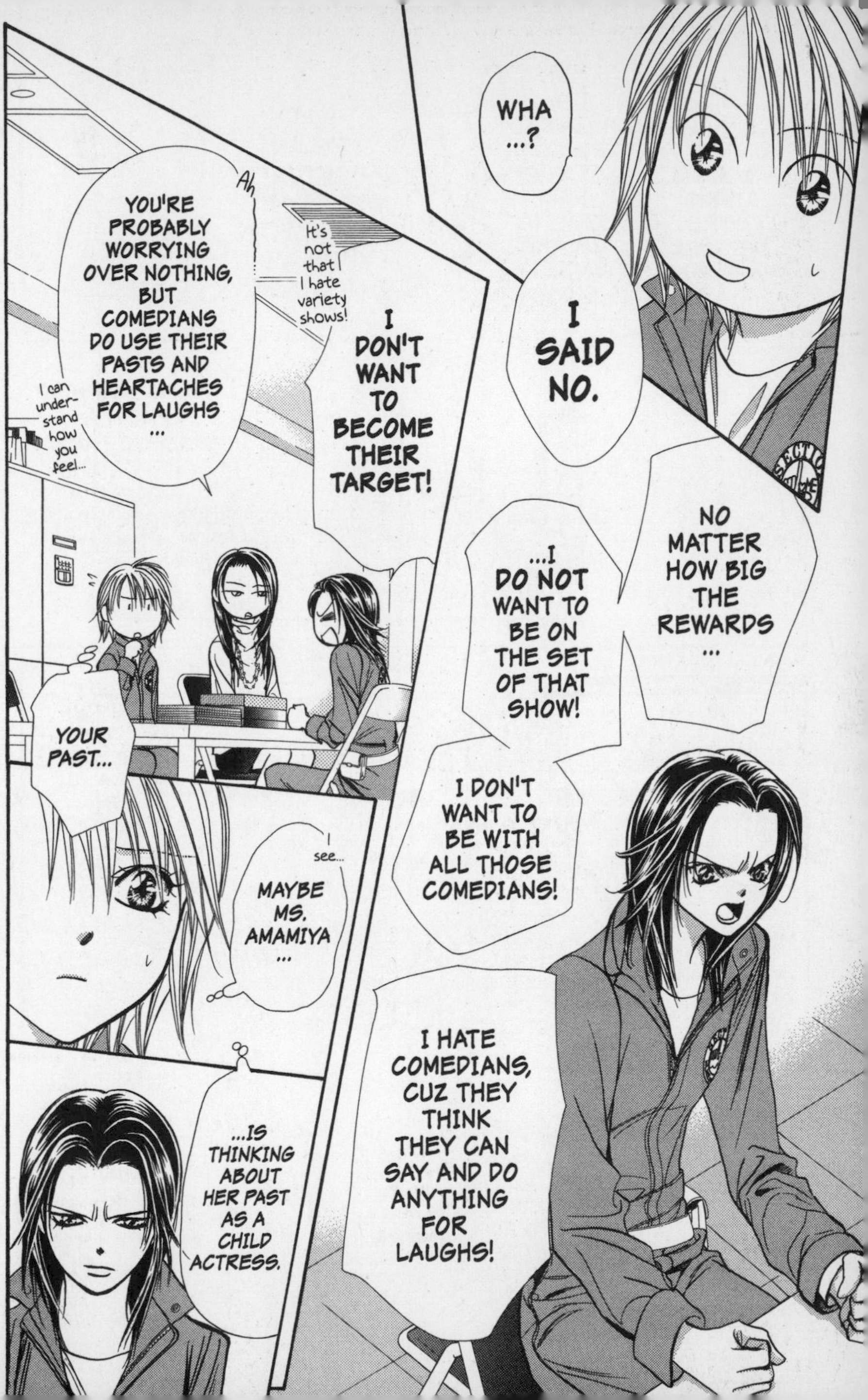
WHA ...?
I SAID NO.
NO MATTER HOW BIG THE REWARDS ...
...I DO NOT WANT TO BE ON THE SET OF THAT SHOW!
I DON'T WANT TO BE WITH ALL THOSE COMEDIANS!
I HATE COMEDIANS, CUZ THEY THINK THEY CAN SAY AND DO ANYTHING FOR LAUGHS!
I DON'T WANT TO BECOME THEIR TARGET!
It's not that I hate variety shows!
Ah
YOU'RE PROBABLY WORRYING OVER NOTHING, BUT COMEDIANS DO USE THEIR PASTS AND HEARTACHES FOR LAUGHS ...
I can under-stand how you feel...
YOUR PAST...
I see...
MAYBE MS. AMAMIYA ...
...IS THINKING ABOUT HER PAST AS A CHILD ACTRESS.

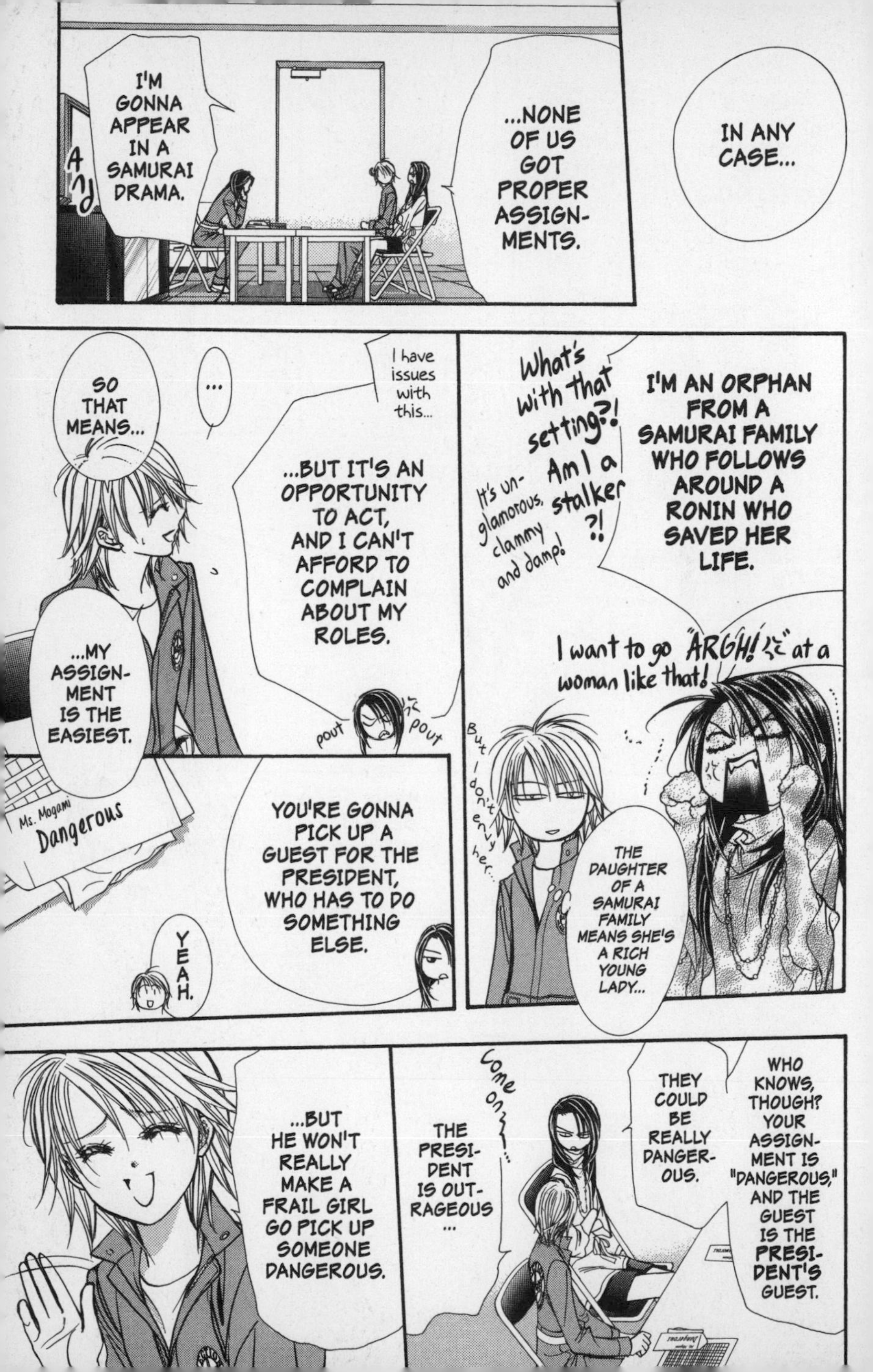
IN ANY CASE...
...NONE OF US GOT PROPER ASSIGNMENTS.
I'M GONNA APPEAR IN A SAMURAI DRAMA.
I'M AN ORPHAN FROM A SAMURAI FAMILY WHO FOLLOWS AROUND A RONIN WHO SAVED HER LIFE.
What's with that setting?! Am I a stalker?!
It's unglamorous, clammy and damp!
I want to go "ARGH!" at a woman like that!
THE DAUGHTER OF A SAMURAI FAMILY MEANS SHE'S A RICH YOUNG LADY...
But I don't envy her...
I have issues with this...
...BUT IT'S AN OPPORTUNITY TO ACT, AND I CAN'T AFFORD TO COMPLAIN ABOUT MY ROLES.
...
SO THAT MEANS...
...MY ASSIGNMENT IS THE EASIEST.
pout pout
YOU'RE GONNA PICK UP A GUEST FOR THE PRESIDENT, WHO HAS TO DO SOMETHING ELSE.
Ms. Mogami
Dangerous
YEAH.
WHO KNOWS, THOUGH? YOUR ASSIGNMENT IS "DANGEROUS," AND THE GUEST IS THE PRESIDENT'S GUEST.
THEY COULD BE REALLY DANGEROUS.
Come on~...
THE PRESIDENT IS OUTRAGEOUS...
...BUT HE WON'T REALLY MAKE A FRAIL GIRL GO PICK UP SOMEONE DANGEROUS.

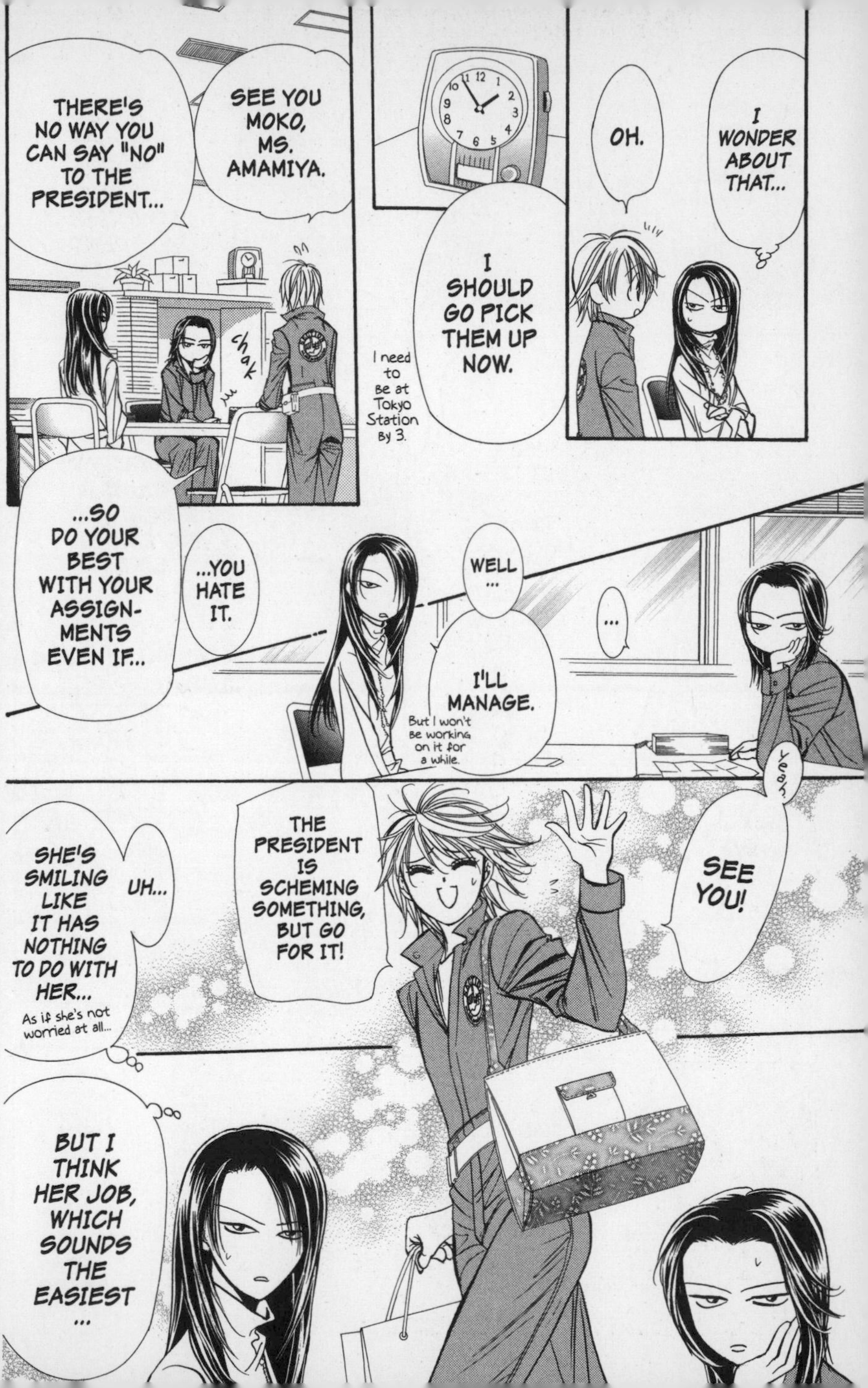
I WONDER ABOUT THAT...
OH.
I SHOULD GO PICK THEM UP NOW.
I need to be at Tokyo Station By 3.
SEE YOU MOKO, MS. AMAMIYA.
chak
THERE'S NO WAY YOU CAN SAY "NO" TO THE PRESIDENT...
...SO DO YOUR BEST WITH YOUR ASSIGNMENTS EVEN IF...
...YOU HATE IT.
...
WELL...
I'LL MANAGE.
But I won't be working on it for a while.
Yeah.
SEE YOU!
THE PRESIDENT IS SCHEMING SOMETHING, BUT GO FOR IT!
UH...
SHE'S SMILING LIKE IT HAS NOTHING TO DO WITH HER...
As if she's not worried at all...
BUT I THINK HER JOB, WHICH SOUNDS THE EASIEST...

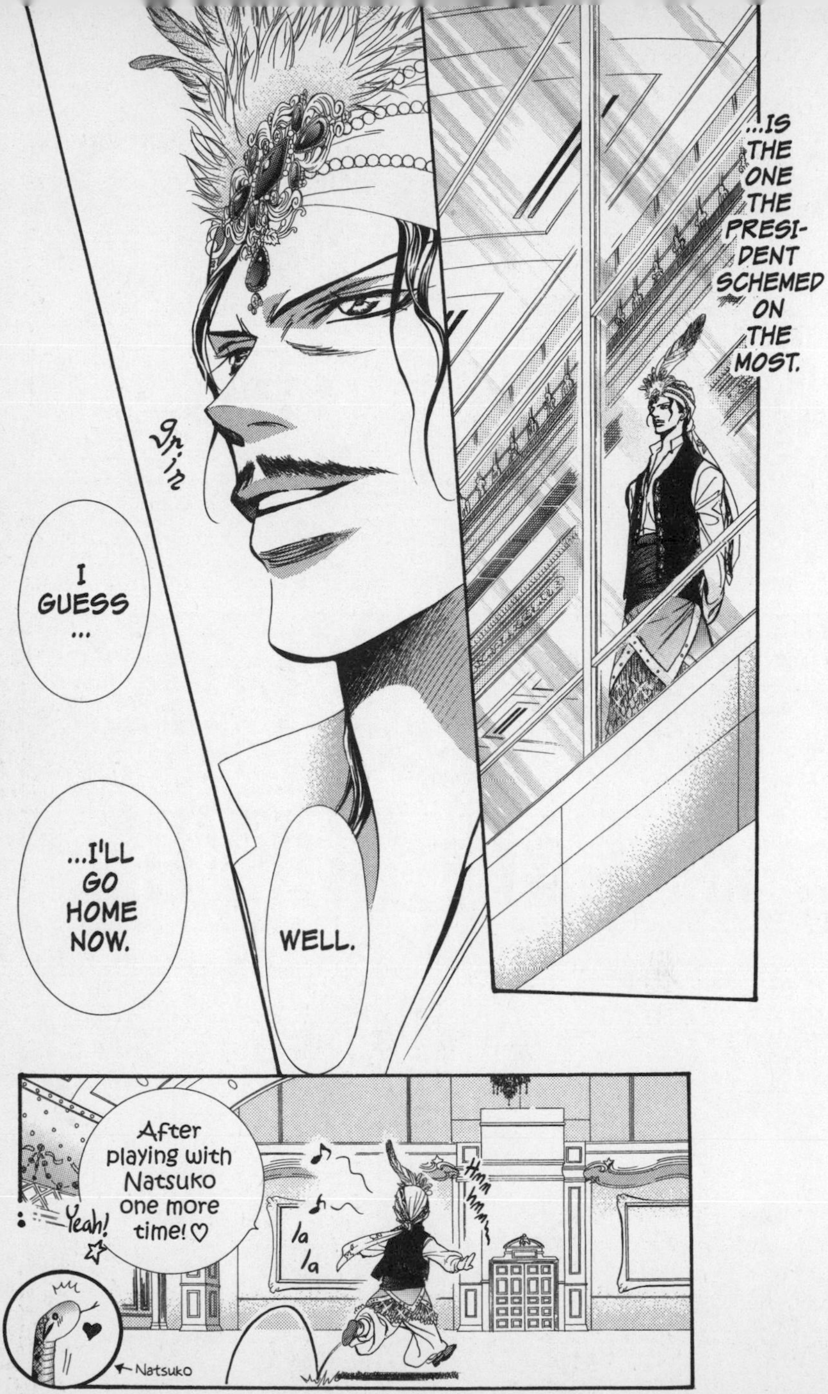
...IS THE ONE THE PRESIDENT SCHEMED ON THE MOST.
Grin
WELL.
I GUESS...
...I'LL GO HOME NOW.
Hmm hmm
la la
After playing with Natsuko one more time! ♡
Yeah!
← Natsuko

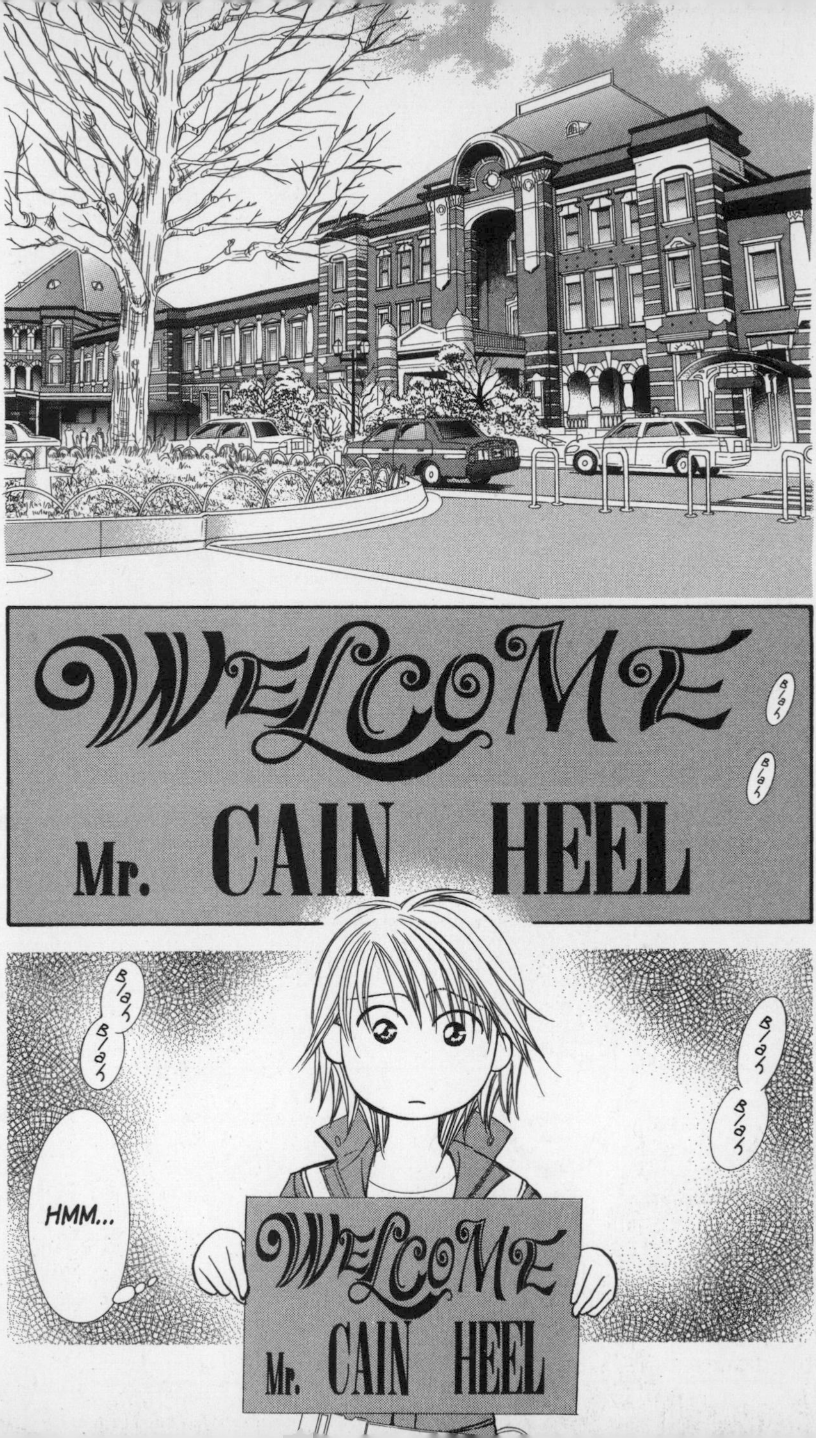
WELCOME
Mr. CAIN HEEL
Blah
Blah
Blah
Blah
Blah
Blah
HMM...
WELCOME
Mr. CAIN HEEL

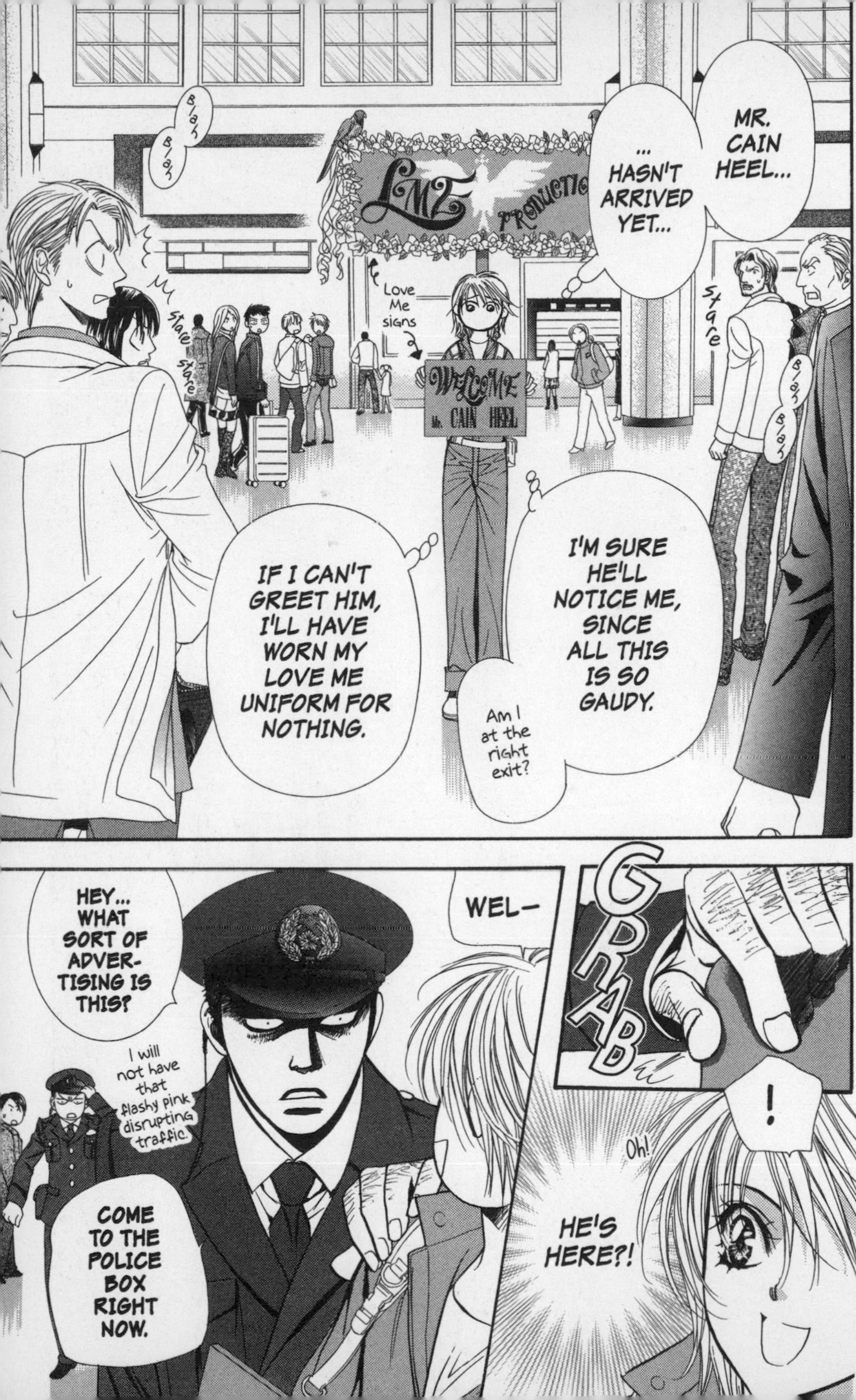
MR. CAIN HEEL...
... HASN'T ARRIVED YET...
Stare
Blah Blah
LME PRODUCTIO
Love Me signs
WELCOME Mr. CAIN HEEL
Stare stare
Blah Blah
I'M SURE HE'LL NOTICE ME, SINCE ALL THIS IS SO GAUDY.
Am I at the right exit?
IF I CAN'T GREET HIM, I'LL HAVE WORN MY LOVE ME UNIFORM FOR NOTHING.
GRAB
!
Oh!
HE'S HERE?!
WEL-
HEY... WHAT SORT OF ADVER-TISING IS THIS?
I will not have that flashy pink disrupting traffic.
COME TO THE POLICE BOX RIGHT NOW.

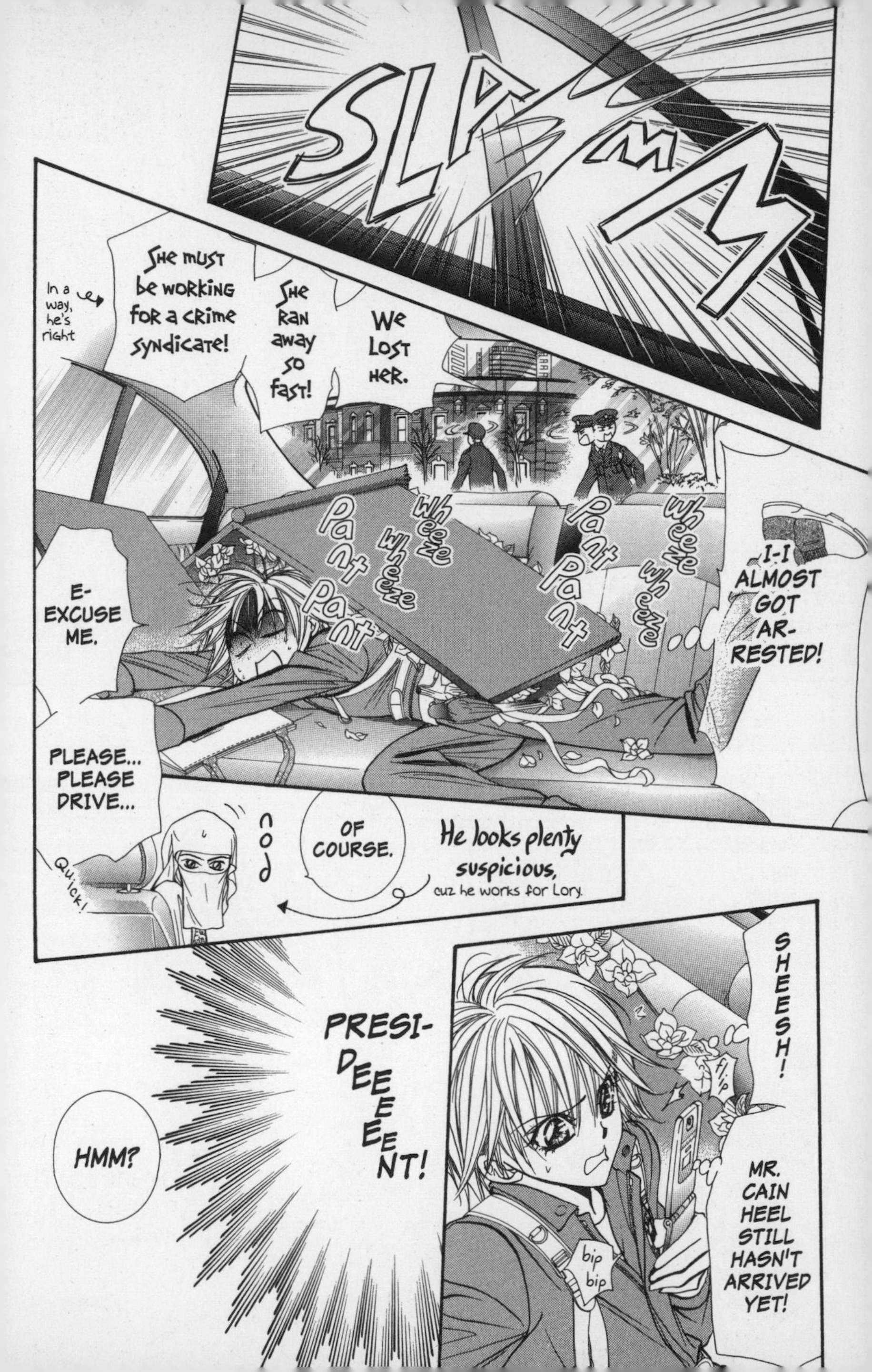
SLAM
I-I ALMOST GOT AR-RESTED!
wheeze wheeze
Pant Pant
WE LOST HER.
She RAN away so fast!
She must be working for a crime syndicate!
In a way, he's right
wheeze wheeze
Pant pant
E-EXCUSE ME.
PLEASE... PLEASE DRIVE...
He looks plenty suspicious, cuz he works for Lory.
OF COURSE.
nod
Quick!
SHEESH!
flip
MR. CAIN HEEL STILL HASN'T ARRIVED YET!
bip bip
PRESI-DEEEEENT!
HMM?

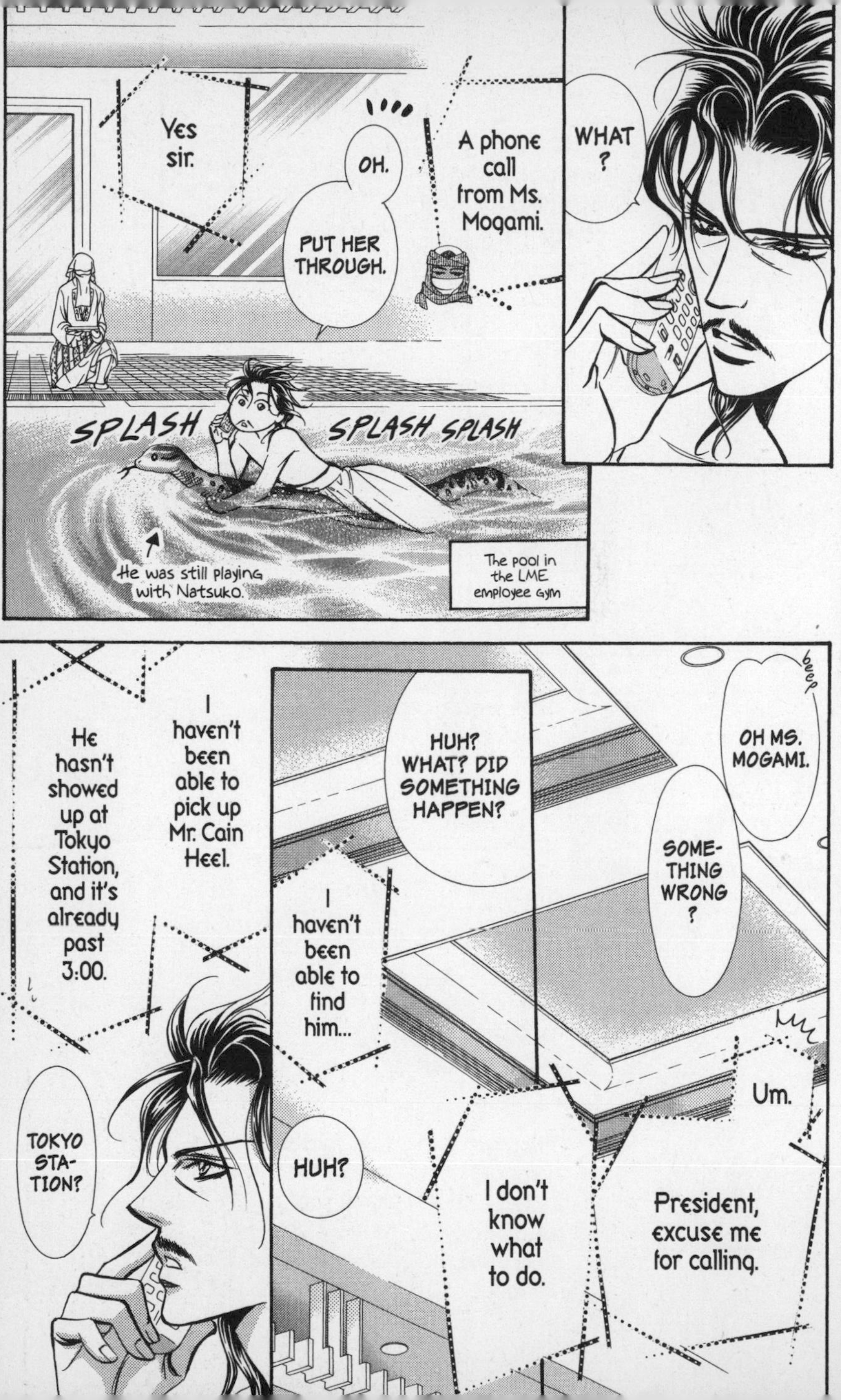
WHAT?
A phone call from Ms. Mogami.
OH.
PUT HER THROUGH.
Yes sir.
SPLASH
SPLASH SPLASH
He was still playing with Natsuko.
The pool in the LME employee gym
beep
OH MS. MOGAMI.
SOMETHING WRONG?
HUH? WHAT? DID SOMETHING HAPPEN?
Um.
President, excuse me for calling.
I don't know what to do.
HUH?
I haven't been able to find him...
I haven't been able to pick up Mr. Cain Heel.
He hasn't showed up at Tokyo Station, and it's already past 3:00.
TOKYO STATION?

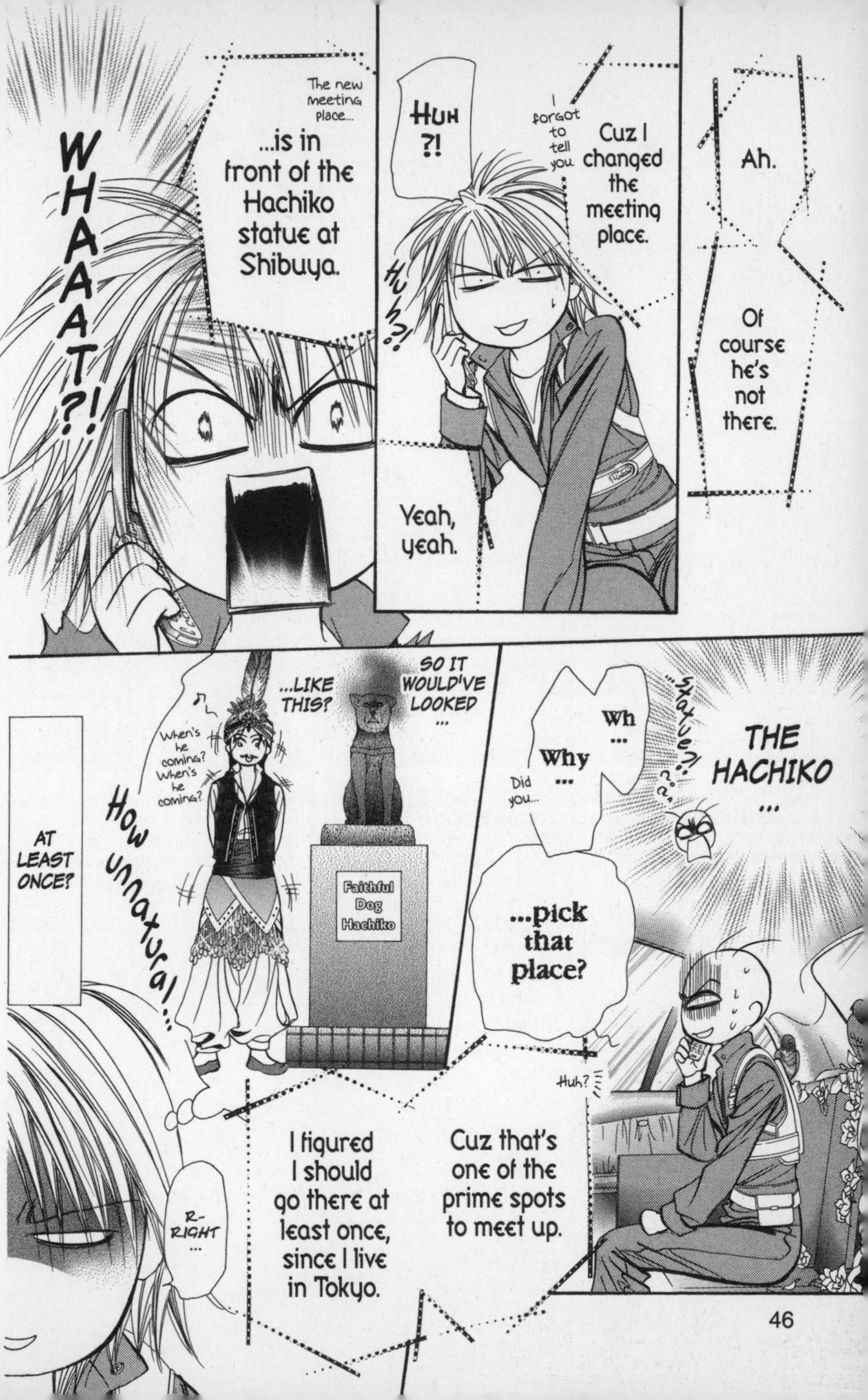
Ah.
Of course he's not there.
HUH?!
I forgot to tell you
Cuz I changed the meeting place.
Huh?!
Yeah, yeah.
The new meeting place...
...is in front of the Hachiko statue at Shibuya.
WHAAAAT?!
THE HACHIKO...
...statue?!
Wh...
Why...
Did you...
...pick that place?
Huh?
Cuz that's one of the prime spots to meet up.
I figured I should go there at least once, since I live in Tokyo.
SO IT WOULD'VE LOOKED...
...LIKE THIS?
When's he coming? When's he coming?
Faithful Dog Hachiko
How unnatural...
AT LEAST ONCE?
R-RIGHT...

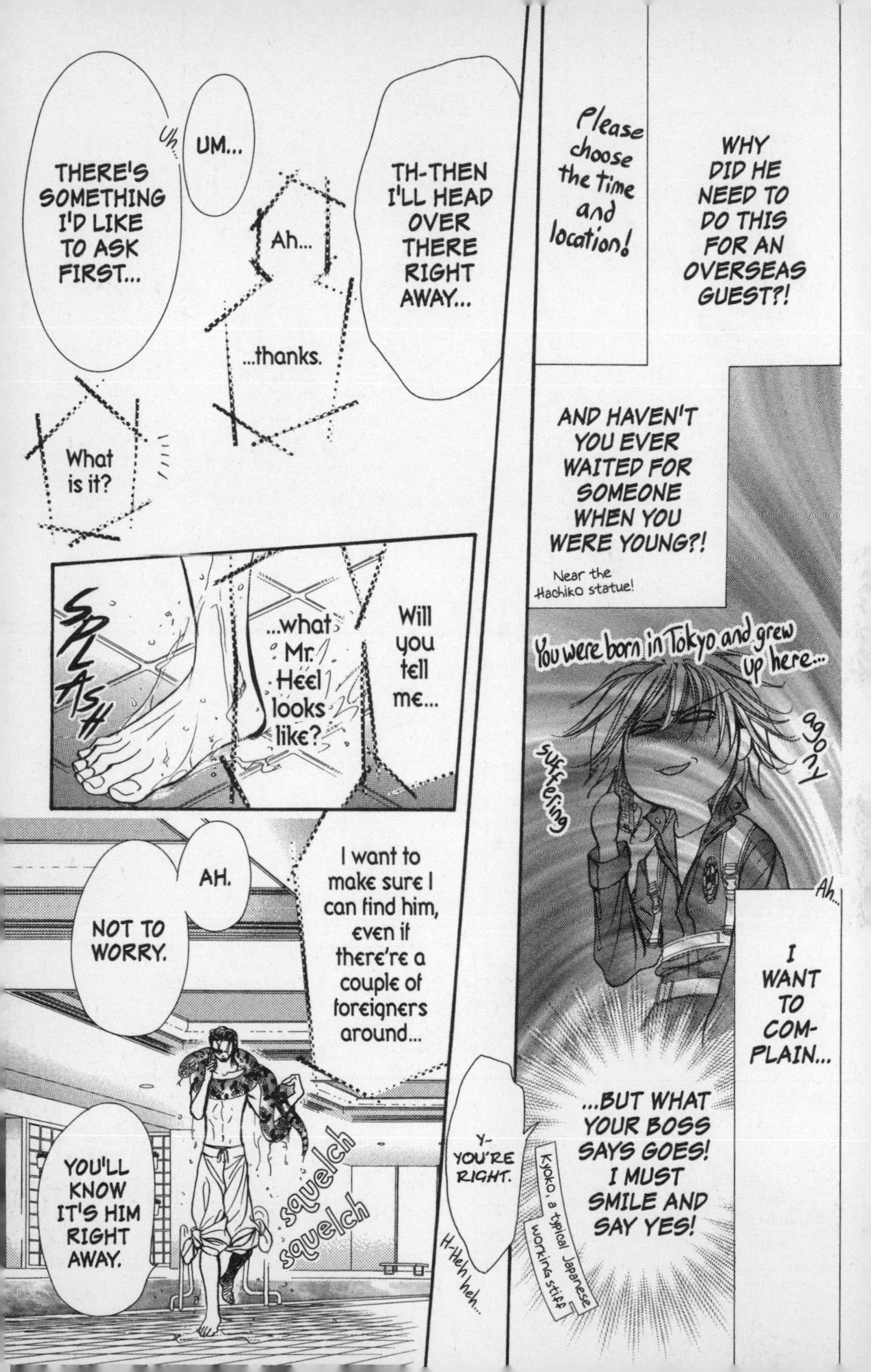
WHY DID HE NEED TO DO THIS FOR AN OVERSEAS GUEST?!
Please choose the time and location!
AND HAVEN'T YOU EVER WAITED FOR SOMEONE WHEN YOU WERE YOUNG?!
Near the Hachiko statue!
You were born in Tokyo and grew up here...
agony
suffering
Ah...
I WANT TO COM-PLAIN...
...BUT WHAT YOUR BOSS SAYS GOES! I MUST SMILE AND SAY YES!
Kyoko, a typical Japanese working stiff
Y-YOU'RE RIGHT.
H-Heh heh...
TH-THEN I'LL HEAD OVER THERE RIGHT AWAY...
Ah...
Uh...
UM...
THERE'S SOMETHING I'D LIKE TO ASK FIRST...
...thanks.
What is it?
Will you tell me...
...what Mr. Heel looks like?
SPLASH
I want to make sure I can find him, even if there're a couple of foreigners around...
AH.
NOT TO WORRY.
YOU'LL KNOW IT'S HIM RIGHT AWAY.
squelch
squelch

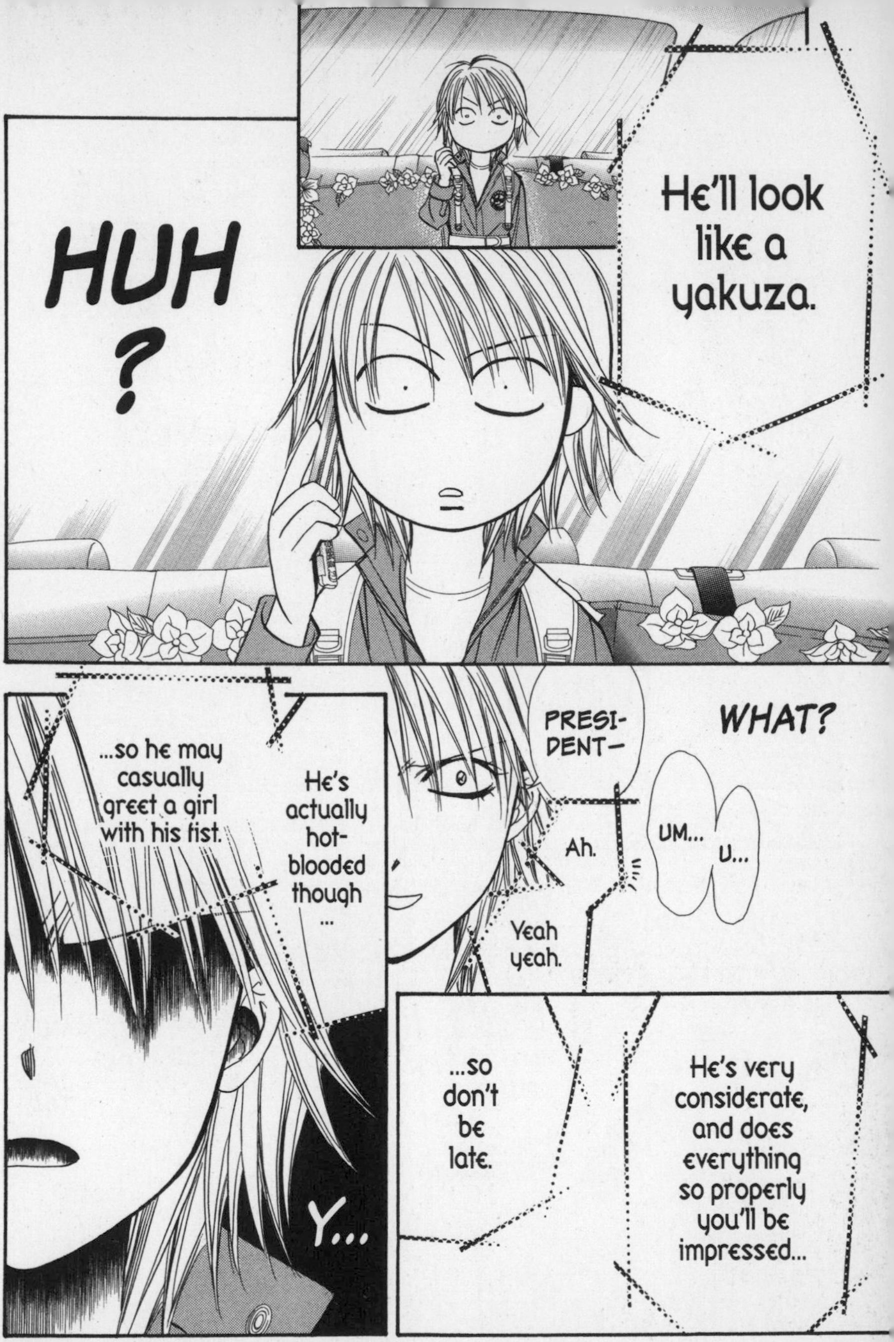
He'll look like a yakuza.
HUH ?
WHAT?
PRESI-DENT—
UM...
U...
Ah.
Yeah yeah.
He's very considerate, and does everything so properly you'll be impressed...
...so don't be late.
He's actually hot-blooded though...
...so he may casually greet a girl with his fist.
Y...

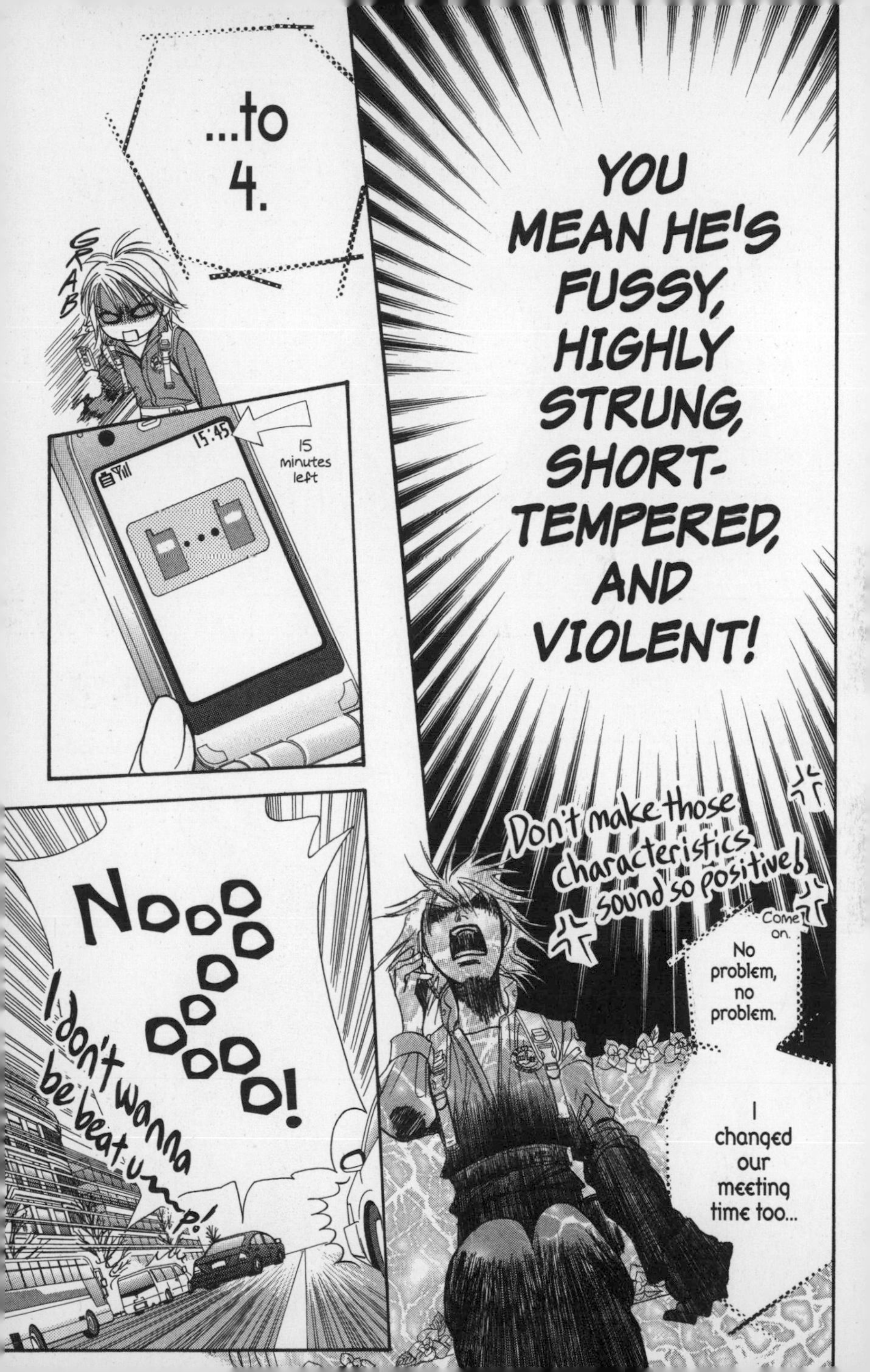
YOU MEAN HE'S FUSSY, HIGHLY STRUNG, SHORT-TEMPERED, AND VIOLENT!
Don't make those characteristics sound so positive!
Come on.
No problem, no problem.
I changed our meeting time too...
...to 4.
GRAB
15:45
15 minutes left
Noooooooooooooo!
I don't wanna be beat u~~p!

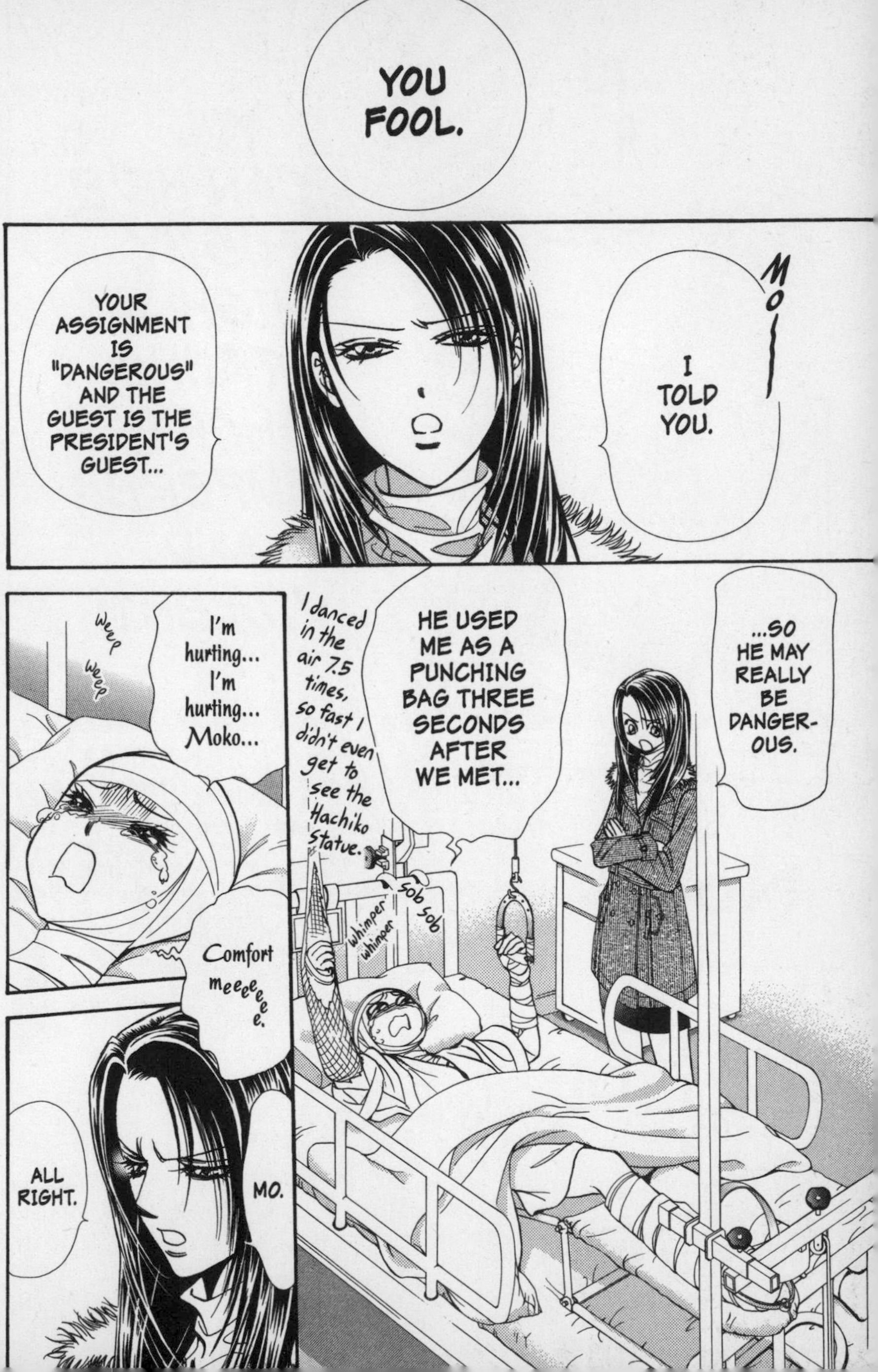
YOU FOOL.
MO———
I TOLD YOU.
YOUR ASSIGNMENT IS "DANGEROUS" AND THE GUEST IS THE PRESIDENT'S GUEST...
...SO HE MAY REALLY BE DANGER-OUS.
HE USED ME AS A PUNCHING BAG THREE SECONDS AFTER WE MET...
I danced in the air 7.5 times, so fast I didn't even get to see the Hachiko Statue.
sob sob
whimper whimper
I'm hurting... I'm hurting... Moko...
weep weep
Comfort meeeeeee.
MO.
ALL RIGHT.

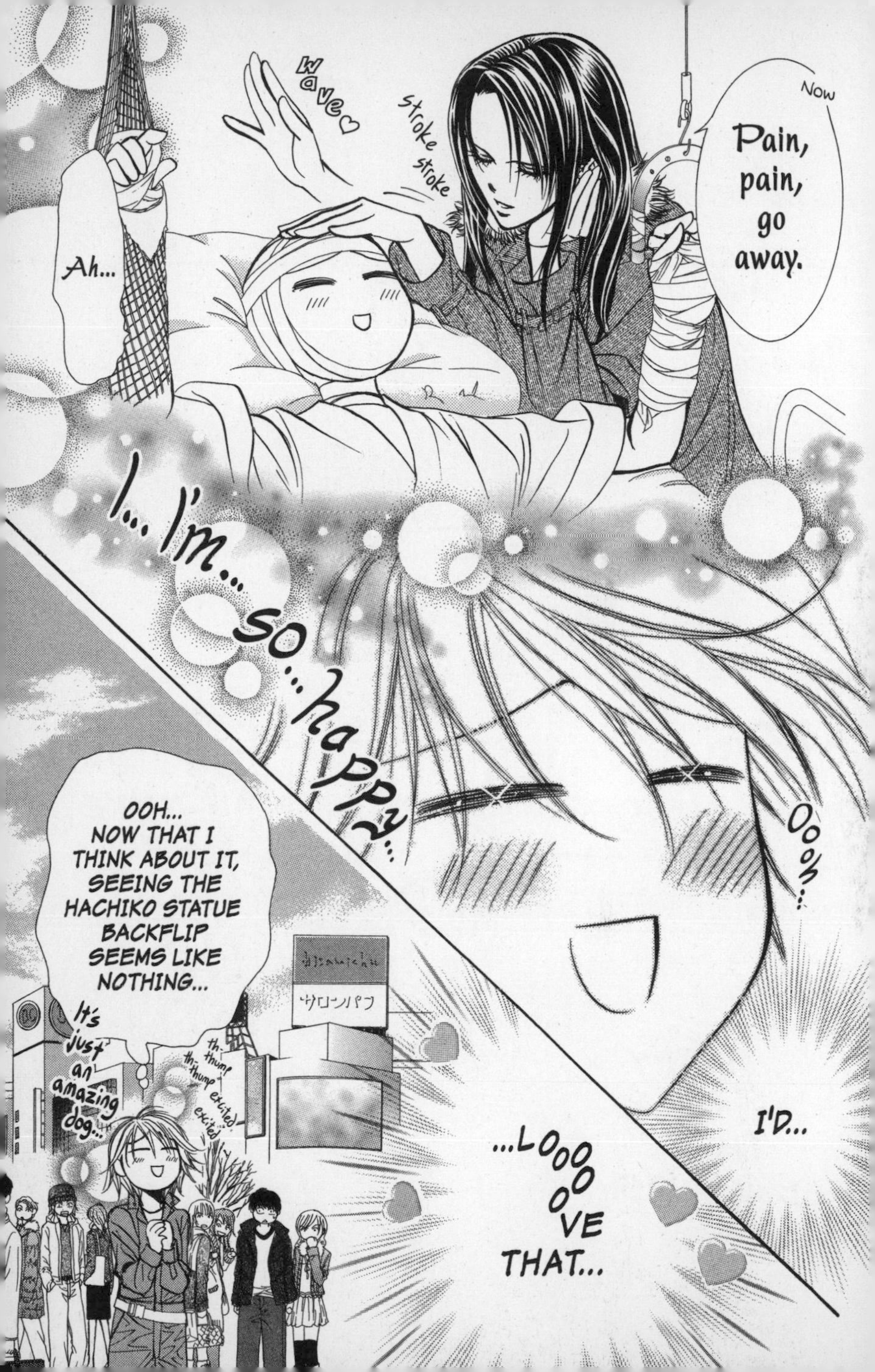
Now
Pain, pain, go away.
stroke stroke
wave♡
Ah...
I... I'm... so... happy...
Oooh...
I'D...
...LOOOOOOVE THAT...
OOH... NOW THAT I THINK ABOUT IT, SEEING THE HACHIKO STATUE BACKFLIP SEEMS LIKE NOTHING...
It's just an amazing dog...
th-thump th-thump
excited excited

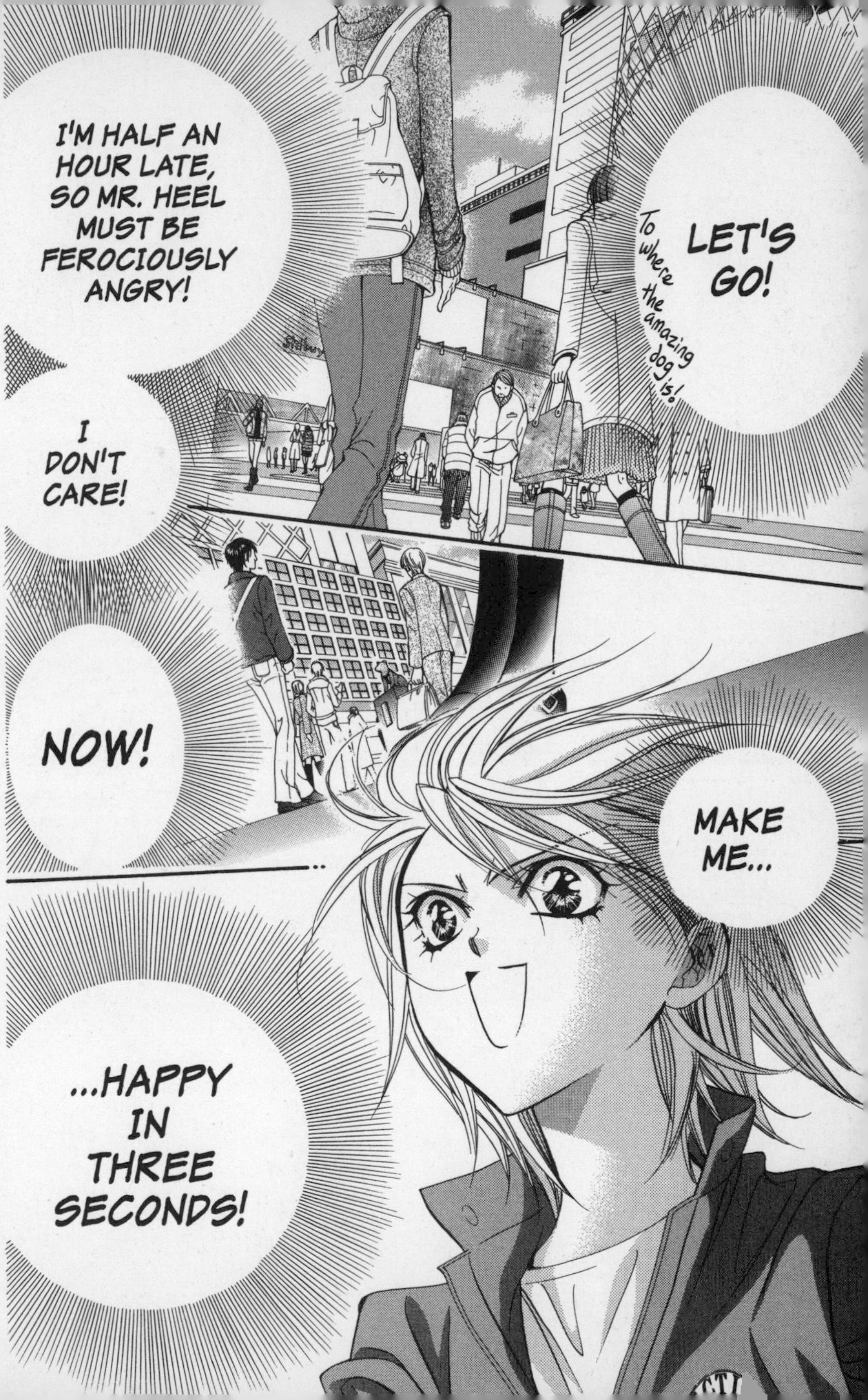
LET'S GO!
To where the amazing dog is!
I'M HALF AN HOUR LATE, SO MR. HEEL MUST BE FEROCIOUSLY ANGRY!
I DON'T CARE!
NOW!
MAKE ME...
...HAPPY IN THREE SECONDS!

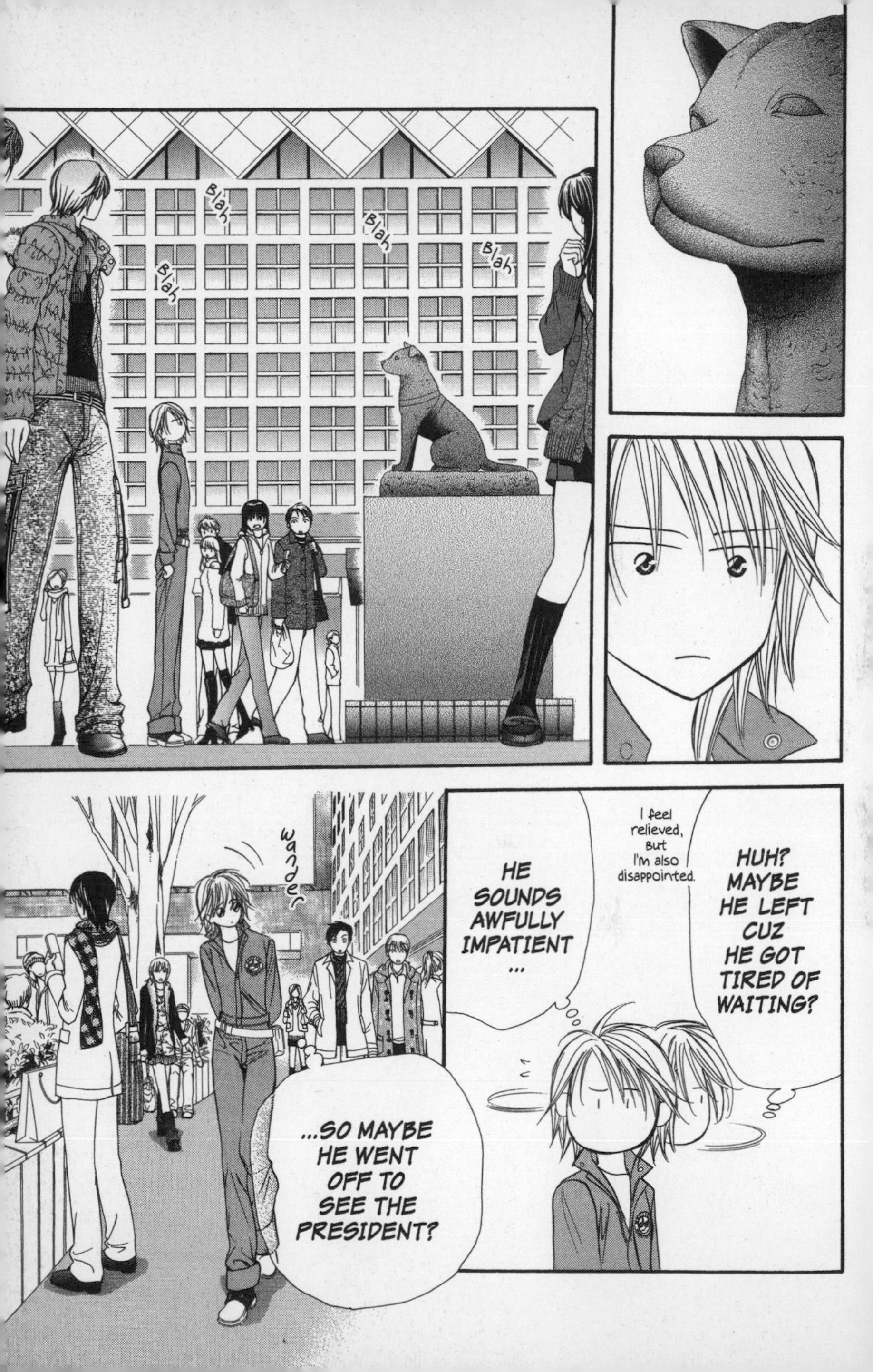
Blah
Blah
Blah
Blah
HUH? MAYBE HE LEFT CUZ HE GOT TIRED OF WAITING?
I feel relieved, but I'm also disappointed.
HE SOUNDS AWFULLY IMPATIENT...
wander
...SO MAYBE HE WENT OFF TO SEE THE PRESIDENT?

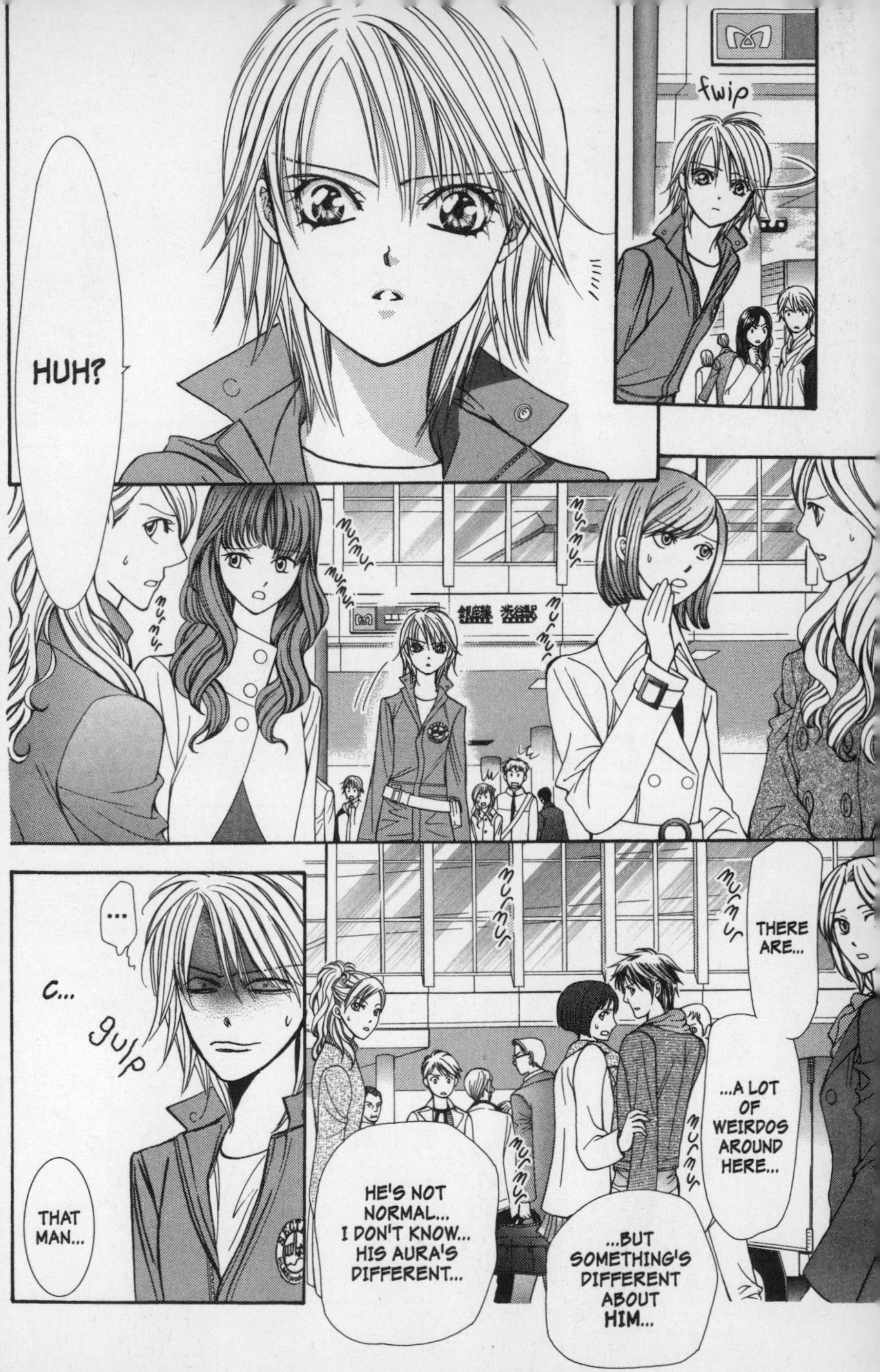
fwip
HUH?
murmur
murmur
murmur
murmur
murmur
銀座線 渋谷駅
murmur
murmur
THERE ARE...
...A LOT OF WEIRDOS AROUND HERE...
murmur
...BUT SOMETHING'S DIFFERENT ABOUT HIM...
murmur
HE'S NOT NORMAL... I DON'T KNOW... HIS AURA'S DIFFERENT...
...
C...
gulp
THAT MAN...

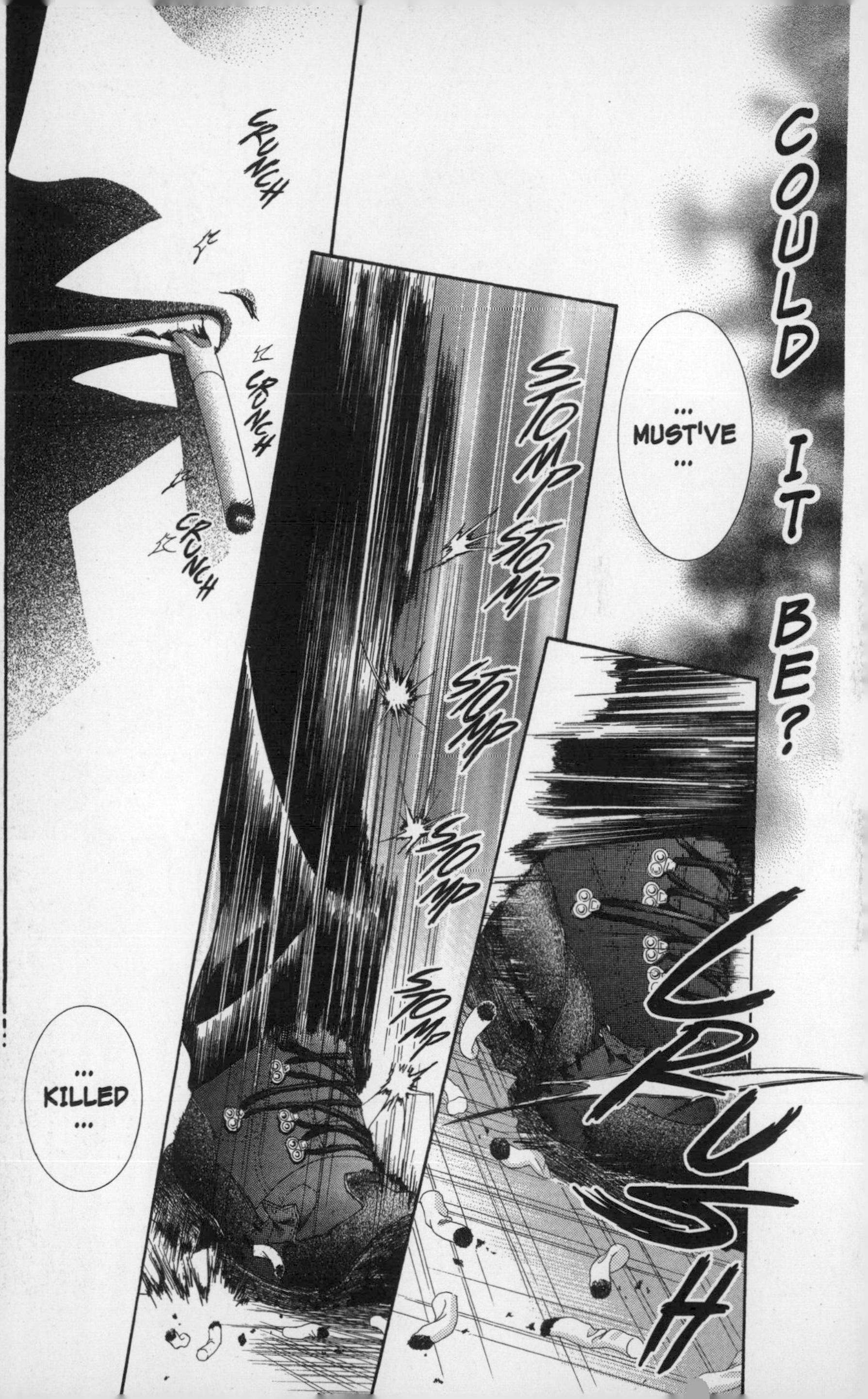
COULD IT BE?
...MUST'VE...
STOMP STOMP STOMP
STOMP
STOMP
STOMP
CRUSH
CRUNCH
CRUNCH
CRUNCH
...KILLED...

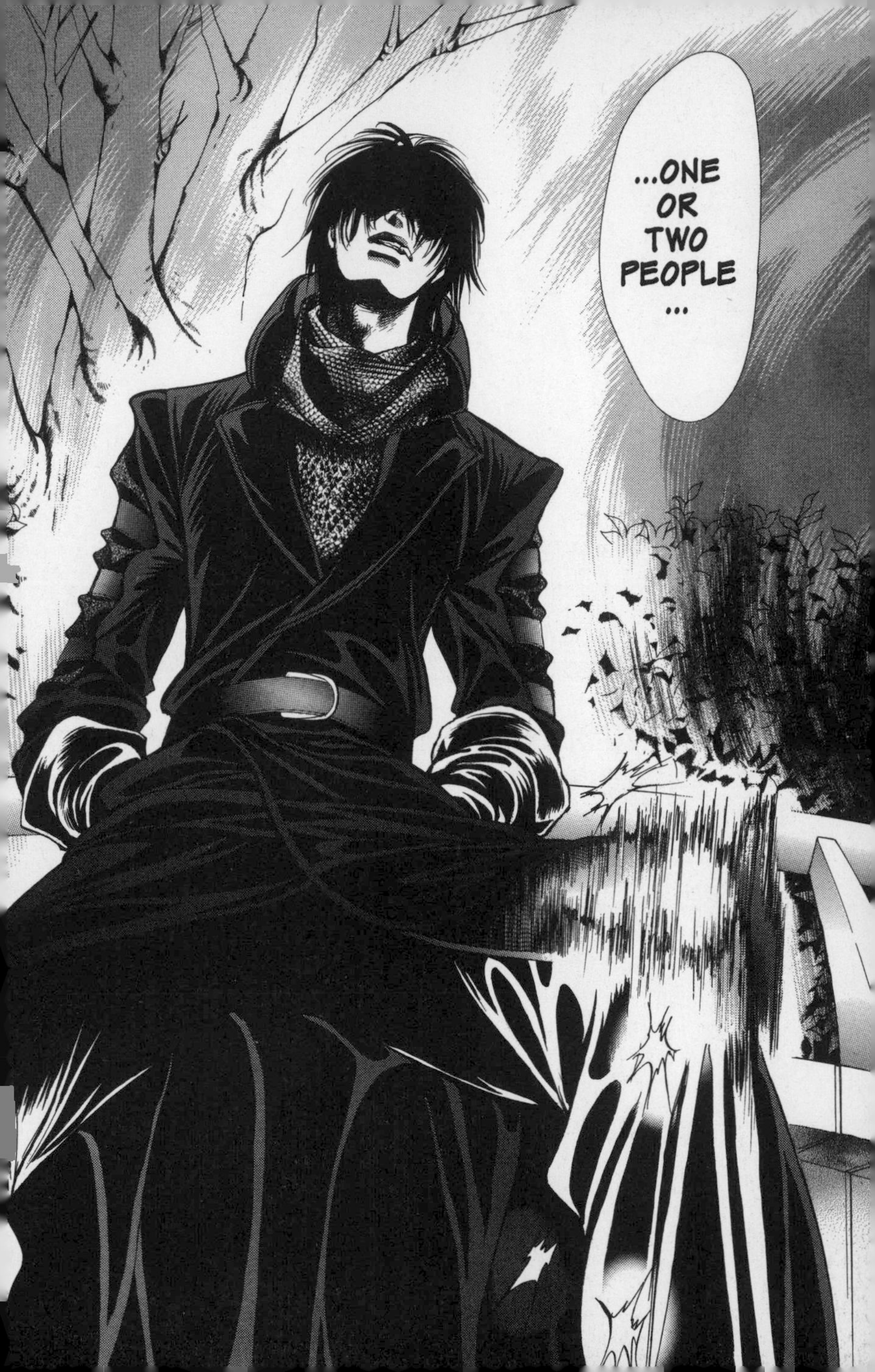
...ONE OR TWO PEOPLE ...

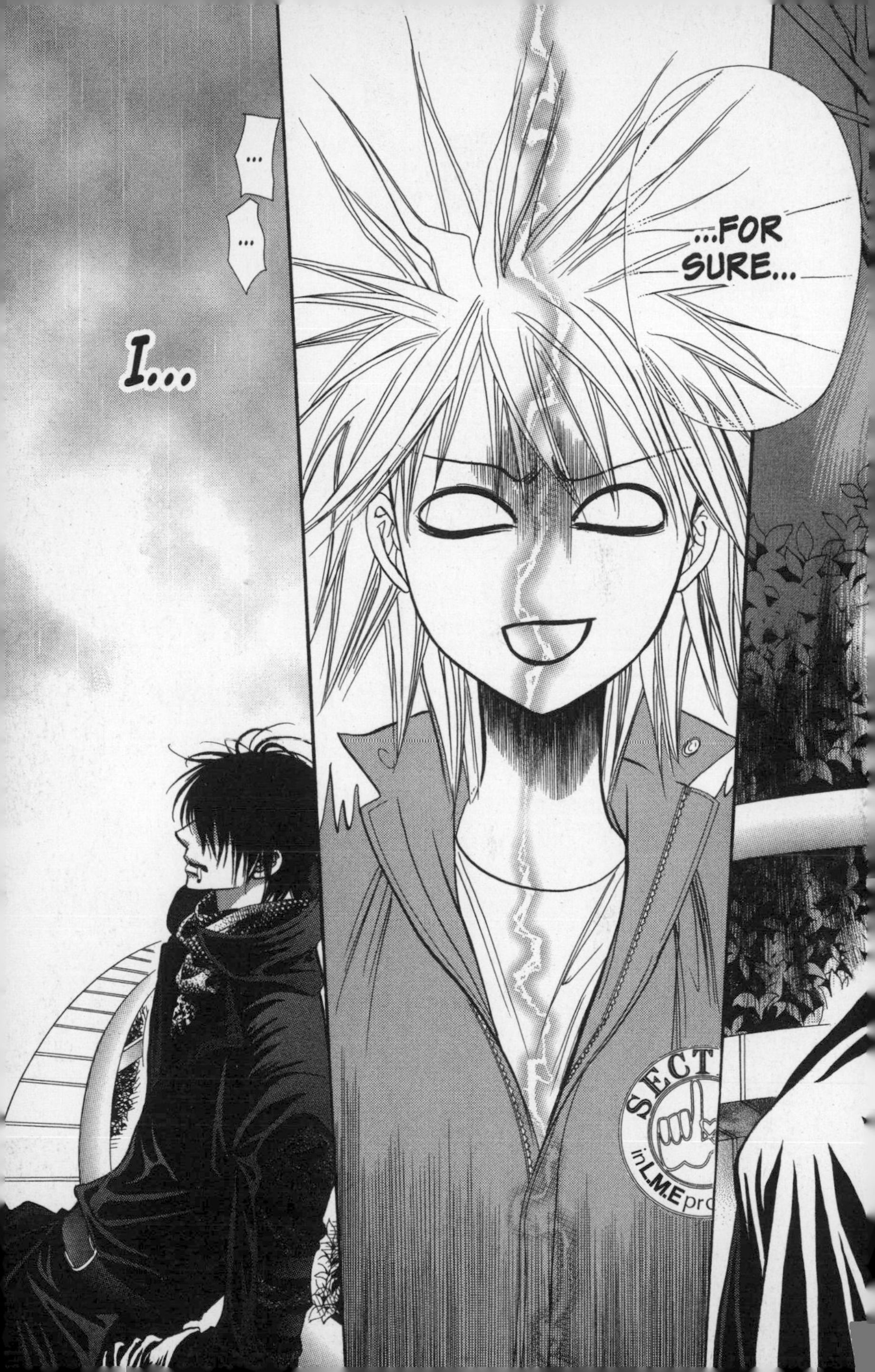
...
...
I...
...FOR SURE...

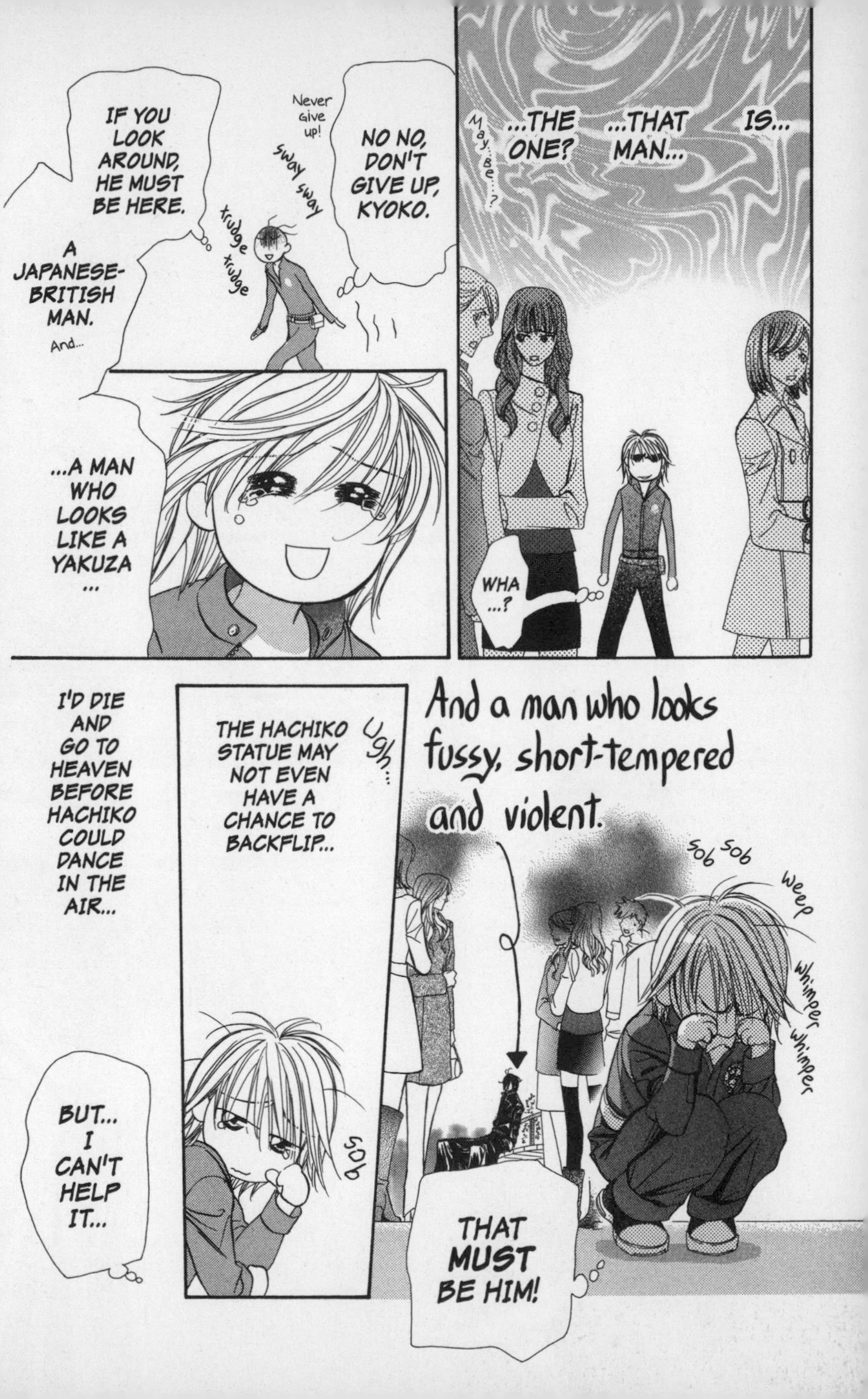
IS...
...THAT MAN...
...THE ONE?
May be...?
WHA ...?
Never give up!
NO NO, DON'T GIVE UP, KYOKO.
sway sway
trudge trudge
IF YOU LOOK AROUND, HE MUST BE HERE.
A JAPANESE-BRITISH MAN.
And...
...A MAN WHO LOOKS LIKE A YAKUZA ...
And a man who looks fussy, short-tempered and violent.
sob sob
weep
whimper whimper
THAT MUST BE HIM!
Ugh...
THE HACHIKO STATUE MAY NOT EVEN HAVE A CHANCE TO BACKFLIP...
I'D DIE AND GO TO HEAVEN BEFORE HACHIKO COULD DANCE IN THE AIR...
sob
BUT... I CAN'T HELP IT...

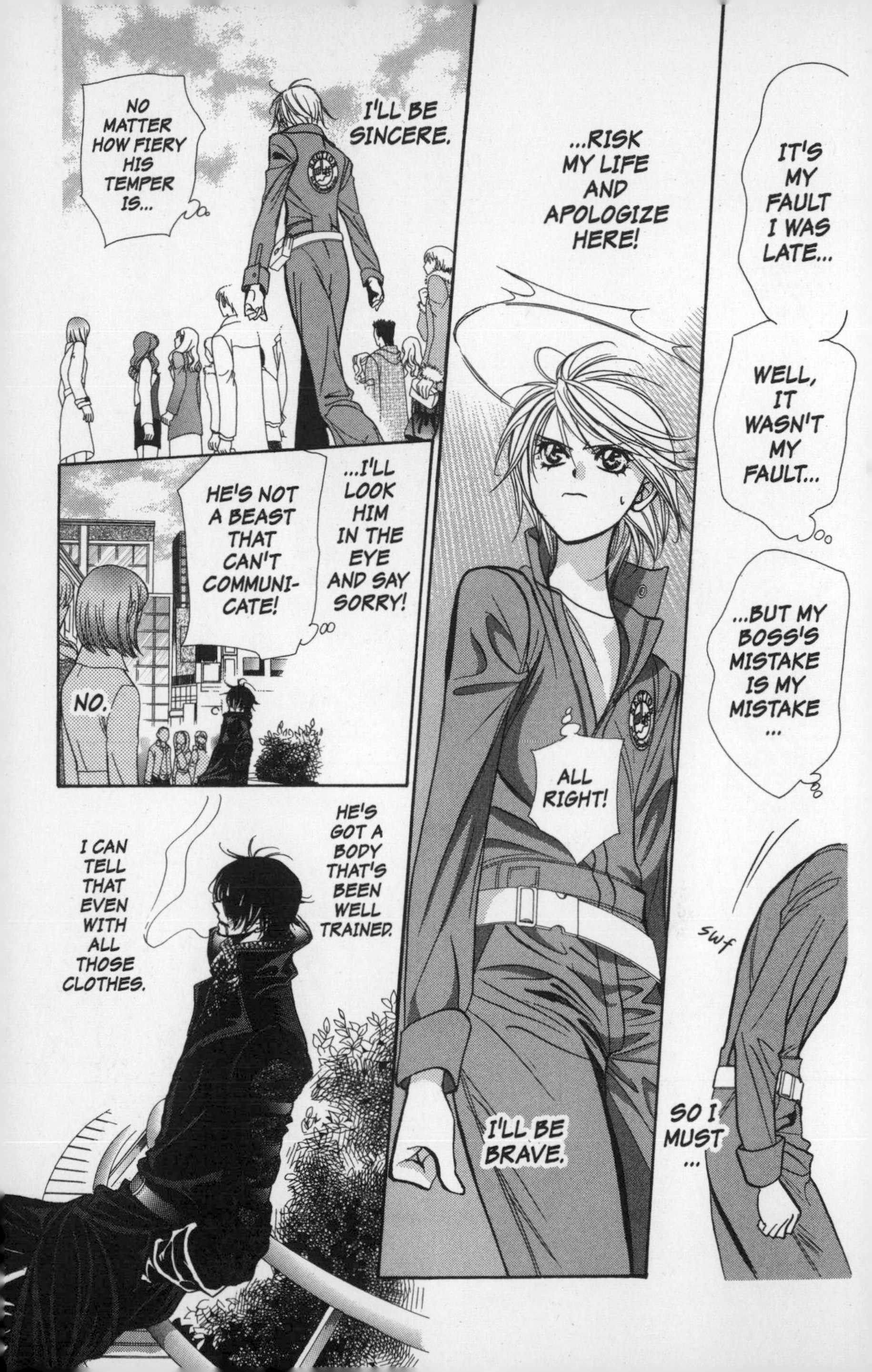
IT'S MY FAULT I WAS LATE...
WELL, IT WASN'T MY FAULT...
...BUT MY BOSS'S MISTAKE IS MY MISTAKE...
swf
SO I MUST...
...RISK MY LIFE AND APOLOGIZE HERE!
ALL RIGHT!
I'LL BE BRAVE.
I'LL BE SINCERE.
NO MATTER HOW FIERY HIS TEMPER IS...
...I'LL LOOK HIM IN THE EYE AND SAY SORRY!
HE'S NOT A BEAST THAT CAN'T COMMUNICATE!
NO.
HE'S GOT A BODY THAT'S BEEN WELL TRAINED.
I CAN TELL THAT EVEN WITH ALL THOSE CLOTHES.

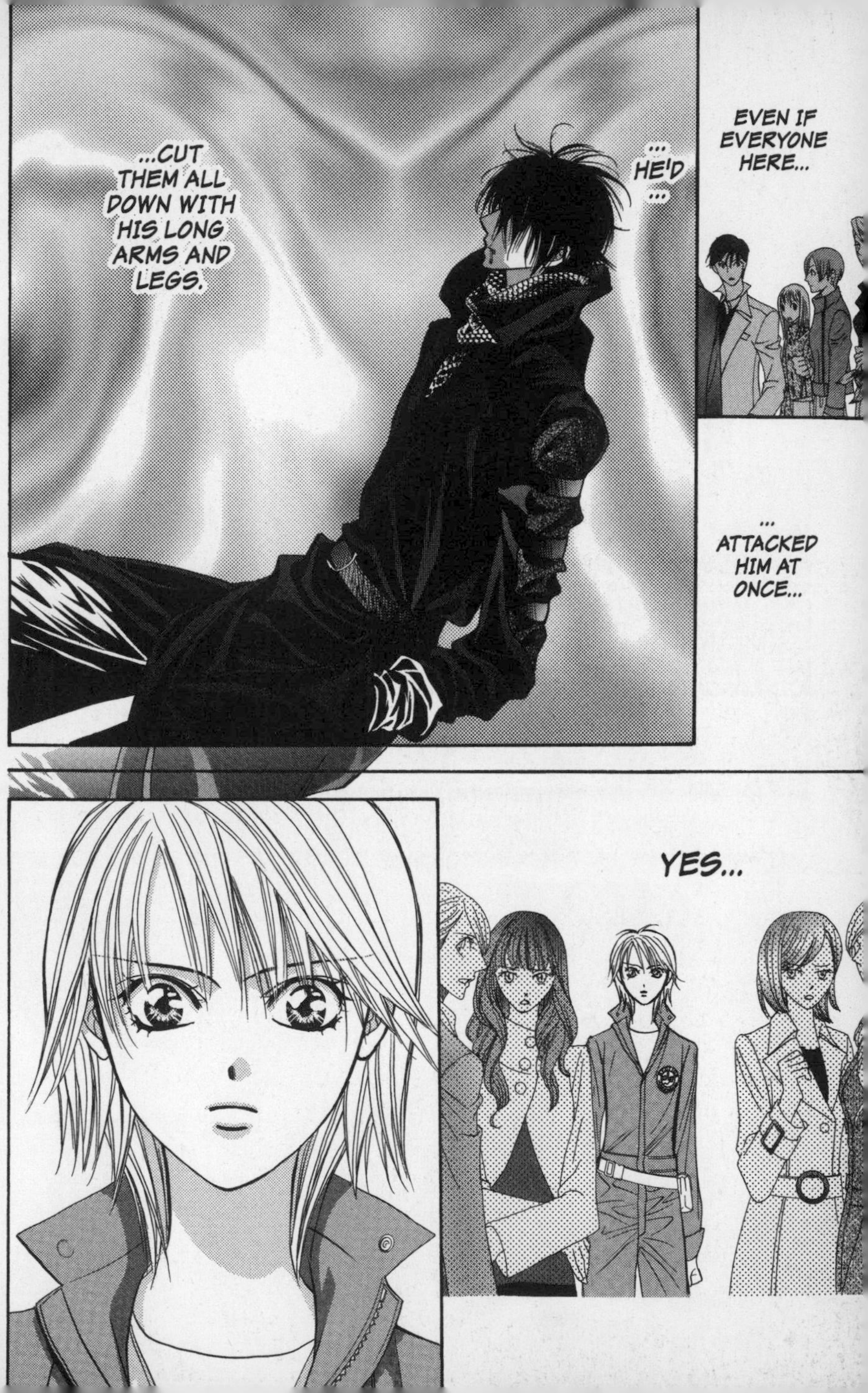
EVEN IF EVERYONE HERE...
...ATTACKED HIM AT ONCE...
...HE'D...
...CUT THEM ALL DOWN WITH HIS LONG ARMS AND LEGS.
YES...

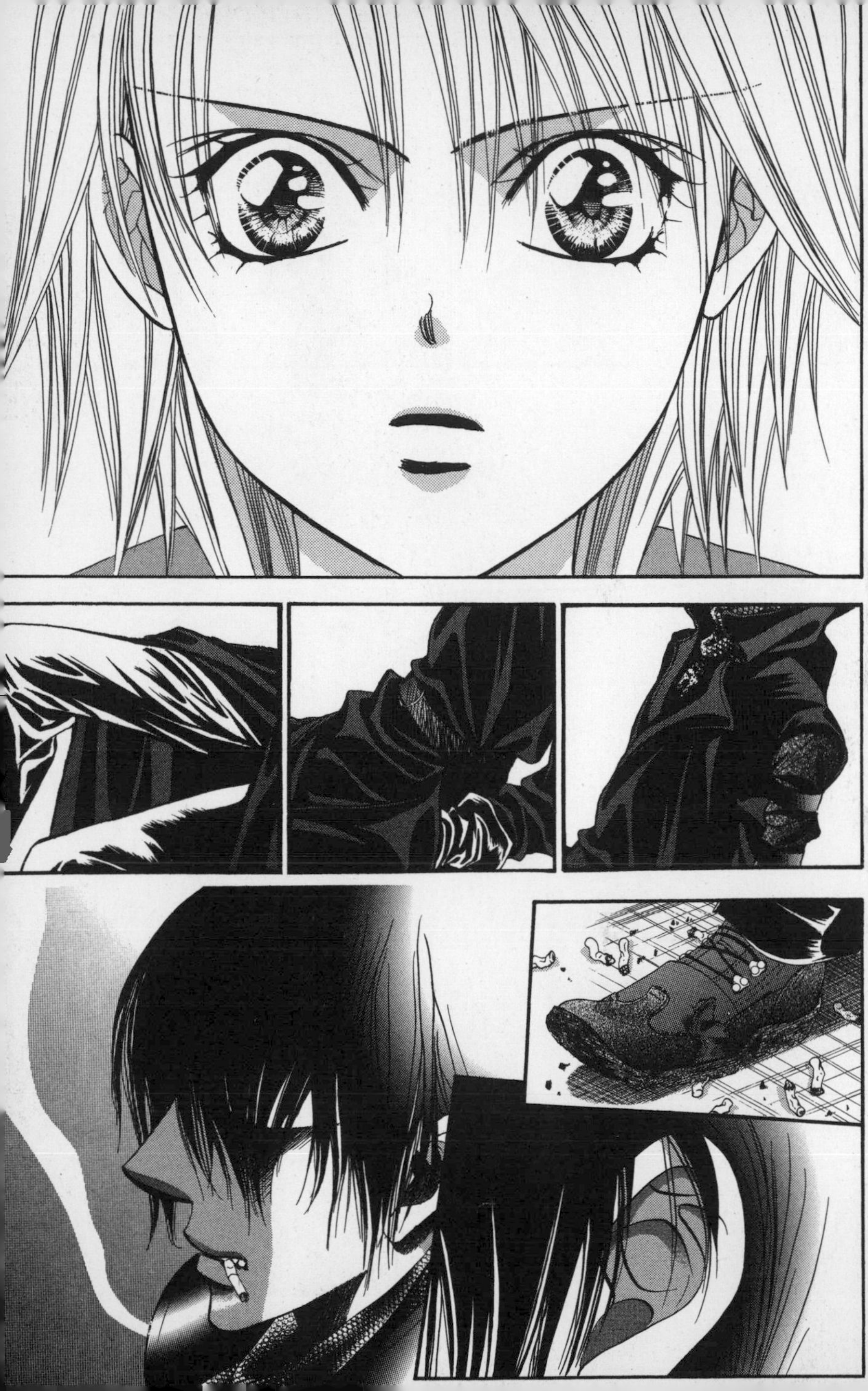

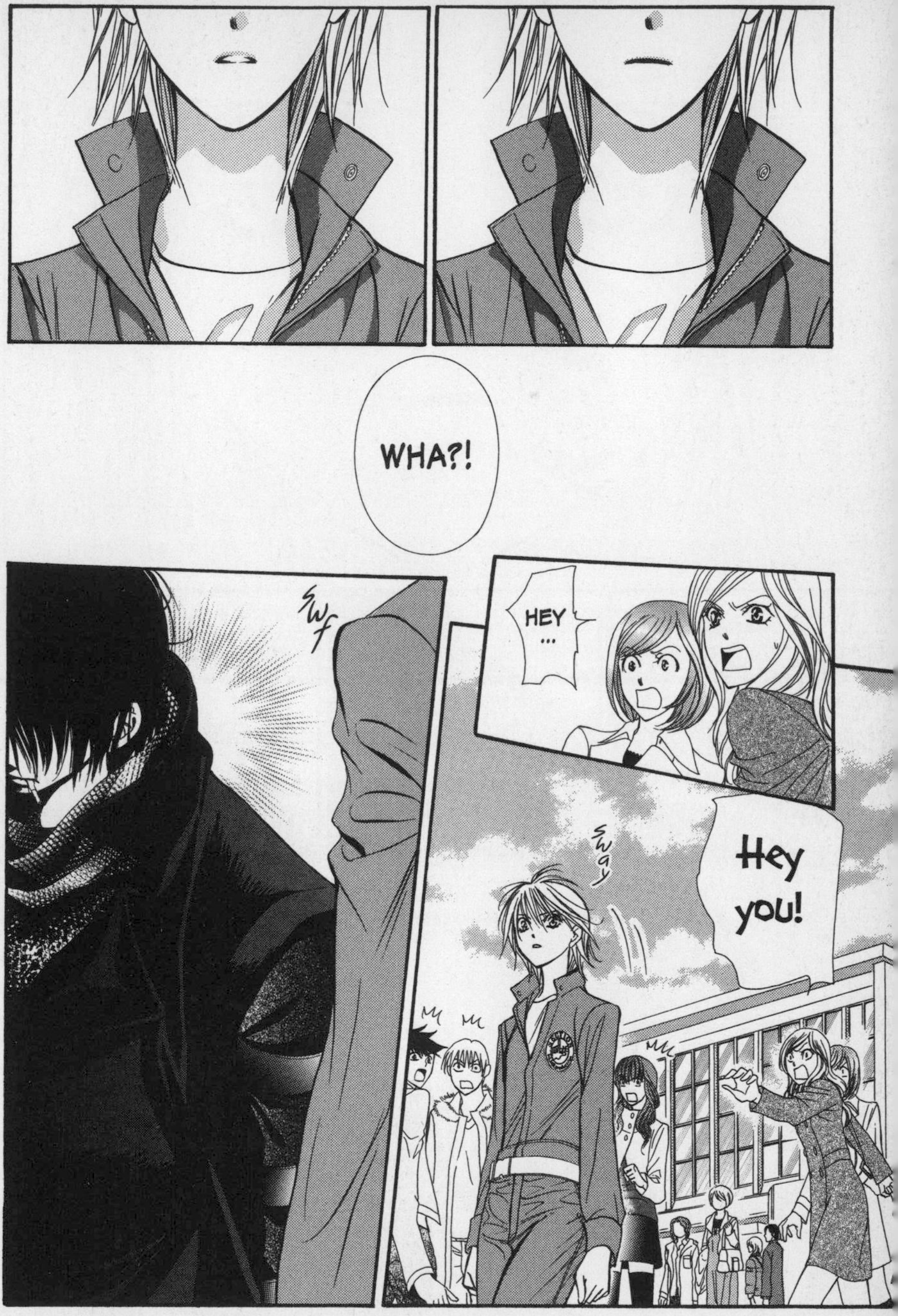
WHA?!
HEY ...
SWAY
Hey you!
SWF

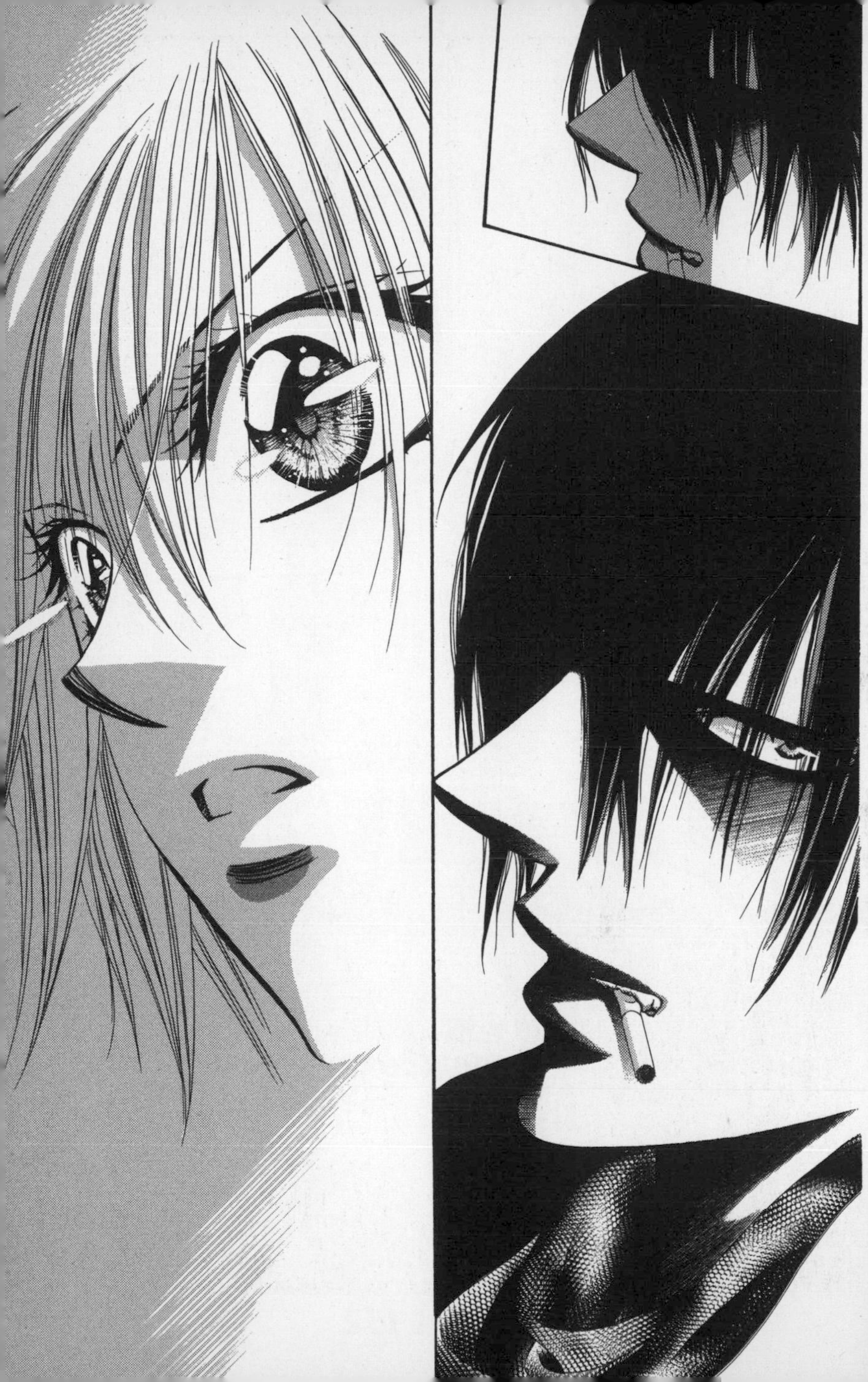

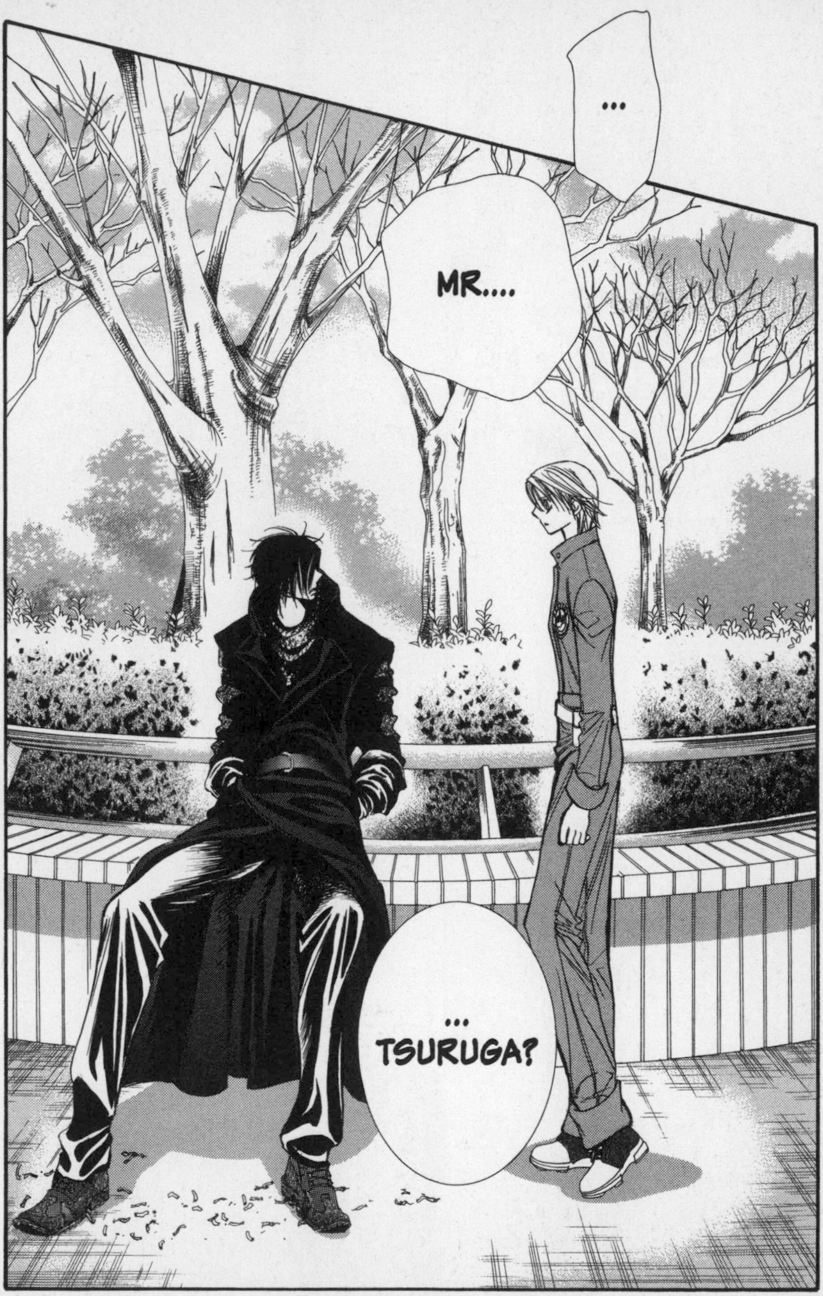
...
MR....
... TSURUGA?

End of Act 152

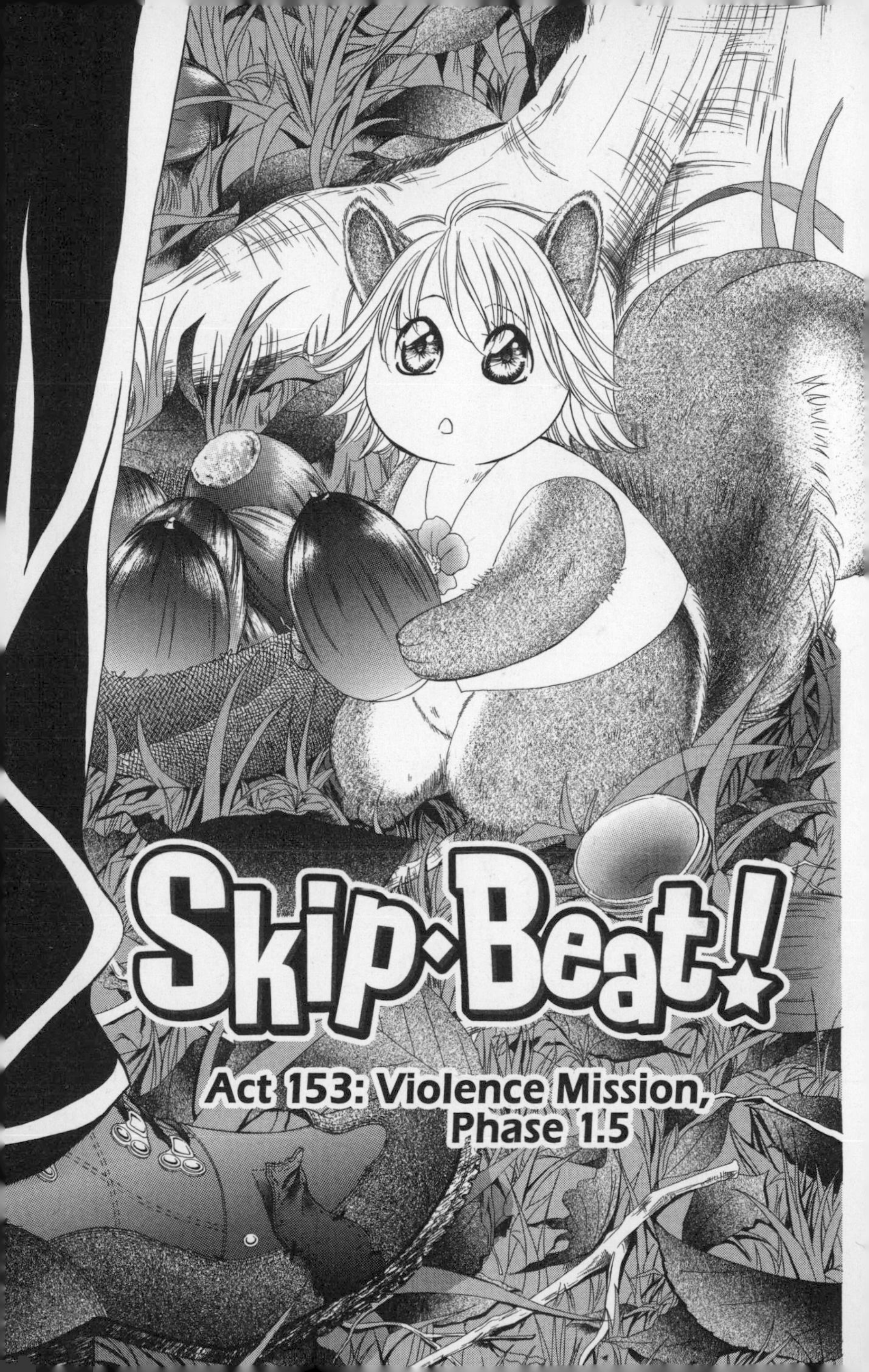
Skip·Beat!
Act 153: Violence Mission, Phase 1.5

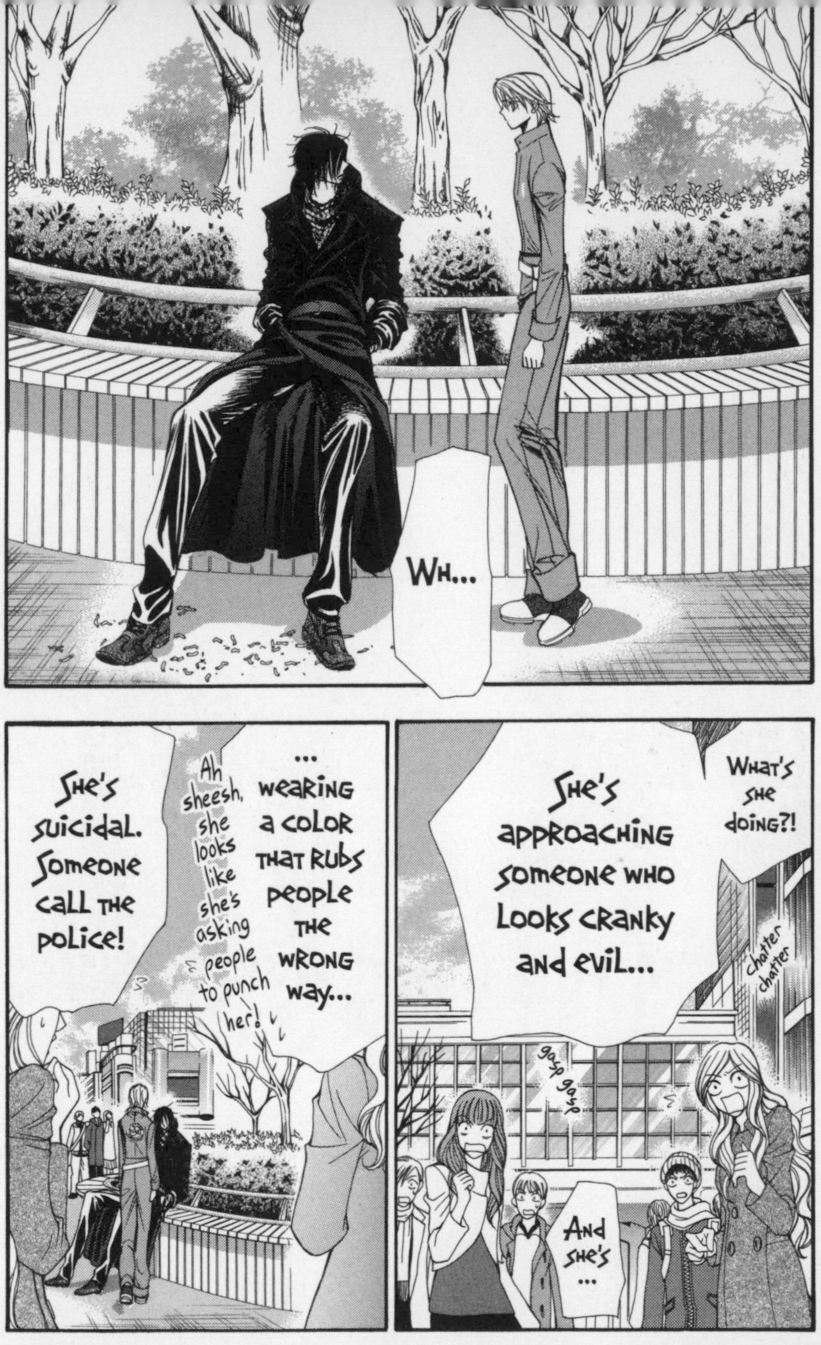
Wh...
What's she doing?!
She's approaching someone who looks cranky and evil...
chatter chatter
gasp gasp
And she's ...
... wearing a color that rubs people the wrong way...
Ah sheesh, she looks like she's asking people to punch her!
She's suicidal. Someone call the police!

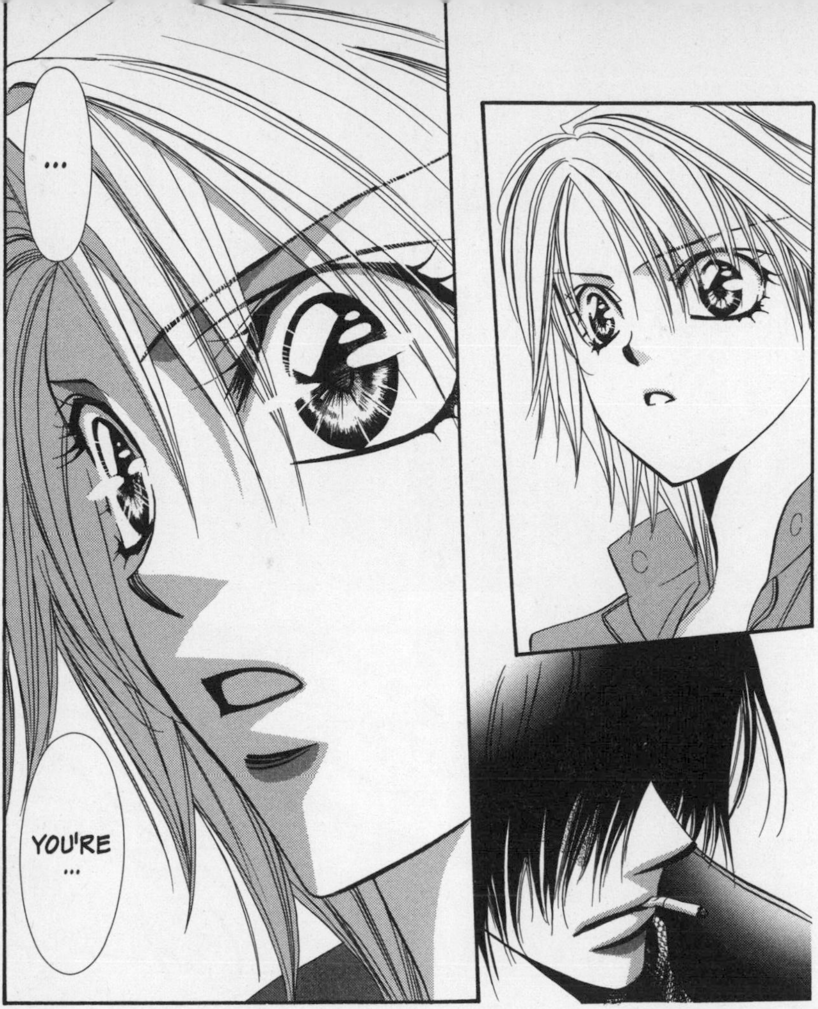
...
YOU'RE ...
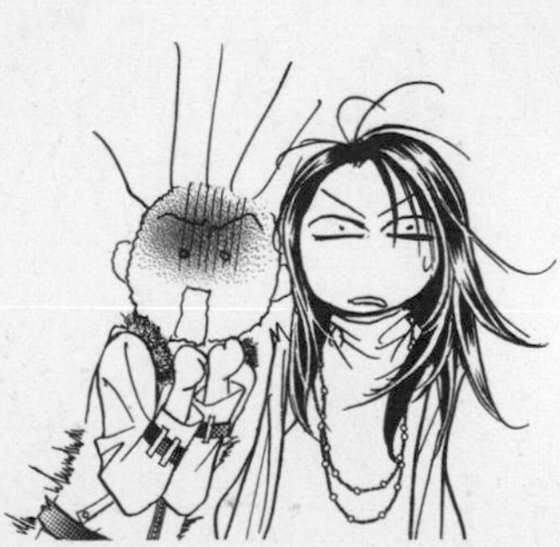

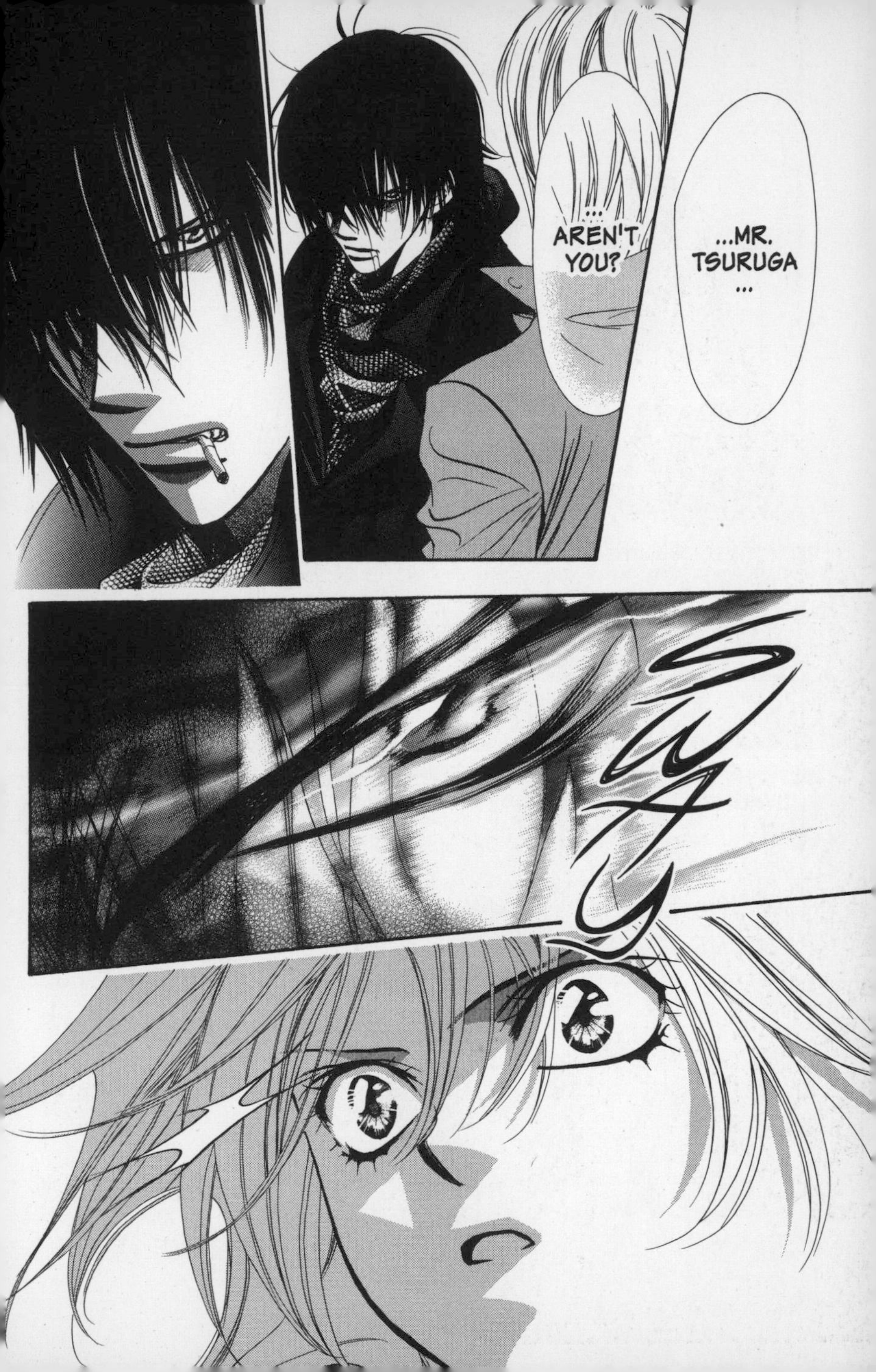
...MR. TSURUGA ...
... AREN'T YOU?
SWAY

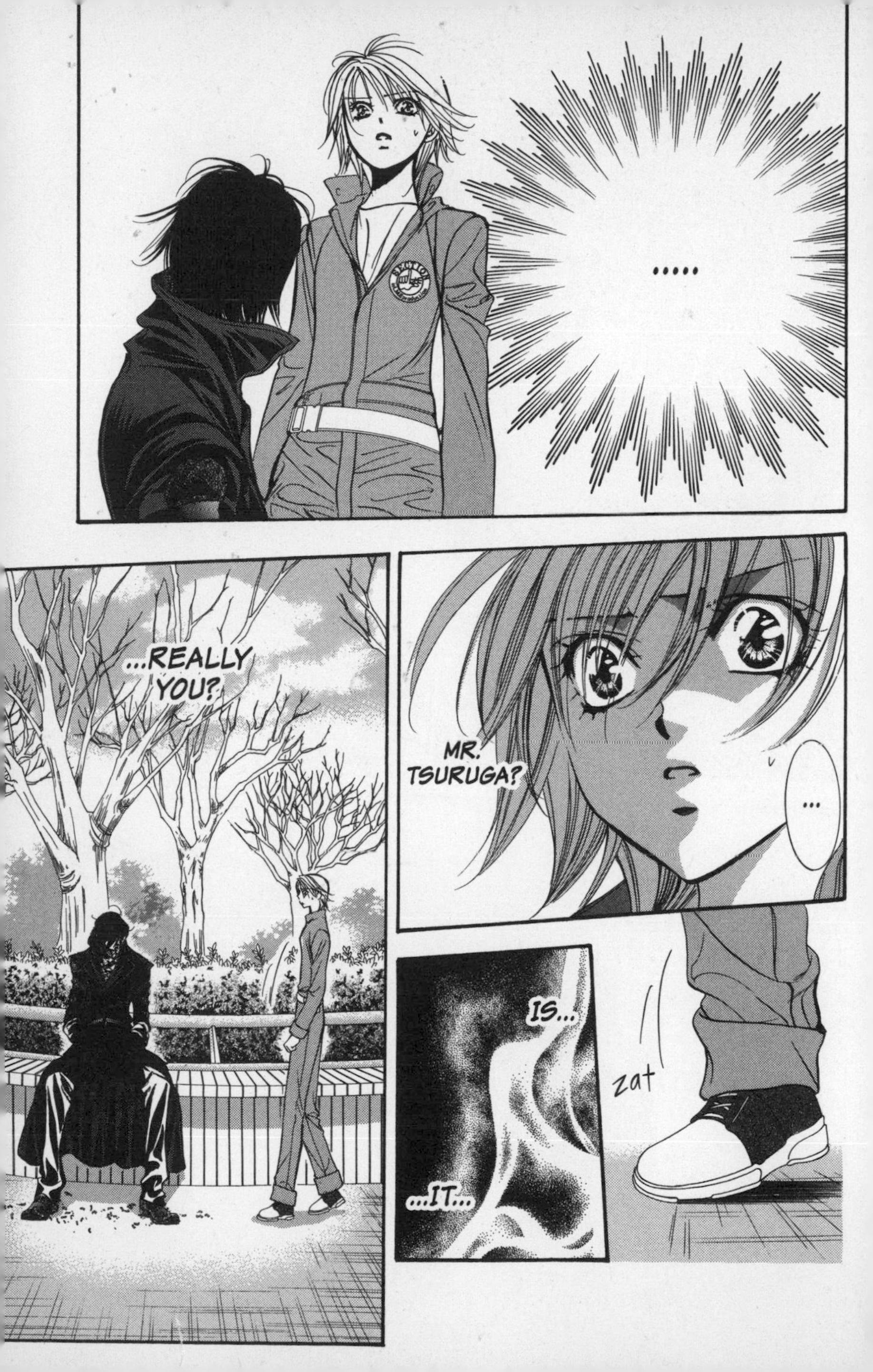
.....
...
MR. TSURUGA?
zat
IS...
...IT...
...REALLY YOU?

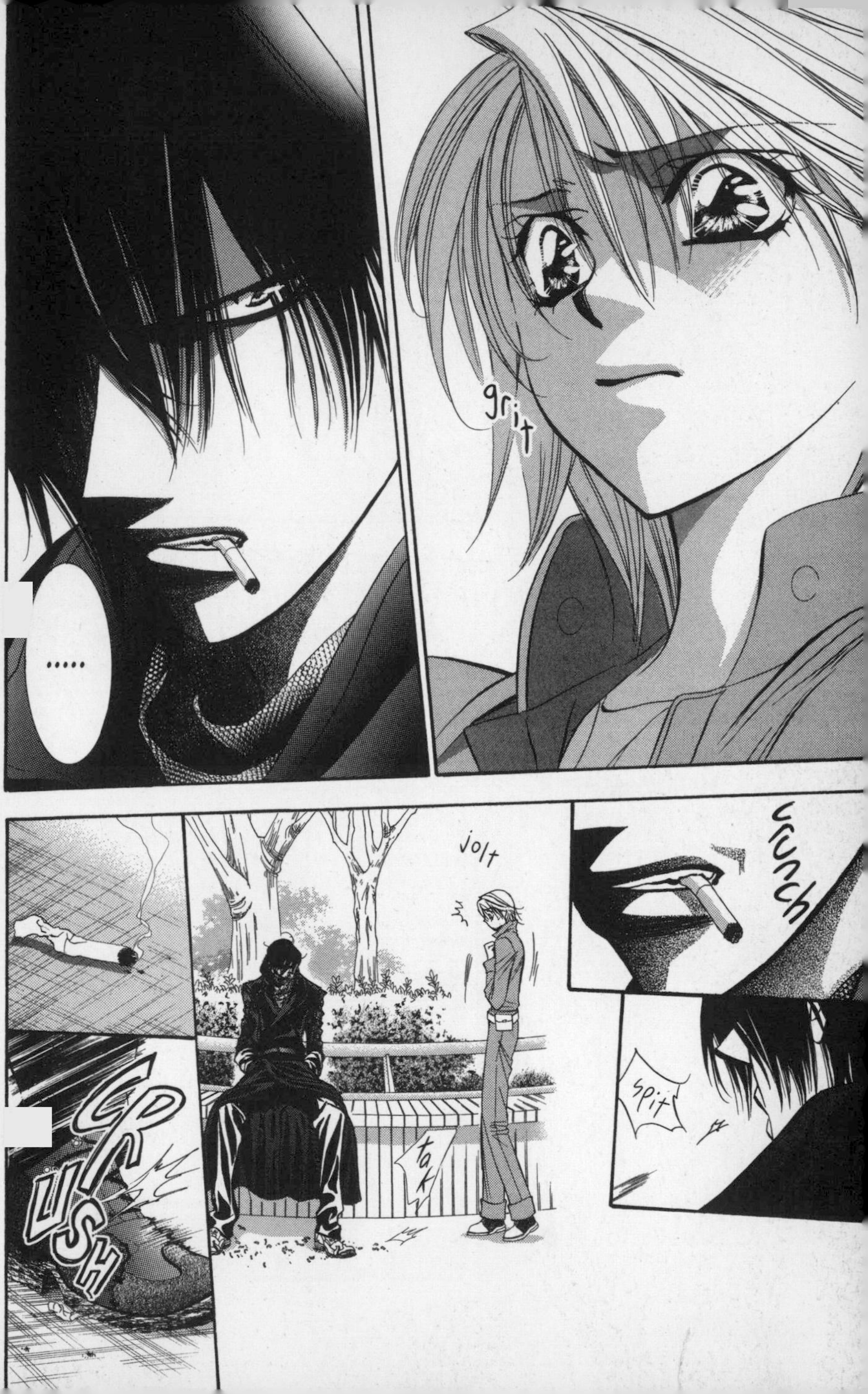
grit
.....
crunch
spit
jolt
tak
CRUSH

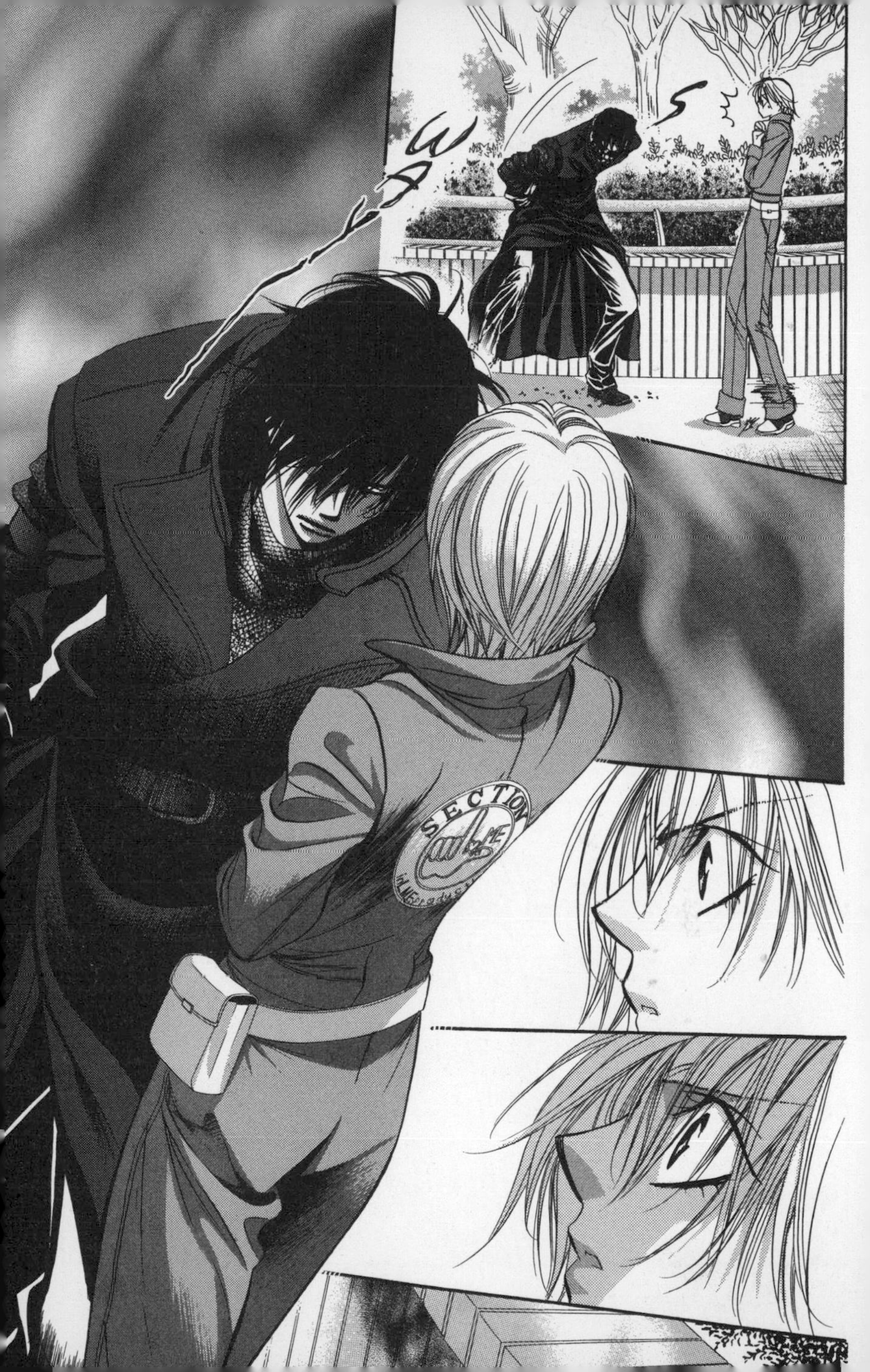
WA

THUD

ZZZok

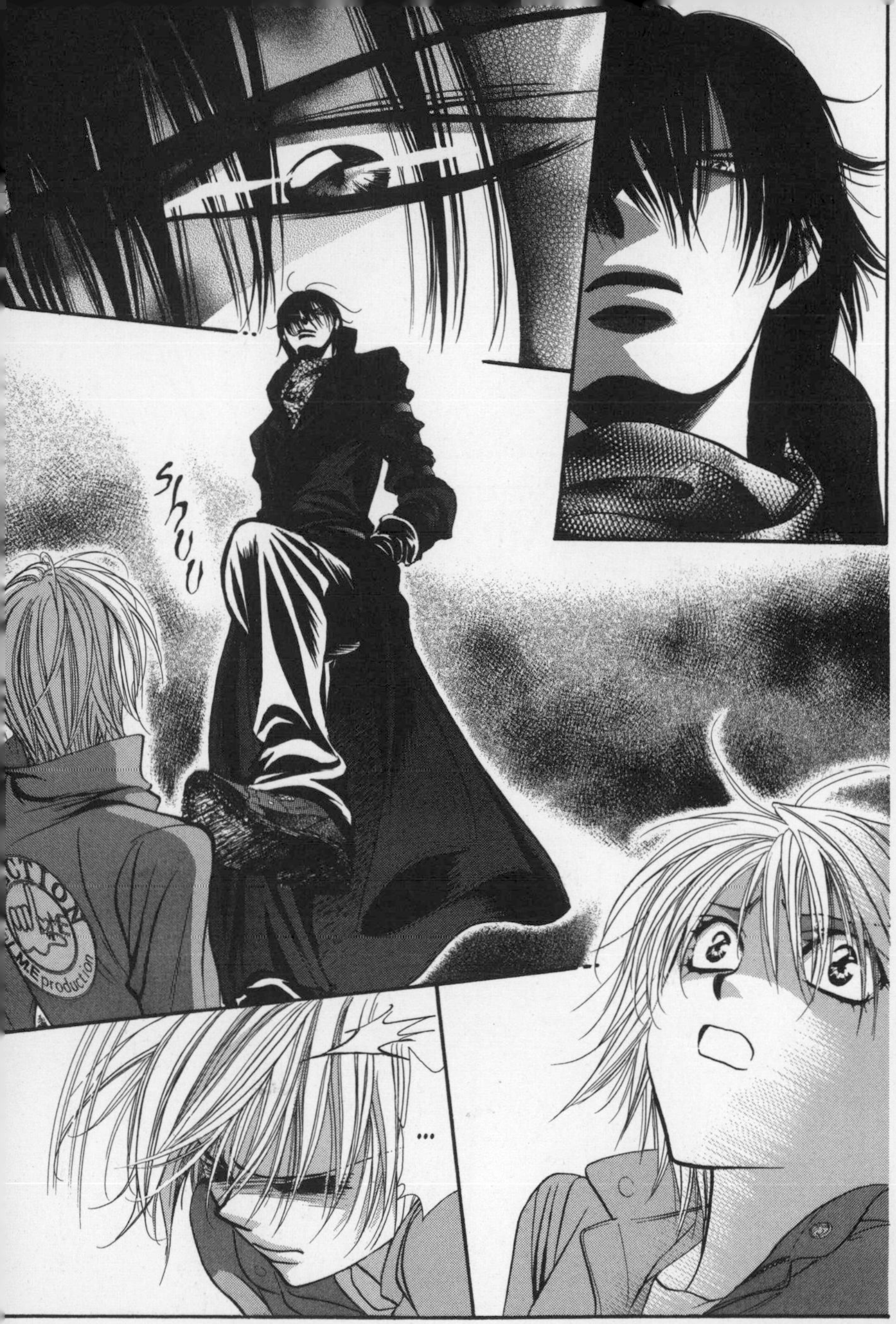
..
SHUU
..
...

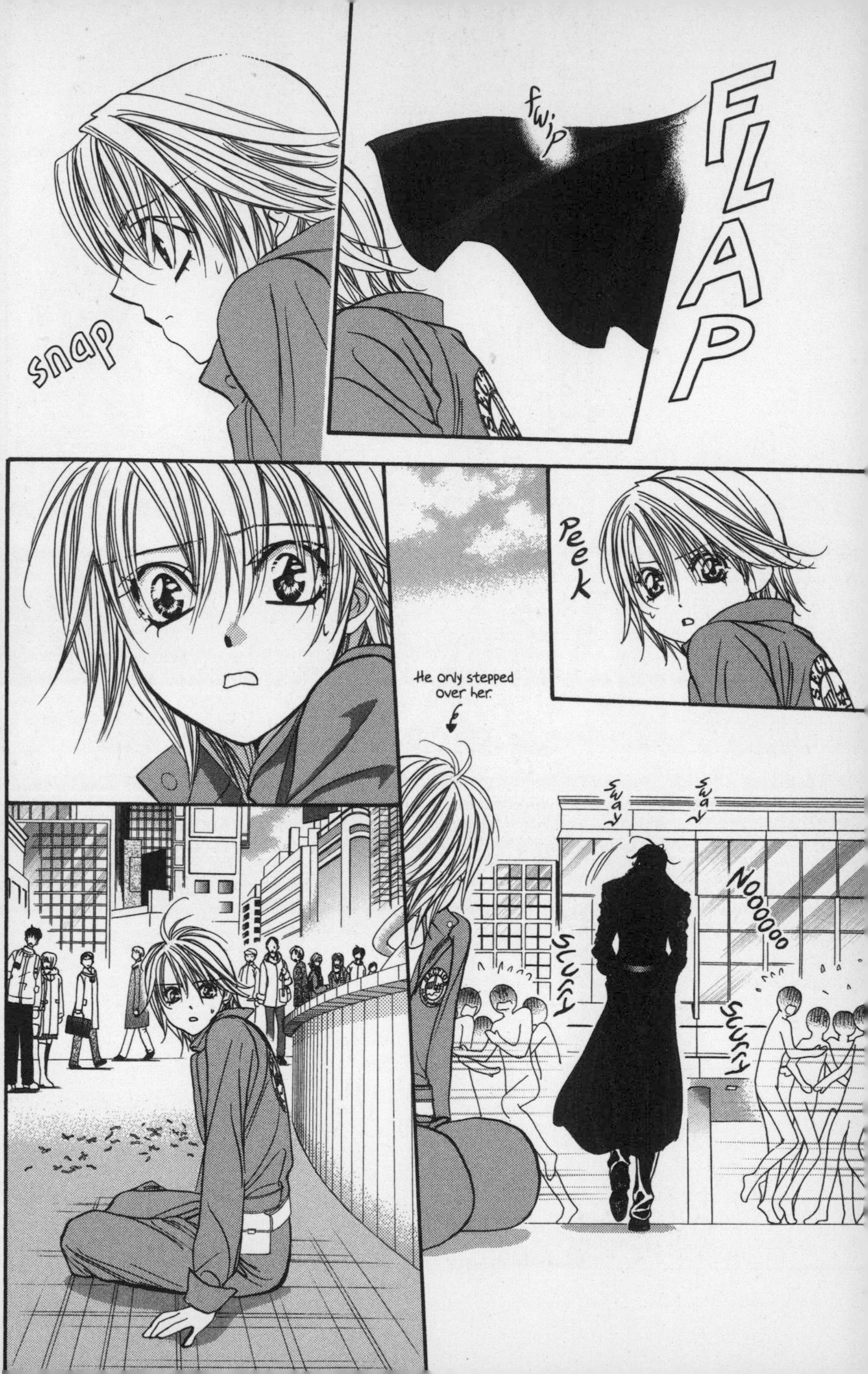

fwip
FLAP
snap
Peek
He only stepped over her.
sway
sway
NOOOOOO
scurry
scurry

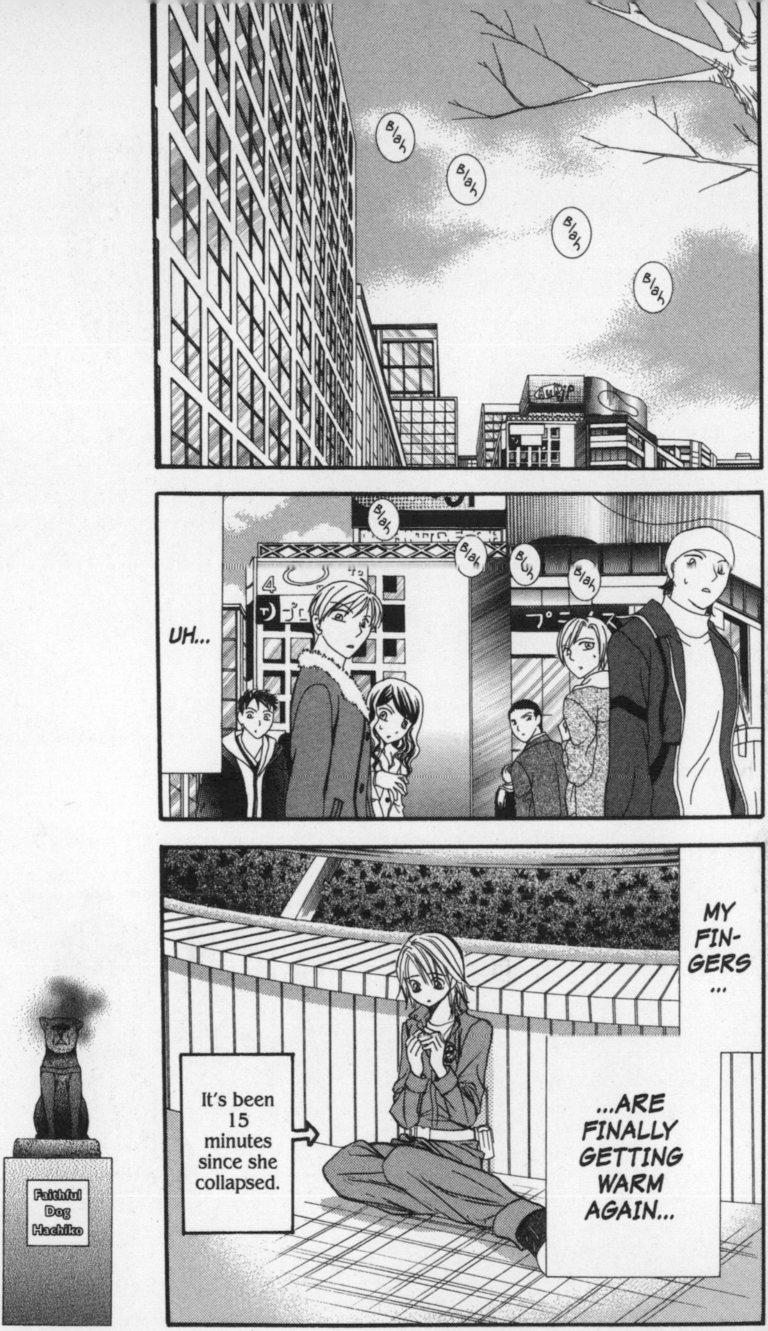
Blah
Blah
Blah
Blah
Blah
Bluh
Blah
Blah
UH...
MY FIN-GERS ...
...ARE FINALLY GETTING WARM AGAIN...
It's been 15 minutes since she collapsed.
Faithful Dog Hachiko

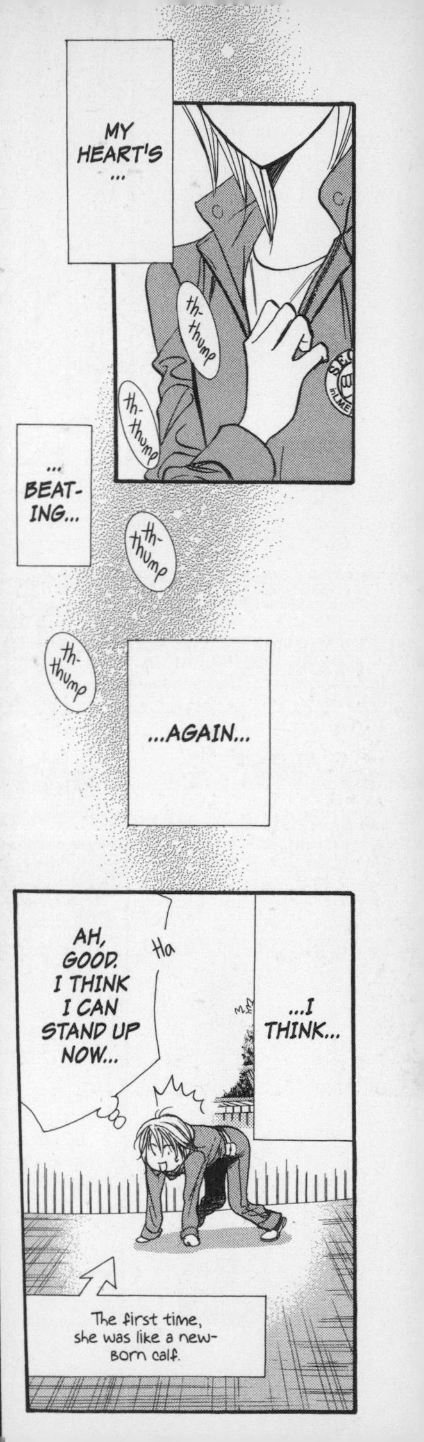
MY HEART'S ...
th-thump
th-thump
... BEATING...
th-thump
th-thump
...AGAIN...
...I THINK...
AH, GOOD. I THINK I CAN STAND UP NOW...
Ha
The first time, she was like a new-born calf.
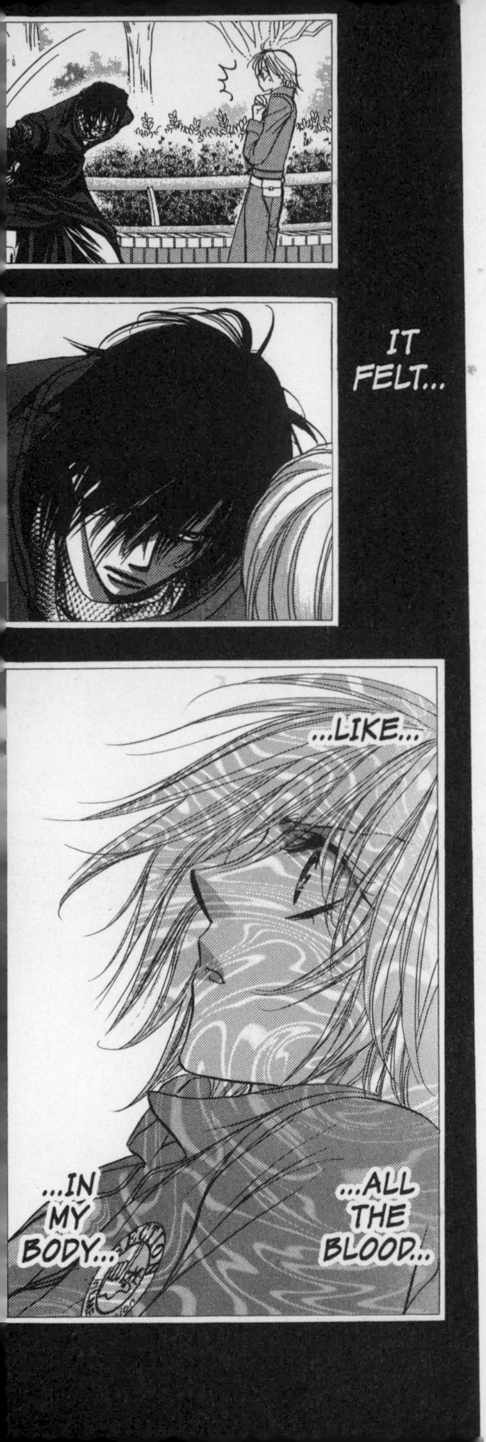
IT FELT...
...LIKE...
...ALL THE BLOOD...
...IN MY BODY...

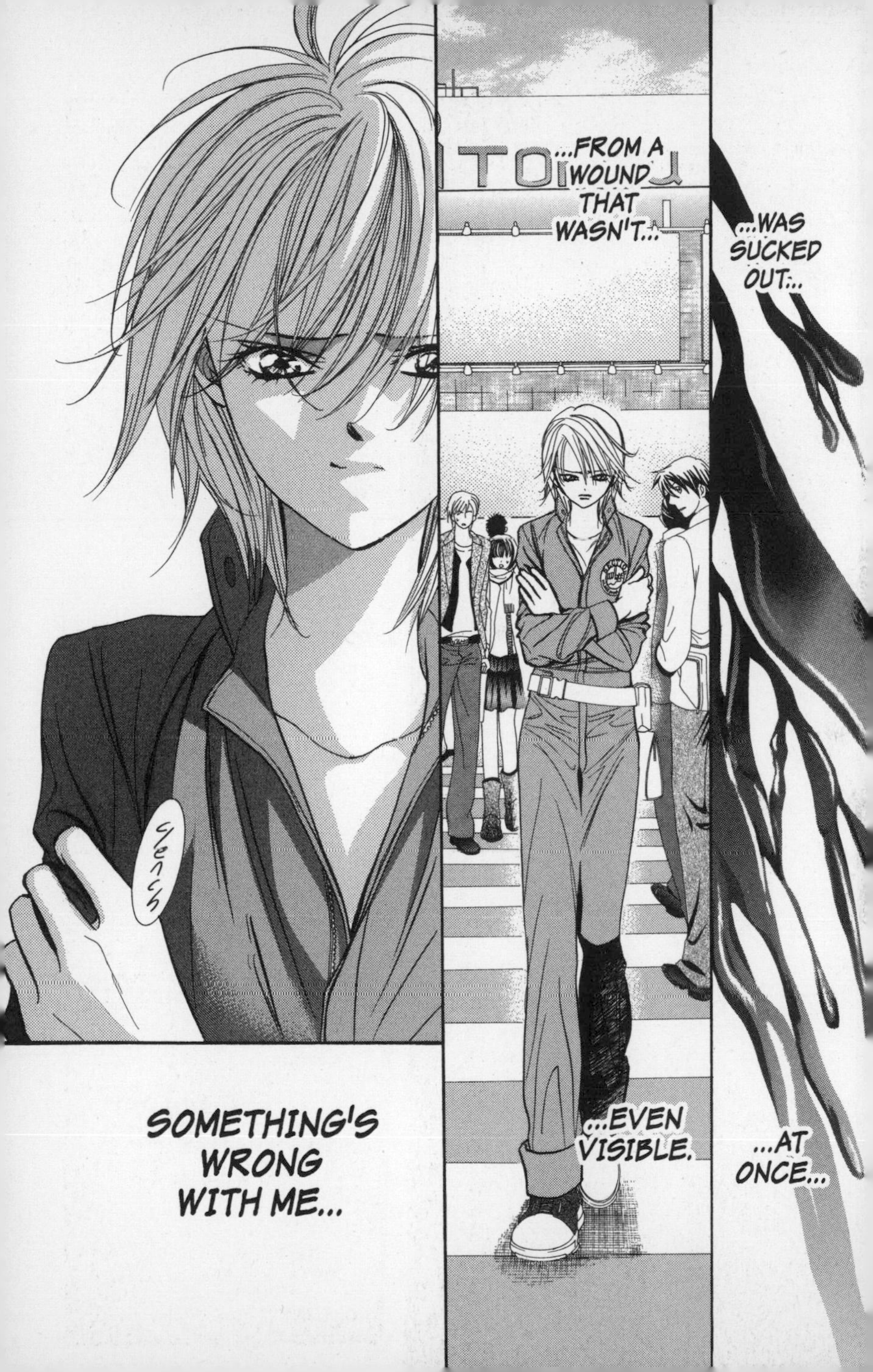
...WAS SUCKED OUT...
...AT ONCE...
...FROM A WOUND THAT WASN'T...
...EVEN VISIBLE.
SOMETHING'S WRONG WITH ME...

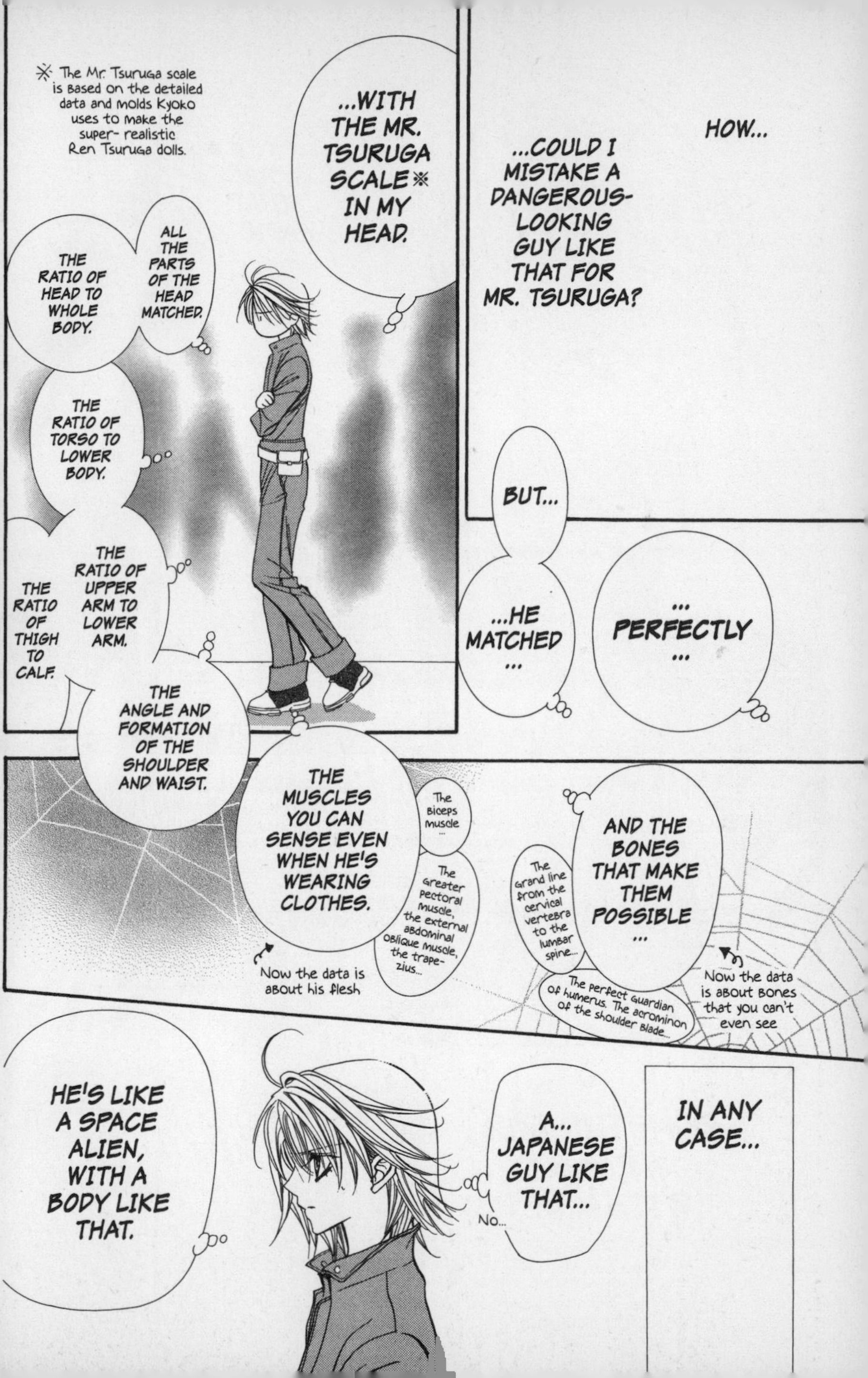

HOW...
...COULD I MISTAKE A DANGEROUS-LOOKING GUY LIKE THAT FOR MR. TSURUGA?
BUT...
...HE MATCHED...
...PERFECTLY...
※ The Mr. Tsuruga scale is based on the detailed data and molds Kyoko uses to make the super- realistic Ren Tsuruga dolls.
...WITH THE MR. TSURUGA SCALE※ IN MY HEAD.
ALL THE PARTS OF THE HEAD MATCHED.
THE RATIO OF HEAD TO WHOLE BODY.
THE RATIO OF TORSO TO LOWER BODY.
THE RATIO OF UPPER ARM TO LOWER ARM.
THE RATIO OF THIGH TO CALF.
THE ANGLE AND FORMATION OF THE SHOULDER AND WAIST.
THE MUSCLES YOU CAN SENSE EVEN WHEN HE'S WEARING CLOTHES.
The Biceps muscle...
The Greater pectoral muscle, the external abdominal oblique muscle, the trapezius...
Now the data is about his flesh
AND THE BONES THAT MAKE THEM POSSIBLE...
The Grand line from the cervical vertebra to the lumbar spine...
The perfect Guardian of humerus. The acrominon of the shoulder Blade...
Now the data is about Bones that you can't even see
IN ANY CASE...
A... JAPANESE GUY LIKE THAT...
No...
HE'S LIKE A SPACE ALIEN, WITH A BODY LIKE THAT.

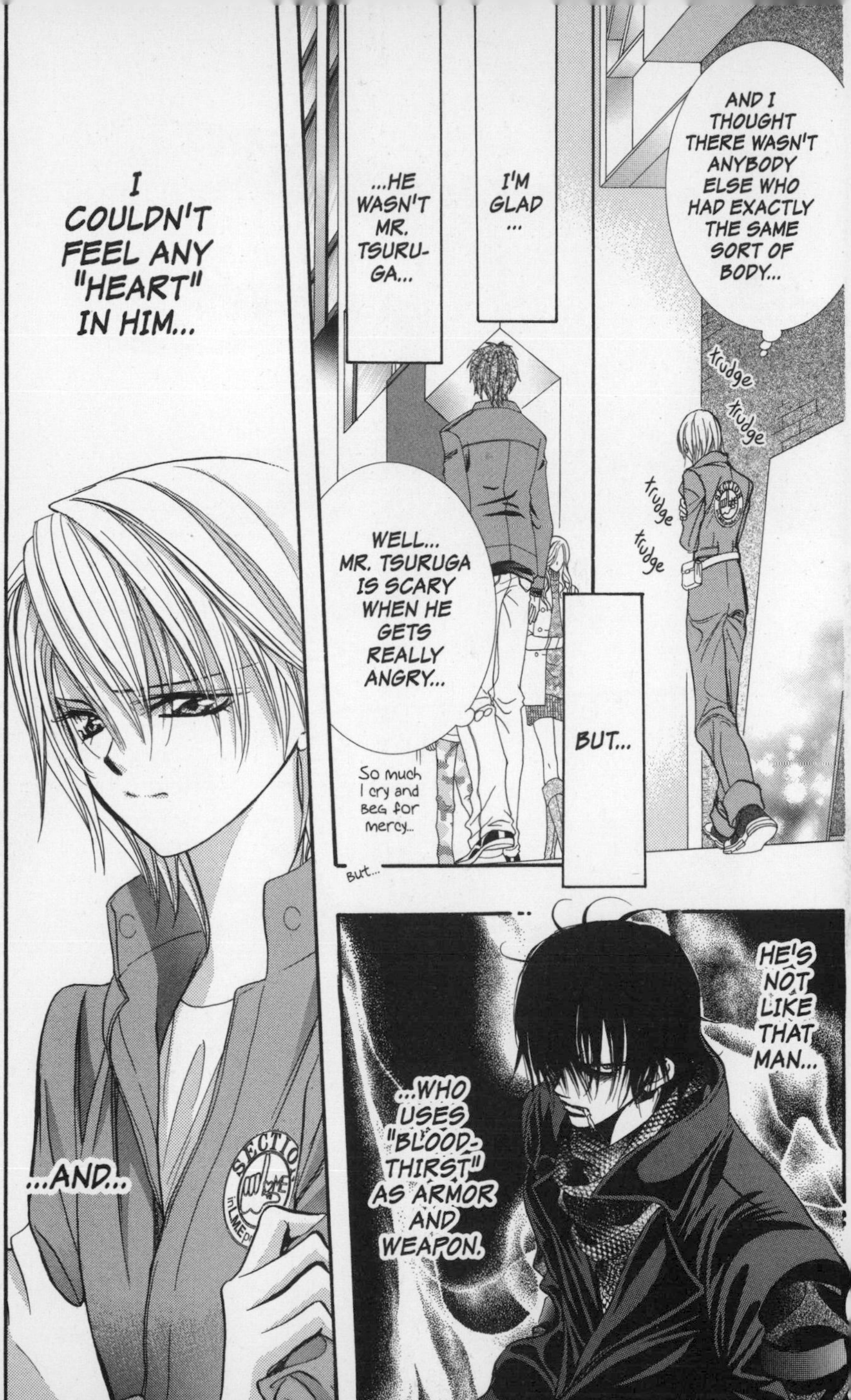
AND I THOUGHT THERE WASN'T ANYBODY ELSE WHO HAD EXACTLY THE SAME SORT OF BODY...
I'M GLAD...
...HE WASN'T MR. TSURUGA...
trudge trudge
trudge trudge
BUT...
WELL... MR. TSURUGA IS SCARY WHEN HE GETS REALLY ANGRY...
So much I cry and beg for mercy...
but...
HE'S NOT LIKE THAT MAN...
...WHO USES "BLOOD-THIRST" AS ARMOR AND WEAPON.
I COULDN'T FEEL ANY "HEART" IN HIM...
...AND...

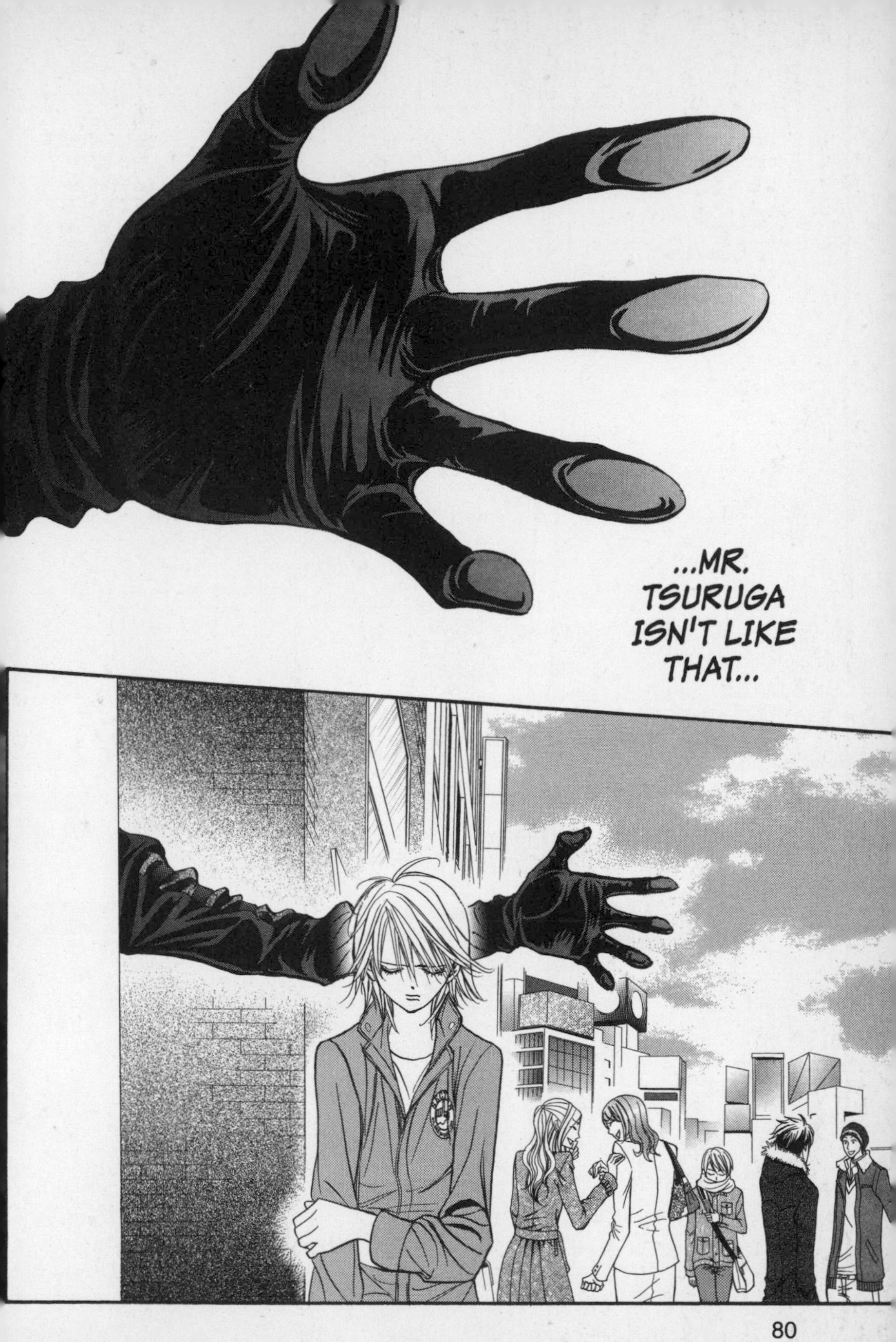
...MR. TSURUGA ISN'T LIKE THAT...

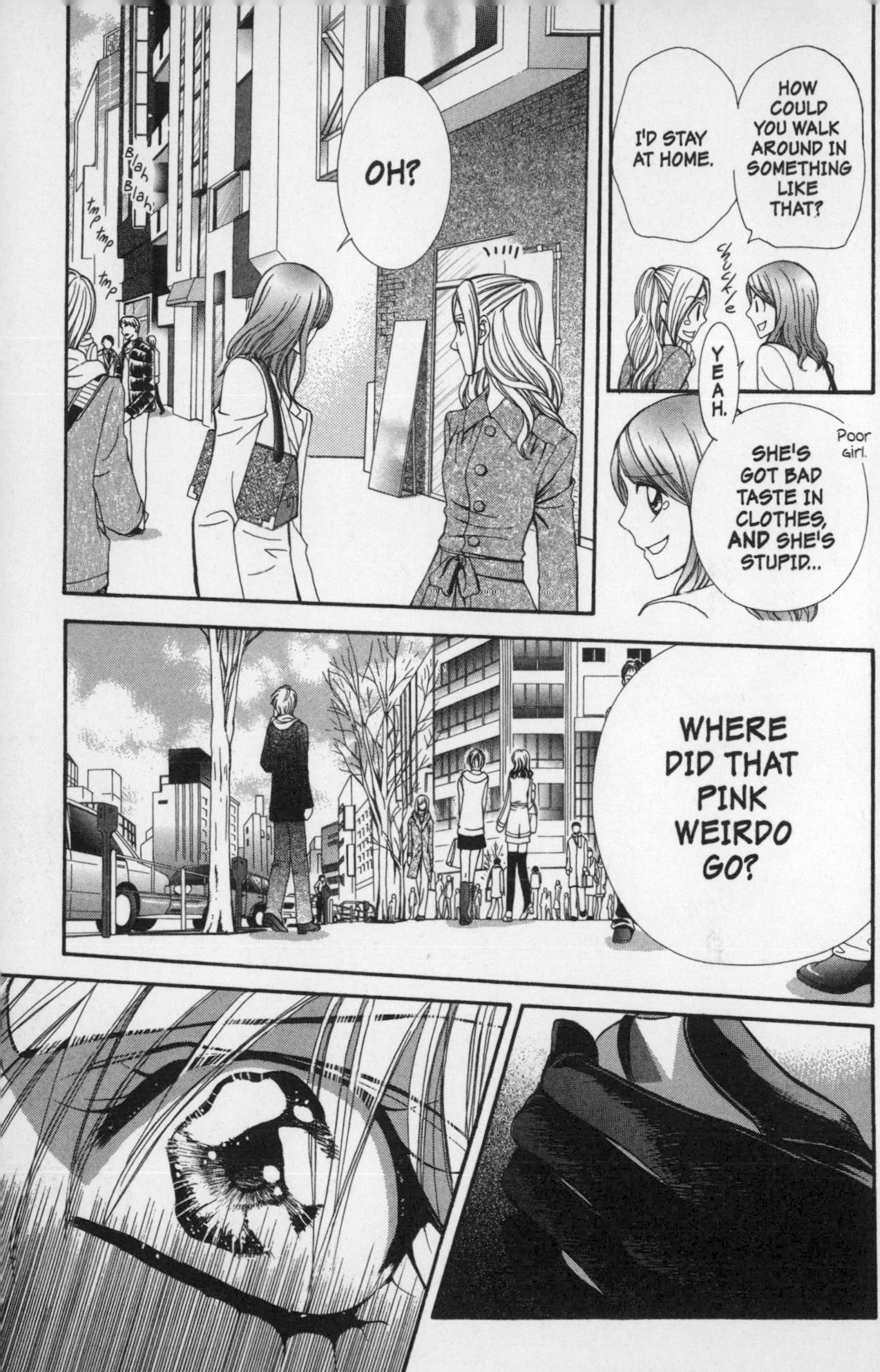
HOW COULD YOU WALK AROUND IN SOMETHING LIKE THAT?
I'D STAY AT HOME.
chuckle
YEAH.
SHE'S GOT BAD TASTE IN CLOTHES, AND SHE'S STUPID...
Poor girl.
OH?
Blah Blah
tmp tmp tmp
WHERE DID THAT PINK WEIRDO GO?

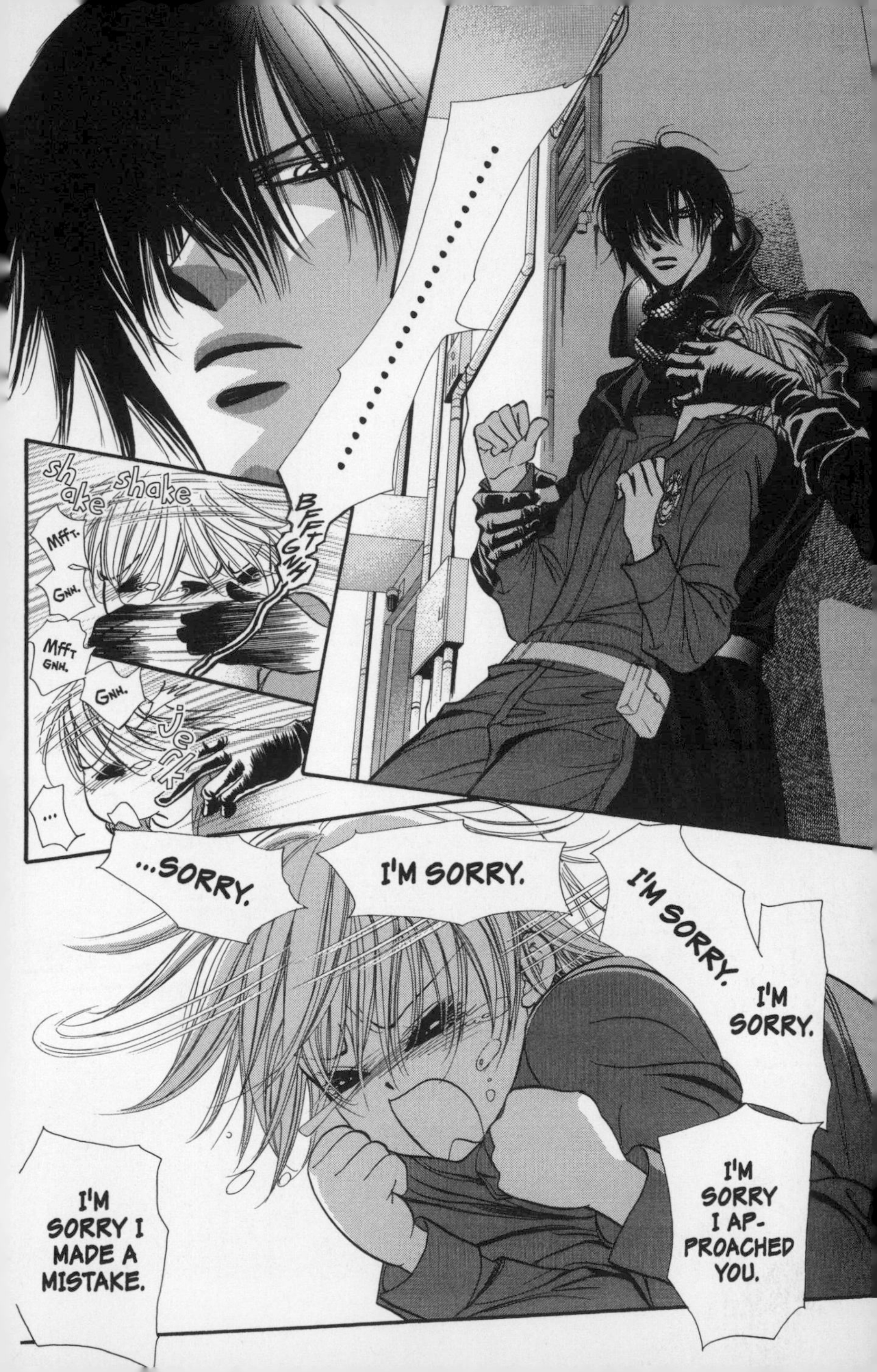
......
shake shake
BFFT GNH
Mfft.
Gnh.
Mfft Gnh.
Gnh.
jerk
...
I'M SORRY.
I'M SORRY.
I'M SORRY.
...SORRY.
I'M SORRY I AP-PROACHED YOU.
I'M SORRY I MADE A MISTAKE.

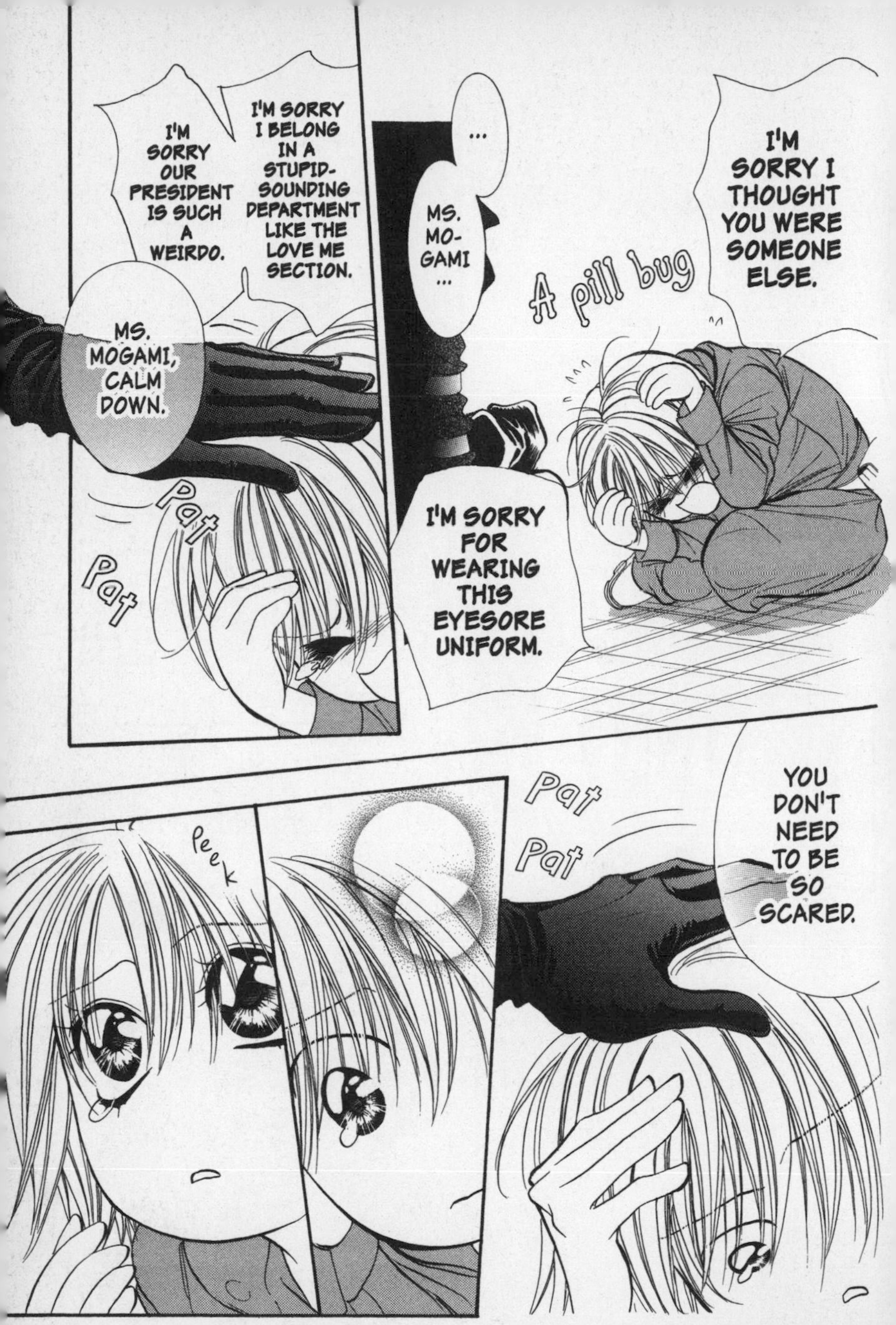
I'M SORRY I THOUGHT YOU WERE SOMEONE ELSE.
A pill bug
I'M SORRY FOR WEARING THIS EYESORE UNIFORM.
...
MS. MOGAMI...
I'M SORRY I BELONG IN A STUPID-SOUNDING DEPARTMENT LIKE THE LOVE ME SECTION.
I'M SORRY OUR PRESIDENT IS SUCH A WEIRDO.
MS. MOGAMI, CALM DOWN.
Pat
Pat
YOU DON'T NEED TO BE SO SCARED.
Pat
Pat
Peek

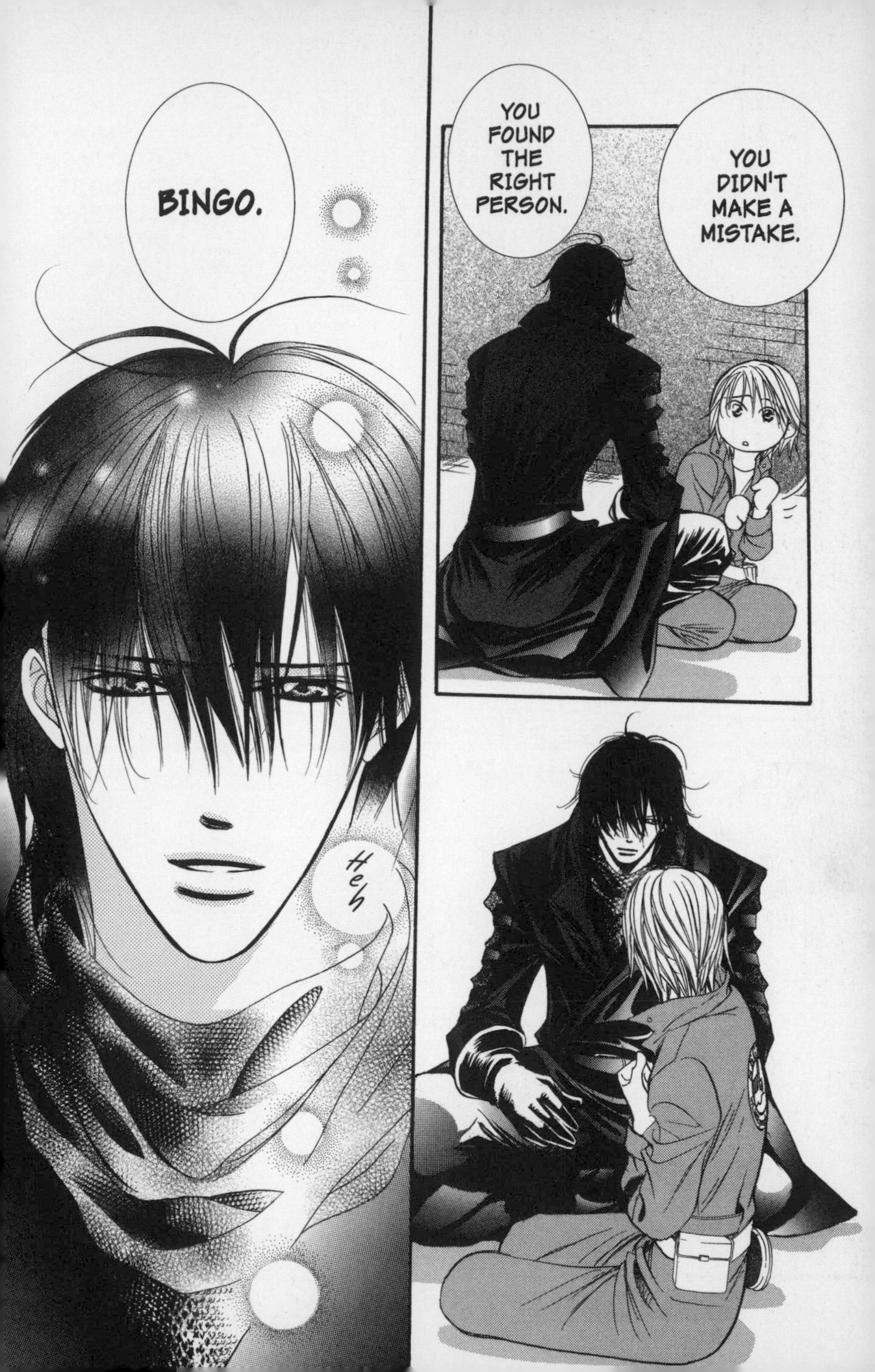
YOU DIDN'T MAKE A MISTAKE.
YOU FOUND THE RIGHT PERSON.
BINGO.
Heh

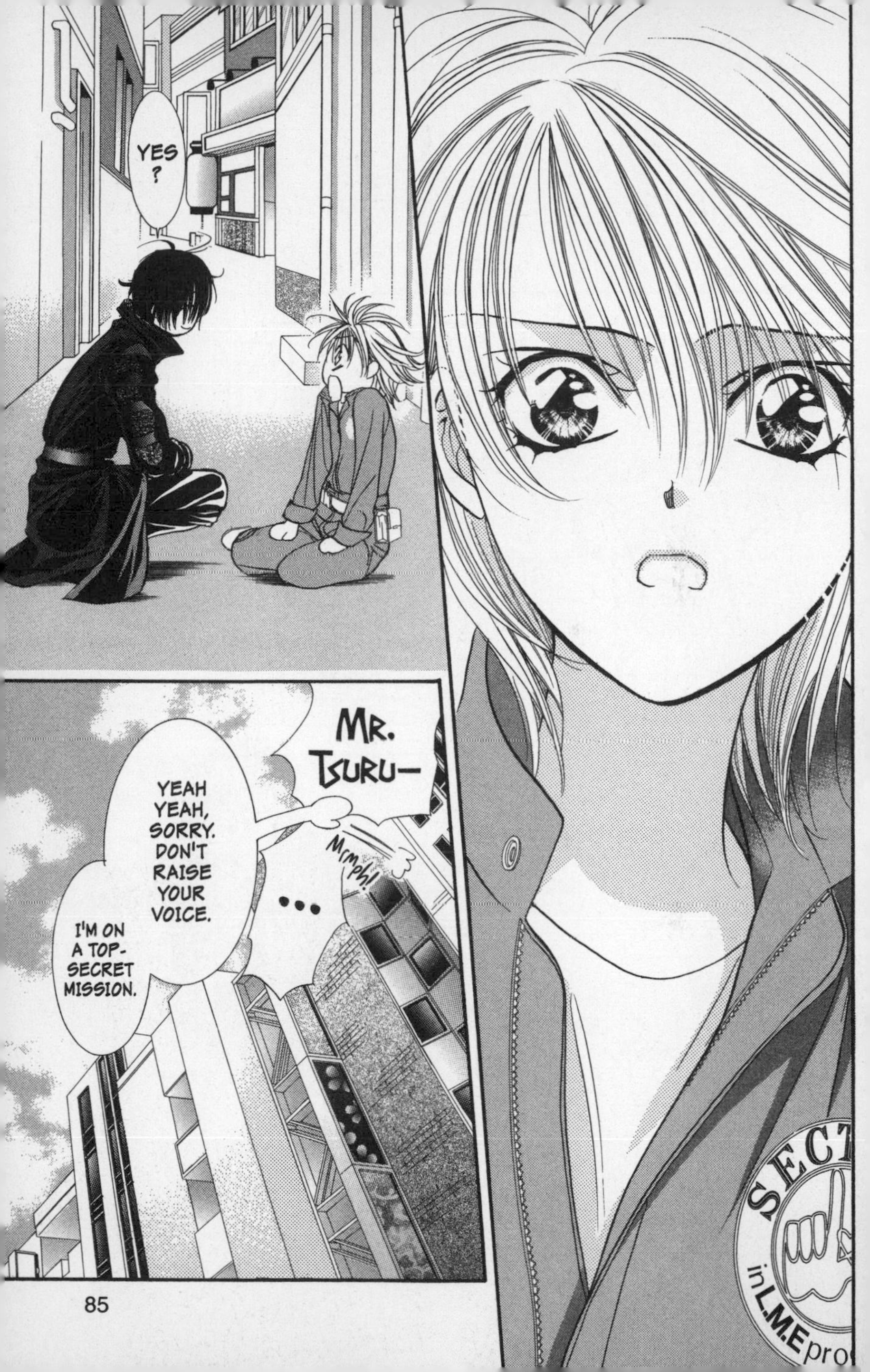
YES ?
MR. TSURU—
Mrmph!
YEAH YEAH, SORRY. DON'T RAISE YOUR VOICE.
...
I'M ON A TOP-SECRET MISSION.

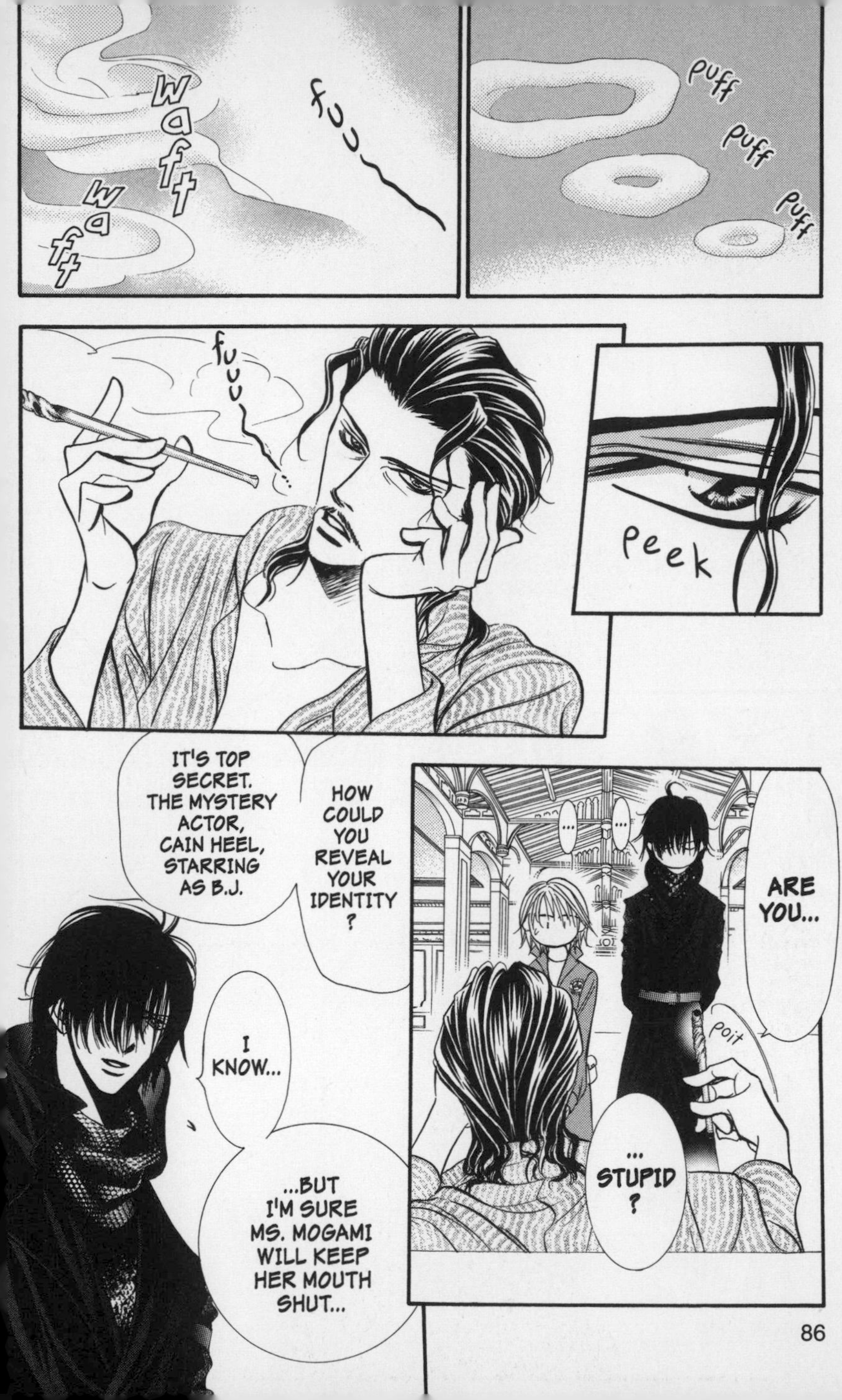
puff
puff
puff
waft
waft
fuuu
peek
fuuu
ARE YOU...
poit
...STUPID?
HOW COULD YOU REVEAL YOUR IDENTITY?
IT'S TOP SECRET. THE MYSTERY ACTOR, CAIN HEEL, STARRING AS B.J.
I KNOW...
...BUT I'M SURE MS. MOGAMI WILL KEEP HER MOUTH SHUT...

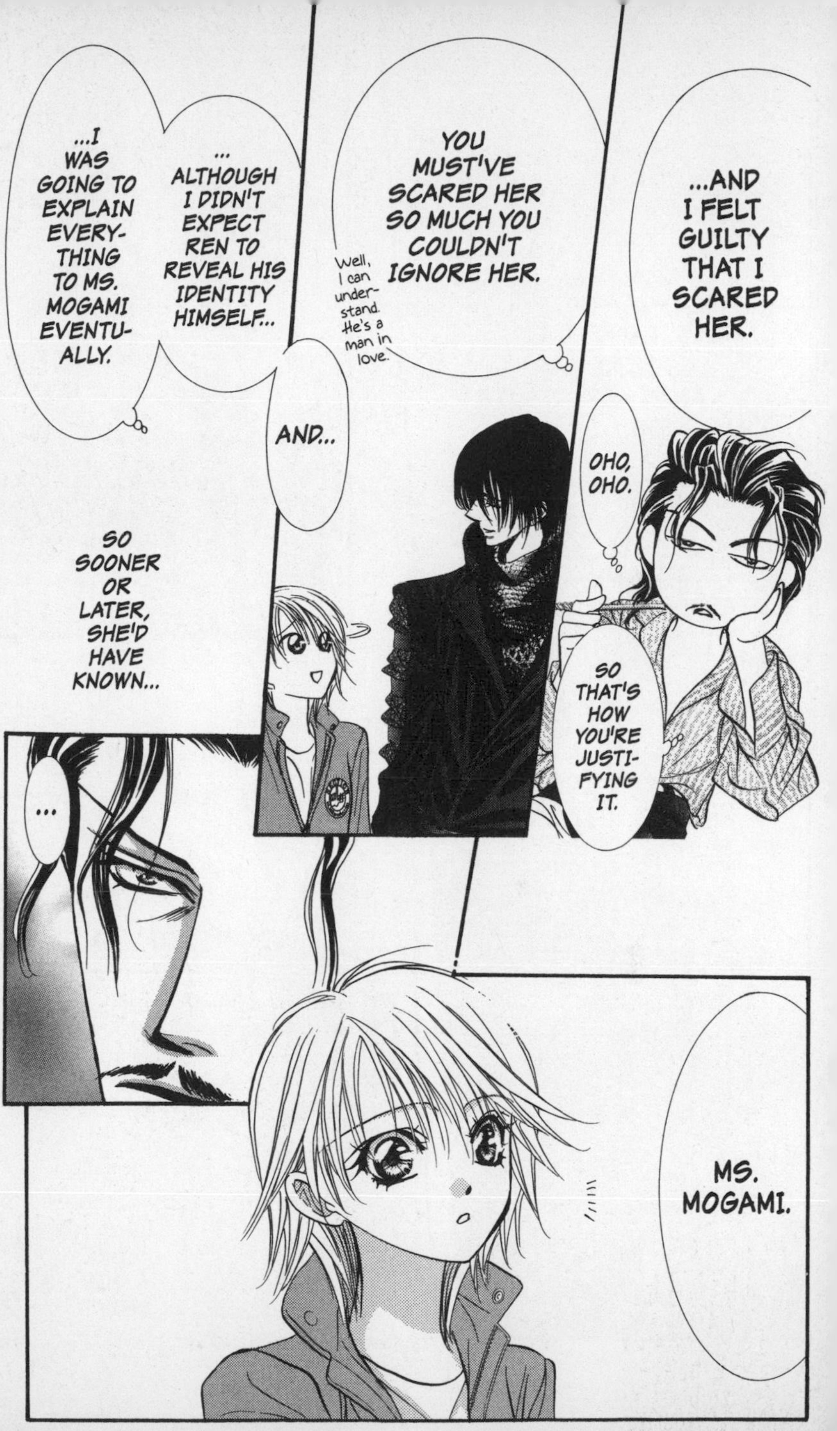
...AND I FELT GUILTY THAT I SCARED HER.
OHO, OHO.
SO THAT'S HOW YOU'RE JUSTI-FYING IT.
YOU MUST'VE SCARED HER SO MUCH YOU COULDN'T IGNORE HER.
Well, I can under-stand. He's a man in love.
AND...
...ALTHOUGH I DIDN'T EXPECT REN TO REVEAL HIS IDENTITY HIMSELF...
...I WAS GOING TO EXPLAIN EVERY-THING TO MS. MOGAMI EVENTU-ALLY.
SO SOONER OR LATER, SHE'D HAVE KNOWN...
MS. MOGAMI.
...

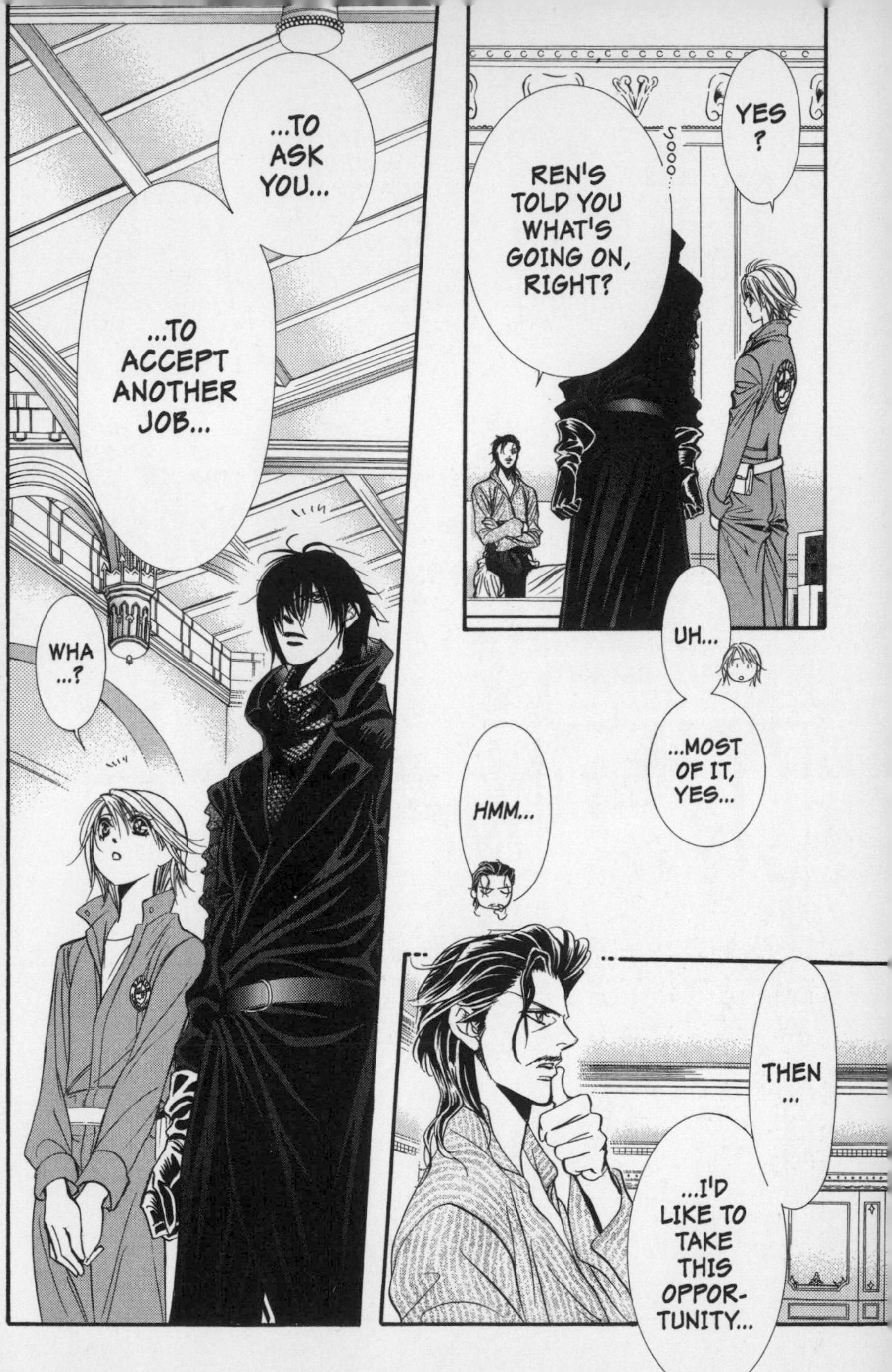
YES?
SOOO...
REN'S TOLD YOU WHAT'S GOING ON, RIGHT?
UH...
...MOST OF IT, YES...
HMM...
THEN...
...I'D LIKE TO TAKE THIS OPPOR-TUNITY...
...TO ASK YOU...
...TO ACCEPT ANOTHER JOB...
WHA...?

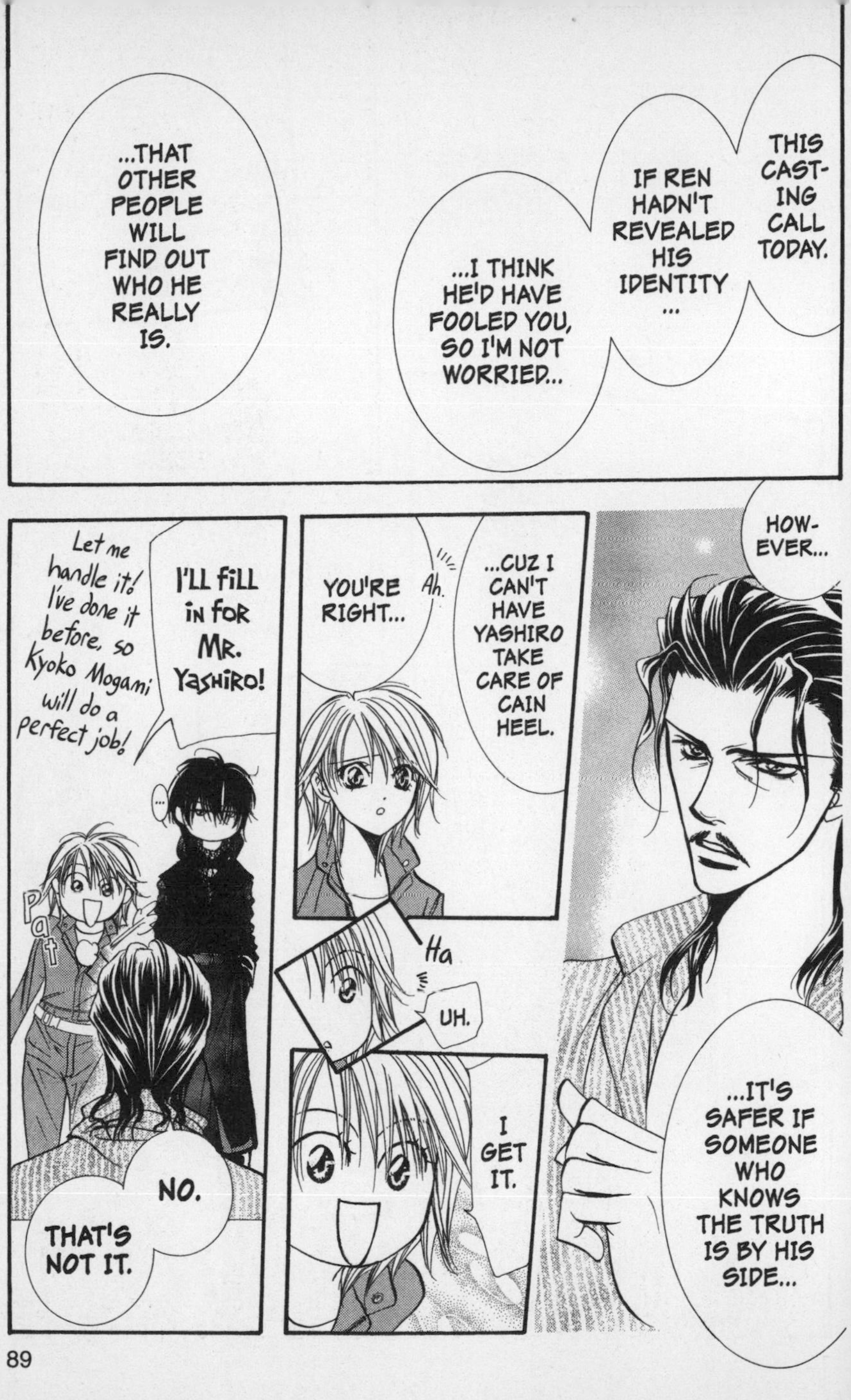
THIS CASTING CALL TODAY.
IF REN HADN'T REVEALED HIS IDENTITY...
...I THINK HE'D HAVE FOOLED YOU, SO I'M NOT WORRIED...
...THAT OTHER PEOPLE WILL FIND OUT WHO HE REALLY IS.
HOW-EVER...
...IT'S SAFER IF SOMEONE WHO KNOWS THE TRUTH IS BY HIS SIDE...
...CUZ I CAN'T HAVE YASHIRO TAKE CARE OF CAIN HEEL.
Ah.
YOU'RE RIGHT...
Ha
UH.
I GET IT.
I'LL FILL IN FOR MR. YASHIRO!
Let me handle it! I've done it before, so Kyoko Mogami will do a perfect job!
Pat
...
NO.
THAT'S NOT IT.

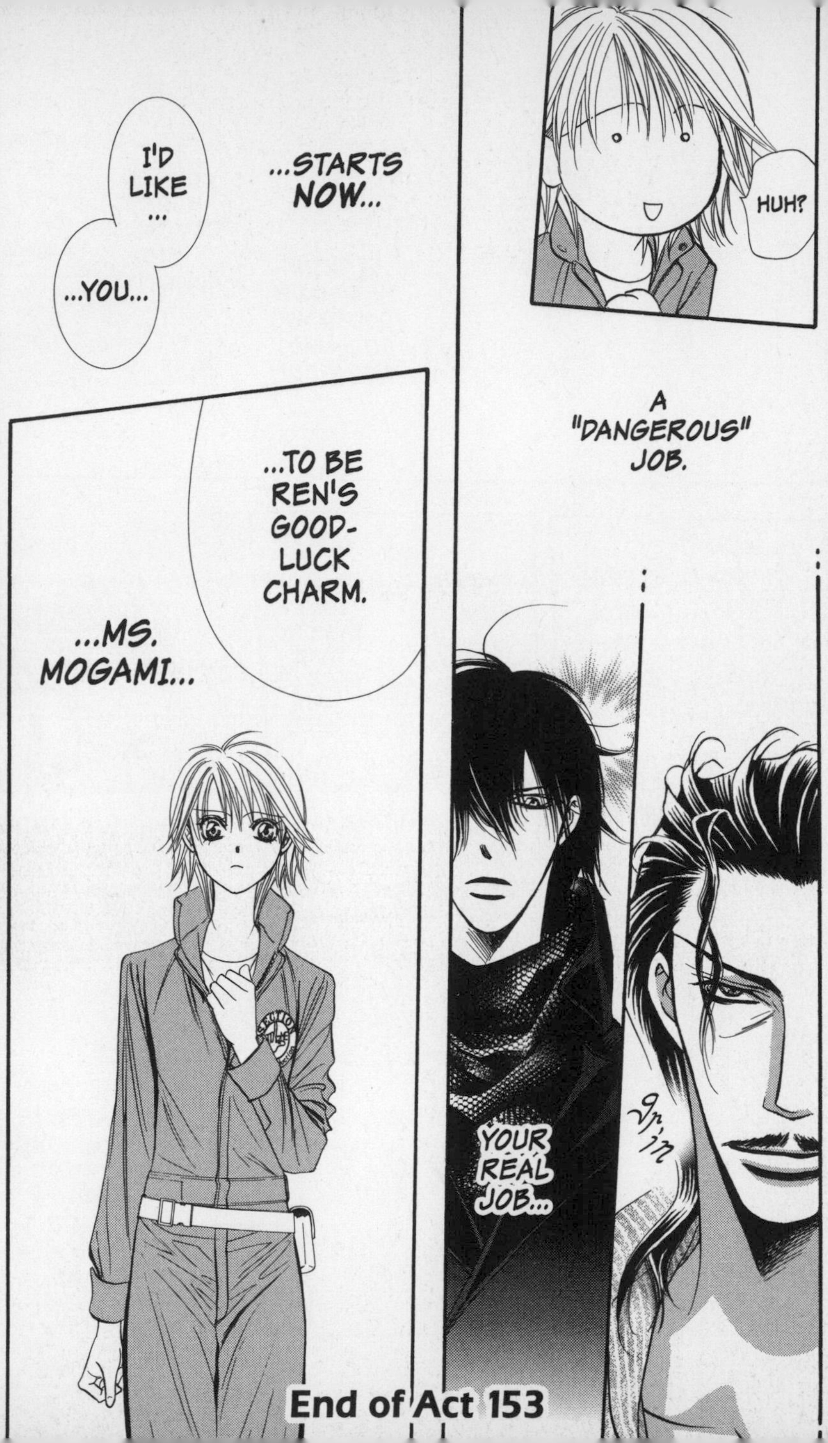
I'D LIKE ...
...YOU...
...TO BE REN'S GOOD-LUCK CHARM.
...MS. MOGAMI...
HUH?
YOUR REAL JOB...
grin
...STARTS NOW...
A "DANGEROUS" JOB.
End of Act 153

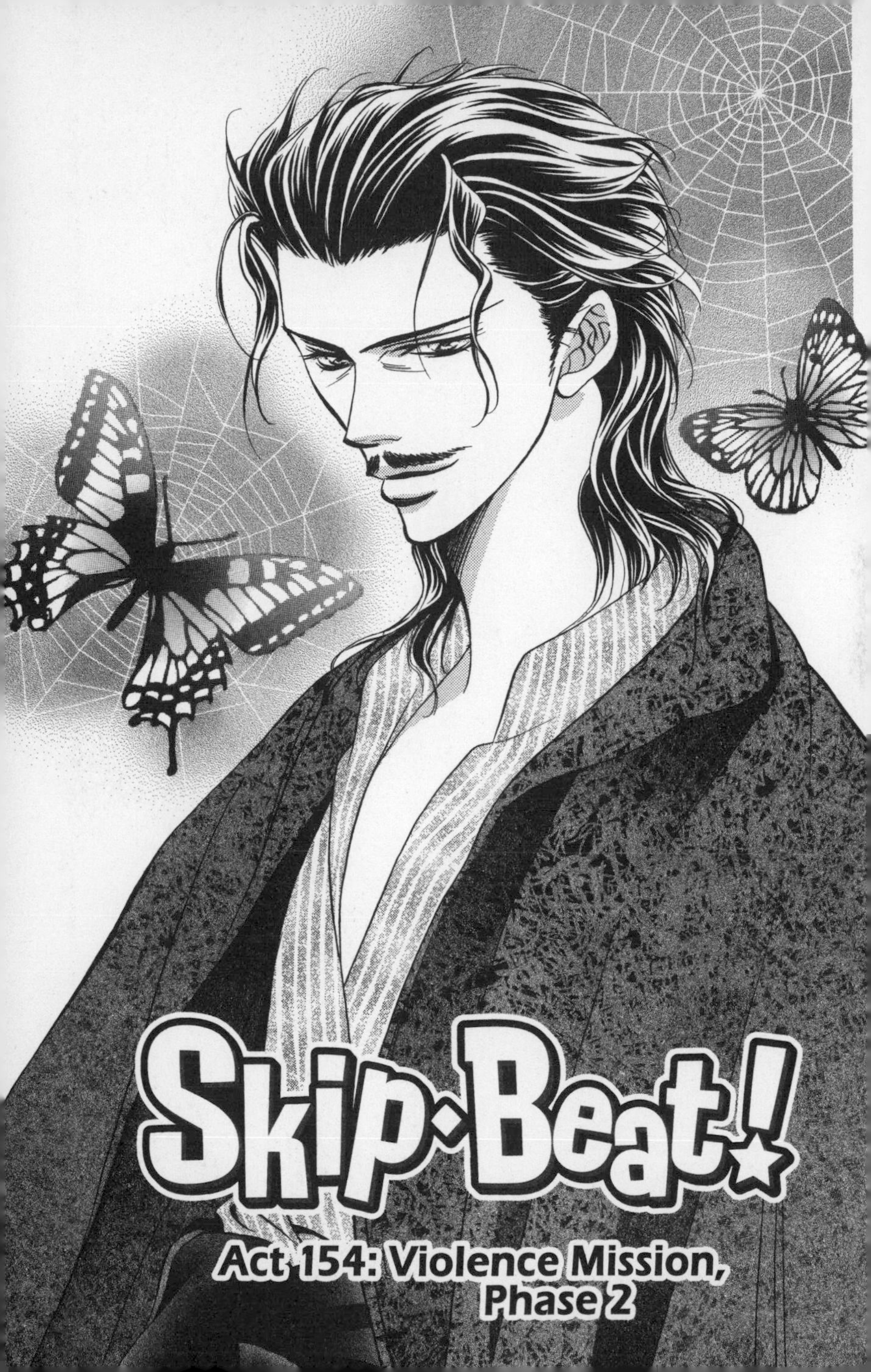
Skip·Beat!
Act 154: Violence Mission, Phase 2

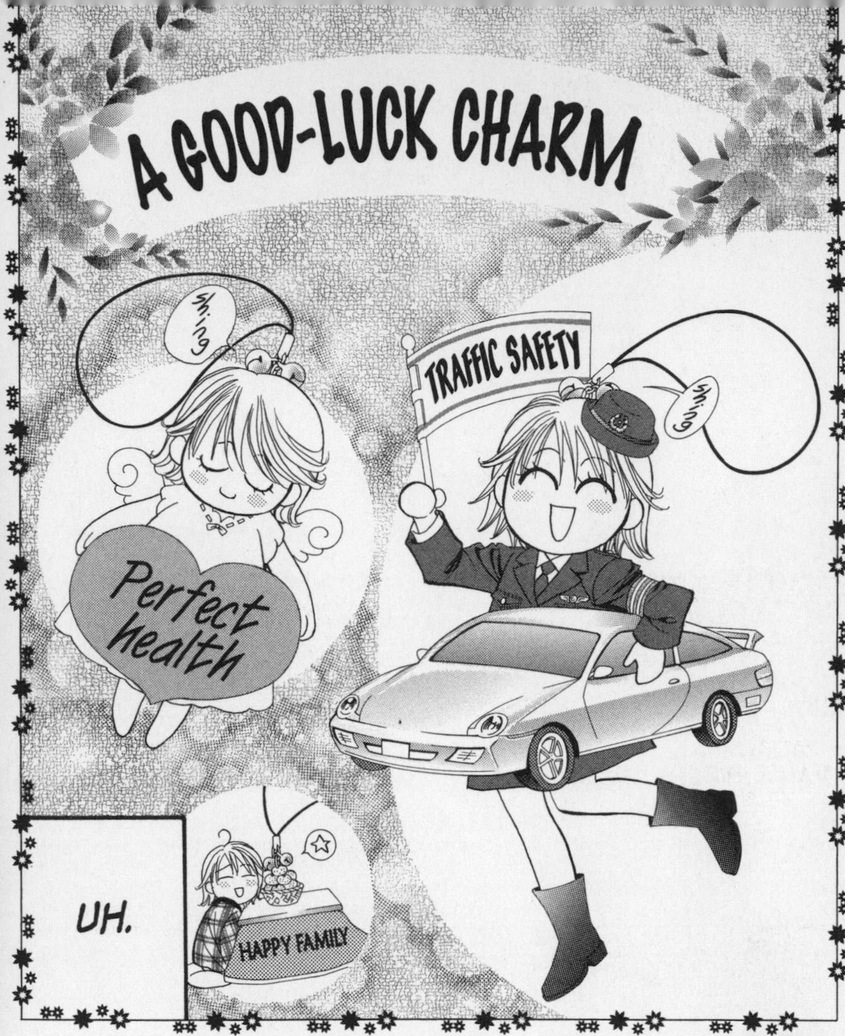
A GOOD-LUCK CHARM
TRAFFIC SAFETY
shing
shing
Perfect health
HAPPY FAMILY
UH.

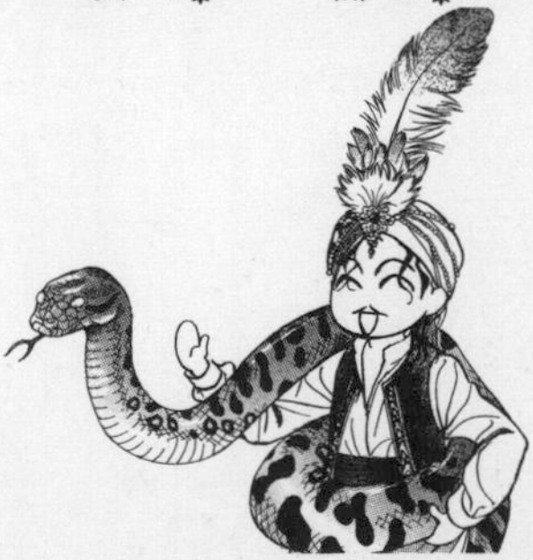

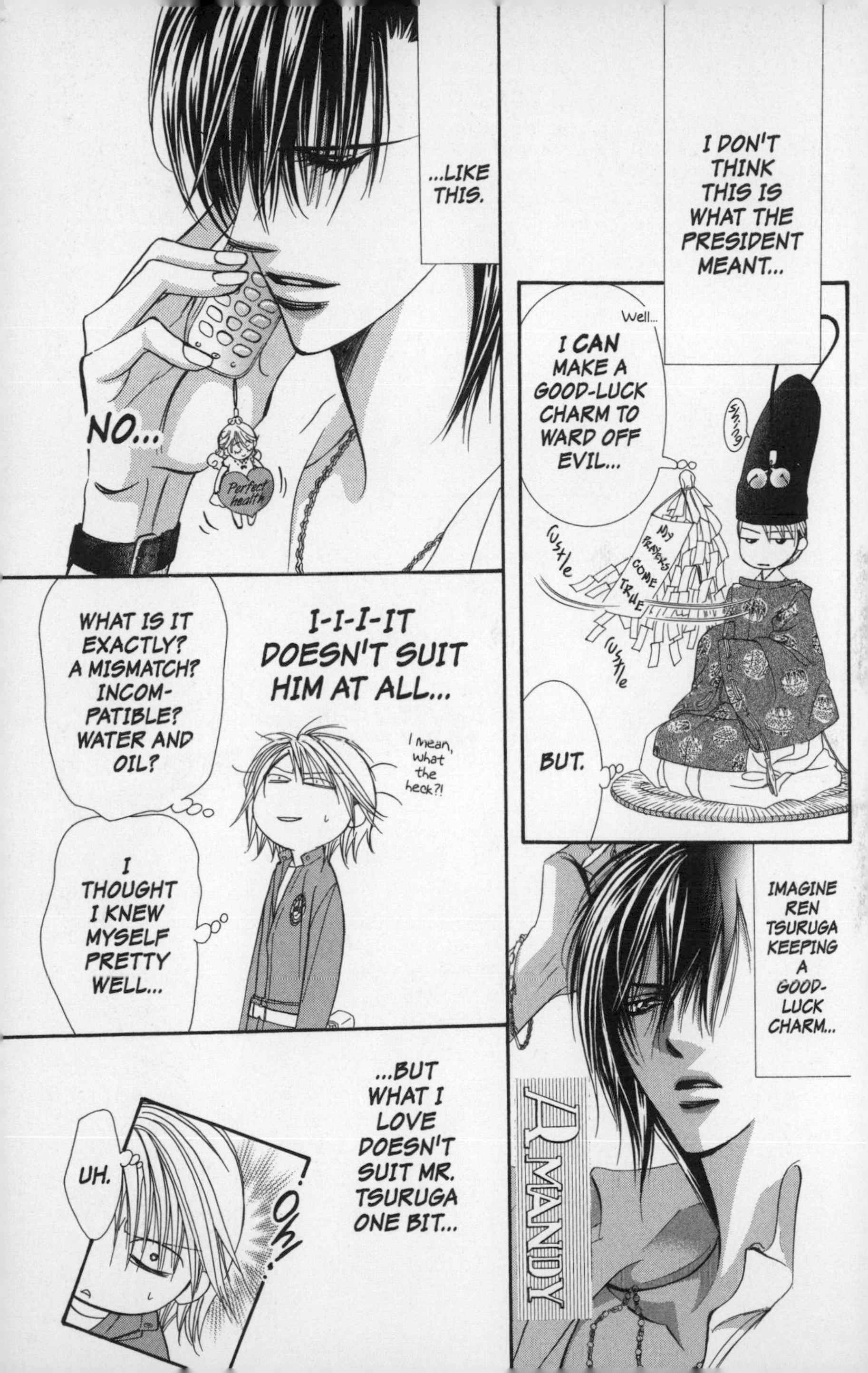
I DON'T THINK THIS IS WHAT THE PRESIDENT MEANT...
Well...
I CAN MAKE A GOOD-LUCK CHARM TO WARD OFF EVIL...
Shing
MY PRAYERS COME TRUE
rustle
rustle
BUT.
IMAGINE REN TSURUGA KEEPING A GOOD-LUCK CHARM...
RMANDY
...LIKE THIS.
NO...
Perfect health
I-I-I-IT DOESN'T SUIT HIM AT ALL...
I mean, what the heck?!
WHAT IS IT EXACTLY? A MISMATCH? INCOM-PATIBLE? WATER AND OIL?
I THOUGHT I KNEW MYSELF PRETTY WELL...
...BUT WHAT I LOVE DOESN'T SUIT MR. TSURUGA ONE BIT...
Oh!
UH.

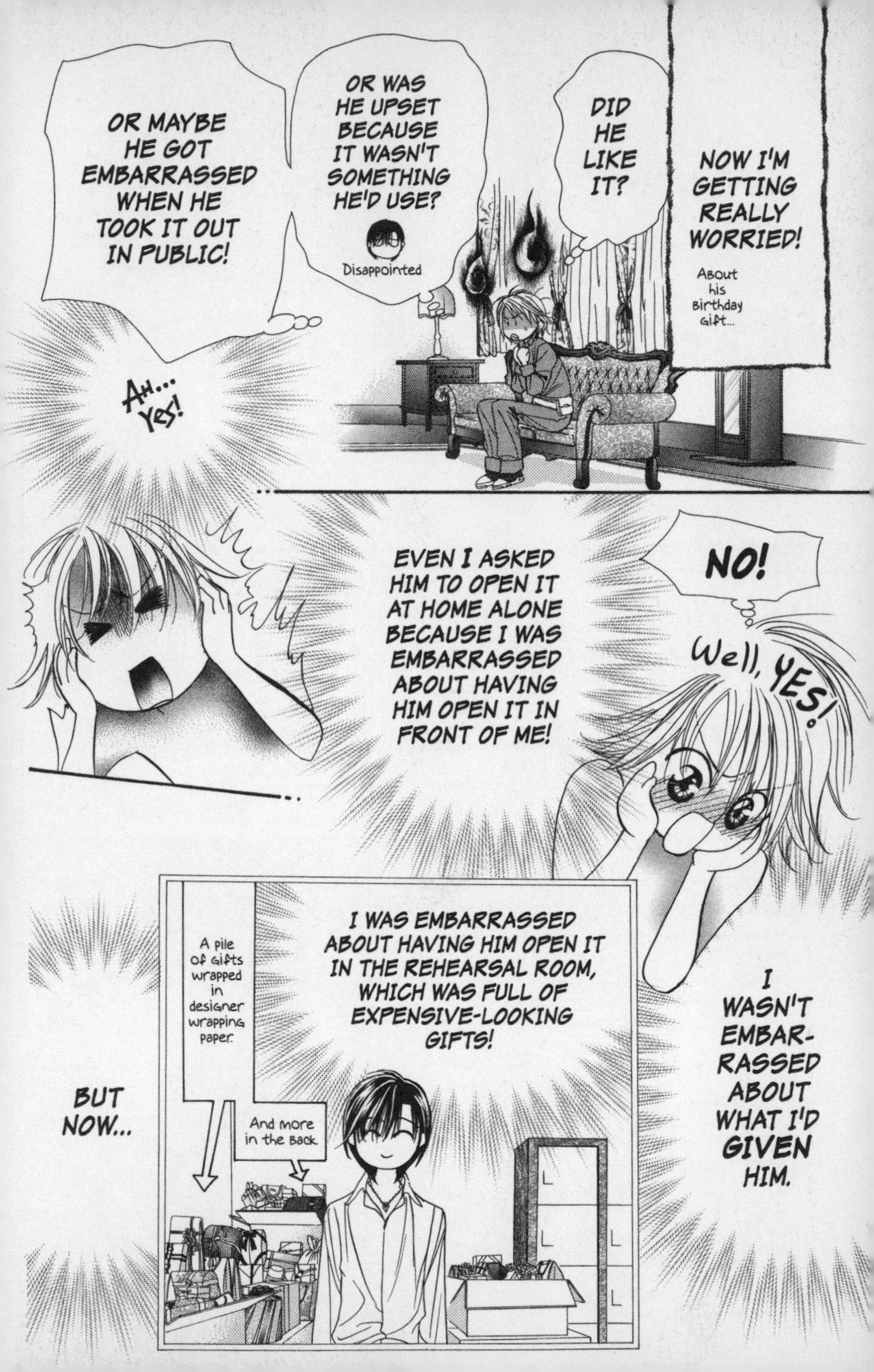
NOW I'M GETTING REALLY WORRIED!
About his Birthday Gift...
DID HE LIKE IT?
OR WAS HE UPSET BECAUSE IT WASN'T SOMETHING HE'D USE?
Disappointed
OR MAYBE HE GOT EMBARRASSED WHEN HE TOOK IT OUT IN PUBLIC!
AH... YES!
NO!
Well, YES!
EVEN I ASKED HIM TO OPEN IT AT HOME ALONE BECAUSE I WAS EMBARRASSED ABOUT HAVING HIM OPEN IT IN FRONT OF ME!
I WASN'T EMBARRASSED ABOUT WHAT I'D GIVEN HIM.
I WAS EMBARRASSED ABOUT HAVING HIM OPEN IT IN THE REHEARSAL ROOM, WHICH WAS FULL OF EXPENSIVE-LOOKING GIFTS!
A pile of gifts wrapped in designer wrapping paper.
And more in the back.
BUT NOW...

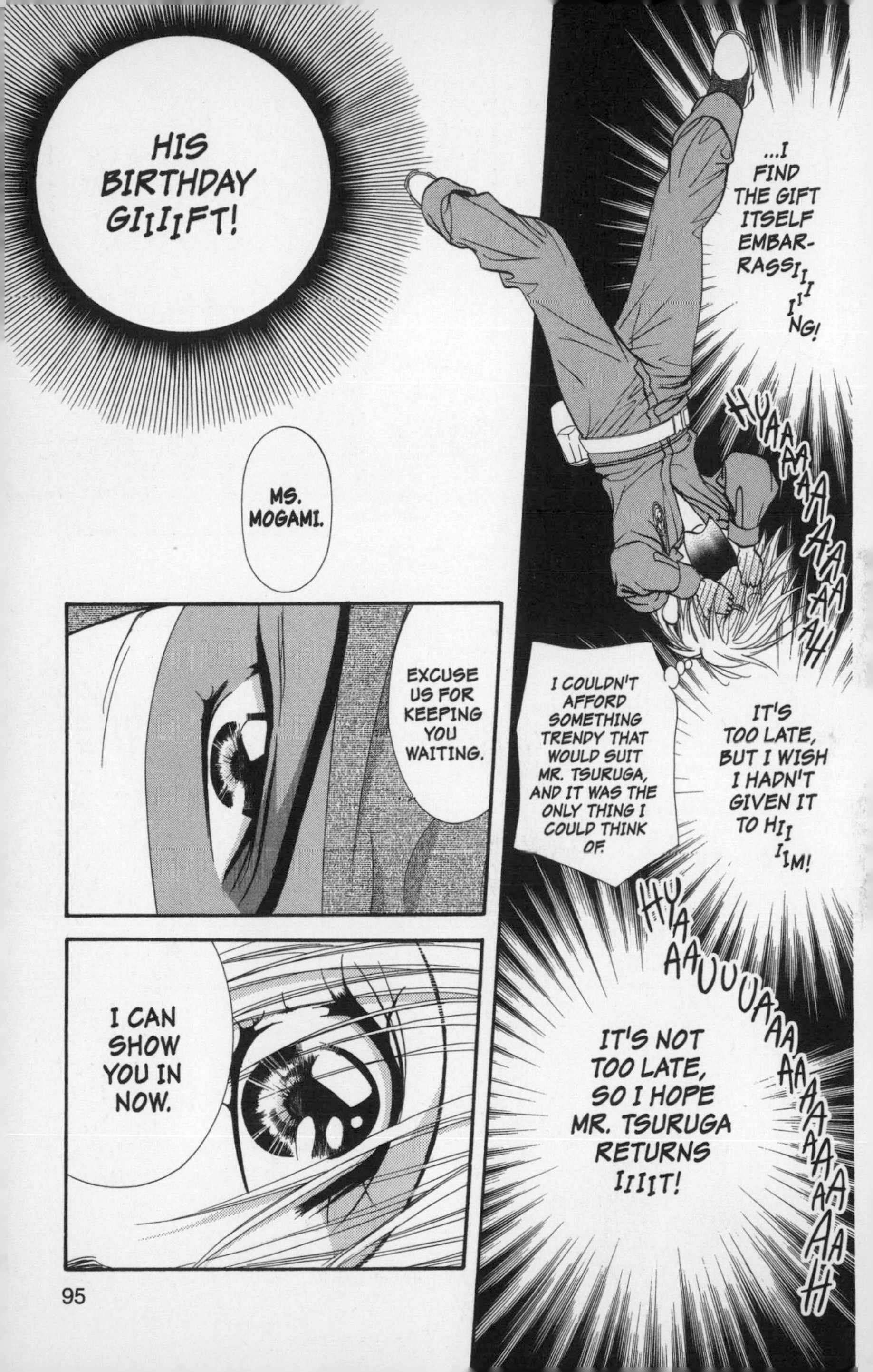
HIS BIRTHDAY GIIIIFT!
...I FIND THE GIFT ITSELF EMBARRASSIIIIING!
HYAAAAAAAAAAAAAAH
I COULDN'T AFFORD SOMETHING TRENDY THAT WOULD SUIT MR. TSURUGA, AND IT WAS THE ONLY THING I COULD THINK OF.
IT'S TOO LATE, BUT I WISH I HADN'T GIVEN IT TO HIIIM!
HYAAAUUUAAAAAAAAAAAAAAH
IT'S NOT TOO LATE, SO I HOPE MR. TSURUGA RETURNS IIIIT!
MS. MOGAMI.
EXCUSE US FOR KEEPING YOU WAITING.
I CAN SHOW YOU IN NOW.

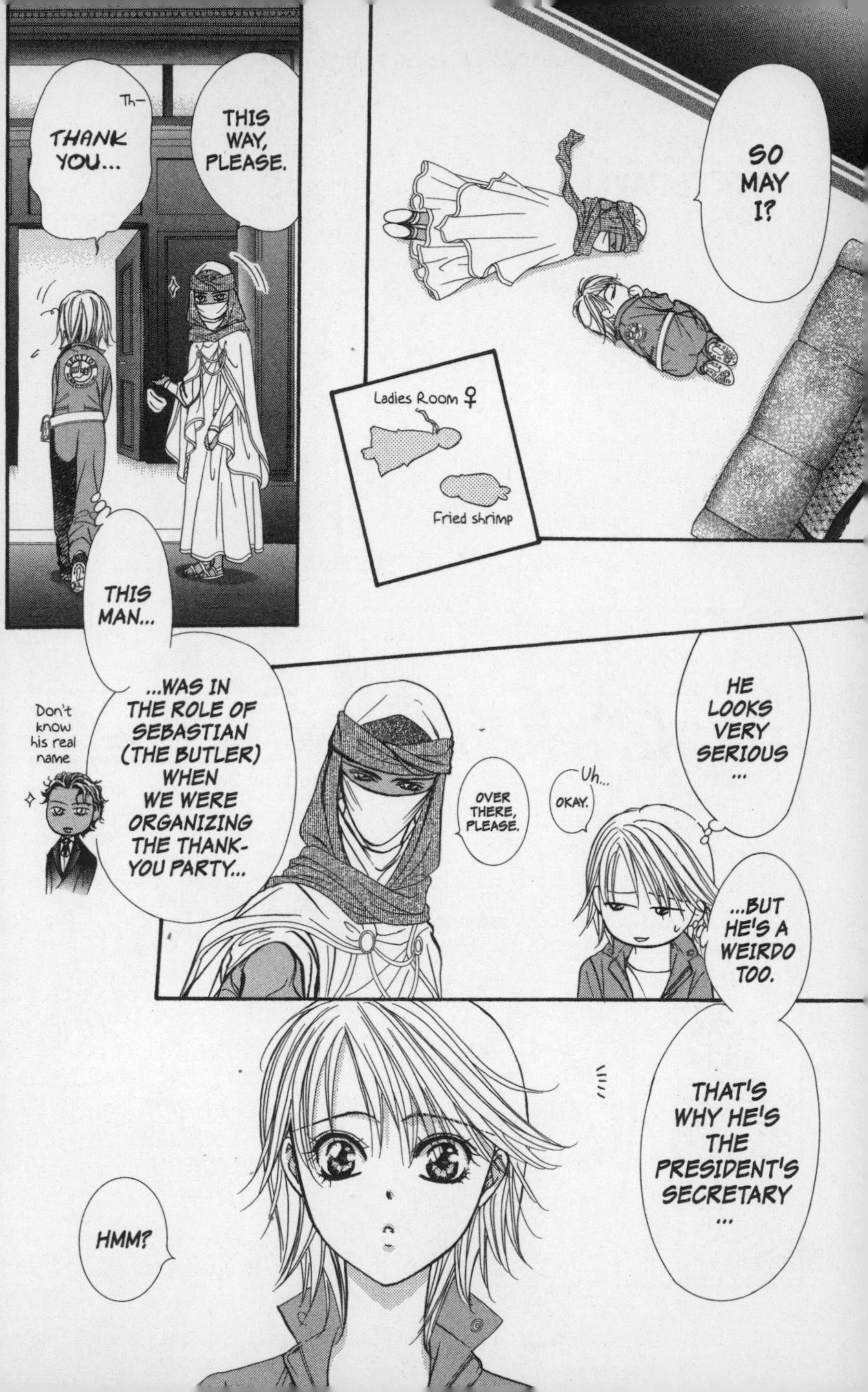
SO MAY I?
Ladies Room ♀
Fried shrimp
THIS WAY, PLEASE.
Th—
THANK YOU...
THIS MAN...
HE LOOKS VERY SERIOUS...
Uh...
OKAY.
OVER THERE, PLEASE.
...WAS IN THE ROLE OF SEBASTIAN (THE BUTLER) WHEN WE WERE ORGANIZING THE THANK-YOU PARTY...
Don't know his real name
...BUT HE'S A WEIRDO TOO.
THAT'S WHY HE'S THE PRESIDENT'S SECRETARY...
HMM?

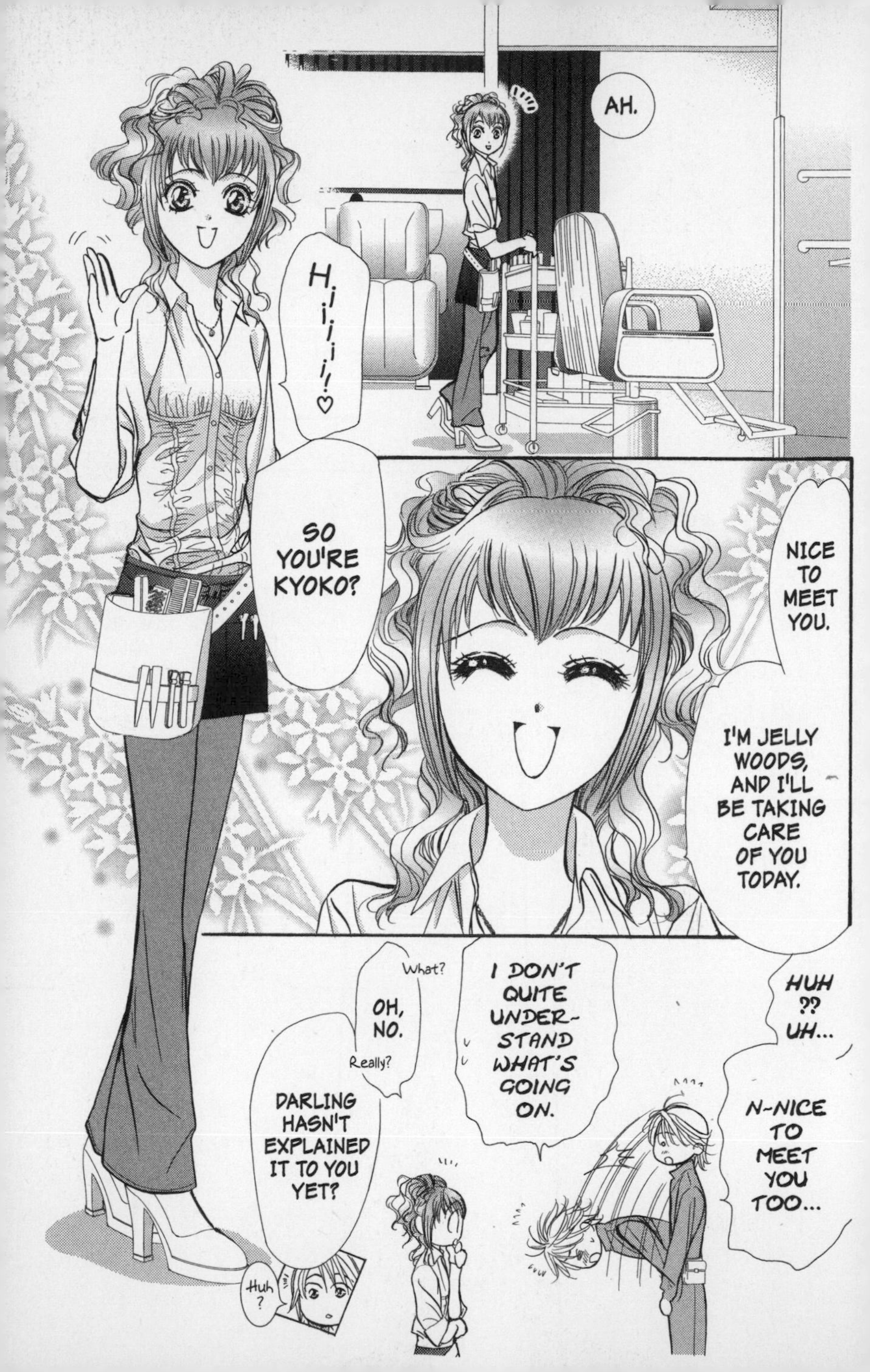
AH.
Hiiiii!♥
SO YOU'RE KYOKO?
NICE TO MEET YOU.
I'M JELLY WOODS, AND I'LL BE TAKING CARE OF YOU TODAY.
HUH ?? UH...
N-NICE TO MEET YOU TOO...
I DON'T QUITE UNDER-STAND WHAT'S GOING ON.
What?
OH, NO.
Really?
DARLING HASN'T EXPLAINED IT TO YOU YET?
Huh ?

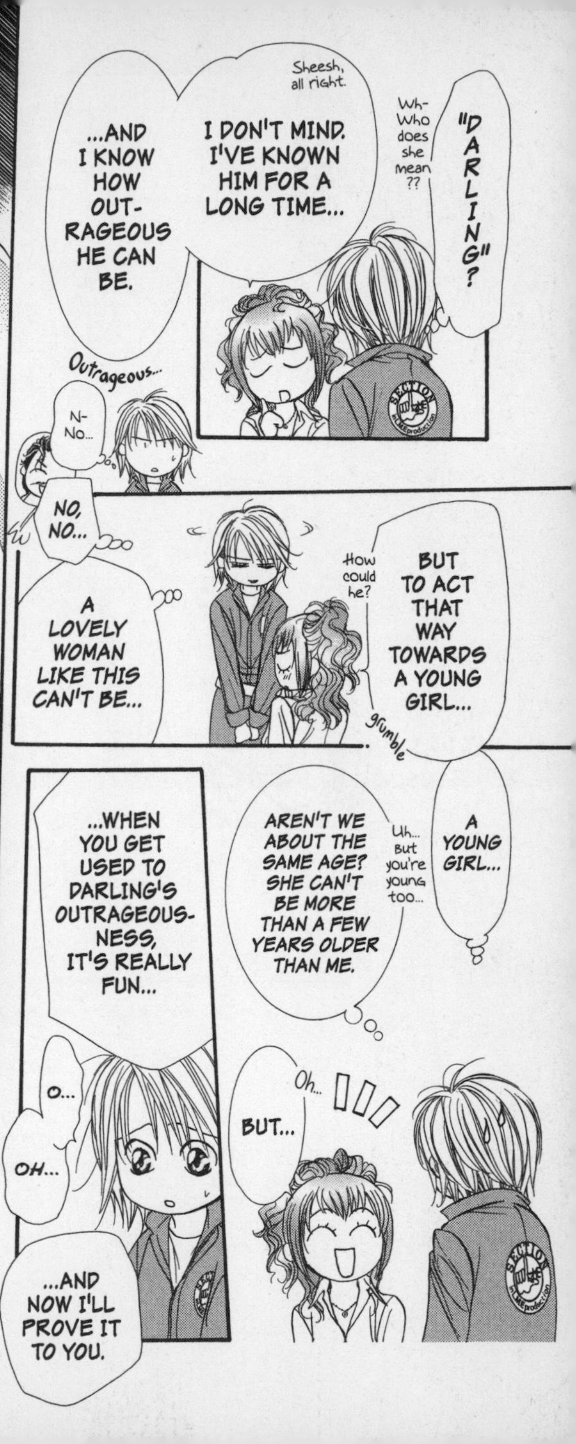
"DARLING"?
Wh-Who does she mean??
I DON'T MIND. I'VE KNOWN HIM FOR A LONG TIME...
Sheesh, all right.
...AND I KNOW HOW OUT-RAGEOUS HE CAN BE.
Outrageous...
N-No...
NO, NO...
BUT TO ACT THAT WAY TOWARDS A YOUNG GIRL...
How could he?
grumble
A LOVELY WOMAN LIKE THIS CAN'T BE...
A YOUNG GIRL...
Uh... But you're young too...
AREN'T WE ABOUT THE SAME AGE? SHE CAN'T BE MORE THAN A FEW YEARS OLDER THAN ME.
...WHEN YOU GET USED TO DARLING'S OUTRAGEOUS-NESS, IT'S REALLY FUN...
Oh...
BUT...
O...
OH...
...AND NOW I'LL PROVE IT TO YOU.
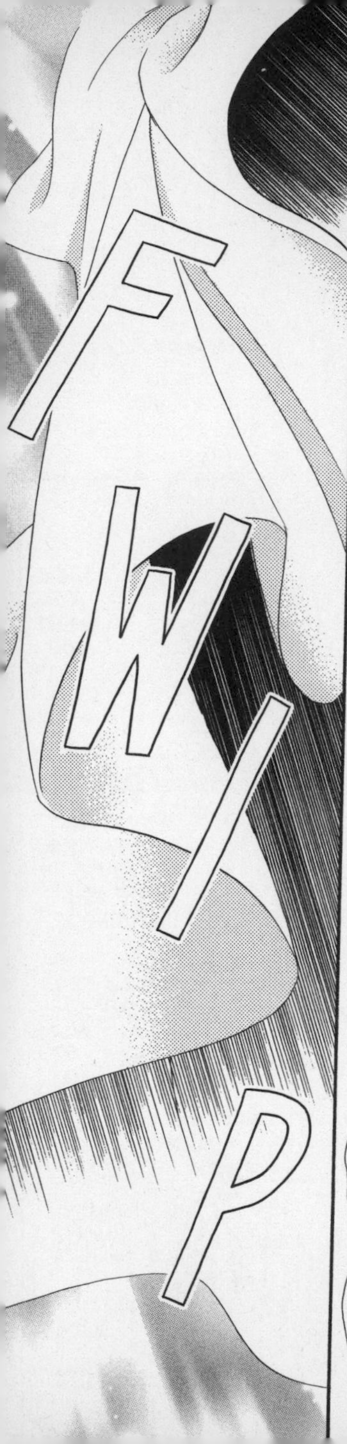
FWIP

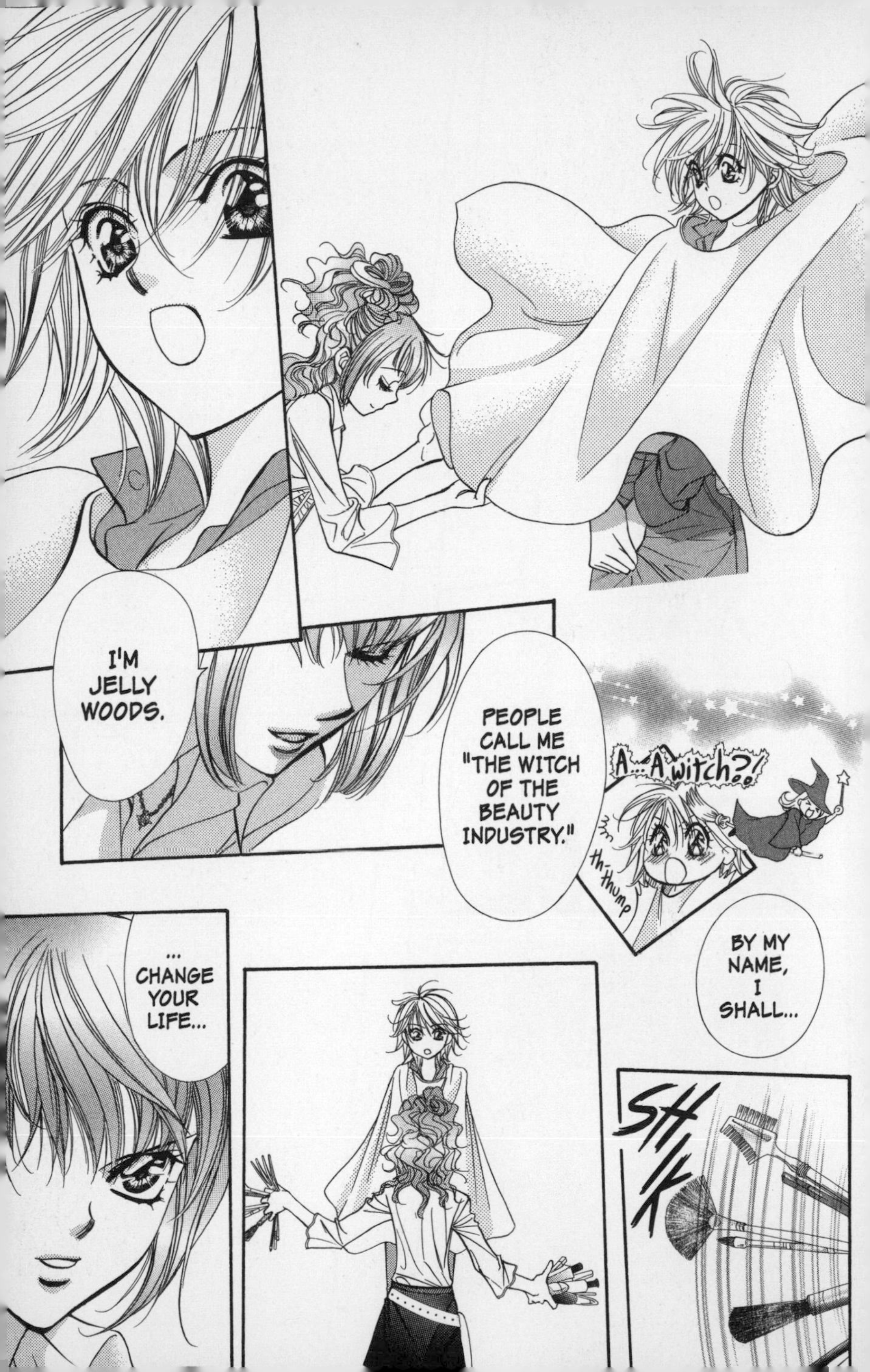
I'M JELLY WOODS.
PEOPLE CALL ME "THE WITCH OF THE BEAUTY INDUSTRY."
A... A witch?!
th-thump
BY MY NAME, I SHALL...
... CHANGE YOUR LIFE...
SHIK

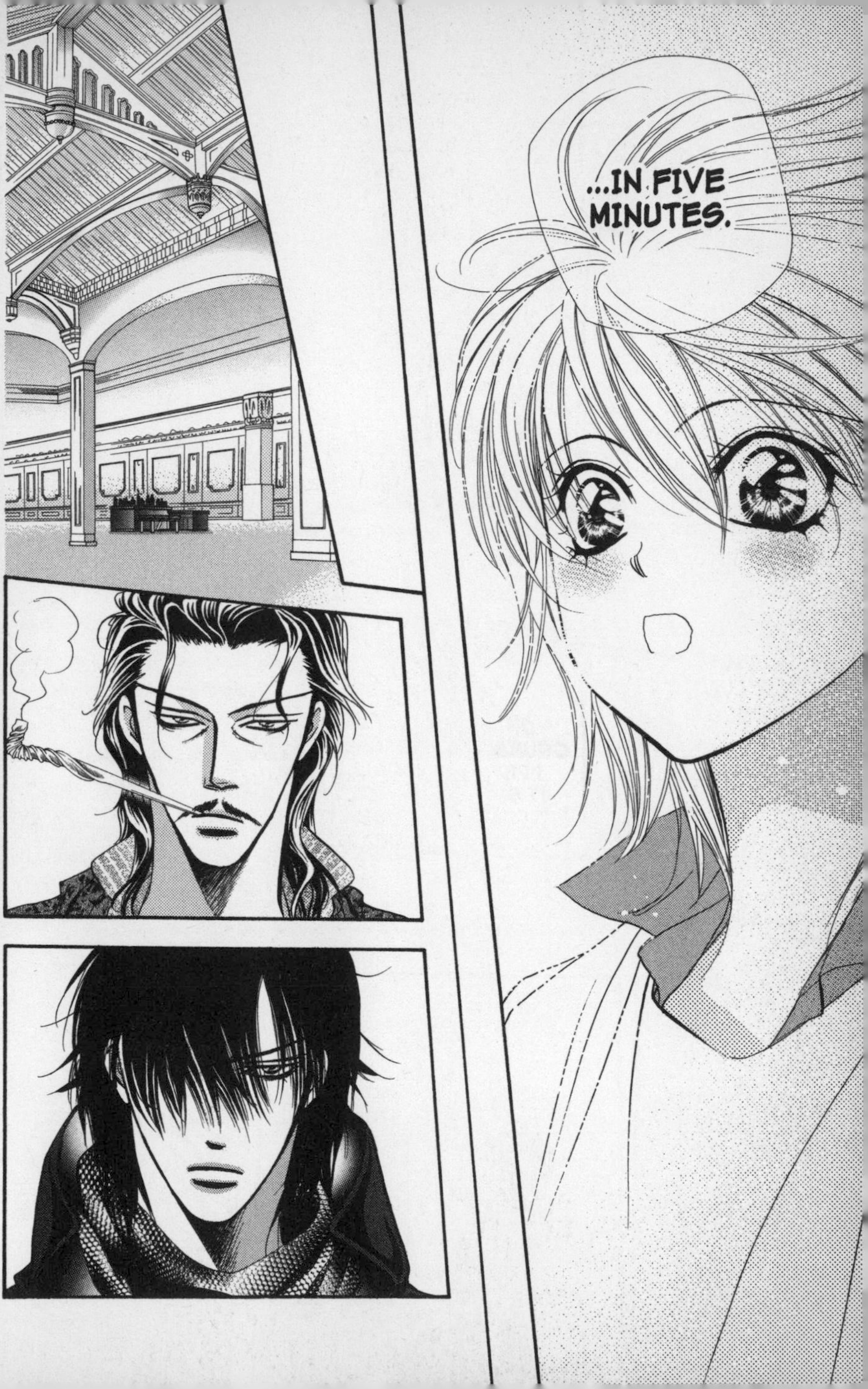
...IN FIVE MINUTES.

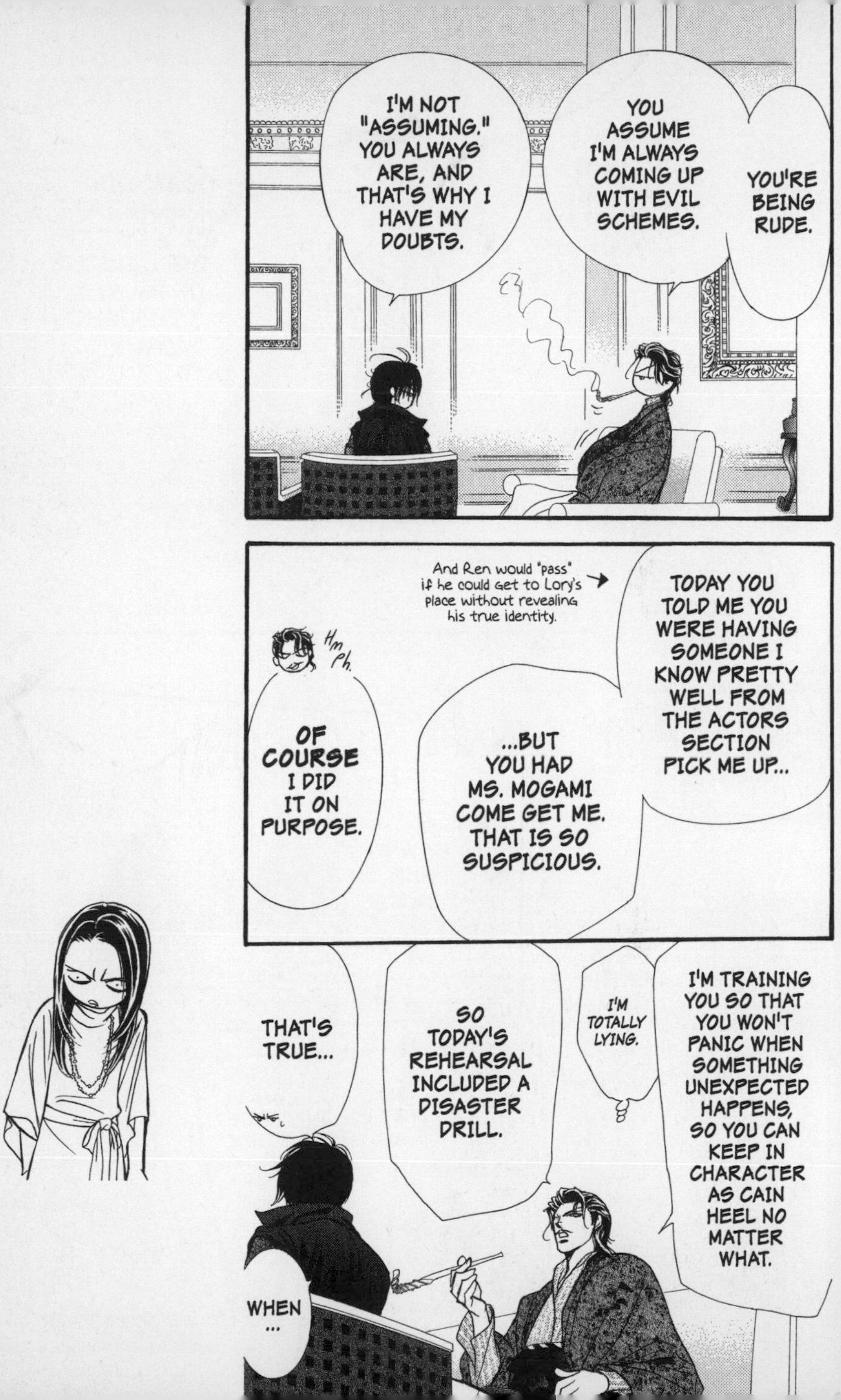
YOU'RE BEING RUDE.
YOU ASSUME I'M ALWAYS COMING UP WITH EVIL SCHEMES.
I'M NOT "ASSUMING." YOU ALWAYS ARE, AND THAT'S WHY I HAVE MY DOUBTS.
TODAY YOU TOLD ME YOU WERE HAVING SOMEONE I KNOW PRETTY WELL FROM THE ACTORS SECTION PICK ME UP...
And Ren would "pass" if he could get to Lory's place without revealing his true identity.
...BUT YOU HAD MS. MOGAMI COME GET ME. THAT IS SO SUSPICIOUS.
Hmph.
OF COURSE I DID IT ON PURPOSE.
I'M TRAINING YOU SO THAT YOU WON'T PANIC WHEN SOMETHING UNEXPECTED HAPPENS, SO YOU CAN KEEP IN CHARACTER AS CAIN HEEL NO MATTER WHAT.
I'M TOTALLY LYING.
SO TODAY'S REHEARSAL INCLUDED A DISASTER DRILL.
THAT'S TRUE...
WHEN ...

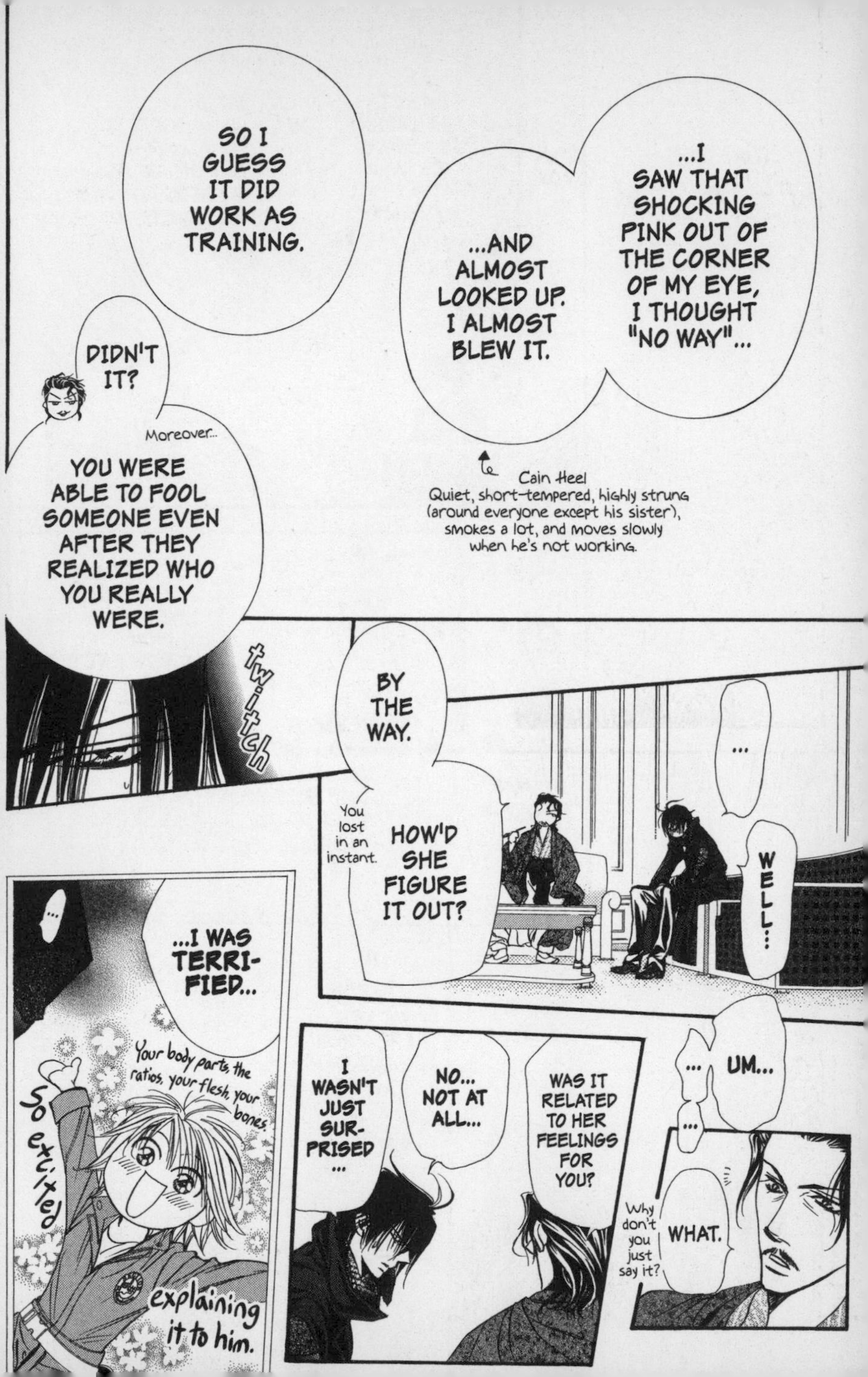
...I SAW THAT SHOCKING PINK OUT OF THE CORNER OF MY EYE, I THOUGHT "NO WAY"...
...AND ALMOST LOOKED UP. I ALMOST BLEW IT.
Cain Heel
Quiet, short-tempered, highly strung (around everyone except his sister), smokes a lot, and moves slowly when he's not working.
SO I GUESS IT DID WORK AS TRAINING.
DIDN'T IT?
Moreover...
YOU WERE ABLE TO FOOL SOMEONE EVEN AFTER THEY REALIZED WHO YOU REALLY WERE.
...
WELL...
BY THE WAY.
HOW'D SHE FIGURE IT OUT?
You lost in an instant.
twitch
... UM...
...
WHAT.
Why don't you just say it?
WAS IT RELATED TO HER FEELINGS FOR YOU?
NO... NOT AT ALL...
I WASN'T JUST SUR-PRISED ...
...I WAS TERRI-FIED...
...
Your body parts, the ratios, your flesh, your bones.
So excited
explaining it to him.

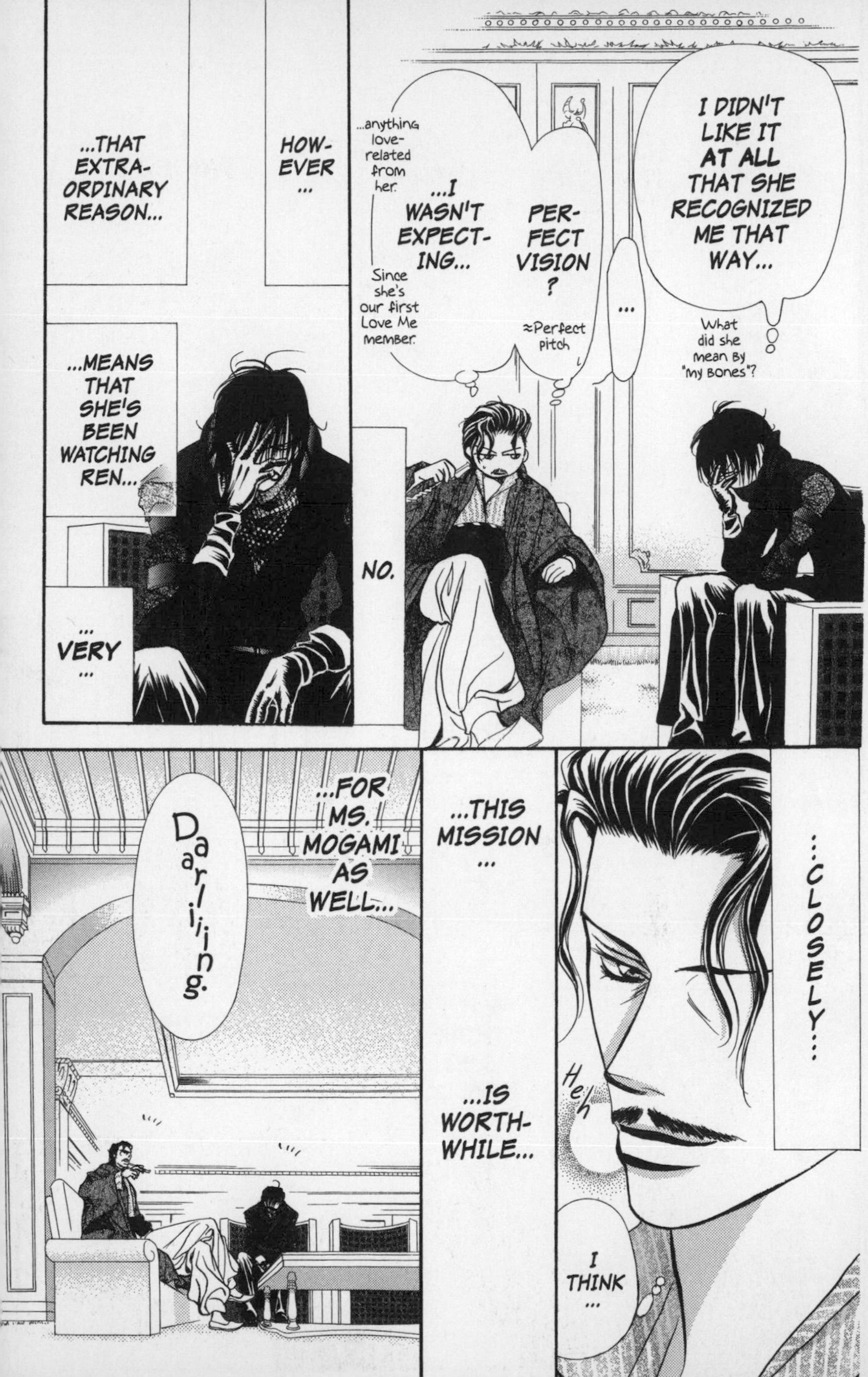
I DIDN'T LIKE IT AT ALL THAT SHE RECOGNIZED ME THAT WAY...
What did she mean By "My Bones"?
...
PERFECT VISION?
≈Perfect pitch
...I WASN'T EXPECTING...
...anything love-related from her.
Since she's our first Love Me member.
NO.
HOWEVER...
...THAT EXTRAORDINARY REASON...
...MEANS THAT SHE'S BEEN WATCHING REN...
...VERY...
...CLOSELY...
Heh
I THINK...
...THIS MISSION...
...IS WORTHWHILE...
...FOR MS. MOGAMI AS WELL...
Darliiing.

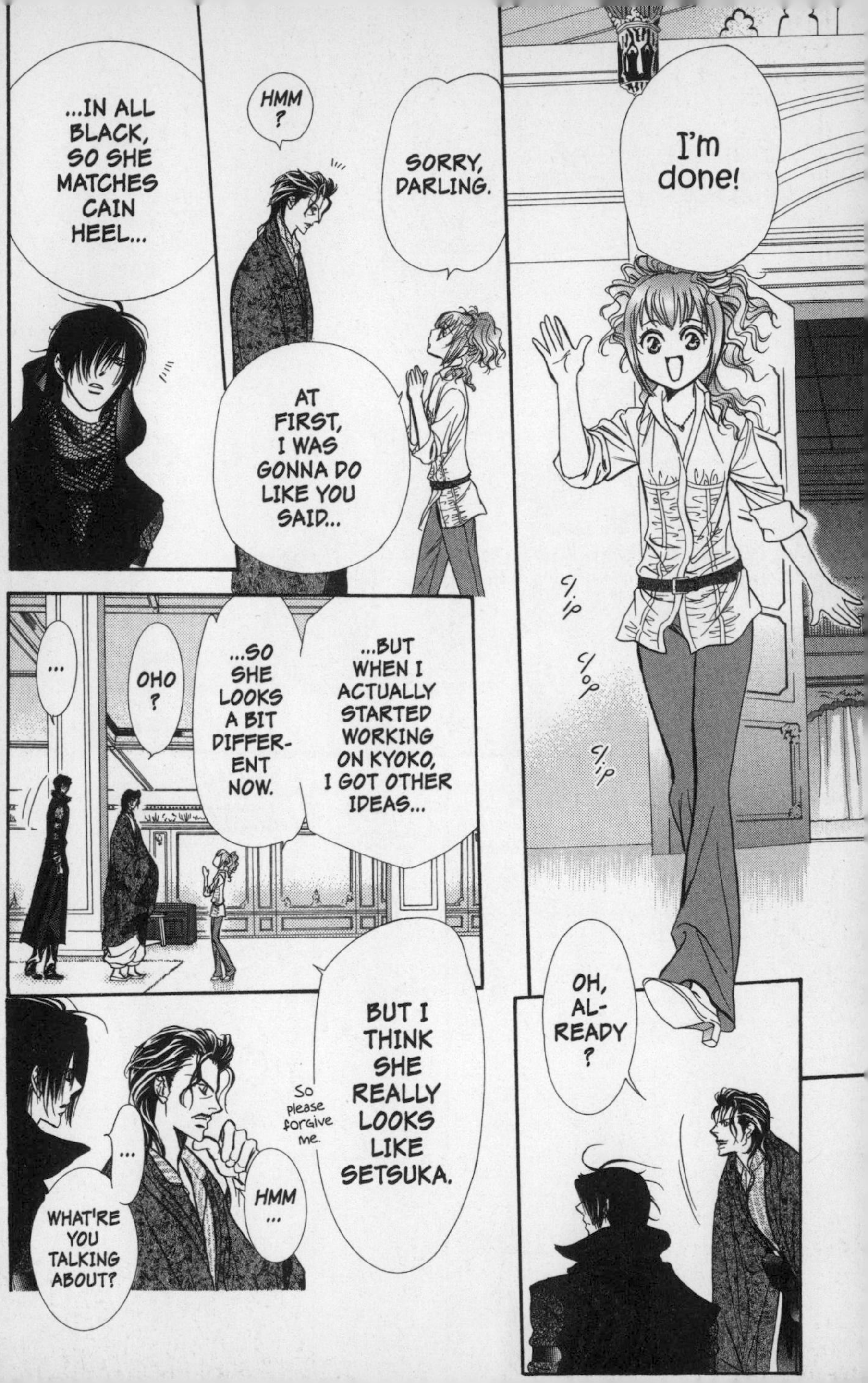
I'm done!
clip
clop
clip
OH, AL-READY?
HMM?
SORRY, DARLING.
AT FIRST, I WAS GONNA DO LIKE YOU SAID...
...IN ALL BLACK, SO SHE MATCHES CAIN HEEL...
...BUT WHEN I ACTUALLY STARTED WORKING ON KYOKO, I GOT OTHER IDEAS...
...SO SHE LOOKS A BIT DIFFER-ENT NOW.
OHO?
...
BUT I THINK SHE REALLY LOOKS LIKE SETSUKA.
So please forgive me.
HMM...
...
WHAT'RE YOU TALKING ABOUT?

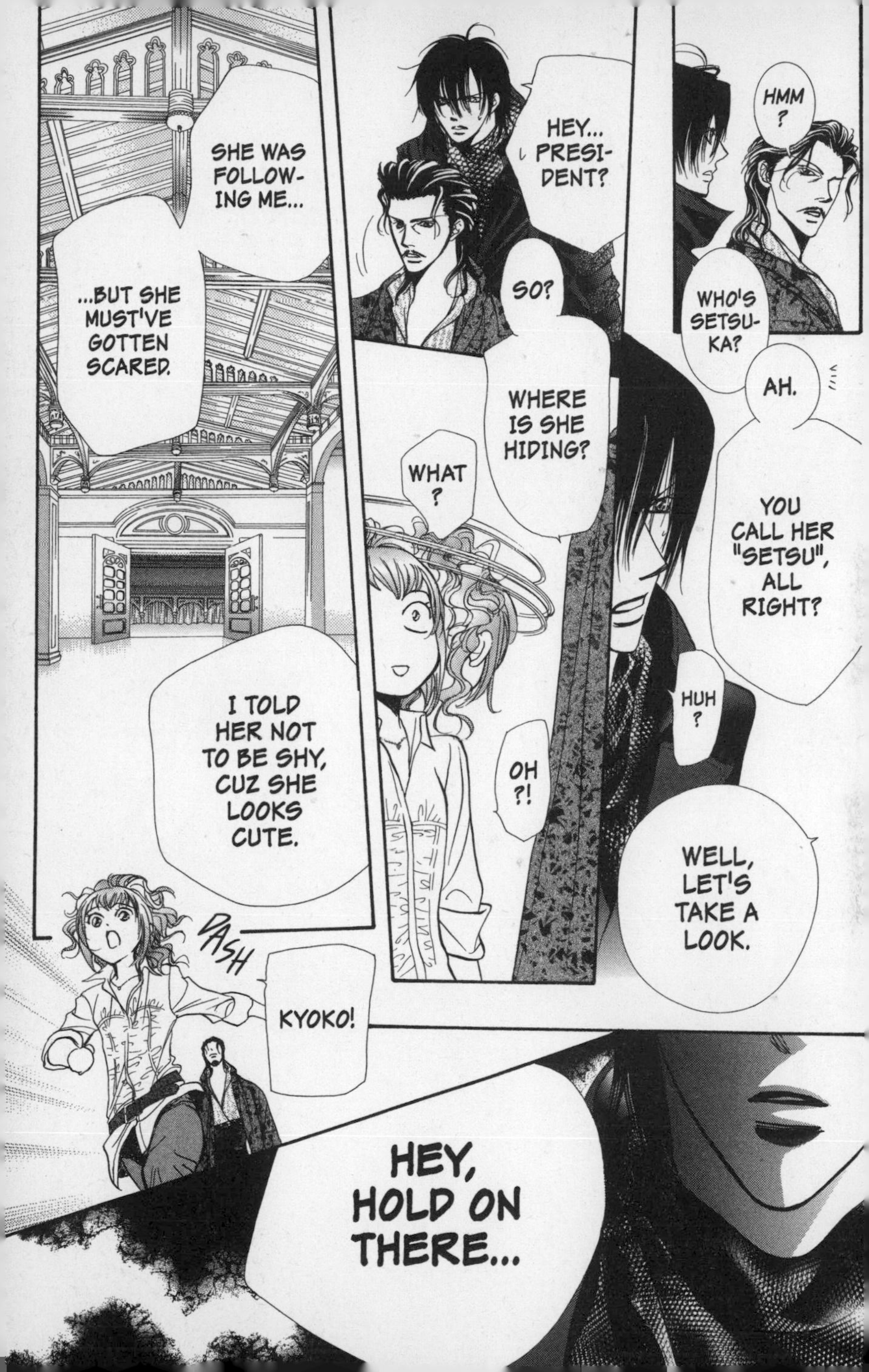
HMM?
WHO'S SETSU-KA?
AH.
YOU CALL HER "SETSU", ALL RIGHT?
HUH?
WELL, LET'S TAKE A LOOK.
HEY... PRESI-DENT?
SO?
WHERE IS SHE HIDING?
WHAT?
OH?!
SHE WAS FOLLOW-ING ME...
...BUT SHE MUST'VE GOTTEN SCARED.
I TOLD HER NOT TO BE SHY, CUZ SHE LOOKS CUTE.
HEY, HOLD ON THERE...
KYOKO!
DASH

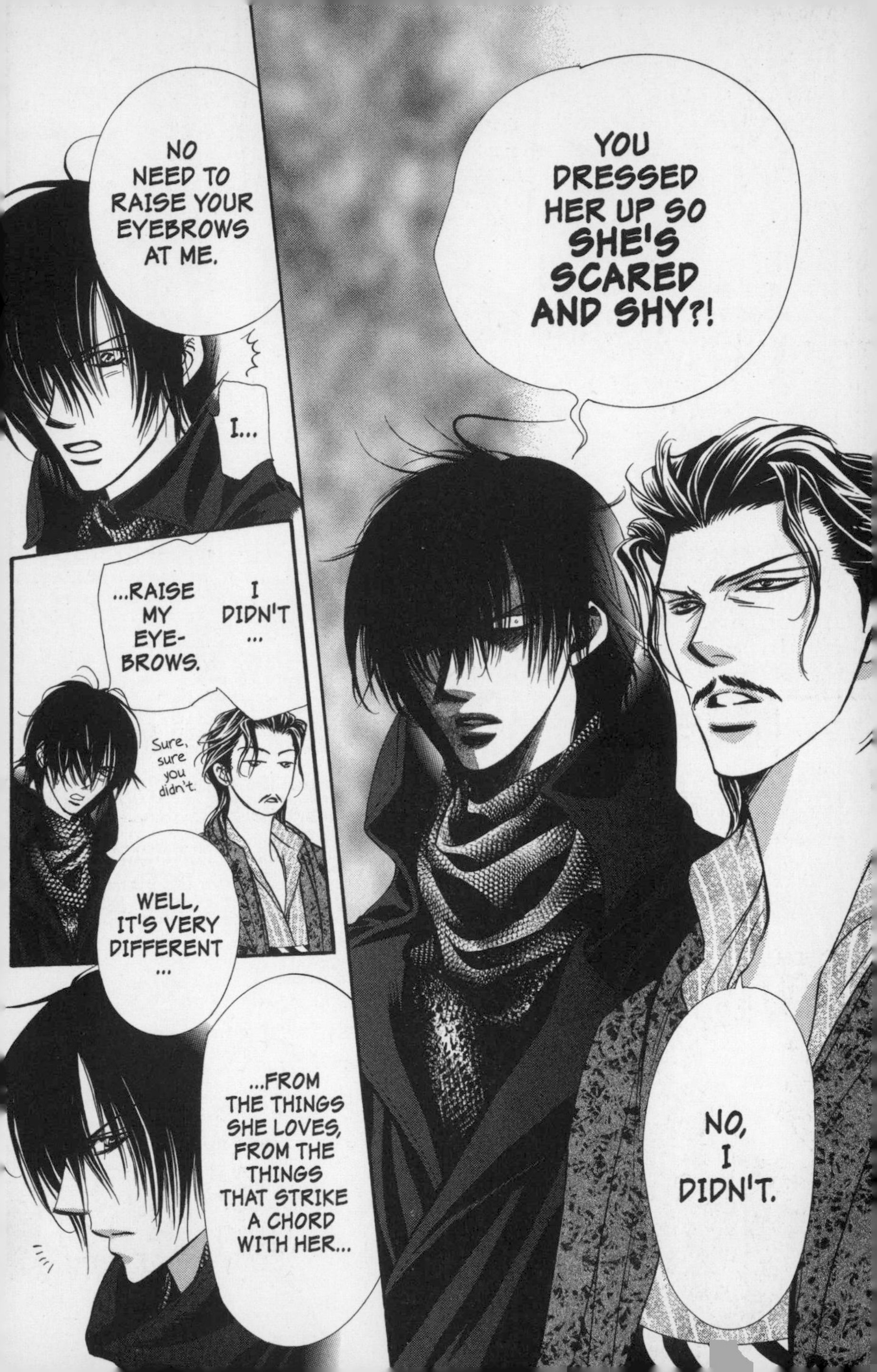
YOU DRESSED HER UP SO SHE'S SCARED AND SHY?!
NO, I DIDN'T.
NO NEED TO RAISE YOUR EYEBROWS AT ME.
I...
I DIDN'T ...
...RAISE MY EYE-BROWS.
Sure, sure you didn't.
WELL, IT'S VERY DIFFERENT ...
...FROM THE THINGS SHE LOVES, FROM THE THINGS THAT STRIKE A CHORD WITH HER...

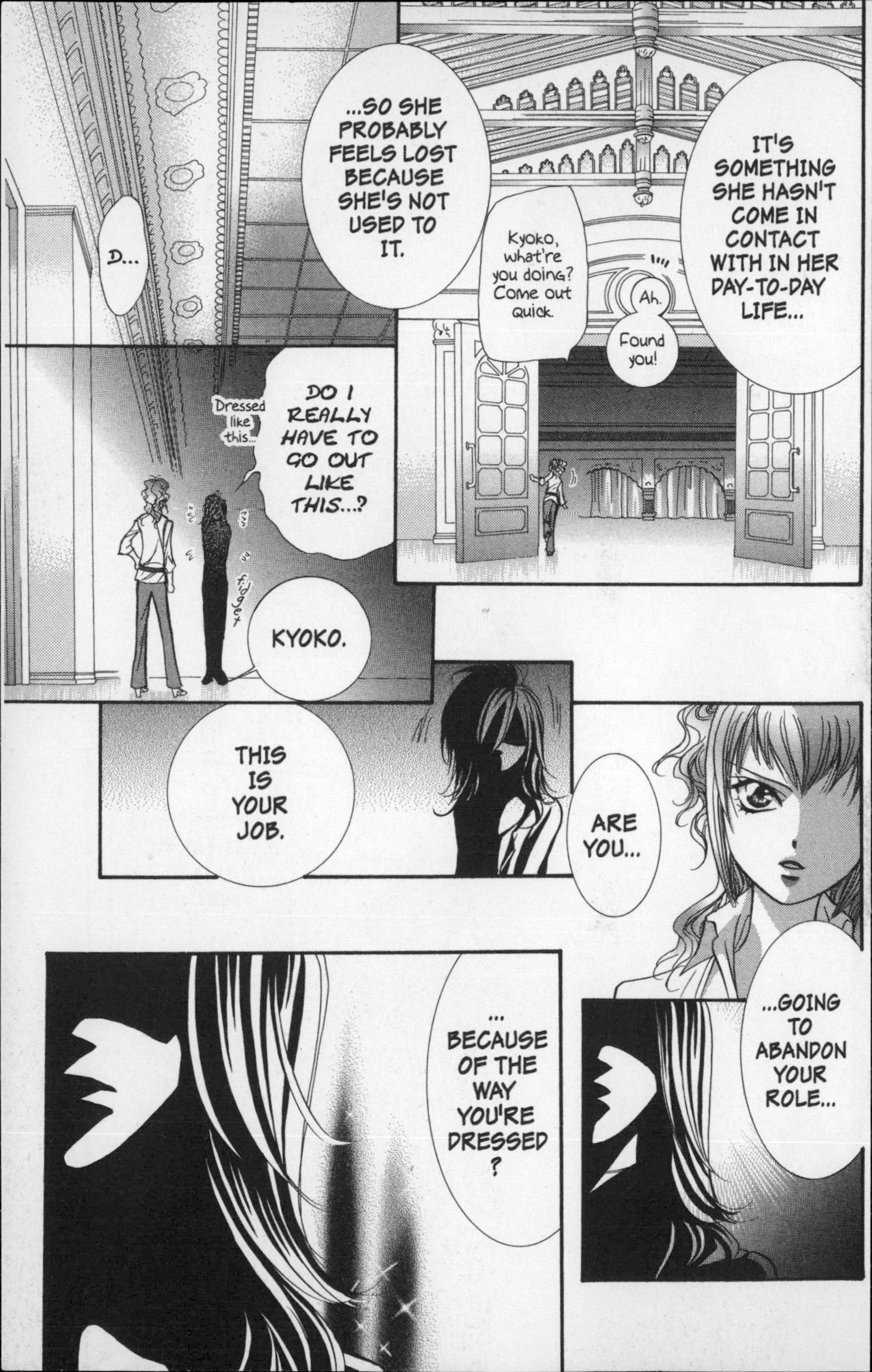
IT'S SOMETHING SHE HASN'T COME IN CONTACT WITH IN HER DAY-TO-DAY LIFE...
...SO SHE PROBABLY FEELS LOST BECAUSE SHE'S NOT USED TO IT.
Ah.
Found you!
Kyoko, what're you doing? Come out quick.
D...
DO I REALLY HAVE TO GO OUT LIKE THIS...?
Dressed like this...
fidget
KYOKO.
ARE YOU...
THIS IS YOUR JOB.
...GOING TO ABANDON YOUR ROLE...
...BECAUSE OF THE WAY YOU'RE DRESSED?

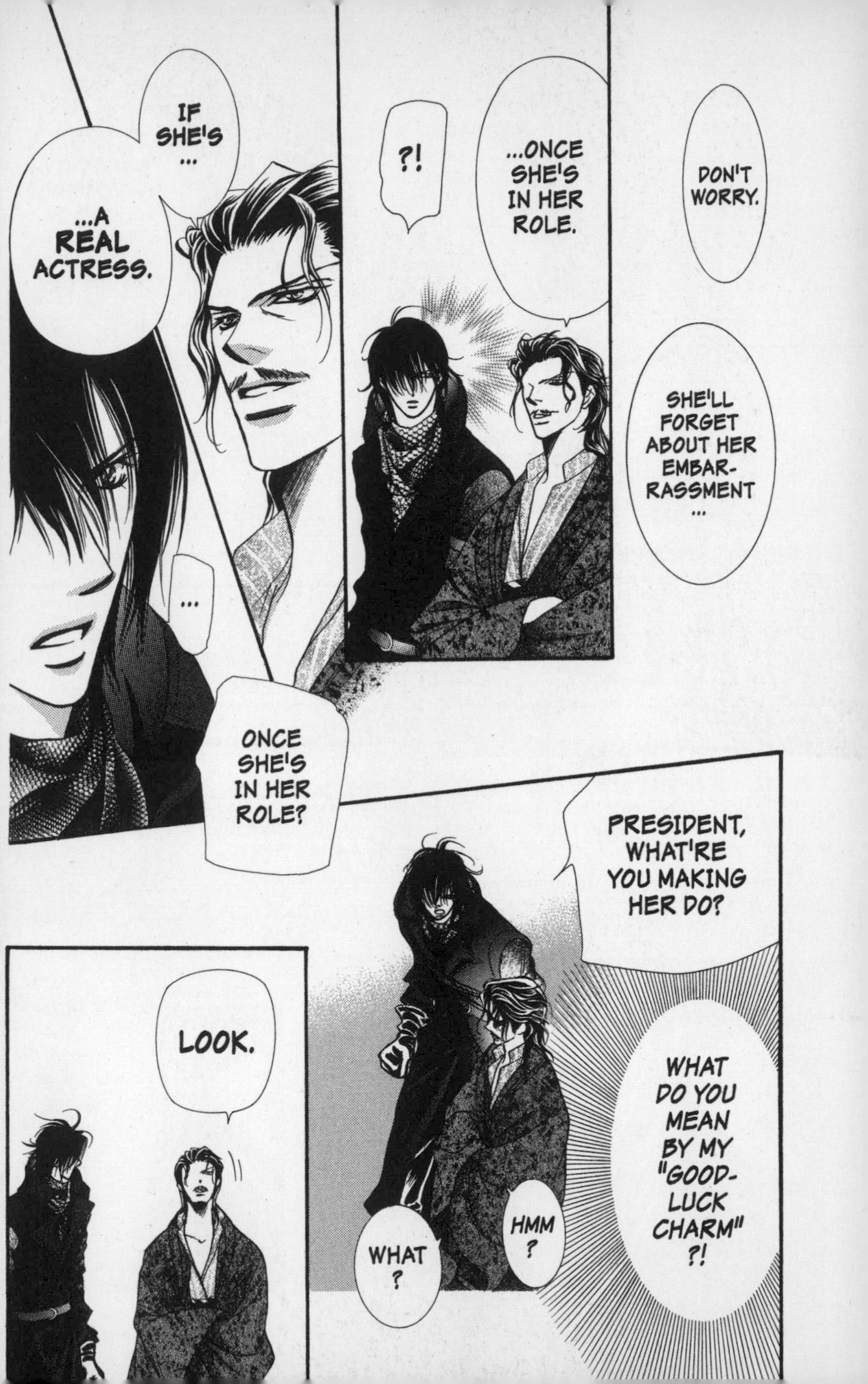
DON'T WORRY.
SHE'LL FORGET ABOUT HER EMBAR-RASSMENT ...
...ONCE SHE'S IN HER ROLE.
?!
IF SHE'S ...
...A REAL ACTRESS.
...
ONCE SHE'S IN HER ROLE?
PRESIDENT, WHAT'RE YOU MAKING HER DO?
WHAT DO YOU MEAN BY MY "GOOD-LUCK CHARM" ?!
HMM ?
WHAT ?
LOOK.

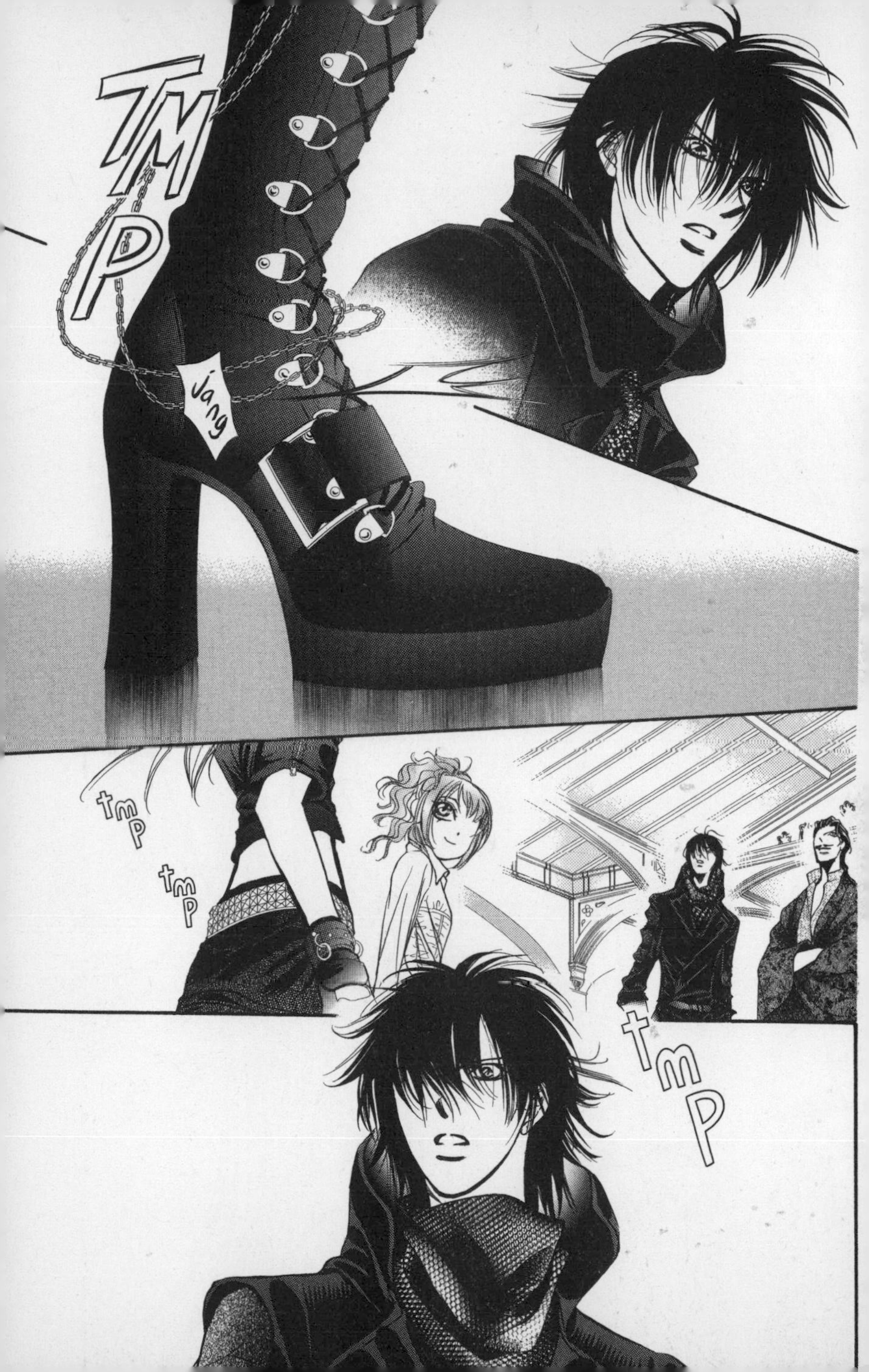
TMP
jang
tmp
tmp
tmp

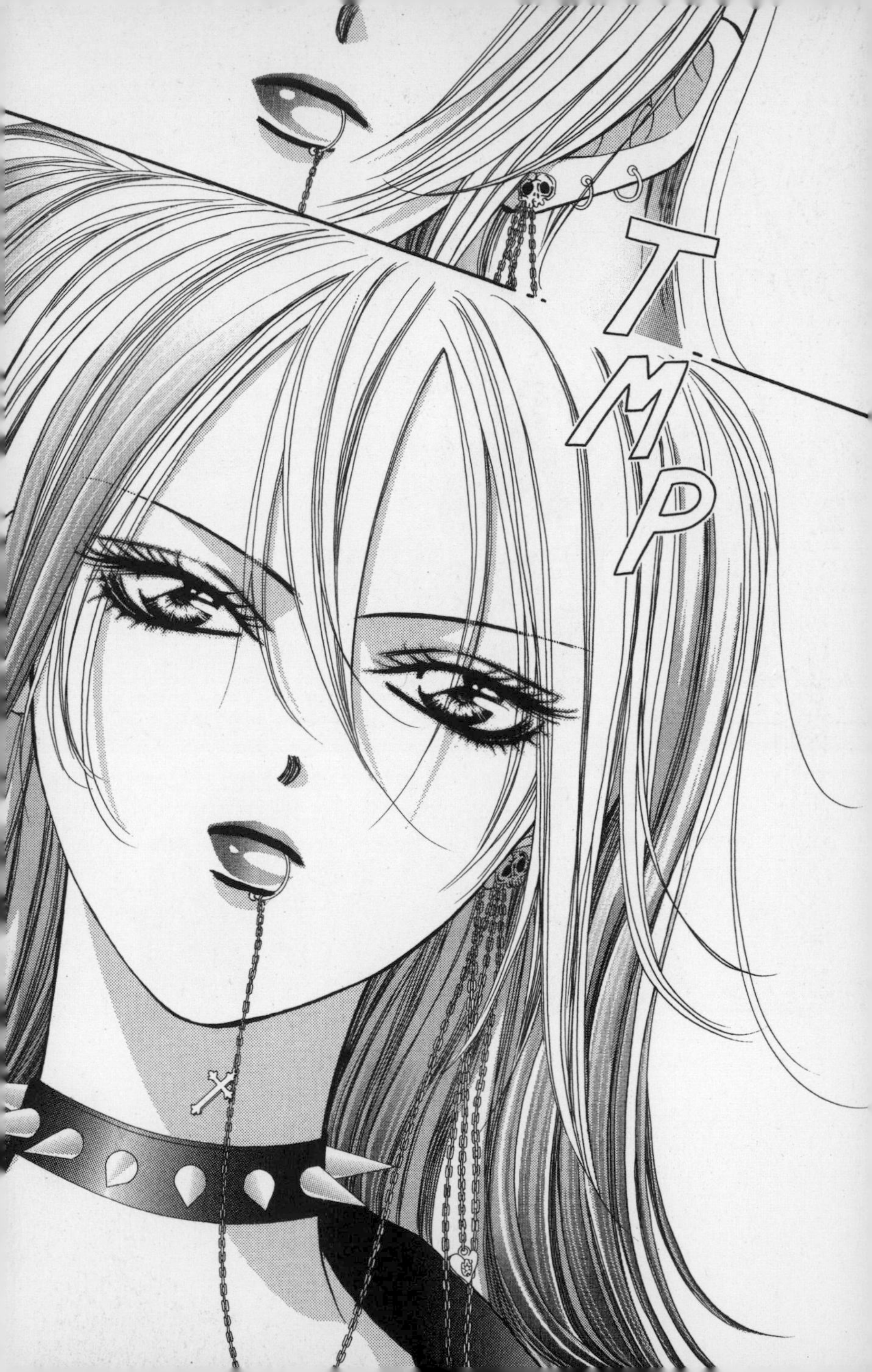
TMP

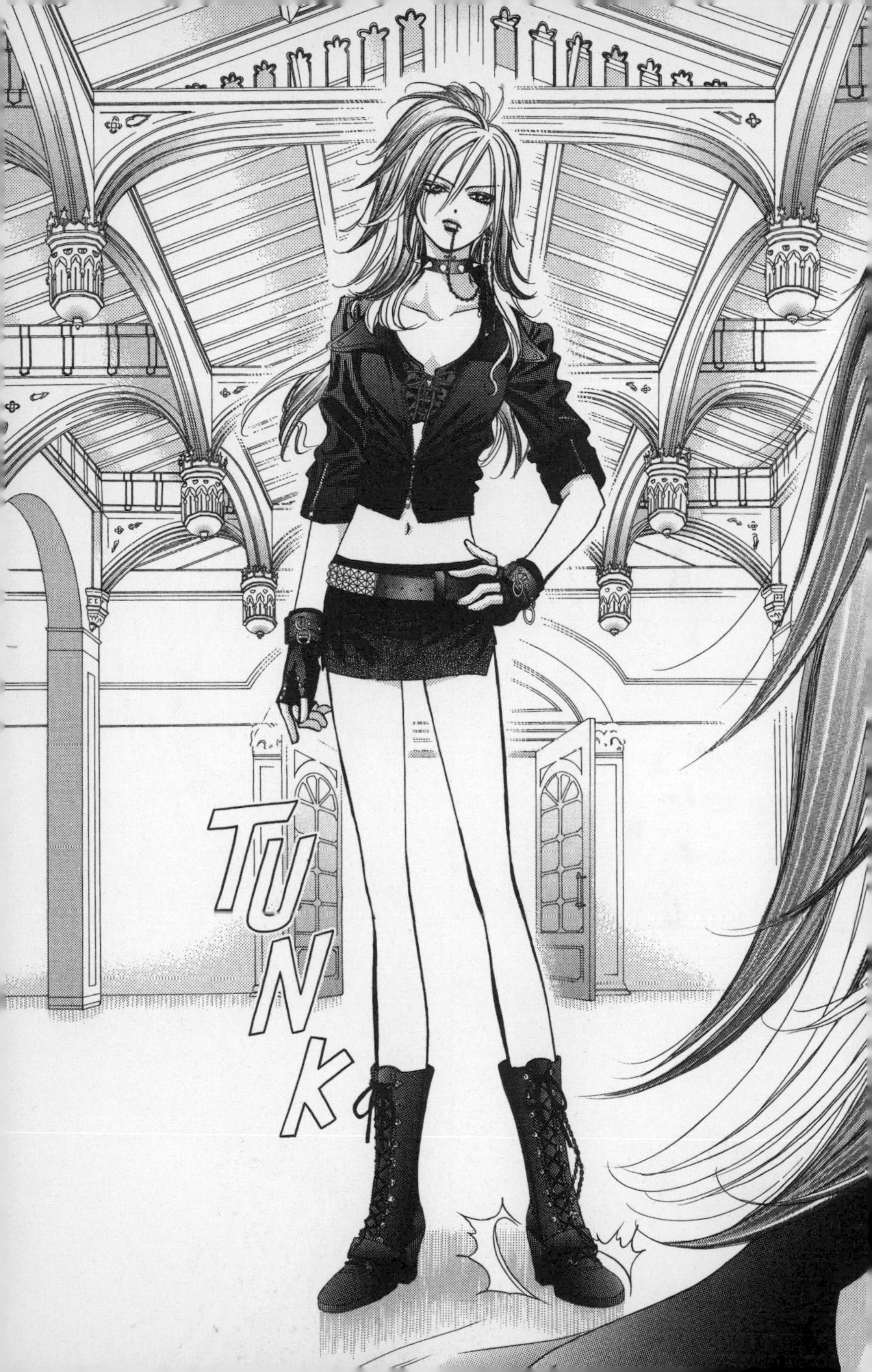
TUNK

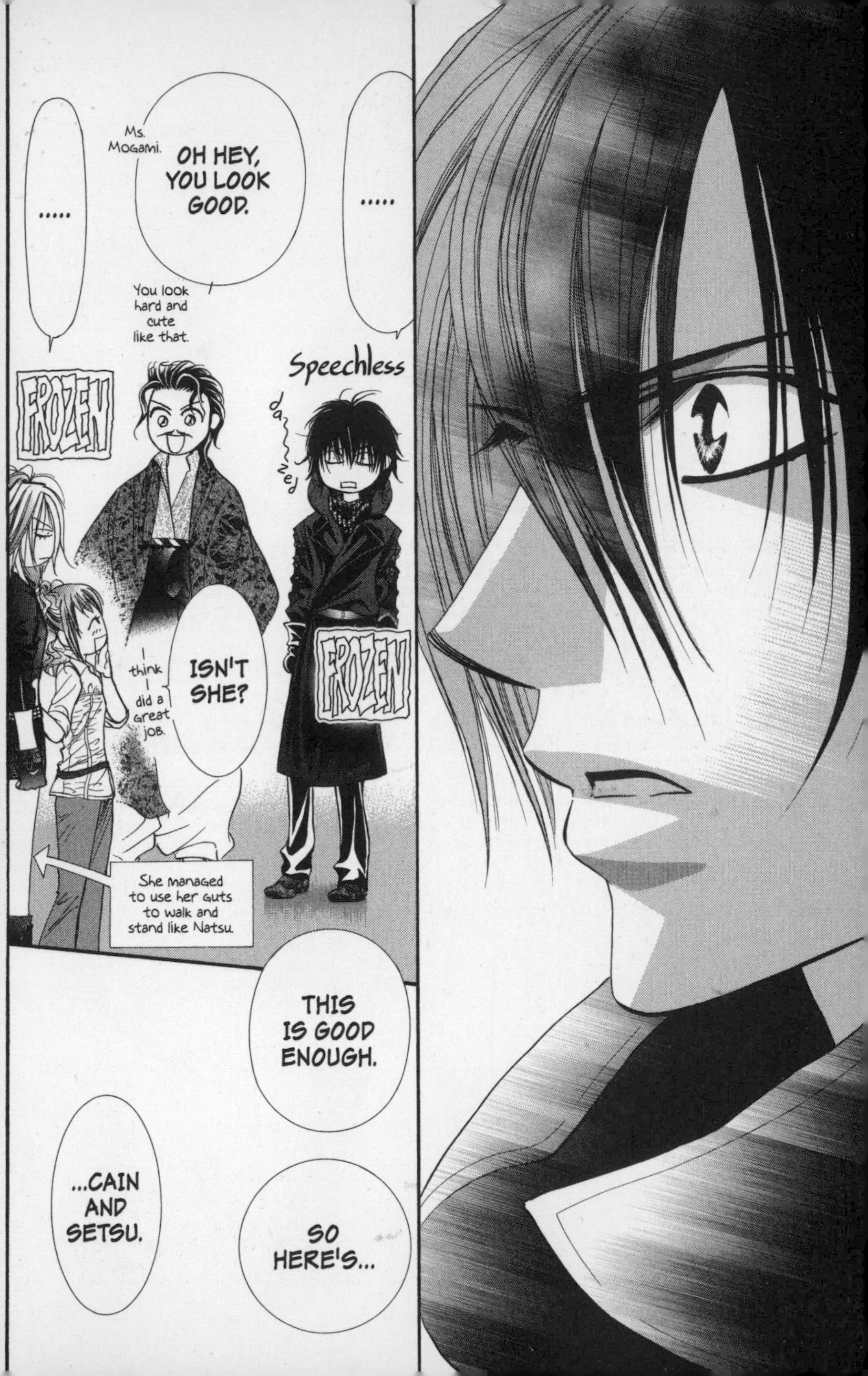
.....
Speechless
dazed
FROZEN
OH HEY, YOU LOOK GOOD.
Ms. Mogami.
You look hard and cute like that.
.....
FROZEN
ISN'T SHE?
I think I did a great job.
FROZEN
She managed to use her guts to walk and stand like Natsu.
THIS IS GOOD ENOUGH.
SO HERE'S...
...CAIN AND SETSU.

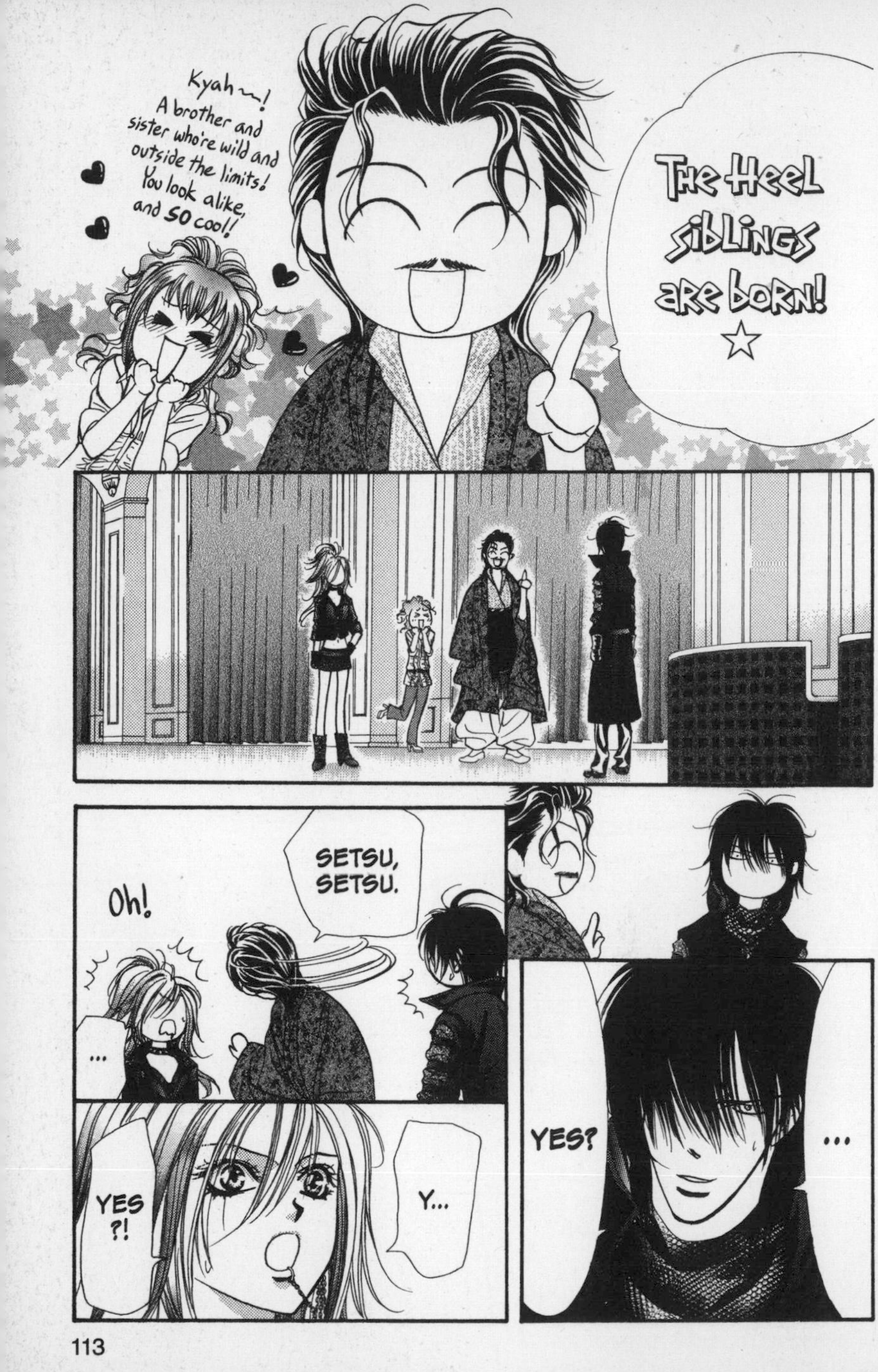
The Heel siblings are born! ☆
Kyah~! A brother and sister who're wild and outside the limits! You look alike, and SO cool!
SETSU, SETSU.
Oh!
...
...
YES?
Y...
YES ?!

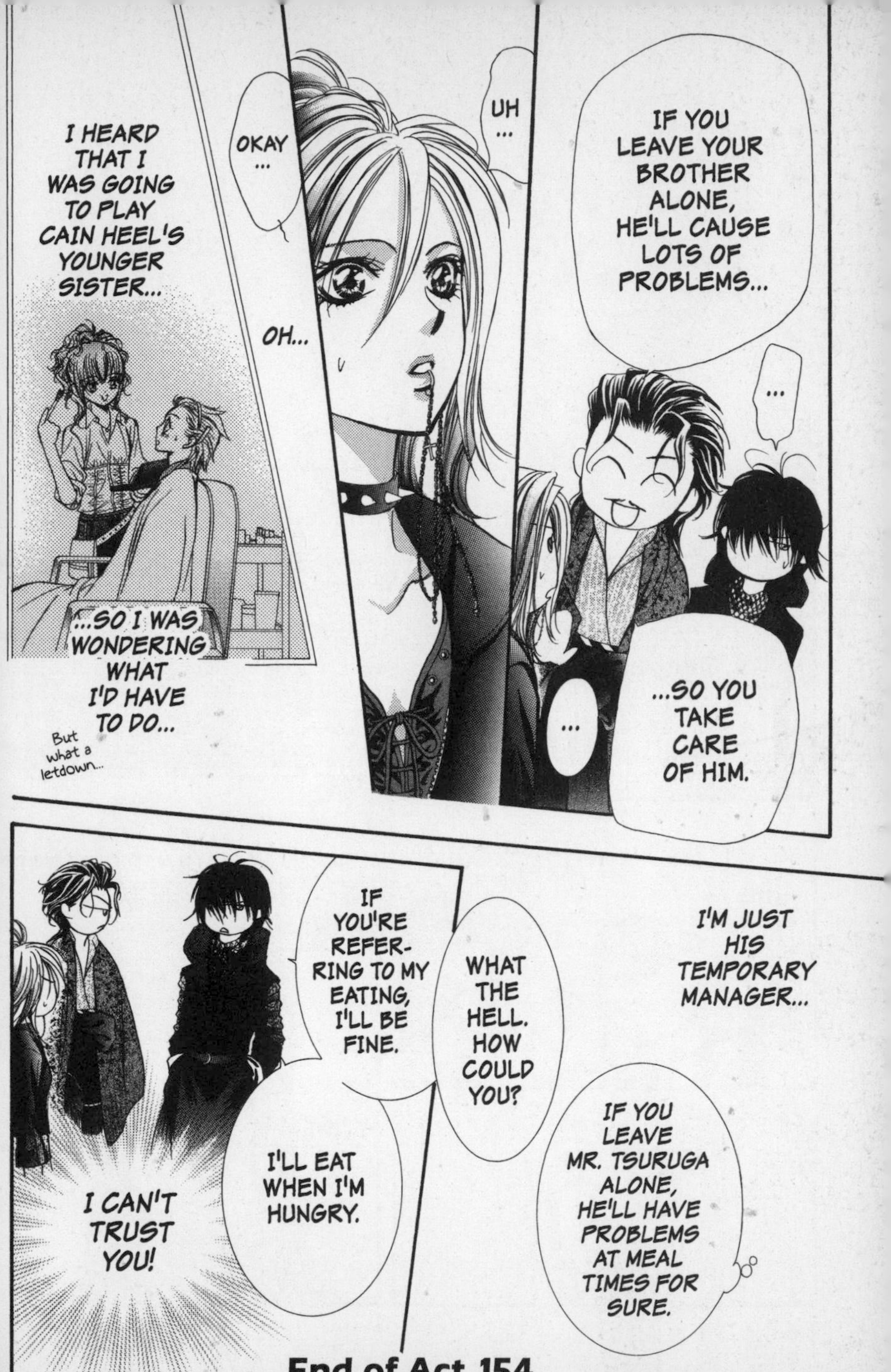
IF YOU LEAVE YOUR BROTHER ALONE, HE'LL CAUSE LOTS OF PROBLEMS...
...
...SO YOU TAKE CARE OF HIM.
...
UH...
OKAY...
OH...
I HEARD THAT I WAS GOING TO PLAY CAIN HEEL'S YOUNGER SISTER...
...SO I WAS WONDERING WHAT I'D HAVE TO DO...
But what a letdown...
I'M JUST HIS TEMPORARY MANAGER...
IF YOU LEAVE MR. TSURUGA ALONE, HE'LL HAVE PROBLEMS AT MEAL TIMES FOR SURE.
WHAT THE HELL. HOW COULD YOU?
IF YOU'RE REFER-RING TO MY EATING, I'LL BE FINE.
I'LL EAT WHEN I'M HUNGRY.
I CAN'T TRUST YOU!

End of Act 154

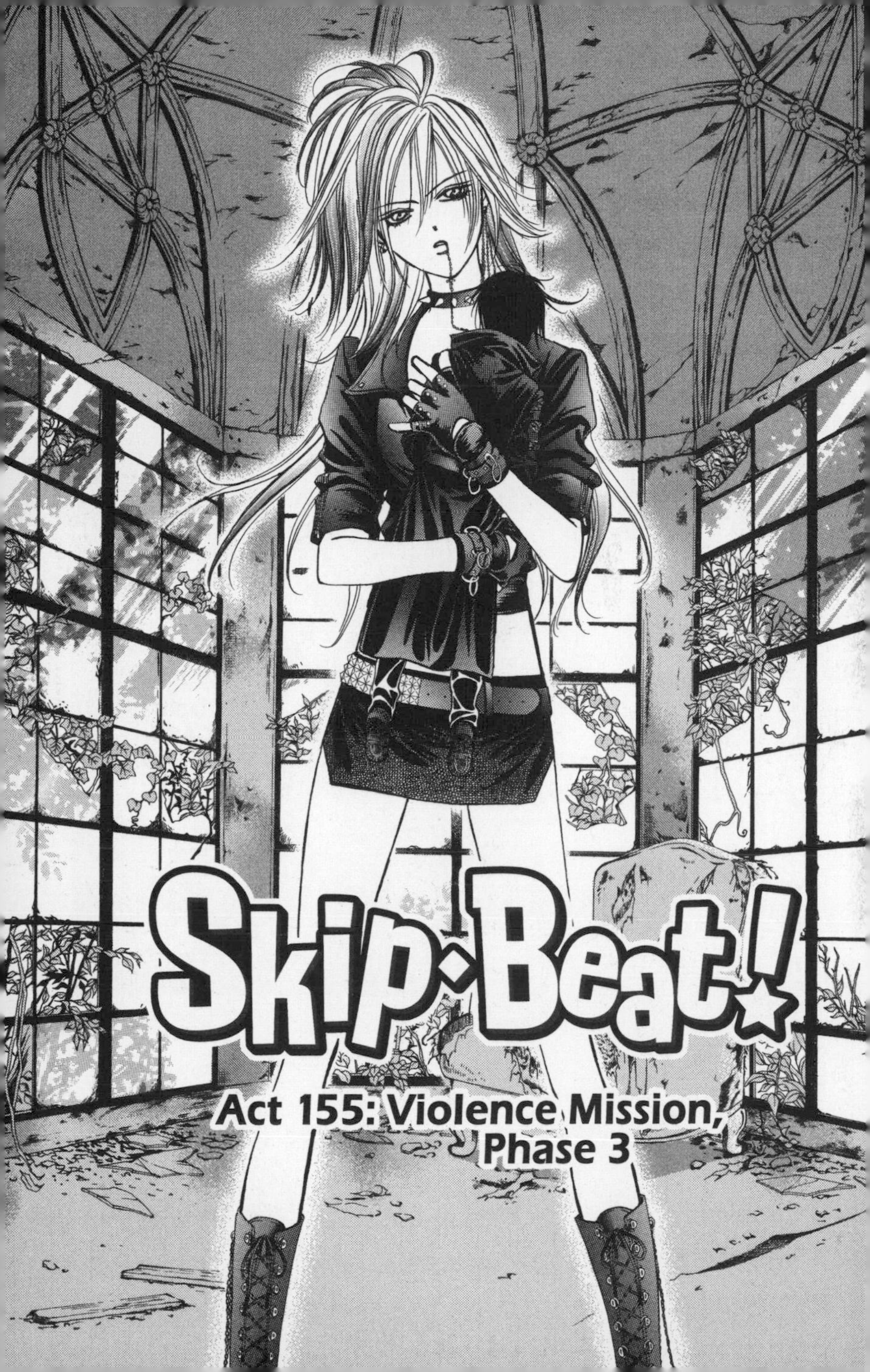
Skip·Beat!
Act 155: Violence Mission, Phase 3

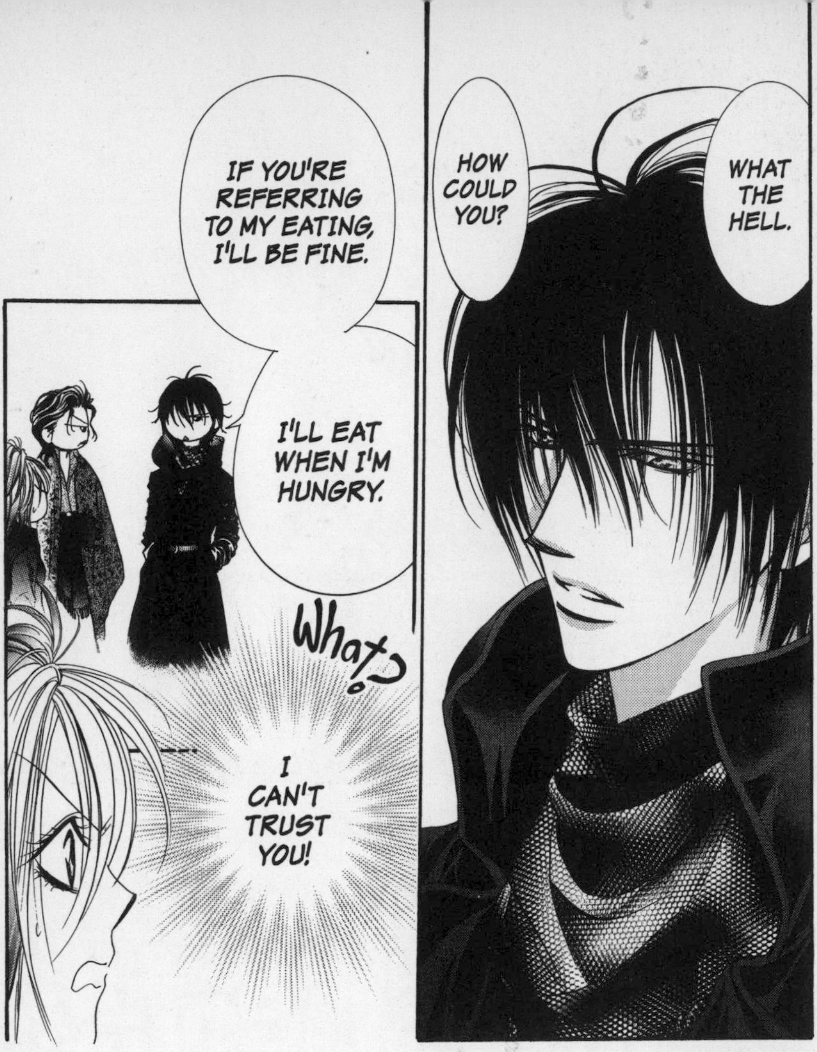
WHAT THE HELL.
HOW COULD YOU?
IF YOU'RE REFERRING TO MY EATING, I'LL BE FINE.
I'LL EAT WHEN I'M HUNGRY.
What?
I CAN'T TRUST YOU!
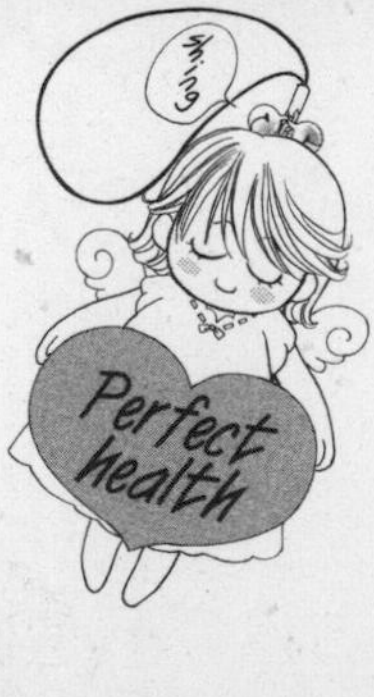
Perfect health

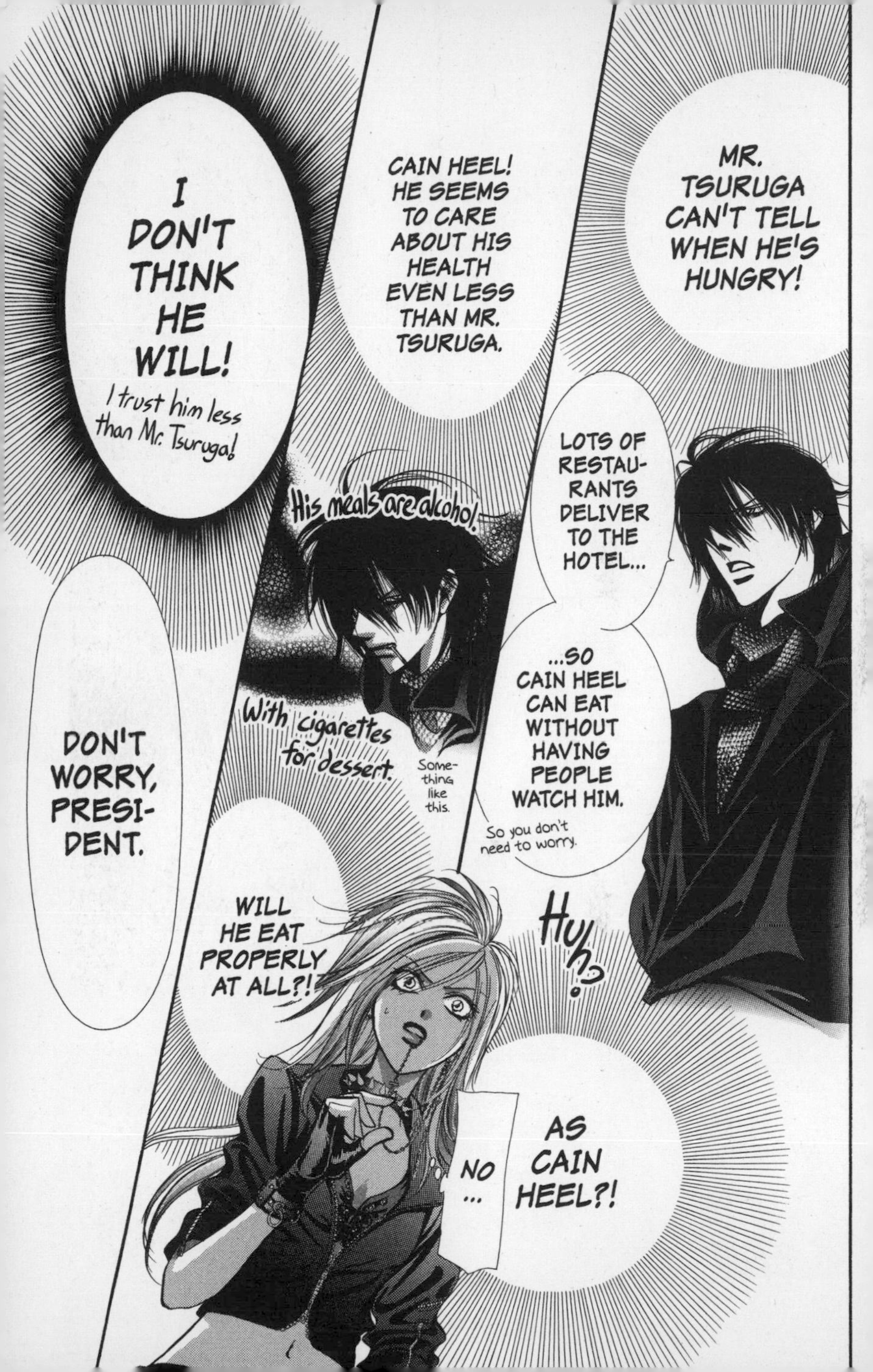
MR. TSURUGA CAN'T TELL WHEN HE'S HUNGRY!
LOTS OF RESTAU-RANTS DELIVER TO THE HOTEL...
...SO CAIN HEEL CAN EAT WITHOUT HAVING PEOPLE WATCH HIM.
So you don't need to worry.
Huh?
AS CAIN HEEL?!
NO...
CAIN HEEL! HE SEEMS TO CARE ABOUT HIS HEALTH EVEN LESS THAN MR. TSURUGA.
His meals are alcohol.
With cigarettes for dessert.
Some-thing like this.
WILL HE EAT PROPERLY AT ALL?!
I DON'T THINK HE WILL!
I trust him less than Mr. Tsuruga!
DON'T WORRY, PRESIDENT.

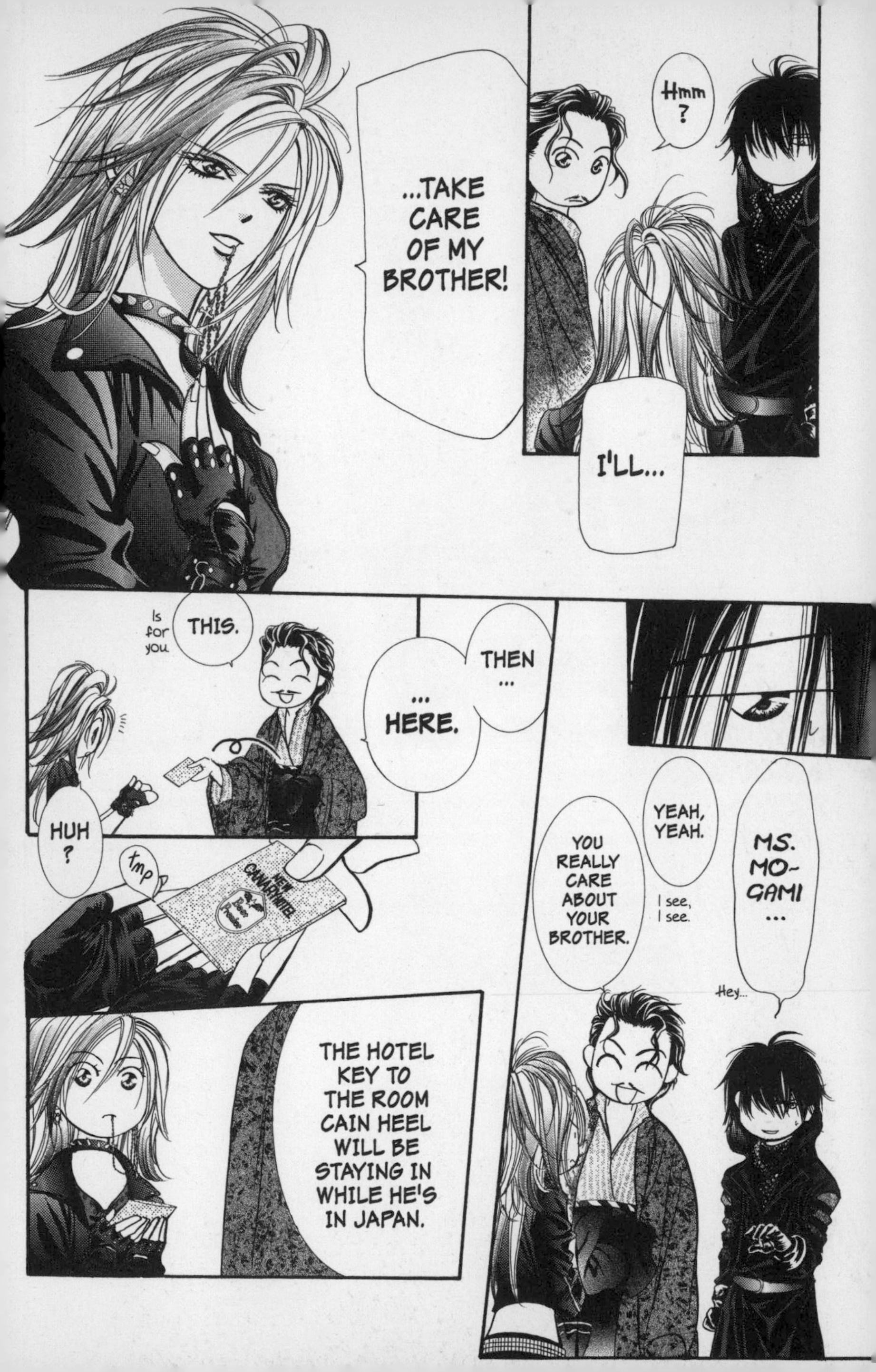
Hmm?
I'LL...
...TAKE CARE OF MY BROTHER!
MS. MO-GAMI...
Hey...
YEAH, YEAH.
I see, I see.
YOU REALLY CARE ABOUT YOUR BROTHER.
THEN...
...HERE.
THIS.
Is for you.
HUH?
tmp
THE HOTEL KEY TO THE ROOM CAIN HEEL WILL BE STAYING IN WHILE HE'S IN JAPAN.

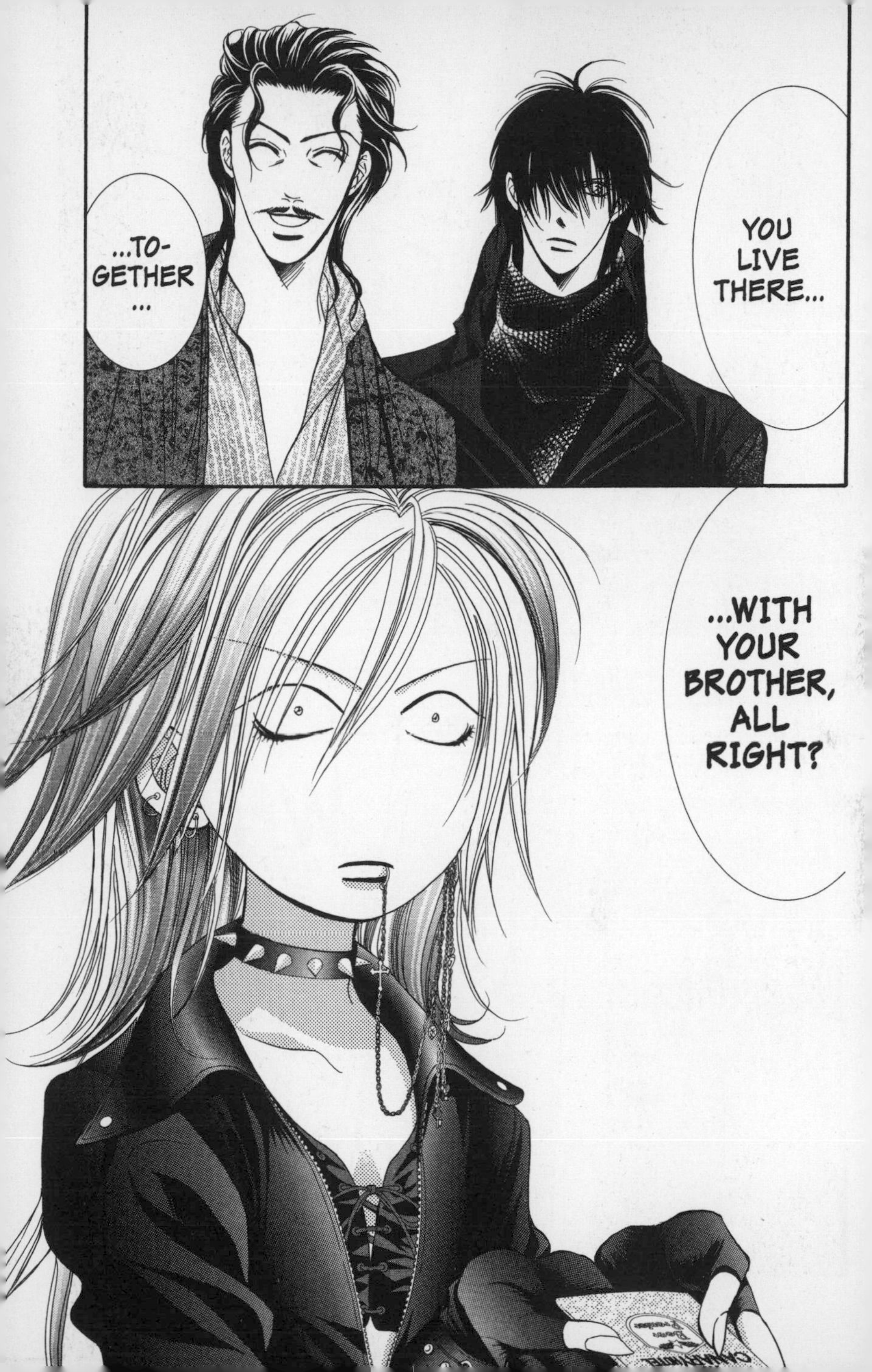
YOU LIVE THERE...
...TO-GETHER...
...WITH YOUR BROTHER, ALL RIGHT?

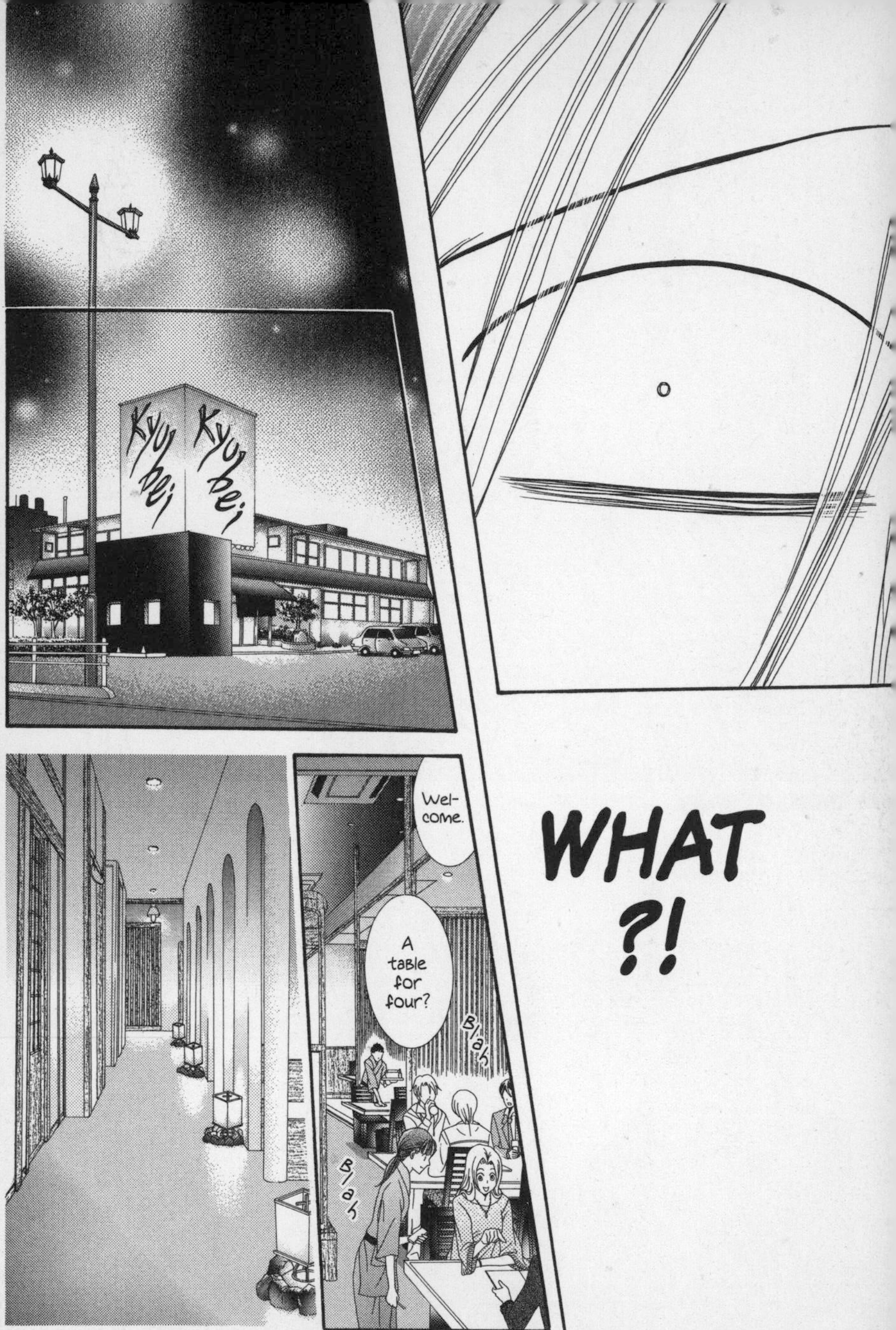
WHAT ?!
Kyubei
Kyubei
Wel-come.
A table for four?
Blah
Blah

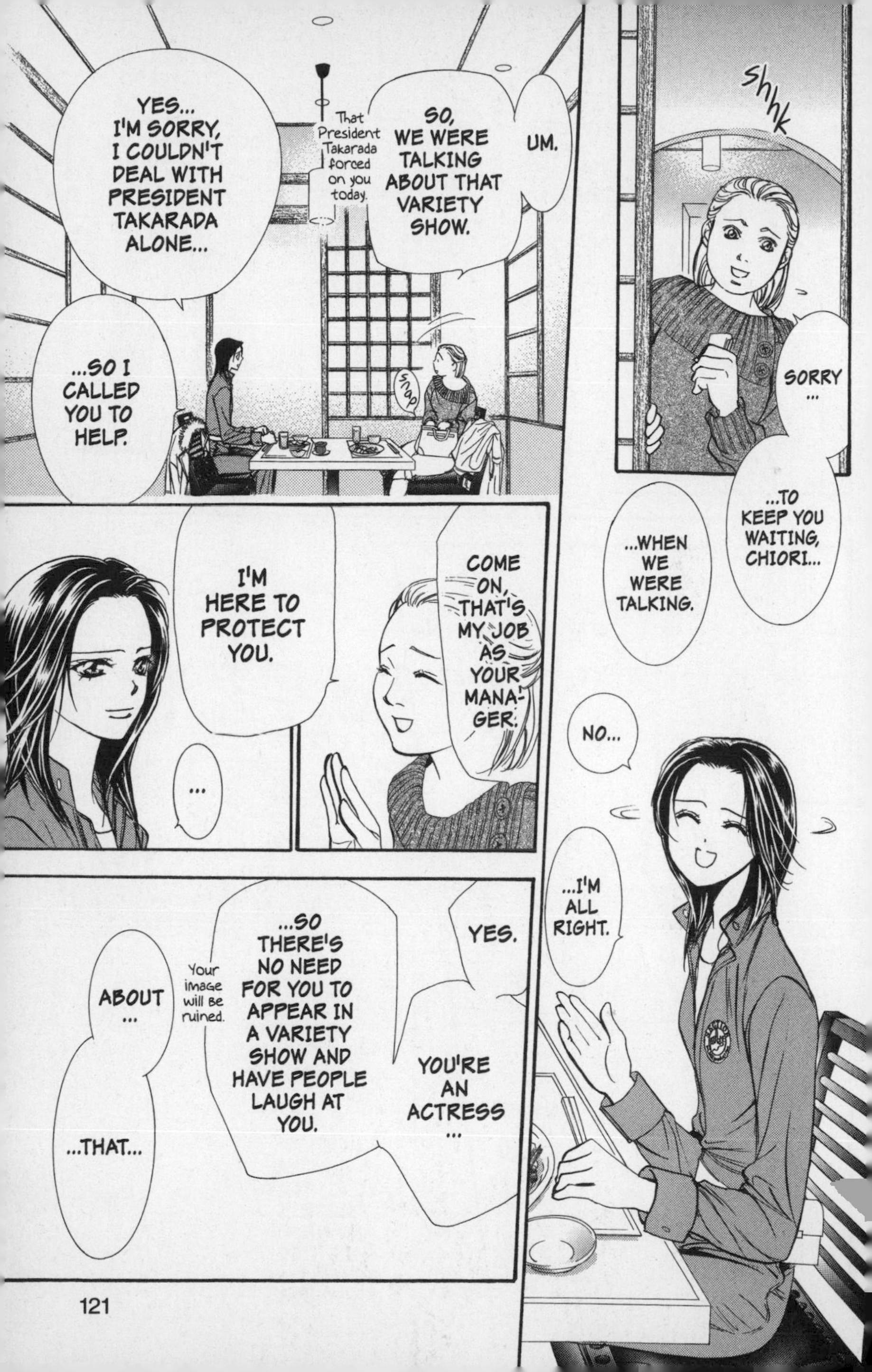
Shhk
SORRY...
...TO KEEP YOU WAITING, CHIORI...
...WHEN WE WERE TALKING.
NO...
...I'M ALL RIGHT.
UM.
SO, WE WERE TALKING ABOUT THAT VARIETY SHOW.
That President Takarada forced on you today.
YES... I'M SORRY, I COULDN'T DEAL WITH PRESIDENT TAKARADA ALONE...
...SO I CALLED YOU TO HELP.
COME ON, THAT'S MY JOB AS YOUR MANAGER.
I'M HERE TO PROTECT YOU.
...
YES.
YOU'RE AN ACTRESS...
...SO THERE'S NO NEED FOR YOU TO APPEAR IN A VARIETY SHOW AND HAVE PEOPLE LAUGH AT YOU.
Your image will be ruined.
ABOUT...
...THAT...

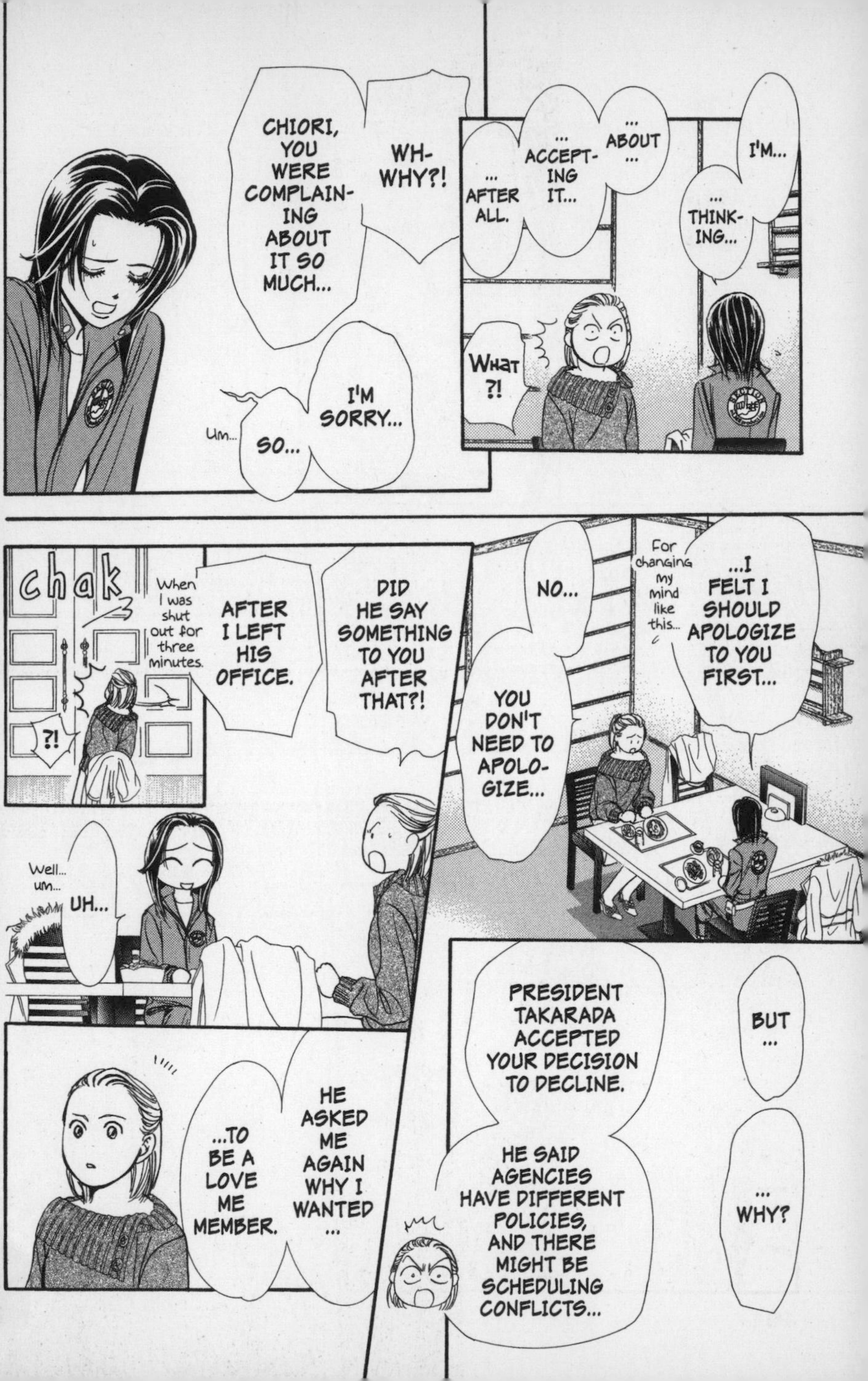
I'M...
...THINKING...
...ABOUT...
...ACCEPTING IT...
...AFTER ALL.
WHAT?!
WH-WHY?!
CHIORI, YOU WERE COMPLAINING ABOUT IT SO MUCH...
I'M SORRY...
SO...
Um...
...I FELT I SHOULD APOLOGIZE TO YOU FIRST...
For changing my mind like this...
NO...
YOU DON'T NEED TO APOLOGIZE...
DID HE SAY SOMETHING TO YOU AFTER THAT?!
AFTER I LEFT HIS OFFICE.
When I was shut out for three minutes.
chak
?!
UH...
Well... um...
BUT...
...WHY?
PRESIDENT TAKARADA ACCEPTED YOUR DECISION TO DECLINE.
HE SAID AGENCIES HAVE DIFFERENT POLICIES, AND THERE MIGHT BE SCHEDULING CONFLICTS...
HE ASKED ME AGAIN WHY I WANTED...
...TO BE A LOVE ME MEMBER.

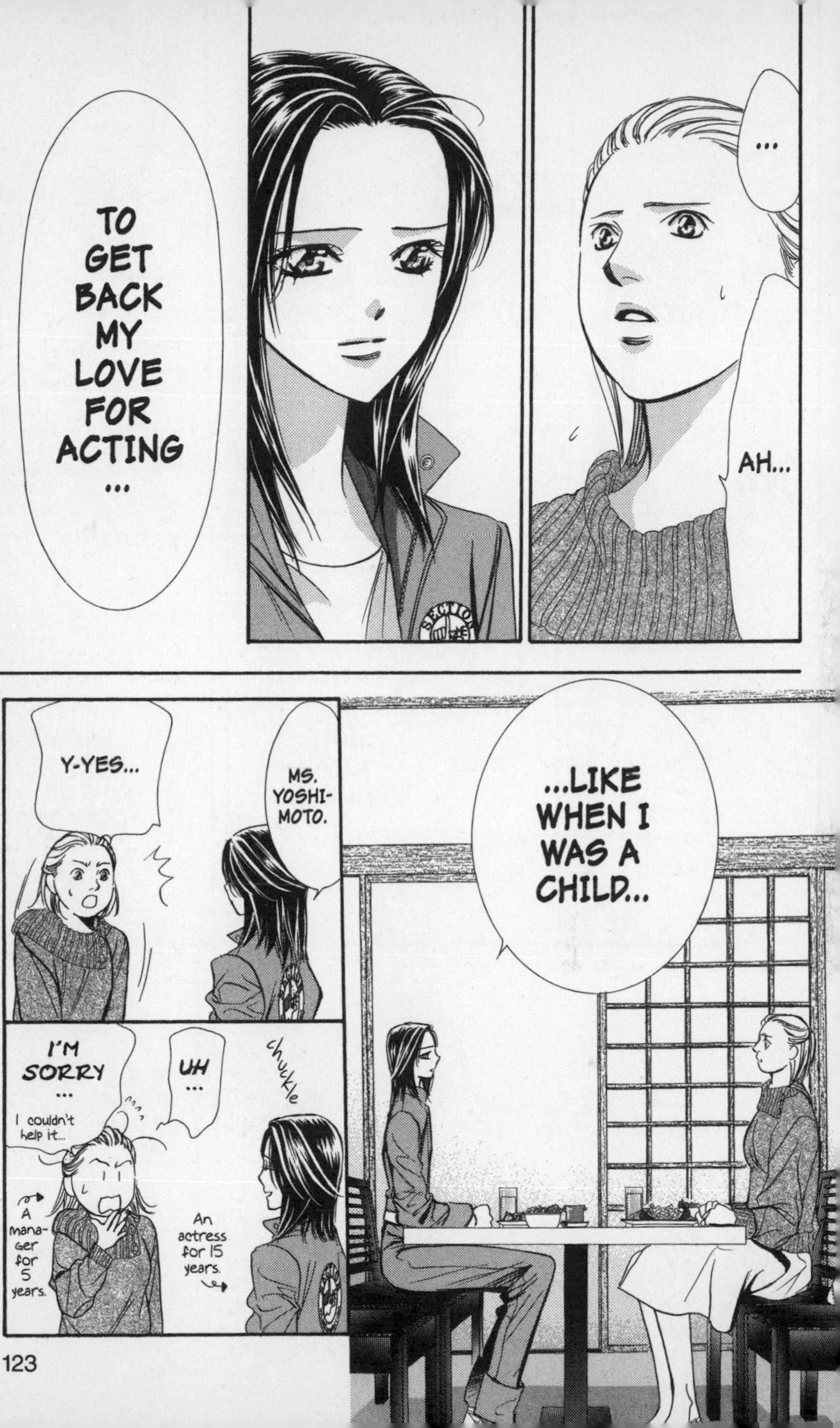
...
AH...
TO GET BACK MY LOVE FOR ACTING...
...LIKE WHEN I WAS A CHILD...
MS. YOSHIMOTO.
Y-YES...
chuckle
UH...
I'M SORRY...
I couldn't help it...
An actress for 15 years.
A manager for 5 years.

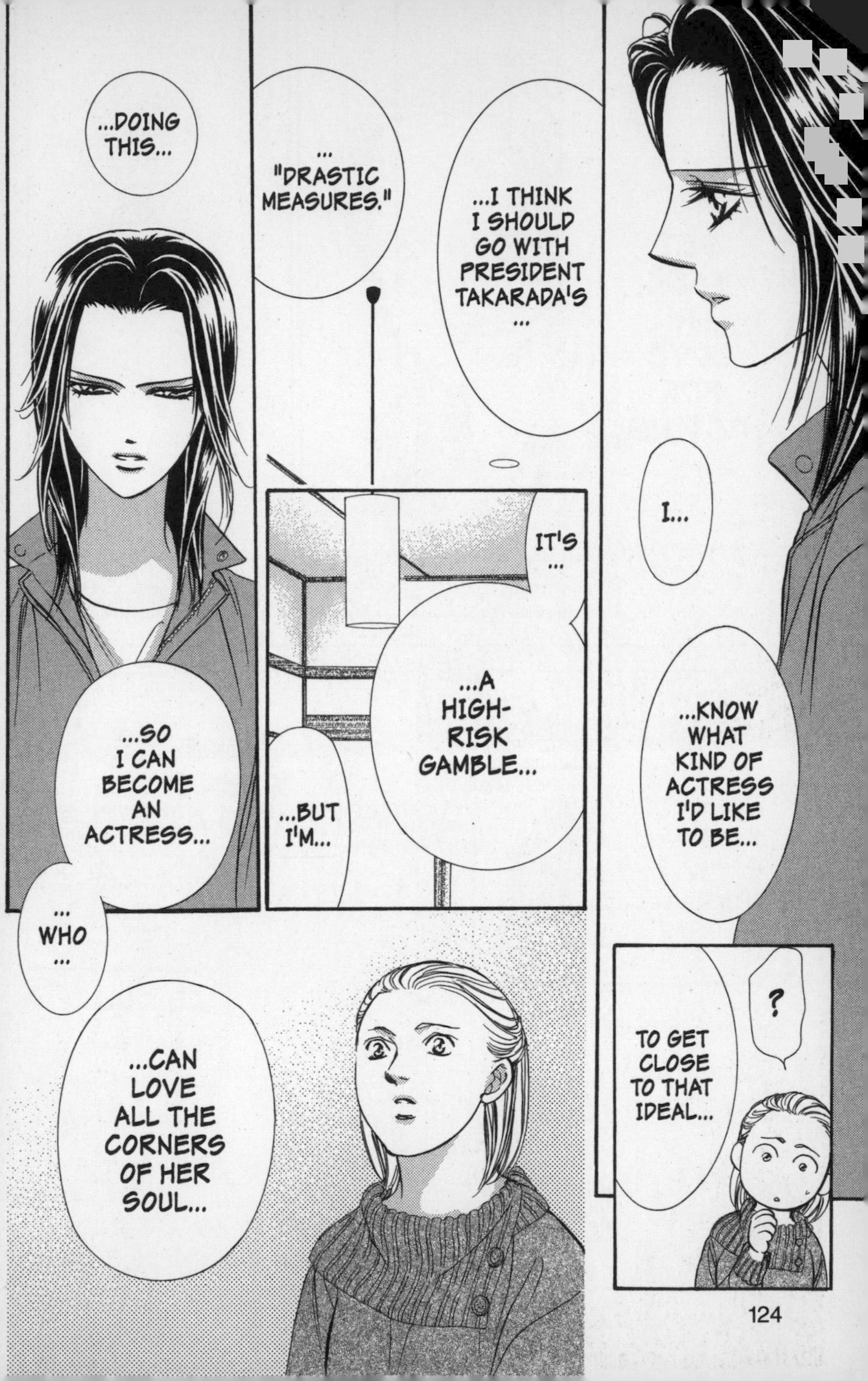
I...
...KNOW WHAT KIND OF ACTRESS I'D LIKE TO BE...
?
TO GET CLOSE TO THAT IDEAL...
...I THINK I SHOULD GO WITH PRESIDENT TAKARADA'S ...
... "DRASTIC MEASURES."
IT'S ...
...A HIGH-RISK GAMBLE...
...BUT I'M...
...DOING THIS...
...SO I CAN BECOME AN ACTRESS...
... WHO ...
...CAN LOVE ALL THE CORNERS OF HER SOUL...

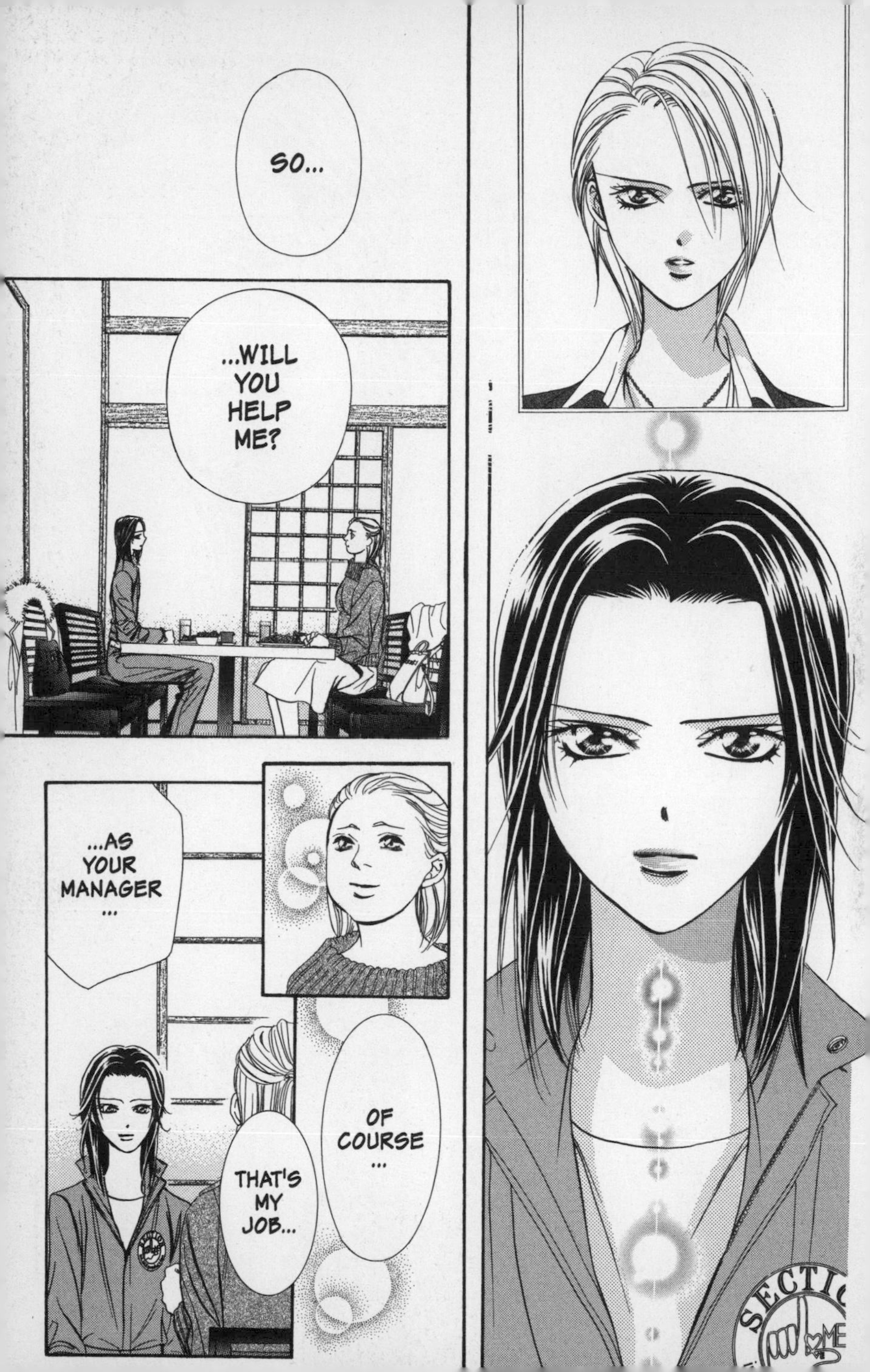
SO...
...WILL YOU HELP ME?
...AS YOUR MANAGER ...
OF COURSE ...
THAT'S MY JOB...

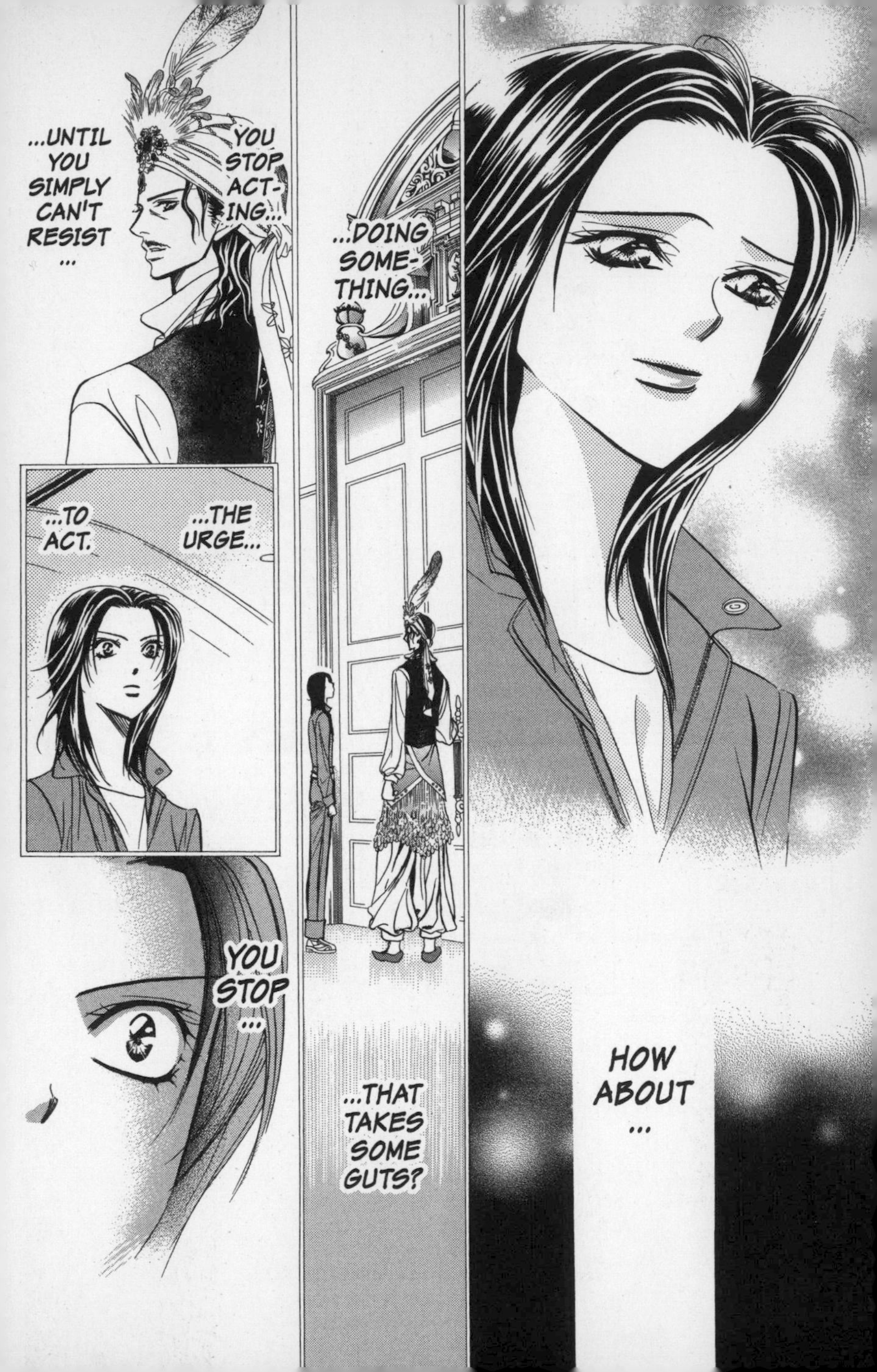
HOW ABOUT ...
...DOING SOME-THING...
...THAT TAKES SOME GUTS?
YOU STOP ACT-ING...
...UNTIL YOU SIMPLY CAN'T RESIST ...
...THE URGE...
...TO ACT.
YOU STOP ...

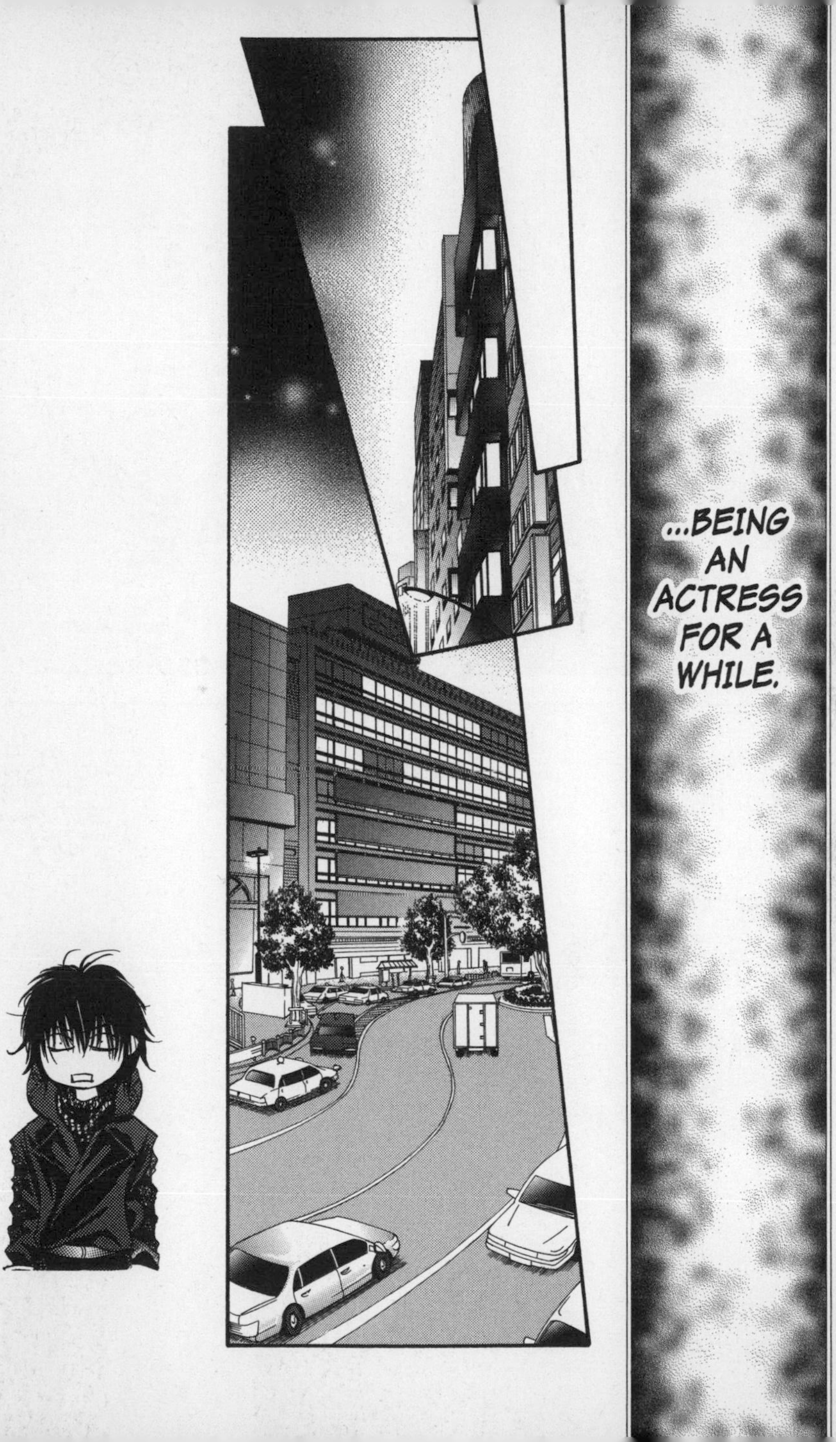
...BEING AN ACTRESS FOR A WHILE.

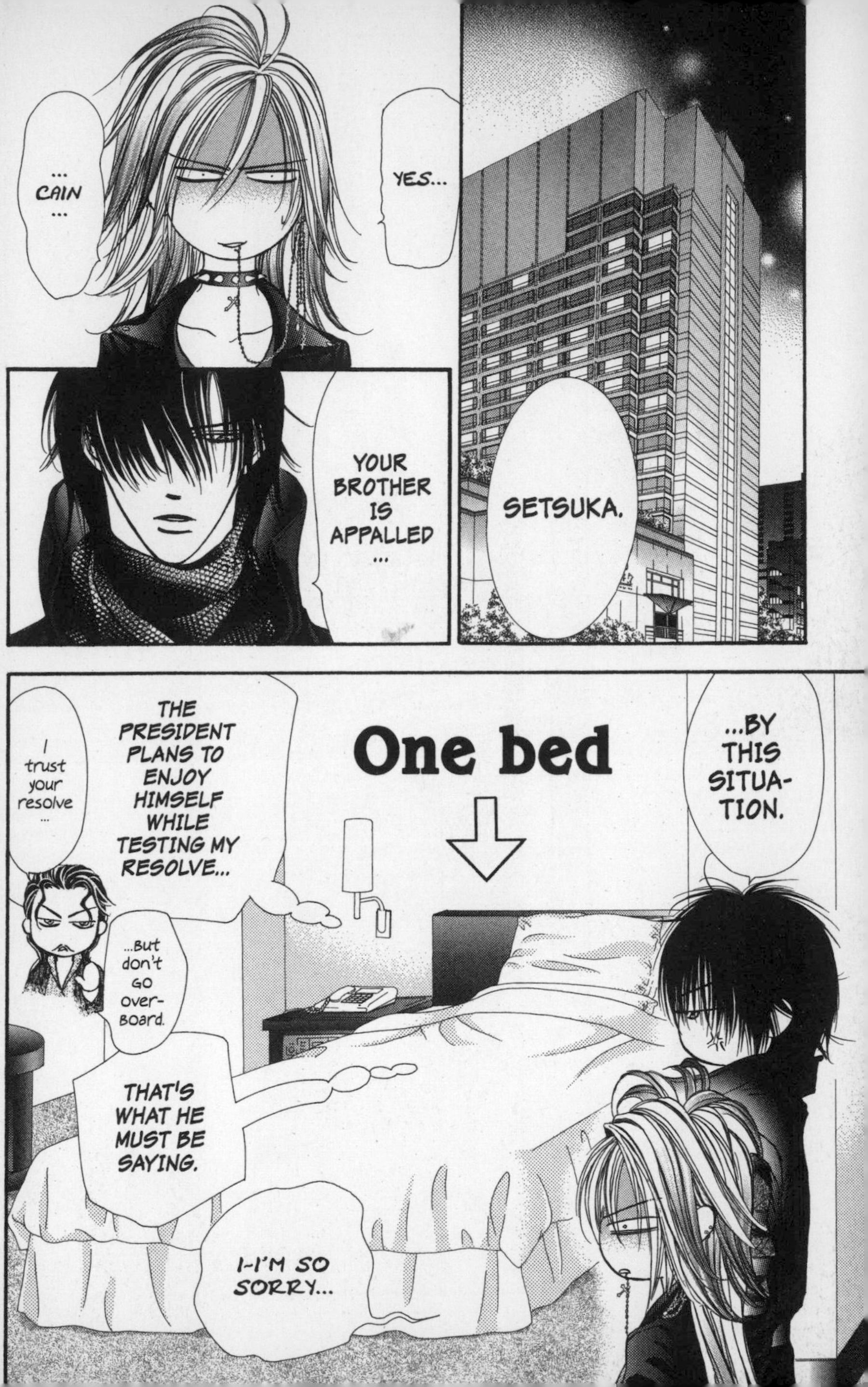
SETSUKA.
YES...
...CAIN...
YOUR BROTHER IS APPALLED...
...BY THIS SITUATION.
One bed
THE PRESIDENT PLANS TO ENJOY HIMSELF WHILE TESTING MY RESOLVE...
I trust your resolve...
...but don't go over-board.
THAT'S WHAT HE MUST BE SAYING.
I-I'M SO SORRY...

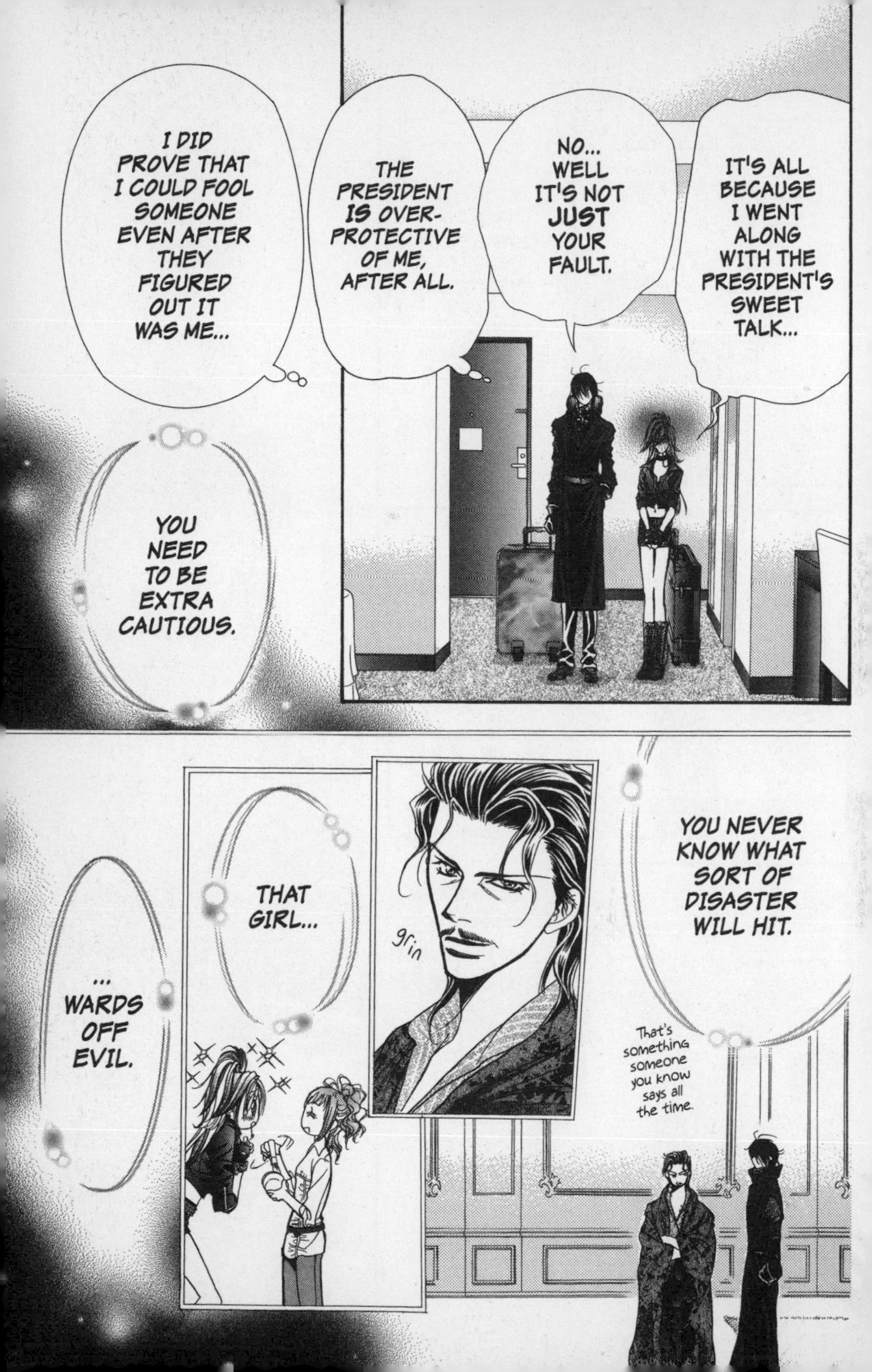
IT'S ALL BECAUSE I WENT ALONG WITH THE PRESIDENT'S SWEET TALK...
NO... WELL IT'S NOT JUST YOUR FAULT.
THE PRESIDENT IS OVER-PROTECTIVE OF ME, AFTER ALL.
I DID PROVE THAT I COULD FOOL SOMEONE EVEN AFTER THEY FIGURED OUT IT WAS ME...
YOU NEED TO BE EXTRA CAUTIOUS.
YOU NEVER KNOW WHAT SORT OF DISASTER WILL HIT.
That's something someone you know says all the time.
grin
THAT GIRL...
... WARDS OFF EVIL.

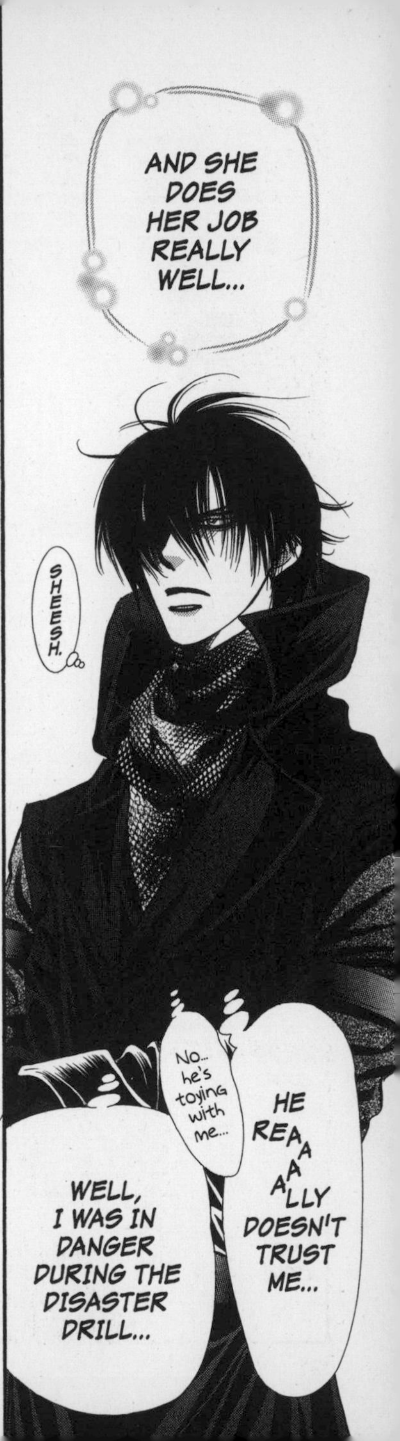
AND SHE DOES HER JOB REALLY WELL...
SHEESH.
HE REAAAALLY DOESN'T TRUST ME...
No... he's toying with me...
WELL, I WAS IN DANGER DURING THE DISASTER DRILL...
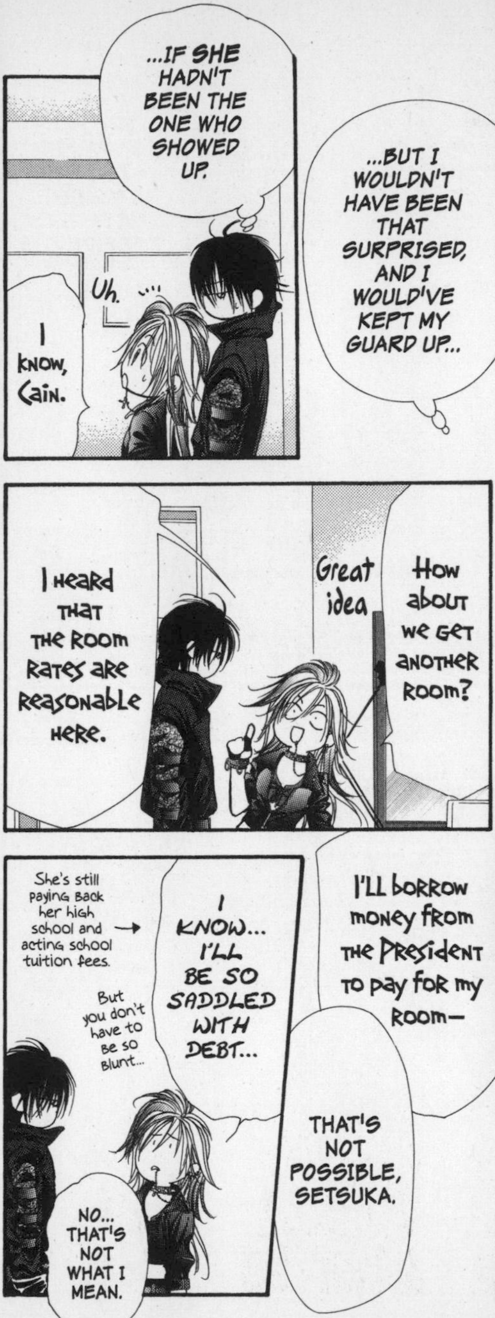
...BUT I WOULDN'T HAVE BEEN THAT SURPRISED, AND I WOULD'VE KEPT MY GUARD UP...
...IF SHE HADN'T BEEN THE ONE WHO SHOWED UP.
Uh. ...
I know, Cain.
How about we get another room?
Great idea
I heard that the room rates are reasonable here.
I'LL borrow money from the President to pay for my room—
THAT'S NOT POSSIBLE, SETSUKA.
I KNOW... I'LL BE SO SADDLED WITH DEBT...
She's still paying back her high school and acting school tuition fees.
But you don't have to be so blunt...
NO... THAT'S NOT WHAT I MEAN.

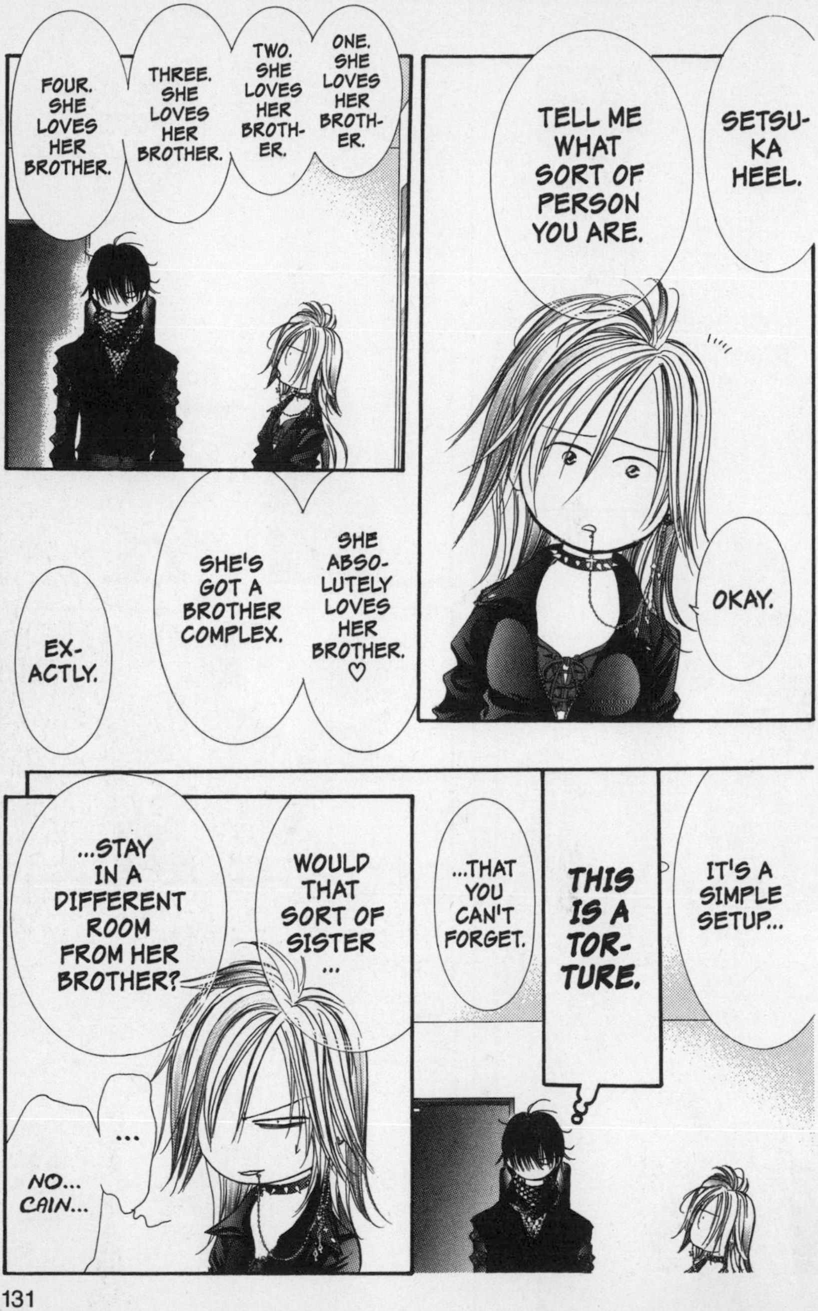
SETSUKA HEEL.
TELL ME WHAT SORT OF PERSON YOU ARE.
OKAY.
ONE. SHE LOVES HER BROTHER.
TWO. SHE LOVES HER BROTHER.
THREE. SHE LOVES HER BROTHER.
FOUR. SHE LOVES HER BROTHER.
SHE ABSOLUTELY LOVES HER BROTHER. ♡
SHE'S GOT A BROTHER COMPLEX.
EXACTLY.
IT'S A SIMPLE SETUP...
THIS IS A TORTURE.
...THAT YOU CAN'T FORGET.
WOULD THAT SORT OF SISTER ...
...STAY IN A DIFFERENT ROOM FROM HER BROTHER?
...
NO... CAIN...

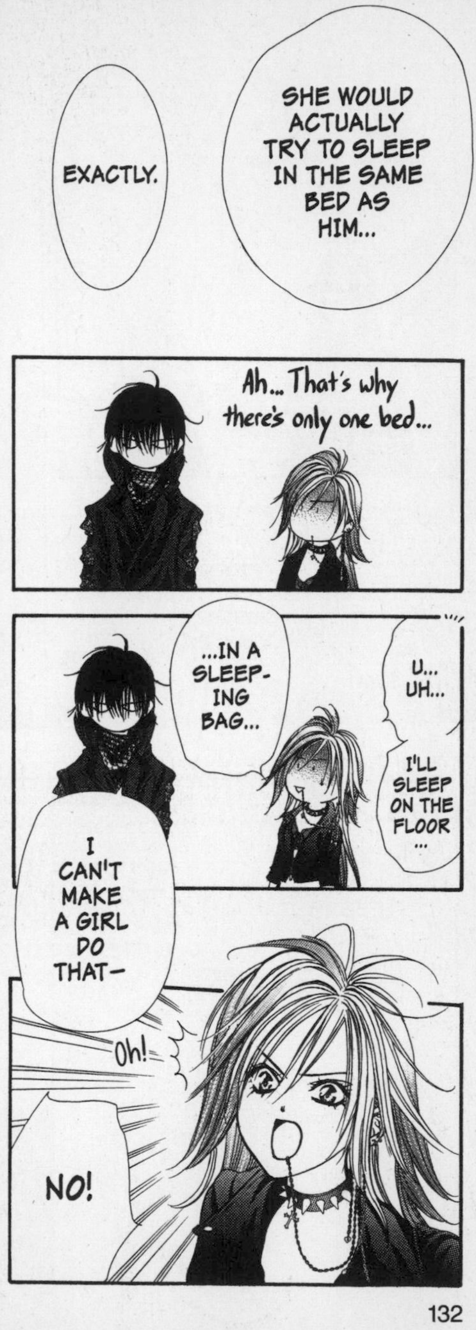
SHE WOULD ACTUALLY TRY TO SLEEP IN THE SAME BED AS HIM...
EXACTLY.
Ah... That's why there's only one bed...
U... UH...
I'LL SLEEP ON THE FLOOR...
...IN A SLEEPING BAG...
I CAN'T MAKE A GIRL DO THAT–
Oh!
NO!

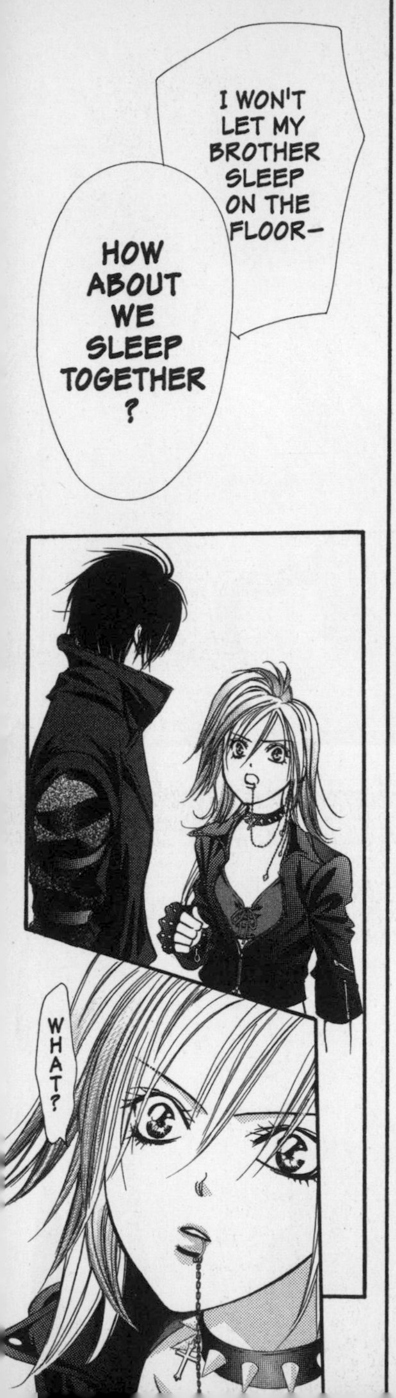
I WON'T LET MY BROTHER SLEEP ON THE FLOOR–
HOW ABOUT WE SLEEP TOGETHER?
WHAT?

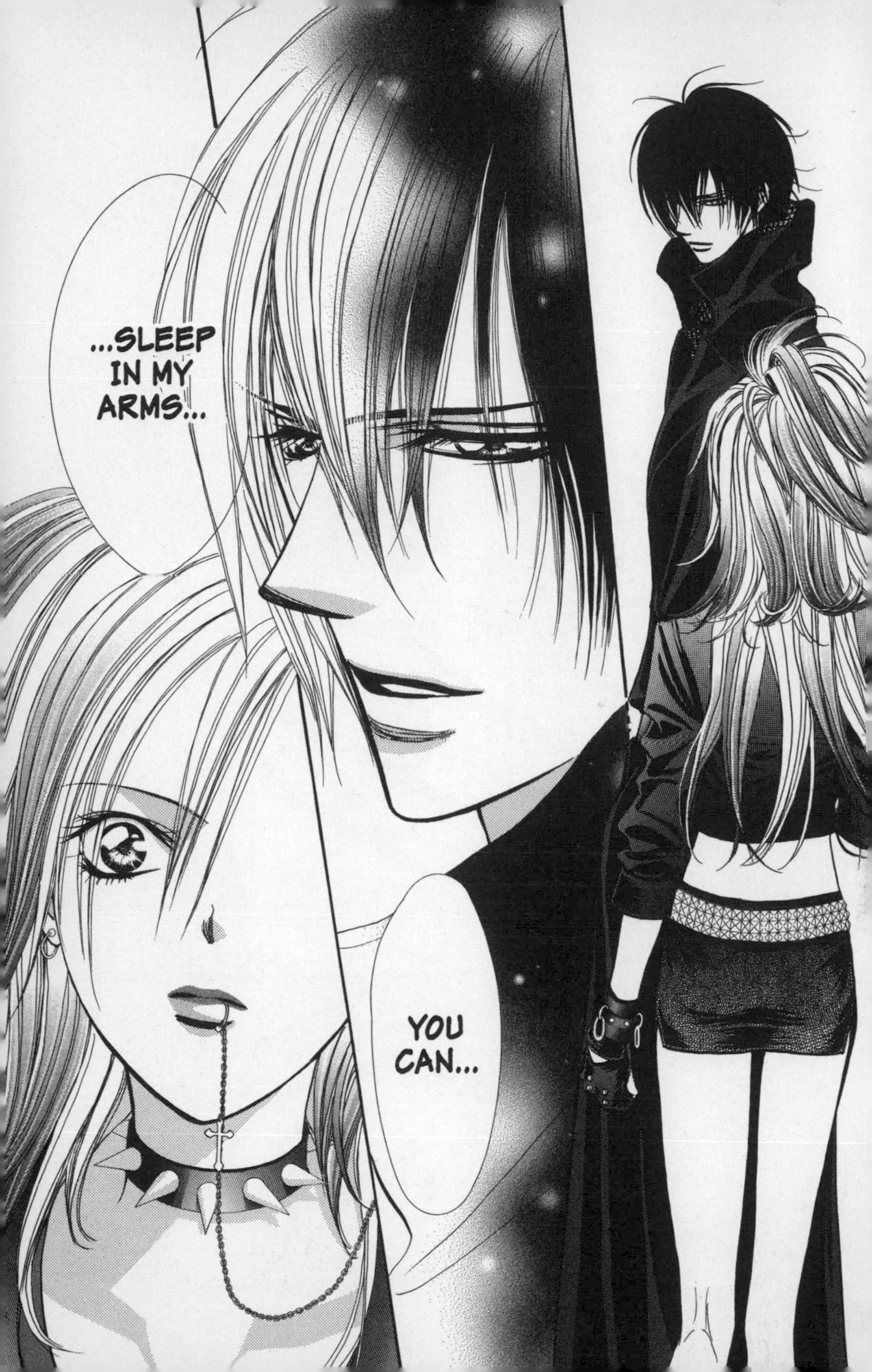
...SLEEP IN MY ARMS...
YOU CAN...

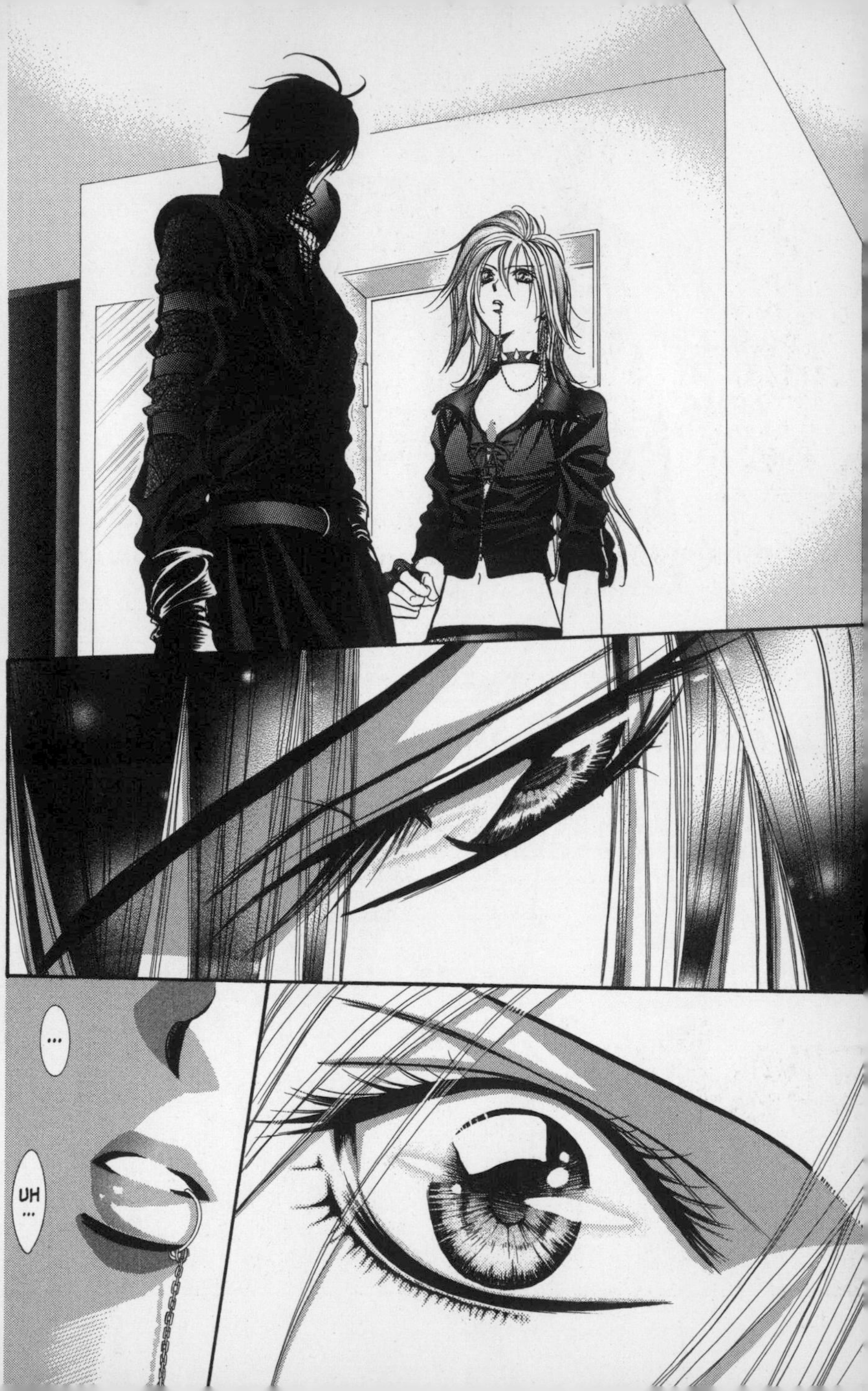
...
UH...

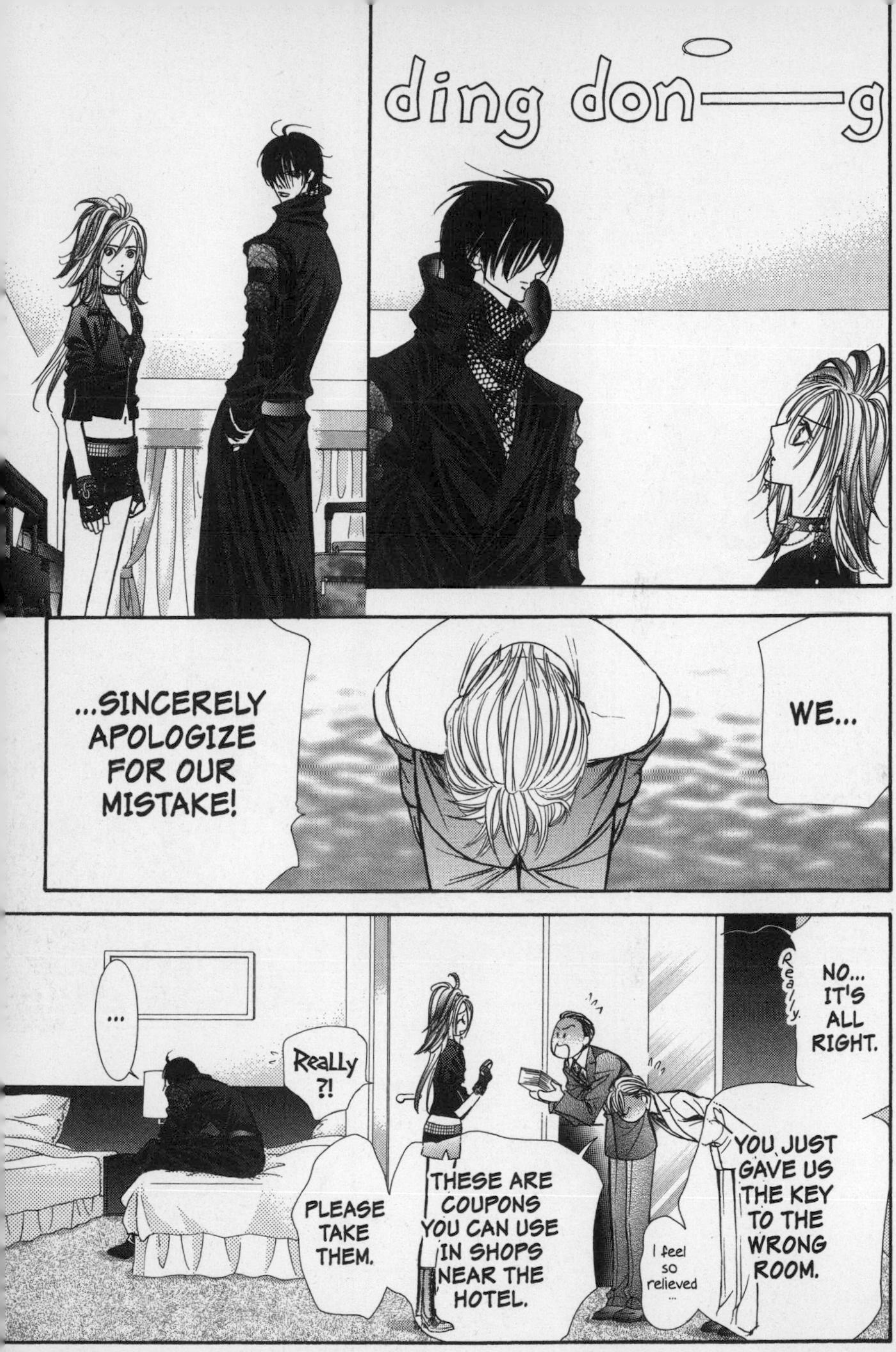
ding don——g
WE...
...SINCERELY APOLOGIZE FOR OUR MISTAKE!
Really.
NO... IT'S ALL RIGHT.
YOU JUST GAVE US THE KEY TO THE WRONG ROOM.
I feel so relieved ...
THESE ARE COUPONS YOU CAN USE IN SHOPS NEAR THE HOTEL.
PLEASE TAKE THEM.
Really ?!
...

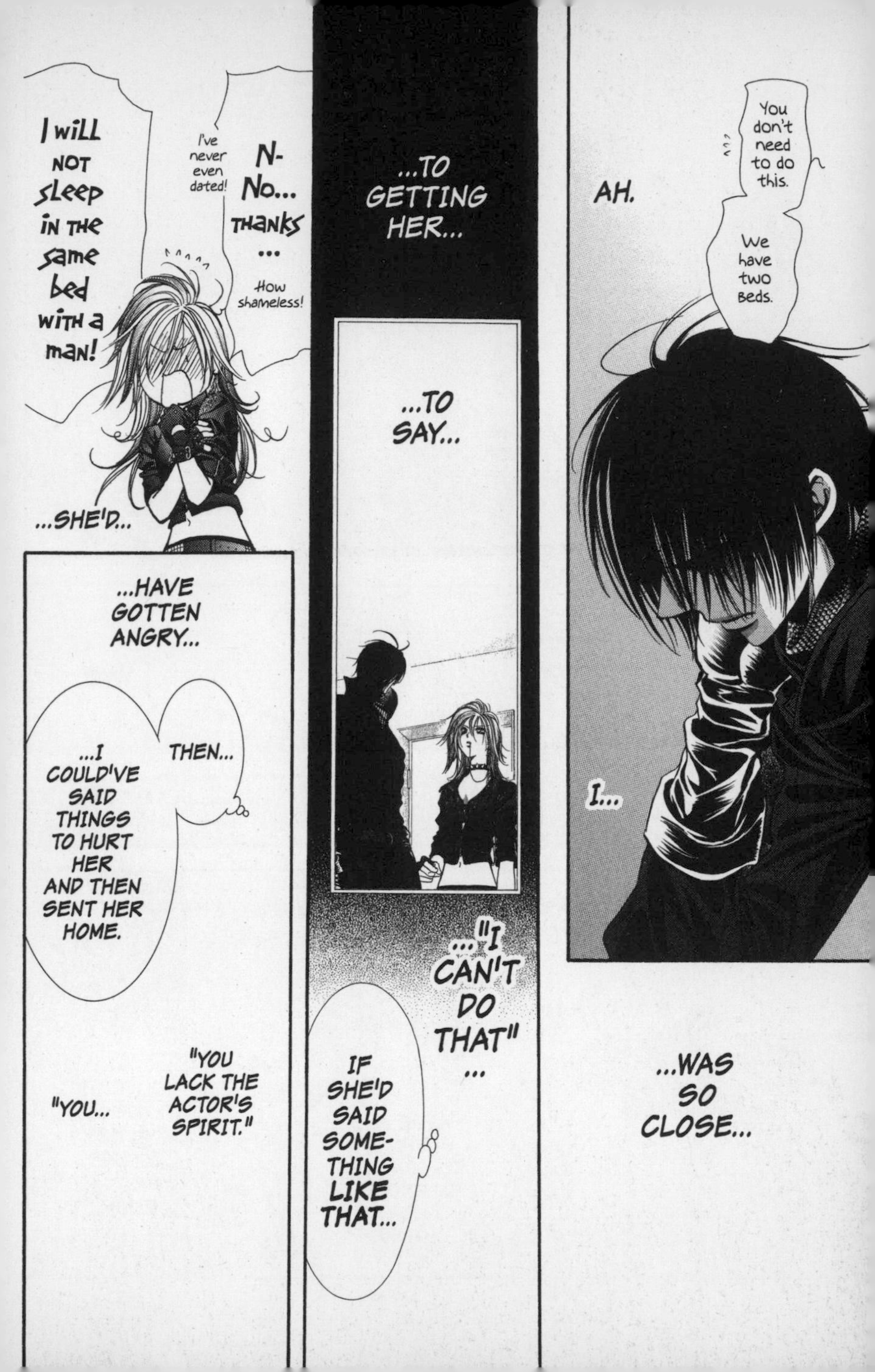

You don't need to do this.
We have two beds.
AH.
I...
...WAS SO CLOSE...
...TO GETTING HER...
...TO SAY...
..."I CAN'T DO THAT"...
IF SHE'D SAID SOMETHING LIKE THAT...
N- No... thanks...
How shameless!
I've never even dated!
I will not sleep in the same bed with a man!
...SHE'D...
...HAVE GOTTEN ANGRY...
THEN...
...I COULD'VE SAID THINGS TO HURT HER AND THEN SENT HER HOME.
"YOU LACK THE ACTOR'S SPIRIT."
"YOU...

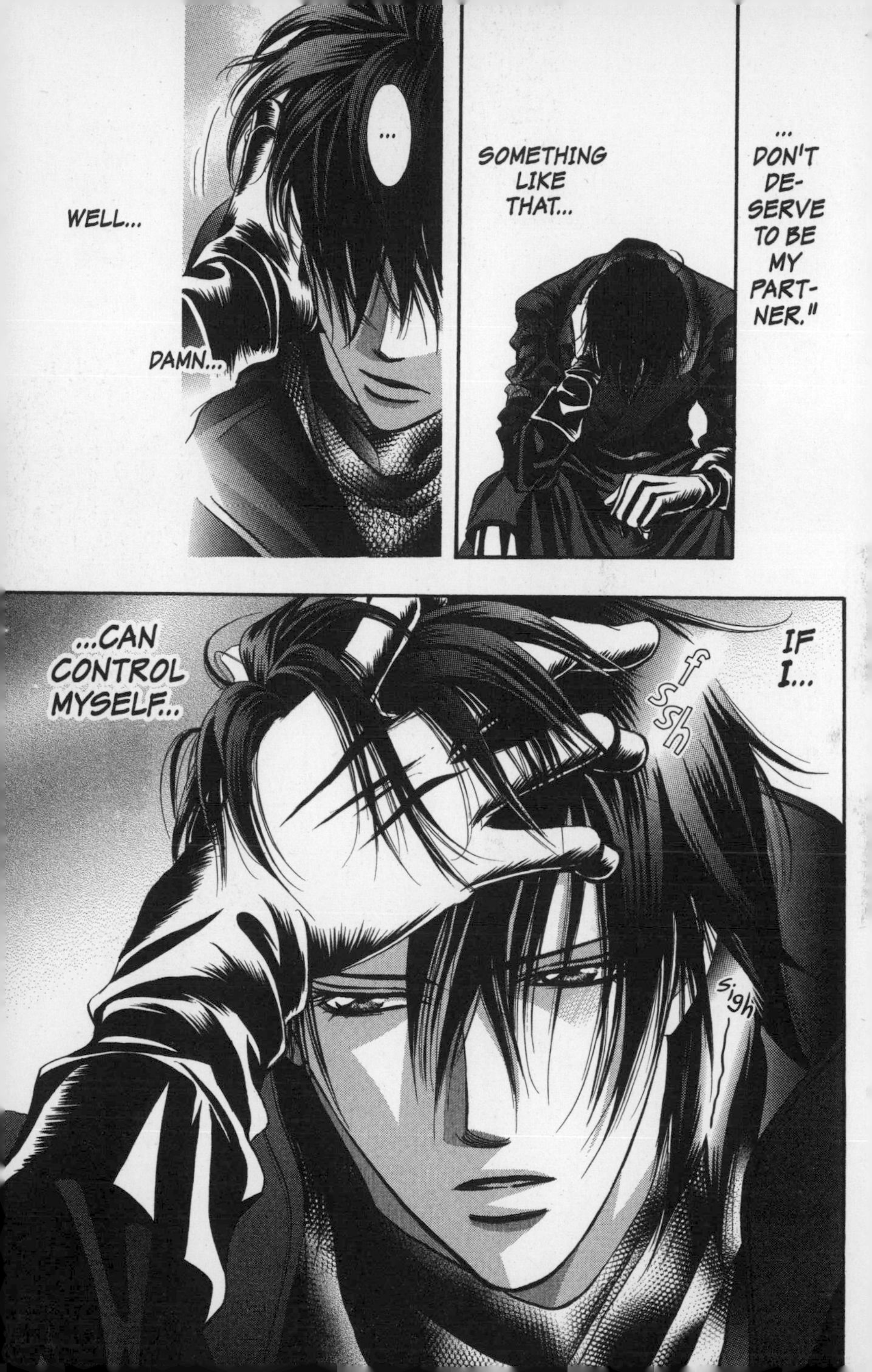

... DON'T DE-SERVE TO BE MY PART-NER."
SOMETHING LIKE THAT...
...
WELL...
DAMN...
IF I...
fssh
...CAN CONTROL MYSELF...
sigh

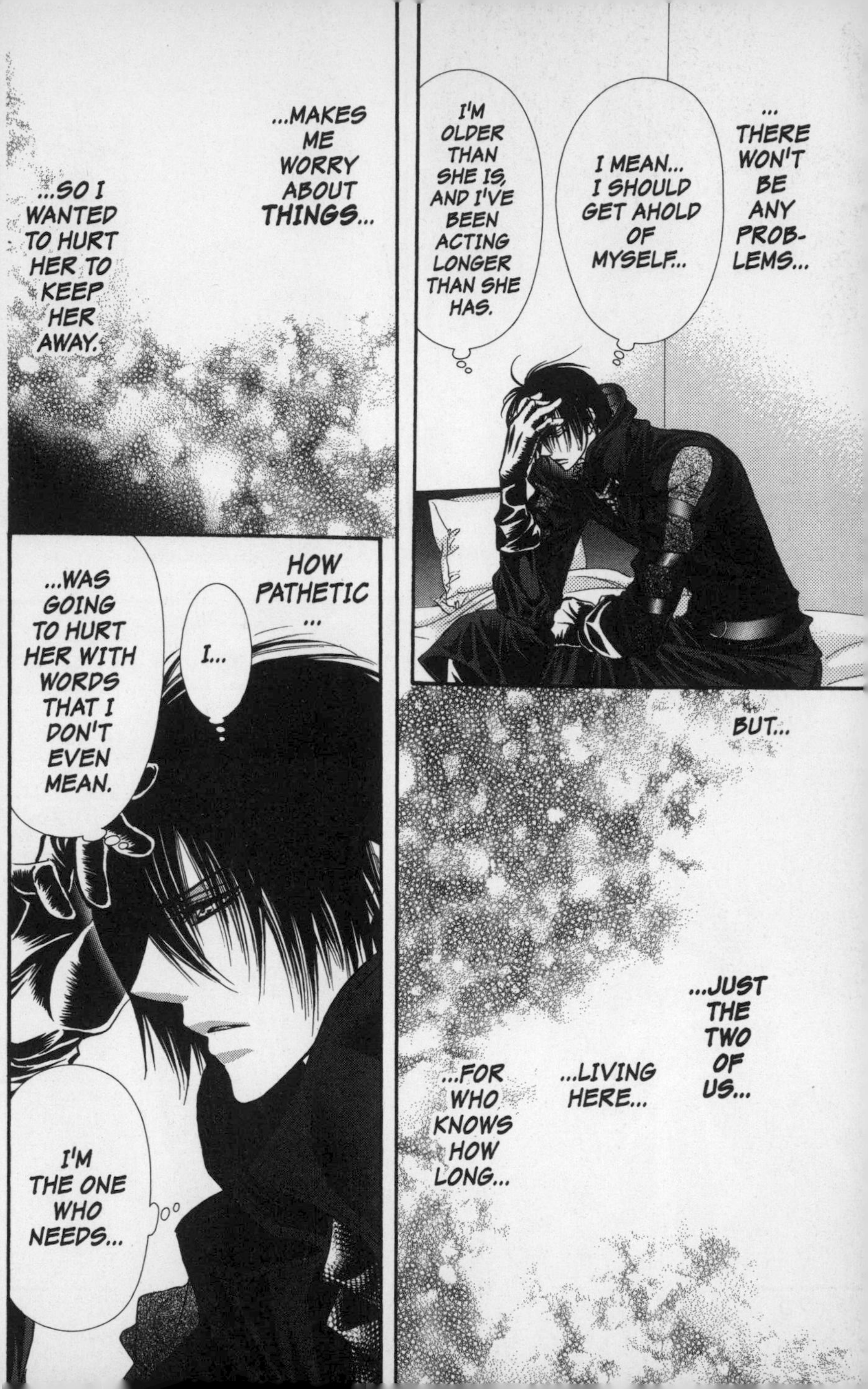
... THERE WON'T BE ANY PROBLEMS...
I MEAN... I SHOULD GET AHOLD OF MYSELF...
I'M OLDER THAN SHE IS, AND I'VE BEEN ACTING LONGER THAN SHE HAS.
BUT...
...JUST THE TWO OF US...
...LIVING HERE...
...FOR WHO KNOWS HOW LONG...
...MAKES ME WORRY ABOUT THINGS...
...SO I WANTED TO HURT HER TO KEEP HER AWAY.
HOW PATHETIC...
I...
...WAS GOING TO HURT HER WITH WORDS THAT I DON'T EVEN MEAN.
I'M THE ONE WHO NEEDS...

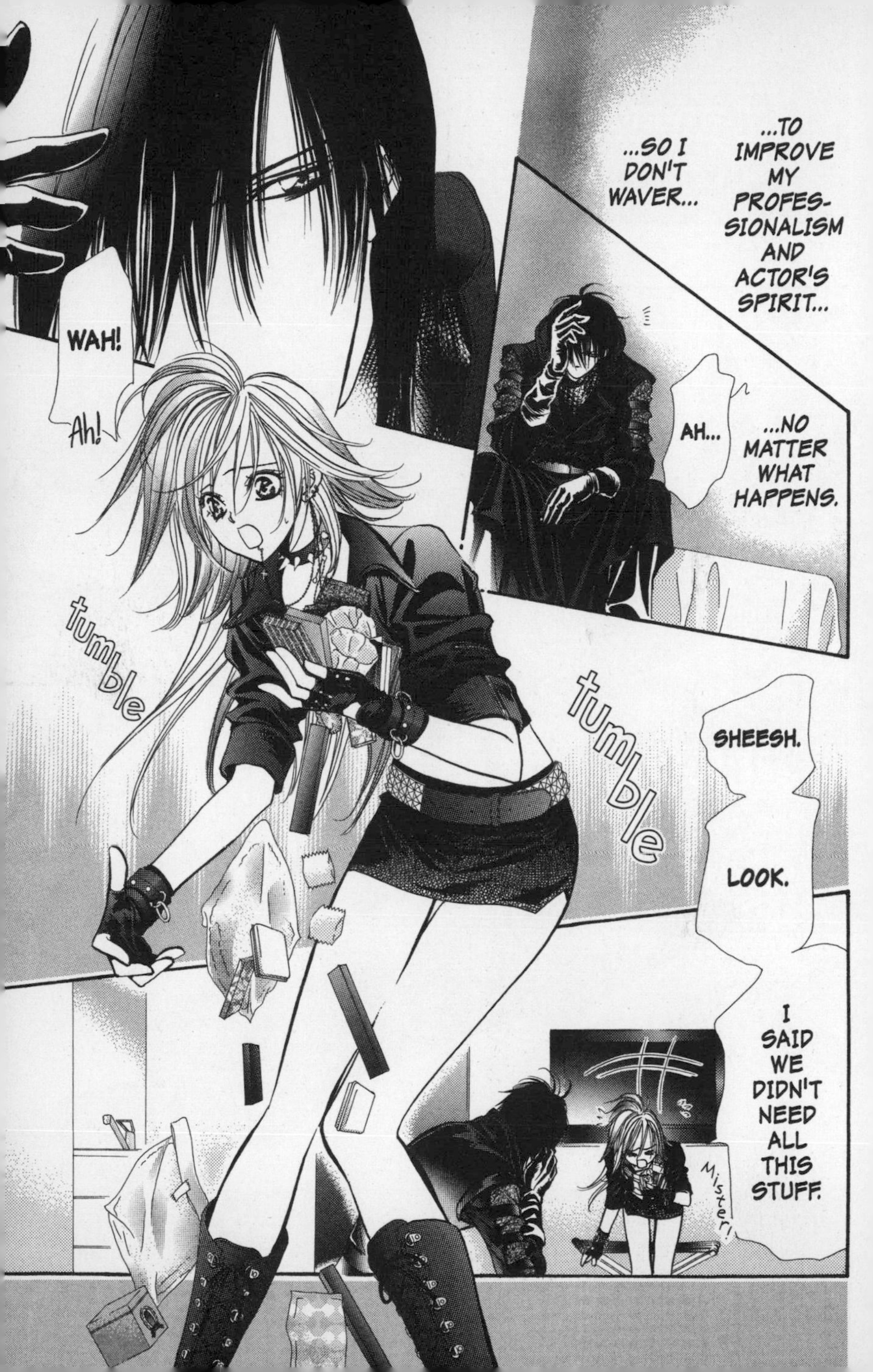
...TO IMPROVE MY PROFESSIONALISM AND ACTOR'S SPIRIT...
...SO I DON'T WAVER...
...NO MATTER WHAT HAPPENS.
AH...
WAH!
Ah!
tumble
tumble
SHEESH.
LOOK.
I SAID WE DIDN'T NEED ALL THIS STUFF.
Mister!

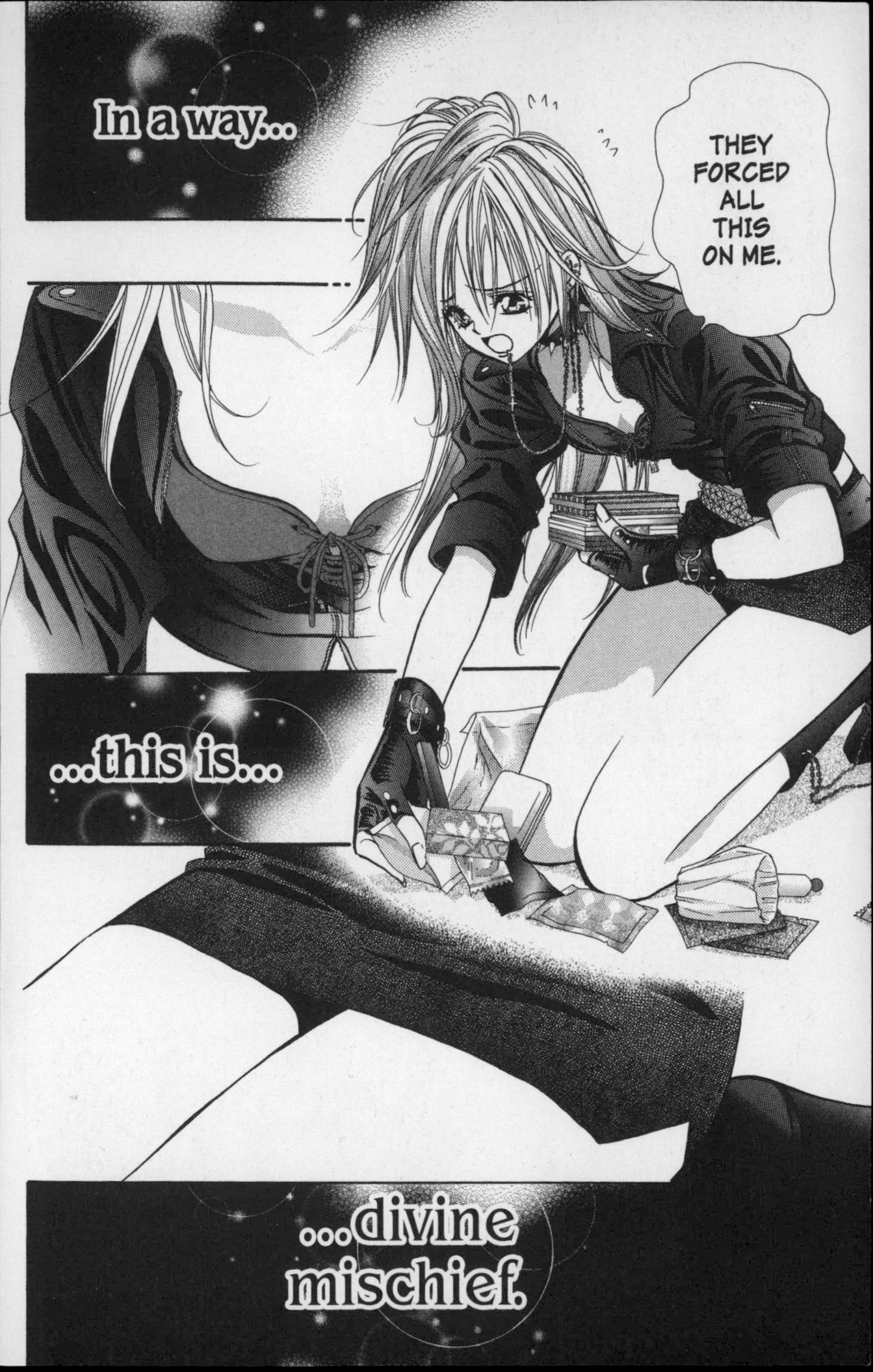
In a way...
THEY FORCED ALL THIS ON ME.
...this is...
...divine mischief.

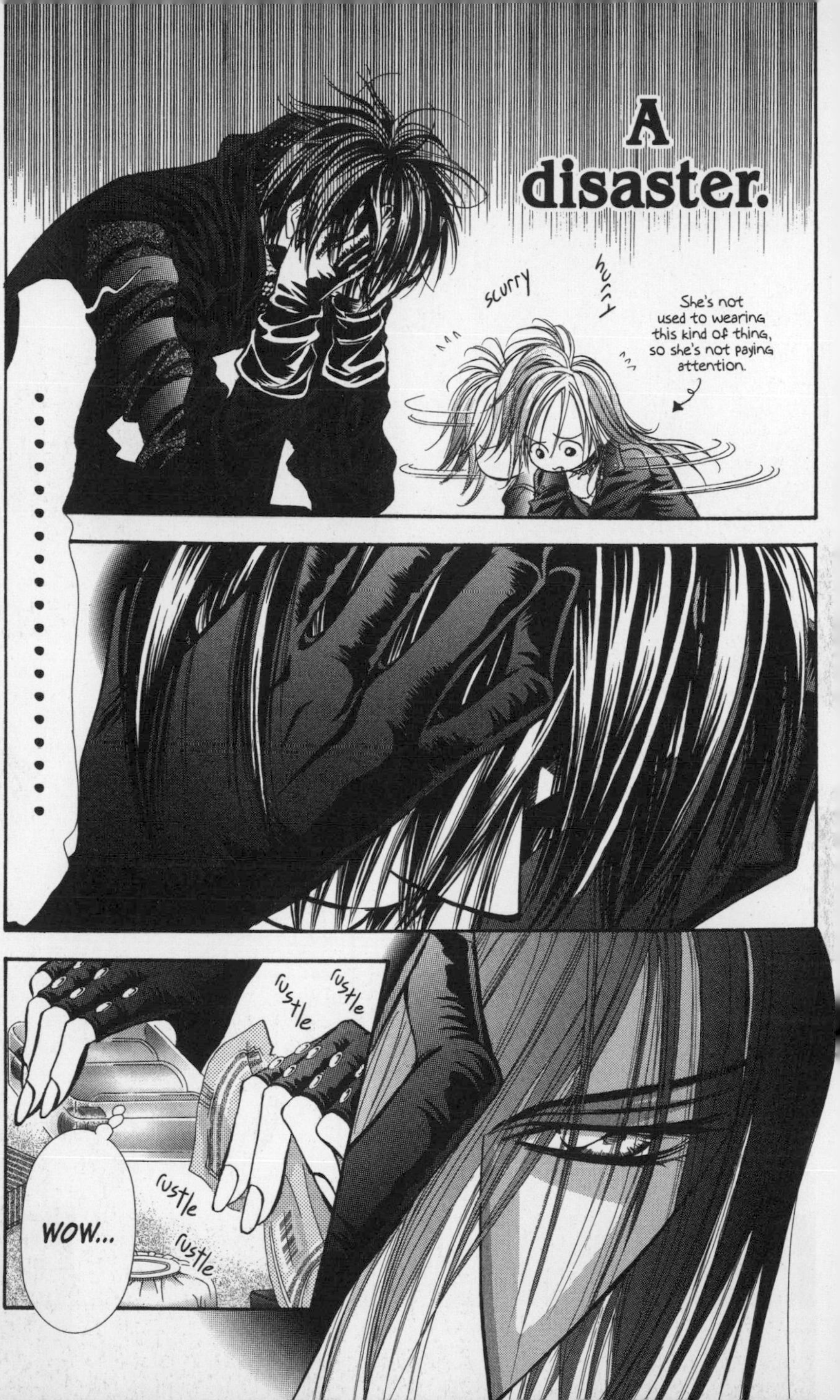
A disaster.
She's not used to wearing this kind of thing, so she's not paying attention.
hurry
scurry
rustle
rustle
rustle
rustle
WOW...

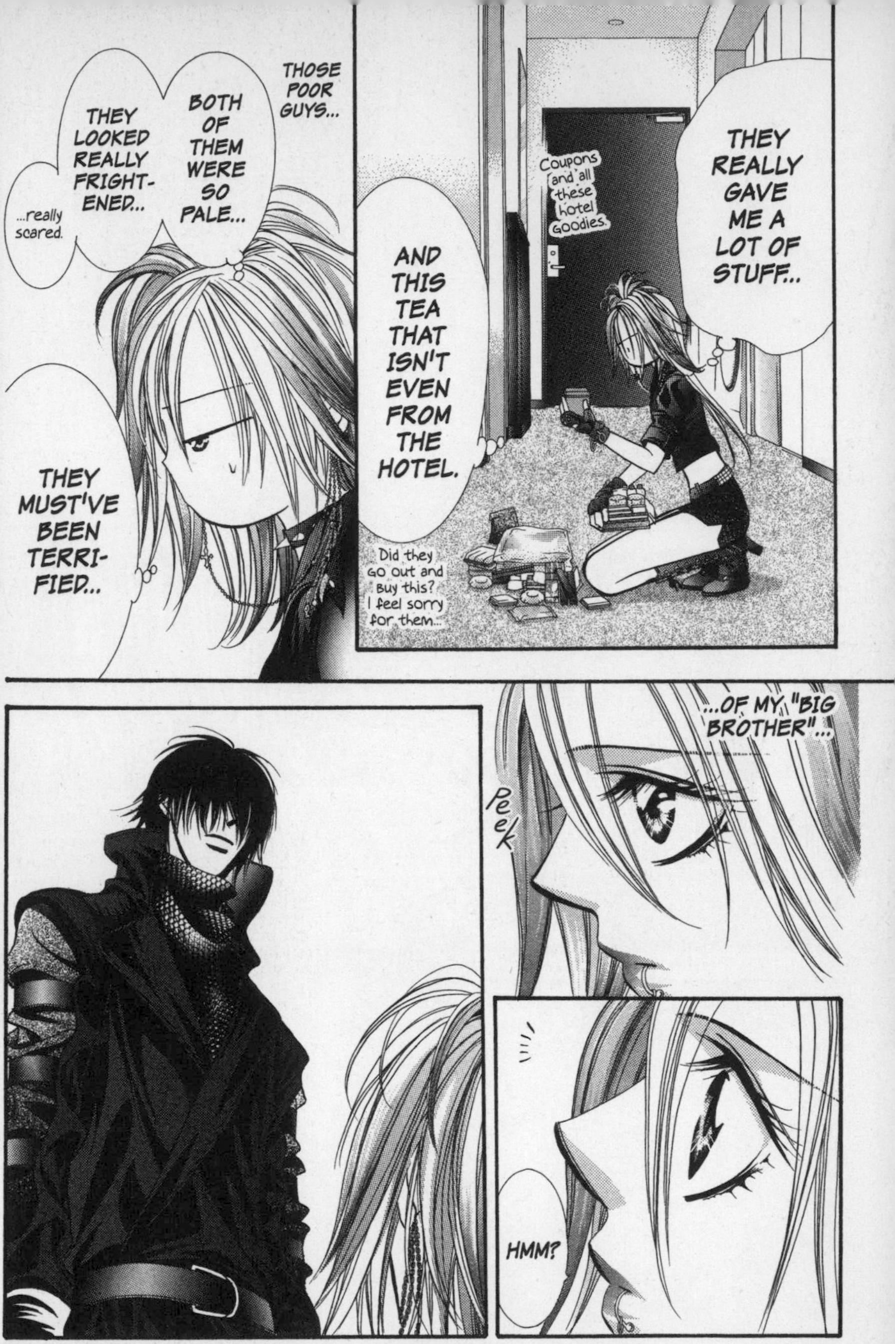
THEY REALLY GAVE ME A LOT OF STUFF...
Coupons and all these hotel Goodies.
AND THIS TEA THAT ISN'T EVEN FROM THE HOTEL.
Did they Go out and Buy this? I feel sorry for them...
THOSE POOR GUYS...
BOTH OF THEM WERE SO PALE...
THEY LOOKED REALLY FRIGHT-ENED...
...really scared.
THEY MUST'VE BEEN TERRI-FIED...
...OF MY "BIG BROTHER"...
Peek
HMM?

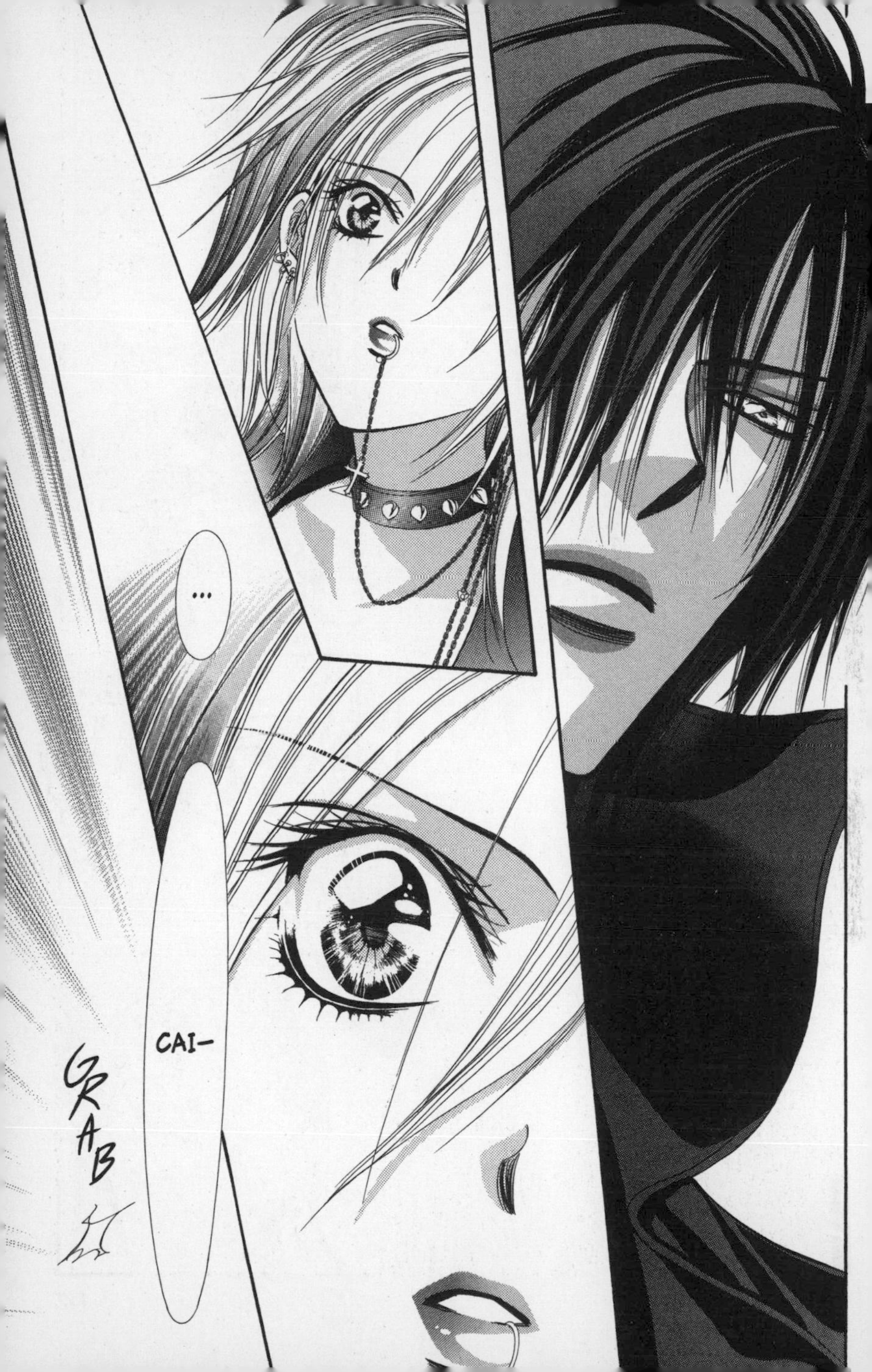
...
CAI–
GRAB

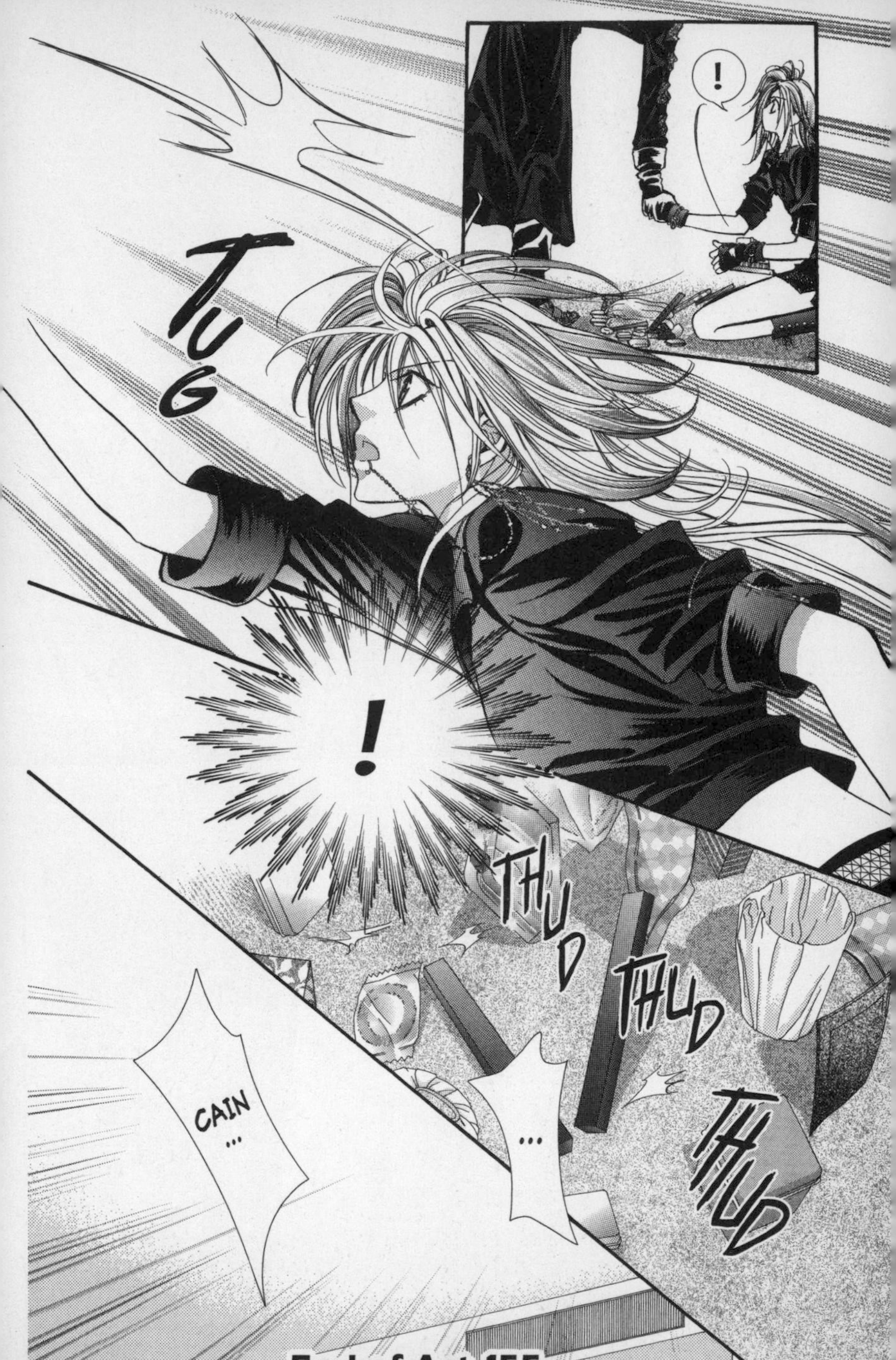
!
TUG
!
THUD
THUD
THUD
...
CAIN ...

End of Act 155

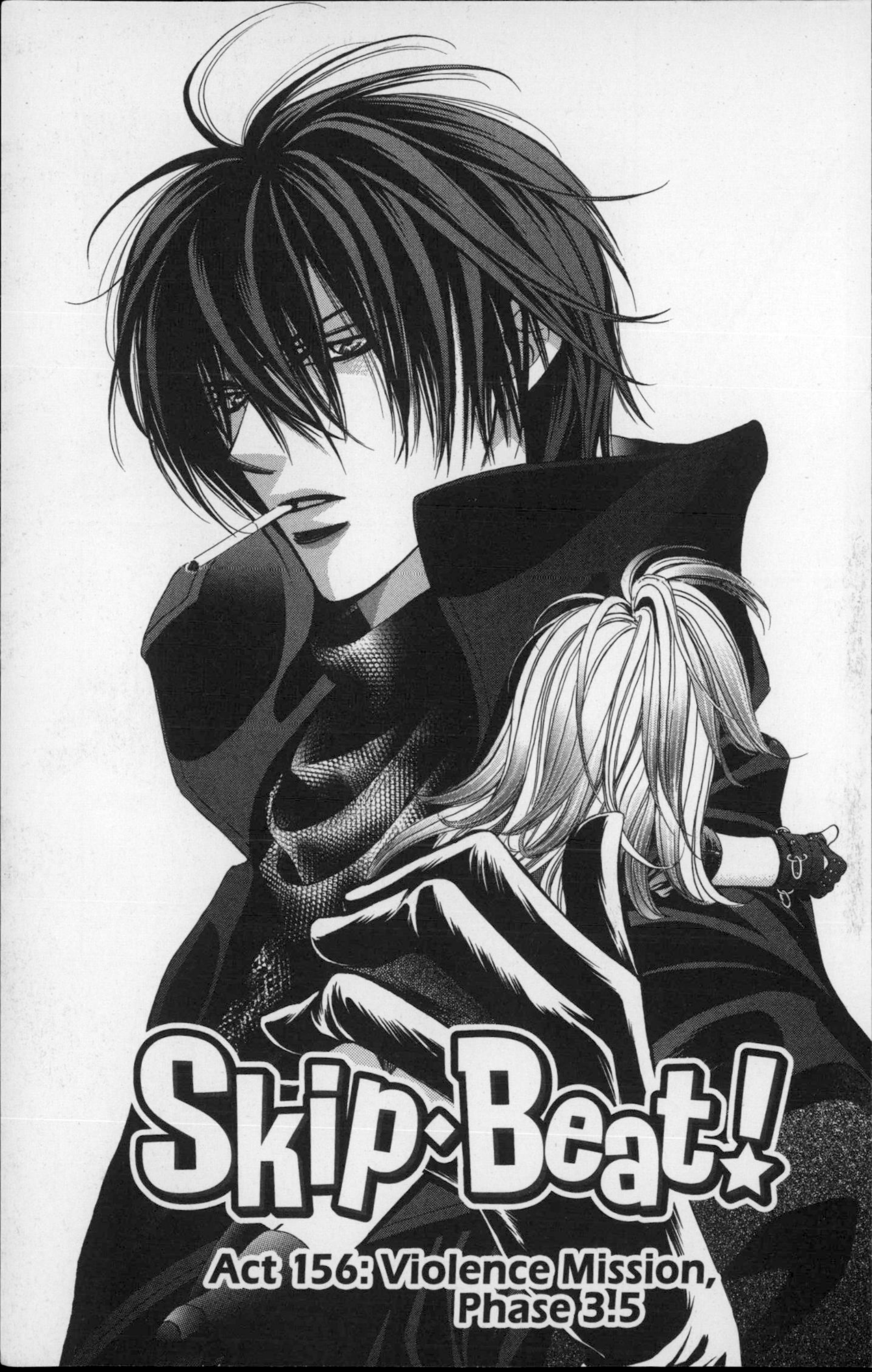
Skip·Beat!
Act 156: Violence Mission, Phase 3.5

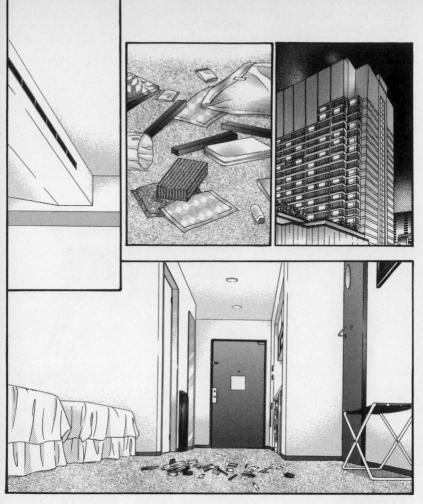

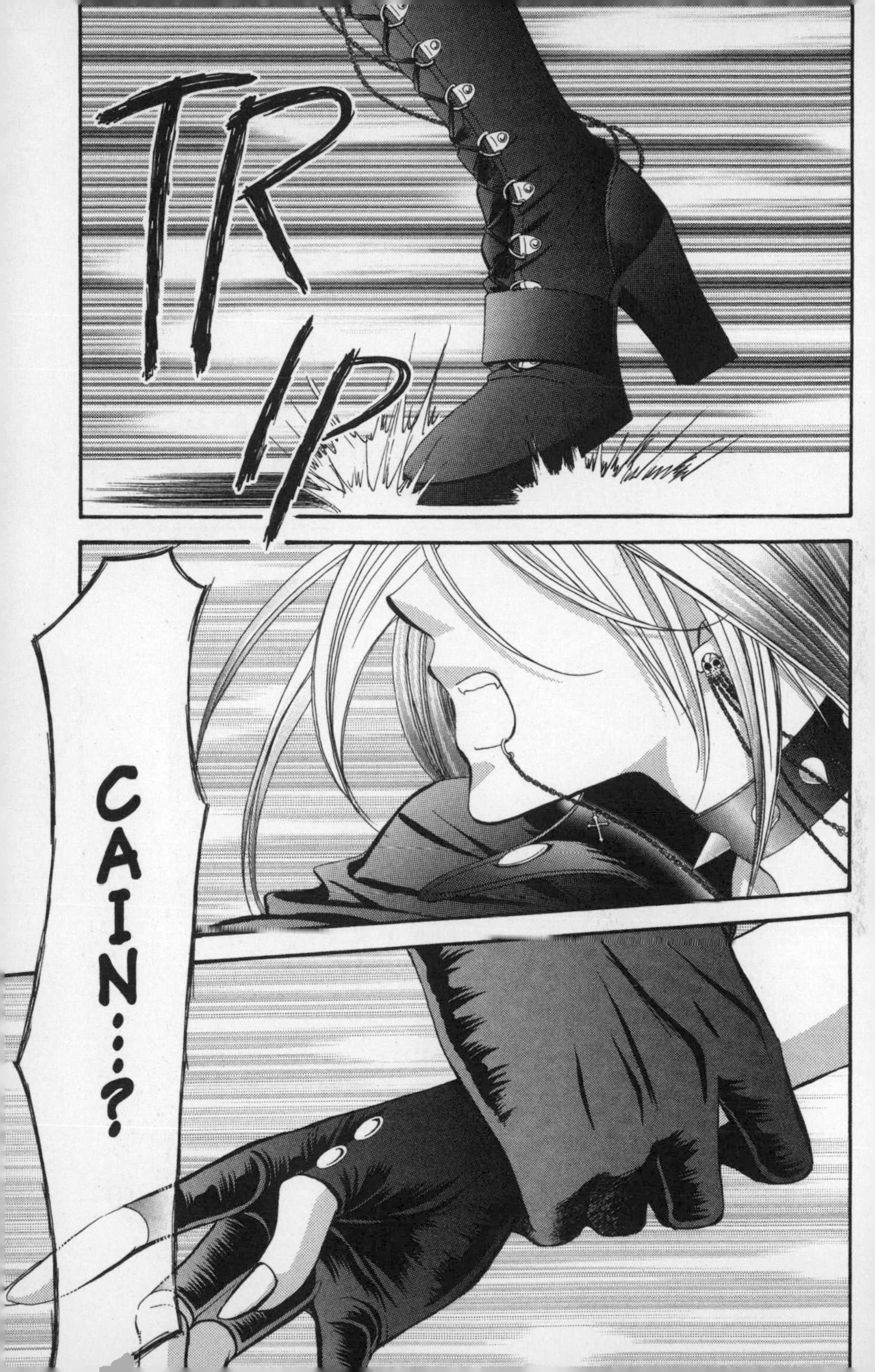
TRIP
CAIN...?

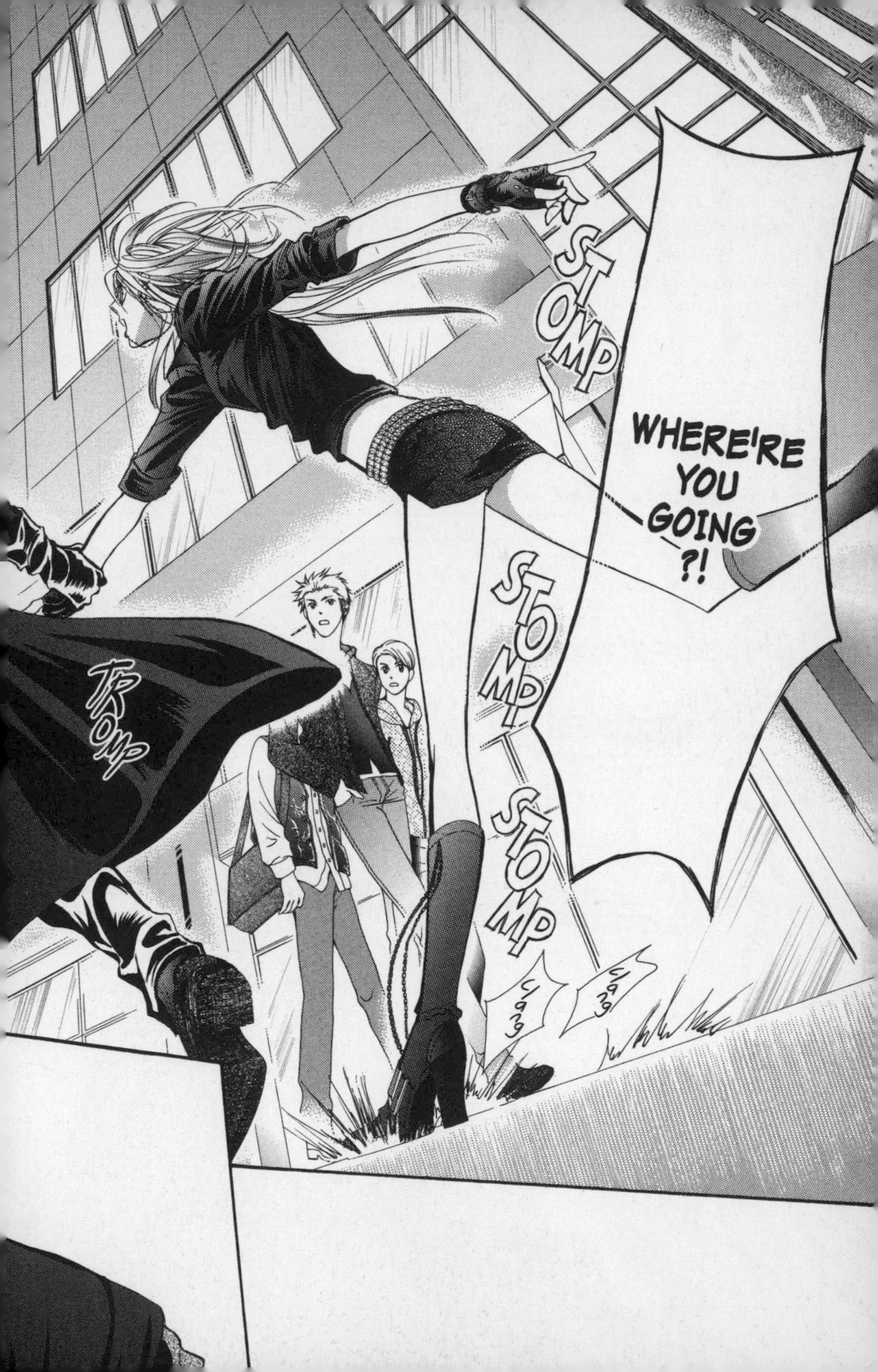
WHERE'RE YOU GOING?!
STOMP
STOMP
STOMP
STOMP
clang
clang
TROMP

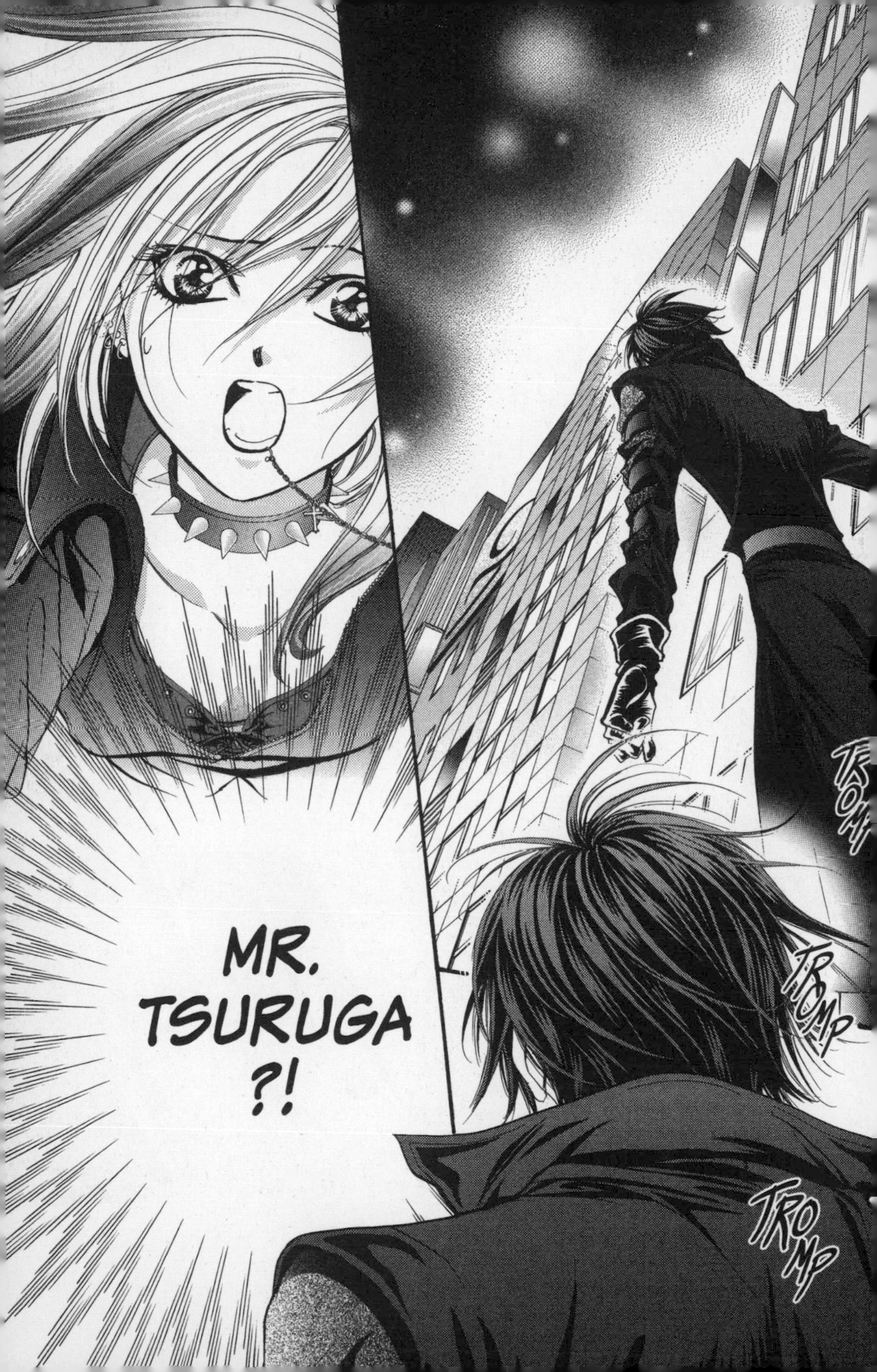
TROM
TROMP
TROMP
MR. TSURUGA ?!

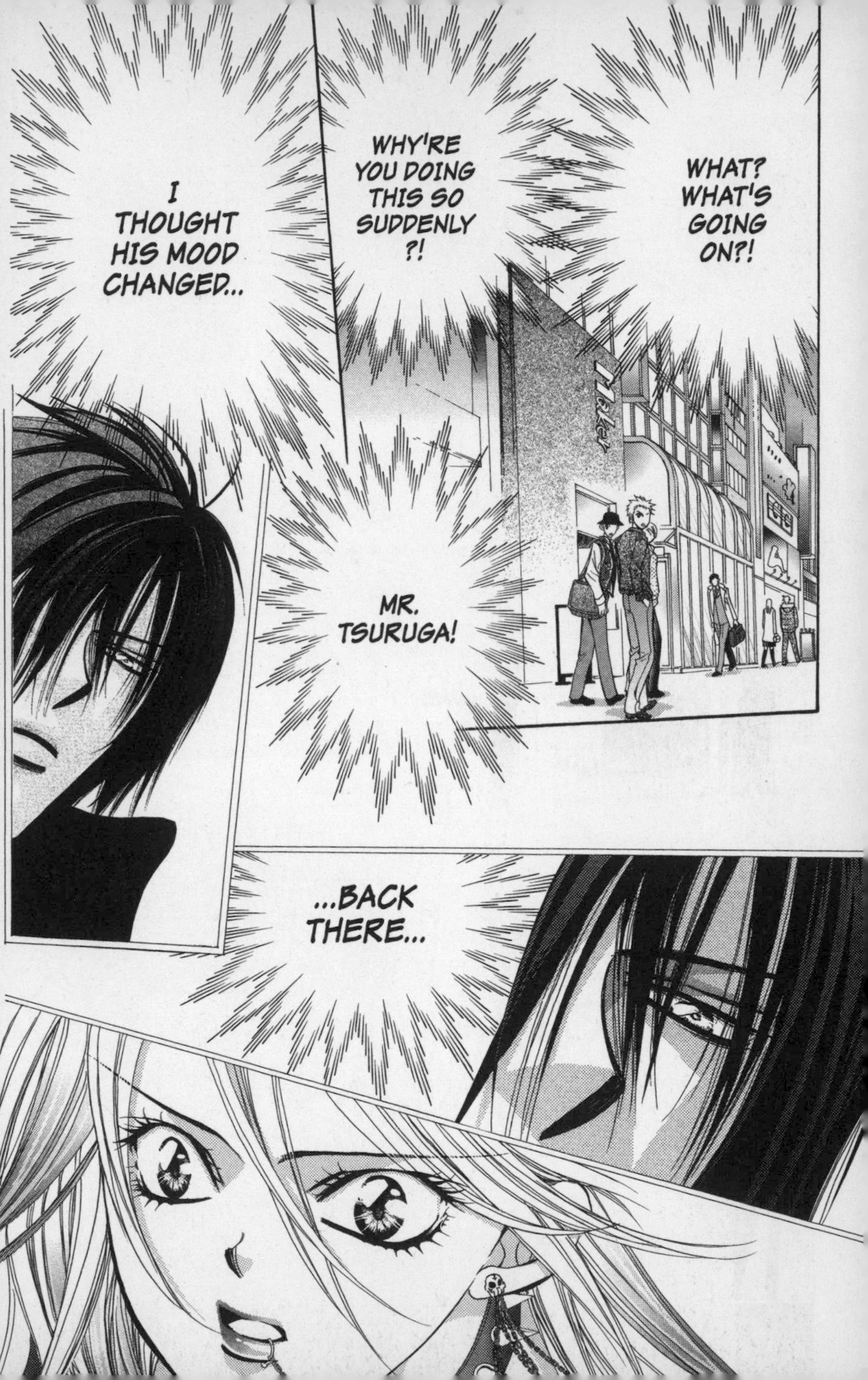
WHAT? WHAT'S GOING ON?!
WHY'RE YOU DOING THIS SO SUDDENLY?!
I THOUGHT HIS MOOD CHANGED...
MR. TSURUGA!
...BACK THERE...

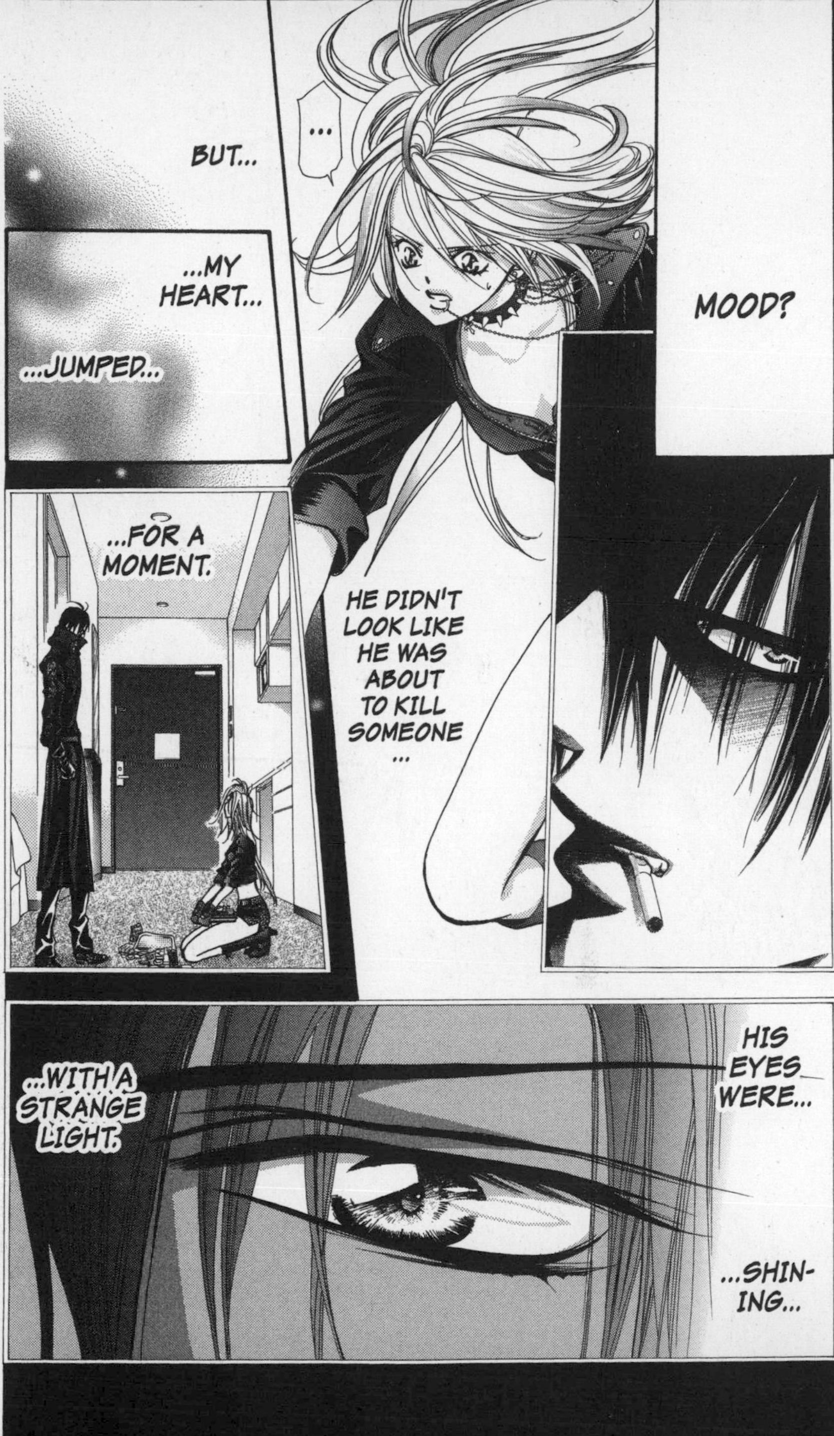
MOOD?
...
HE DIDN'T LOOK LIKE HE WAS ABOUT TO KILL SOMEONE ...
BUT...
...MY HEART...
...JUMPED...
...FOR A MOMENT.
HIS EYES WERE...
...SHIN-ING...
...WITH A STRANGE LIGHT.

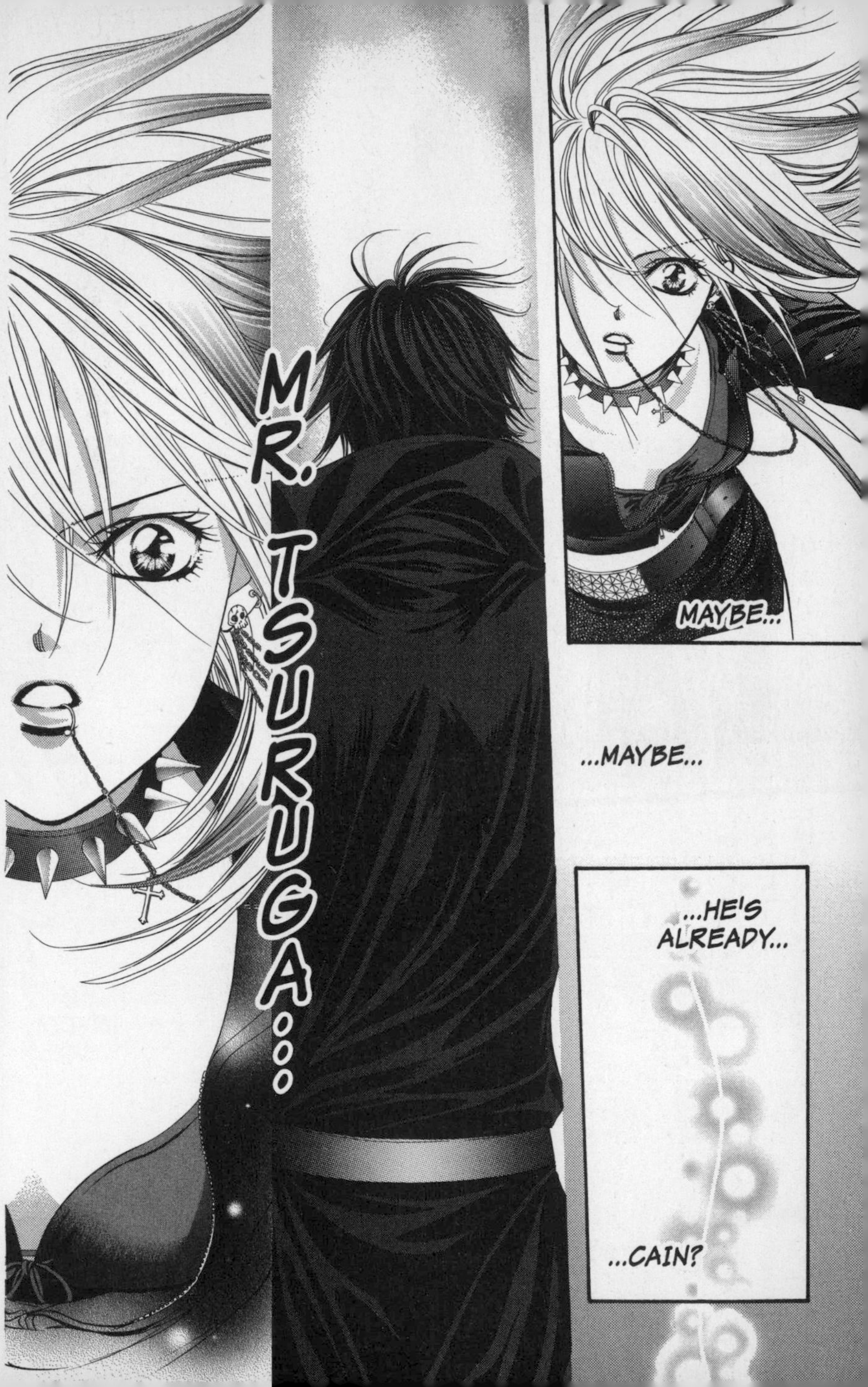
MAYBE...
...MAYBE...
...HE'S ALREADY...
...CAIN?
MR. TSURUGA...

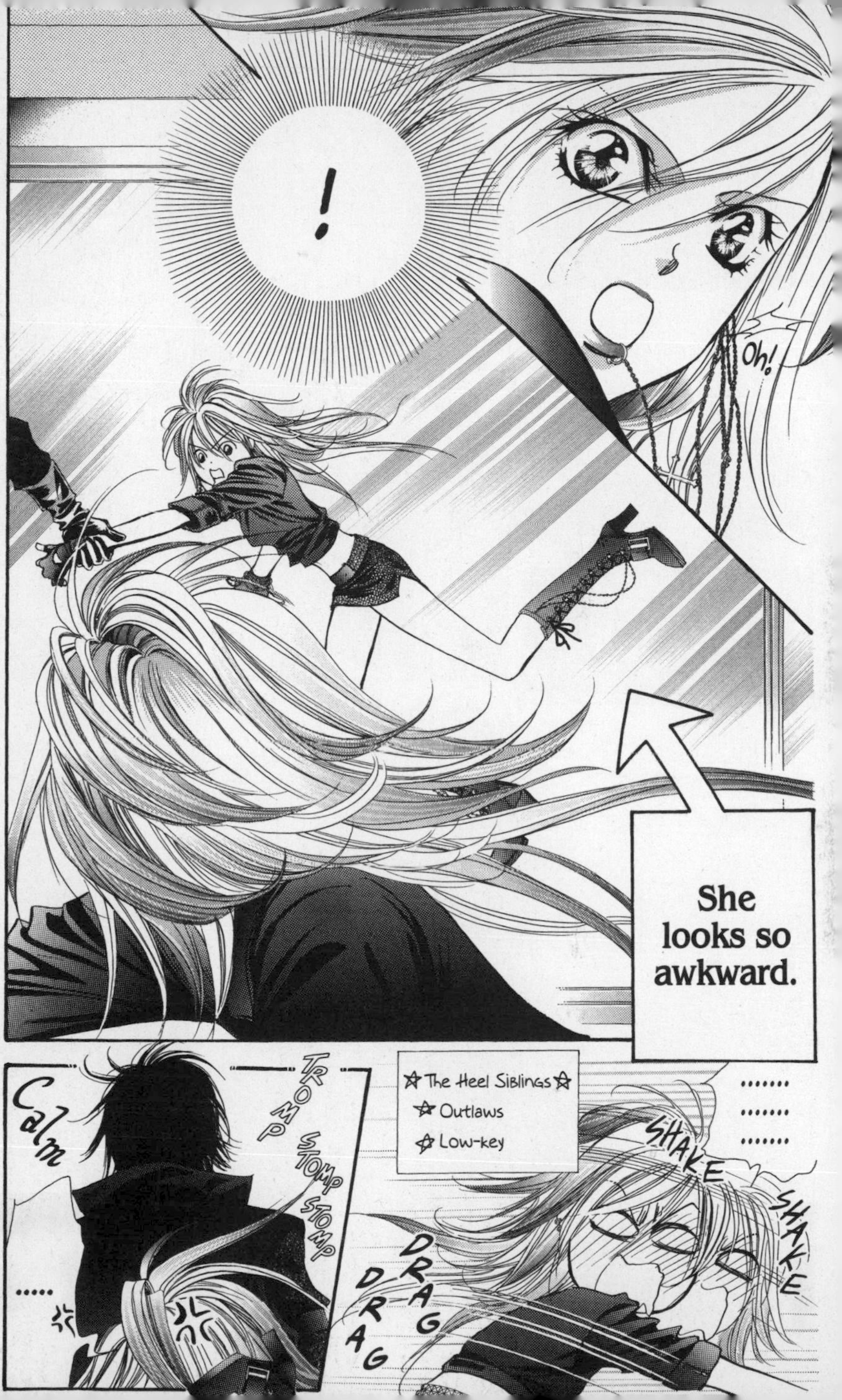
!
Oh!
She looks so awkward.
☆The Heel Siblings☆
☆Outlaws
☆Low-key
......
......
......
SHAKE
SHAKE
DRAG
DRAG
Calm
TROMP
STOMP
STOMP
......

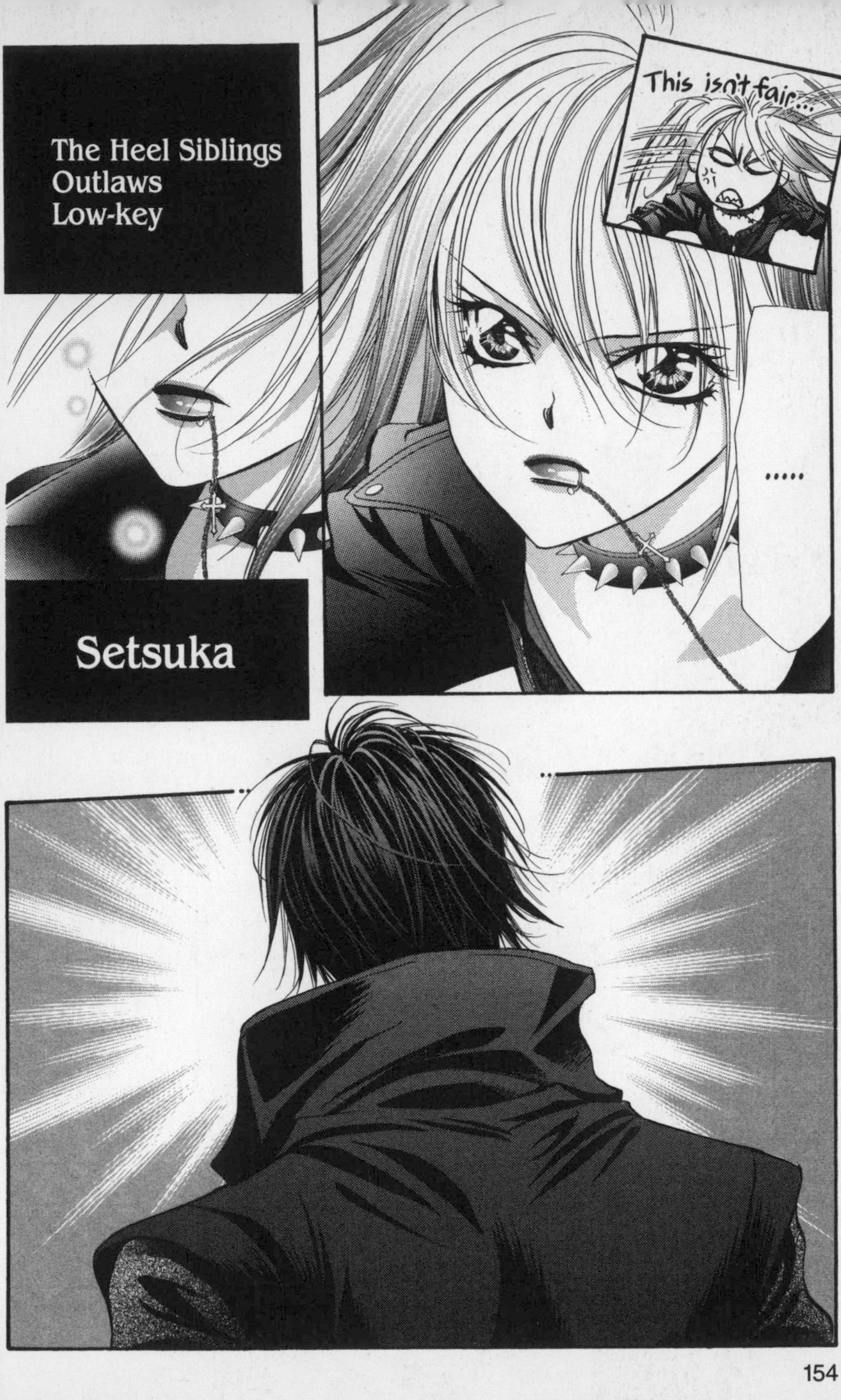
This isn't fair...
.....
The Heel Siblings
Outlaws
Low-key
Setsuka

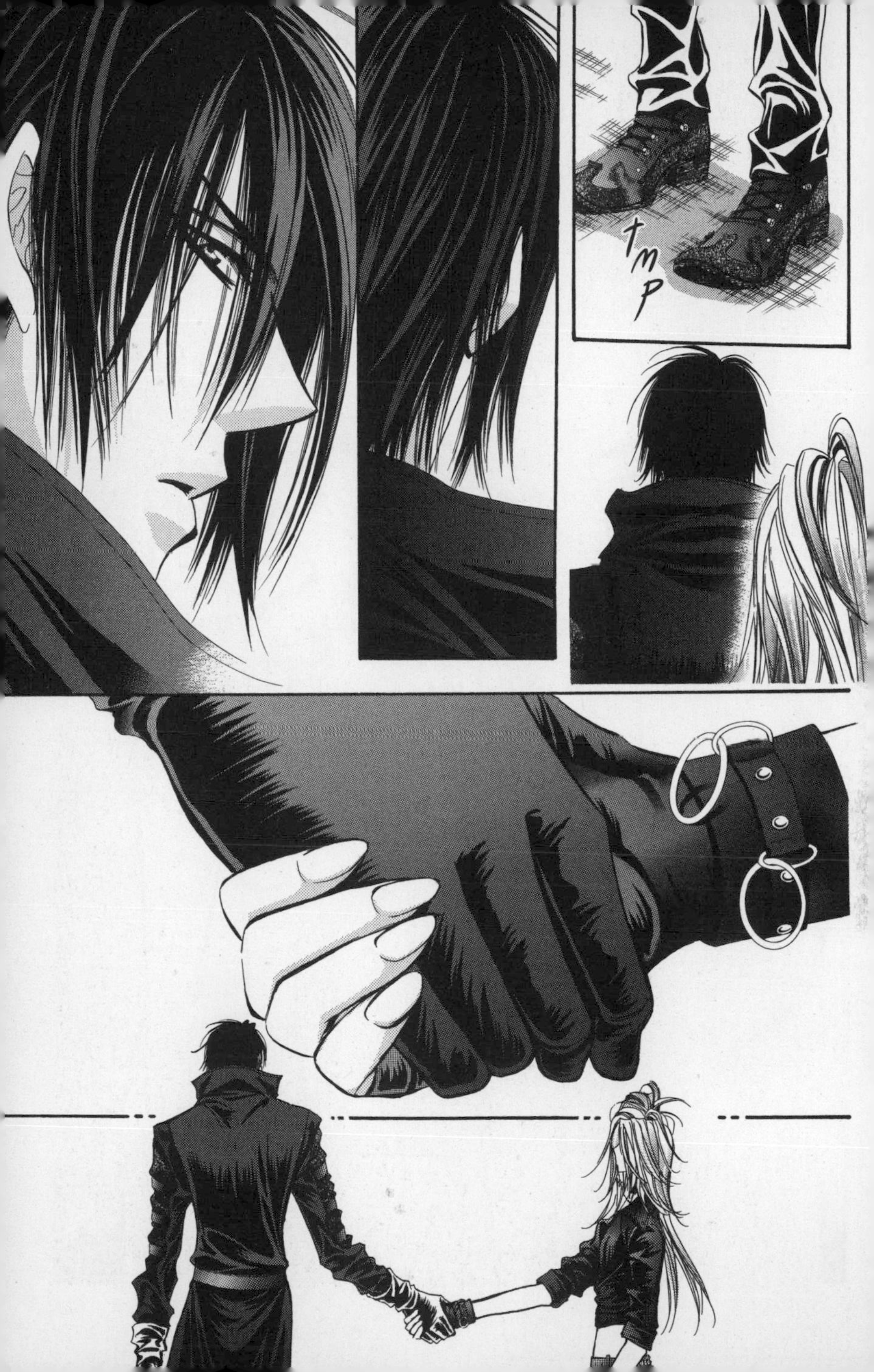
TMP

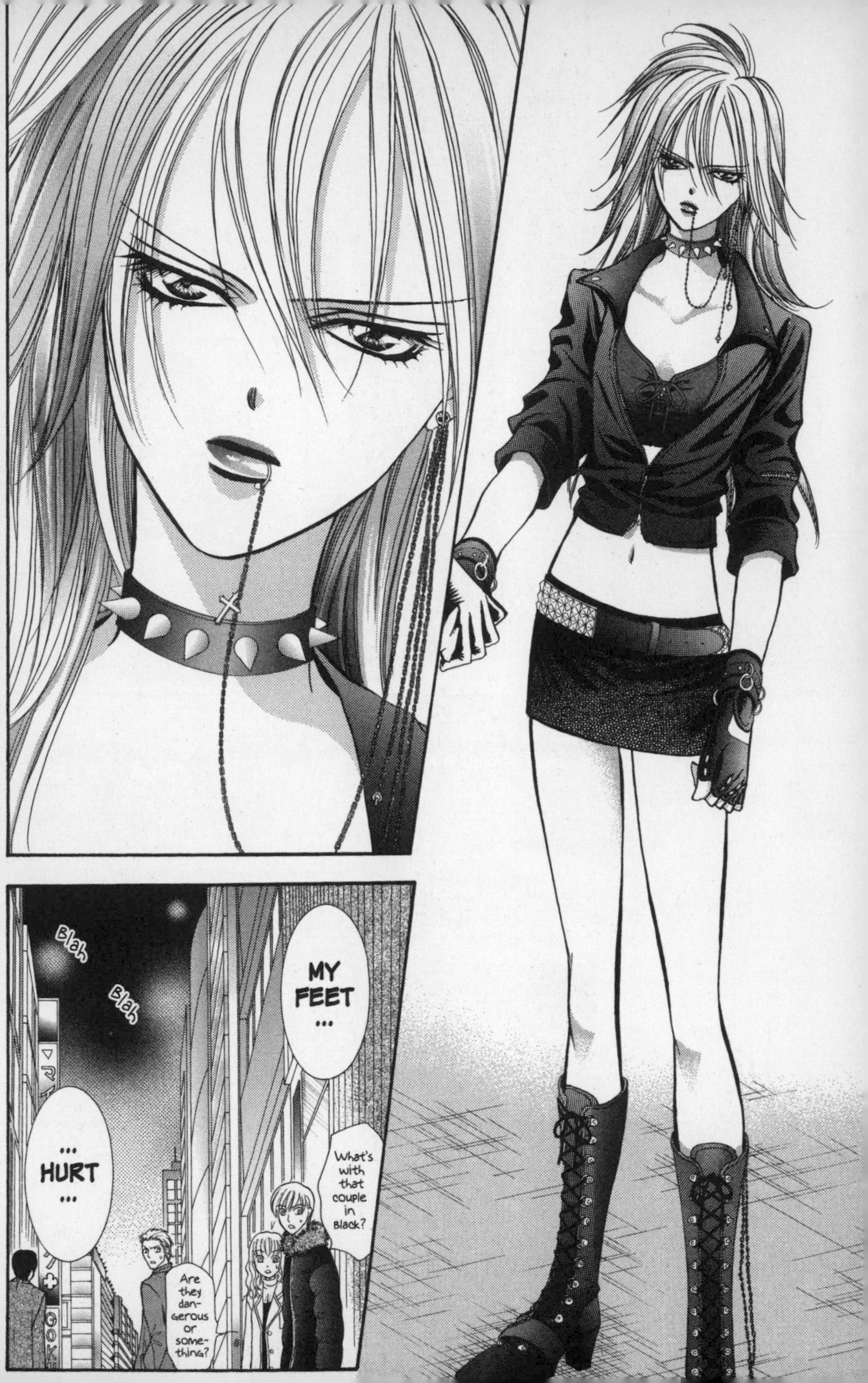
MY FEET ...
... HURT ...
What's with that couple in black?
Are they dangerous or something?
Blah
Blah

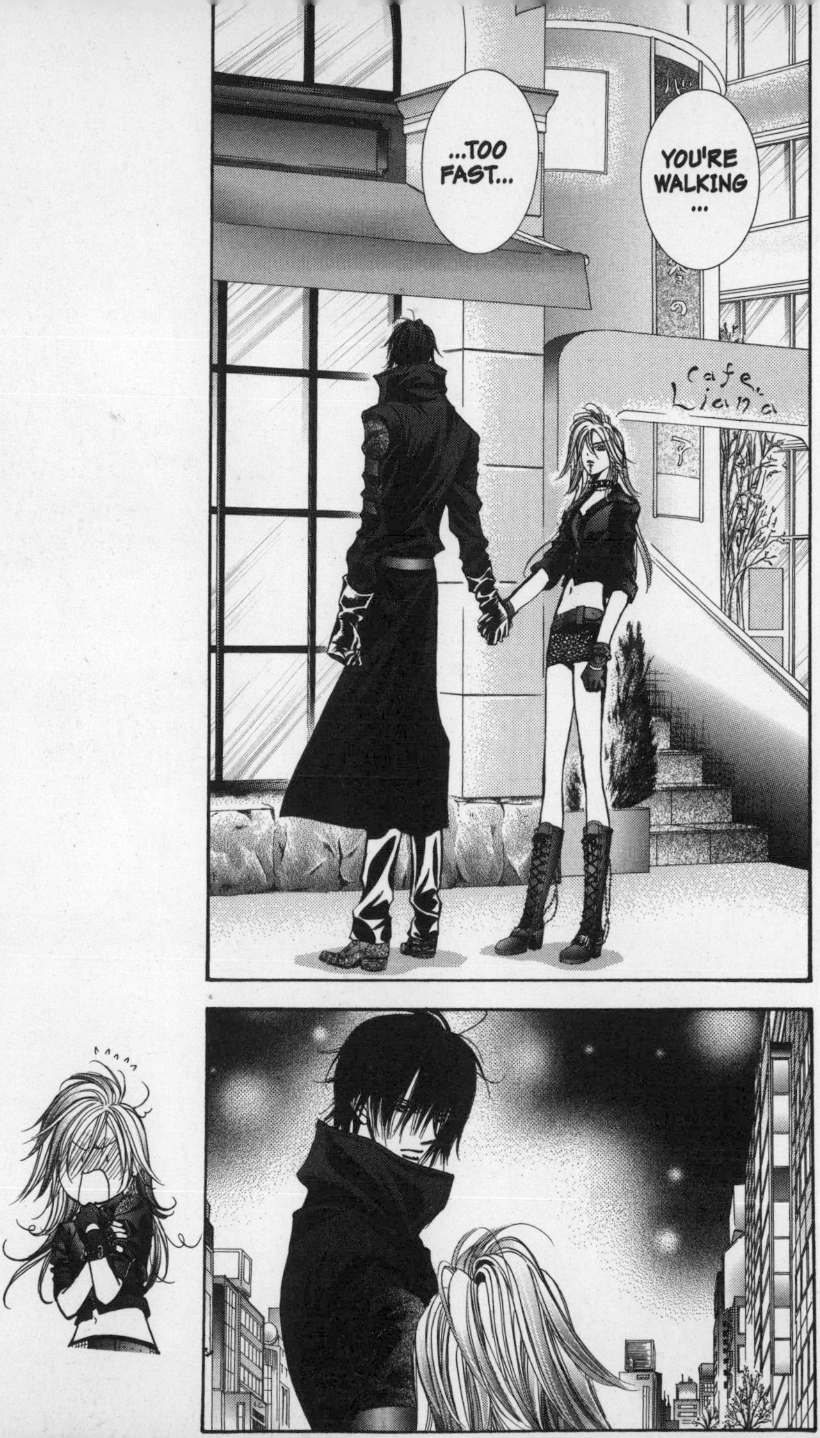
YOU'RE WALKING ...
...TOO FAST...
Cafe Liana

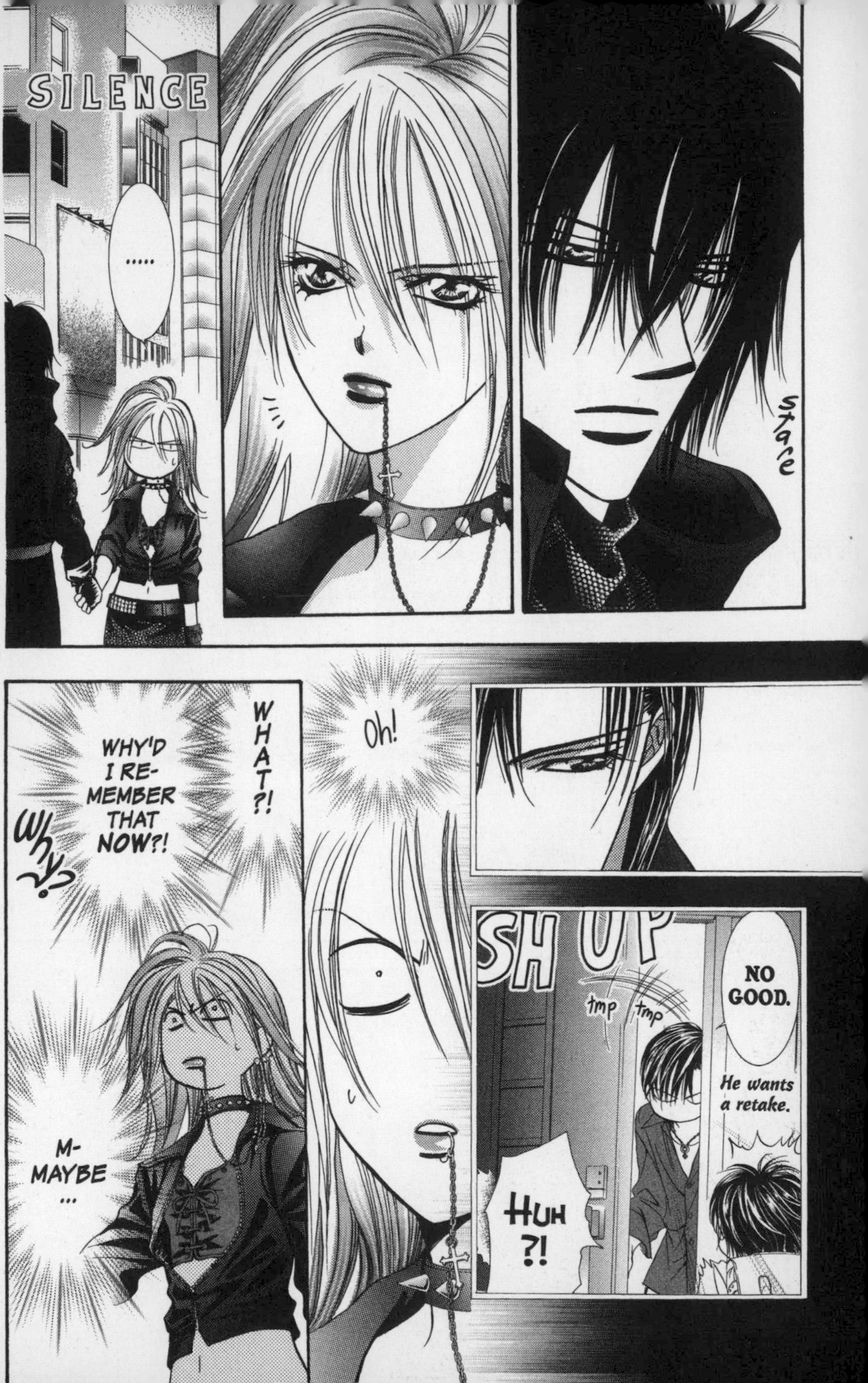
stare
SILENCE
.....
Oh!
SHUP
tmp tmp
NO GOOD.
He wants a retake.
HUH ?!
WHAT?!
WHY'D I RE-MEMBER THAT NOW?!
Why?
M-MAYBE ...

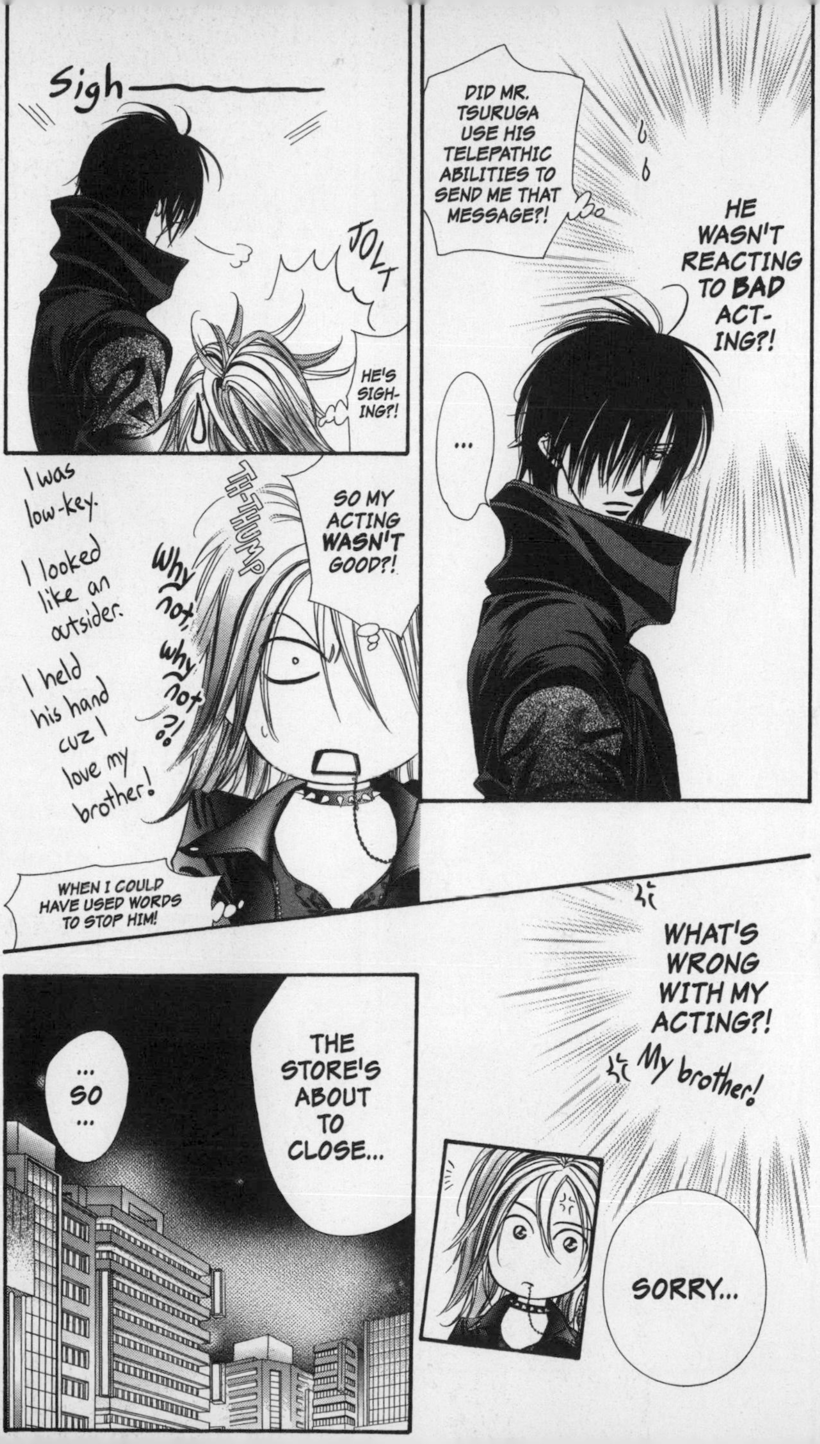

DID MR. TSURUGA USE HIS TELEPATHIC ABILITIES TO SEND ME THAT MESSAGE?!
HE WASN'T REACTING TO BAD ACTING?!
...
Sigh
JOLT
HE'S SIGHING?!
SO MY ACTING WASN'T GOOD?!
TH-THUMP
Why not, why not?!
I was low-key.
I looked like an outsider.
I held his hand cuz I love my brother!
WHEN I COULD HAVE USED WORDS TO STOP HIM!
WHAT'S WRONG WITH MY ACTING?!
My brother!
SORRY...
THE STORE'S ABOUT TO CLOSE...
... SO ...

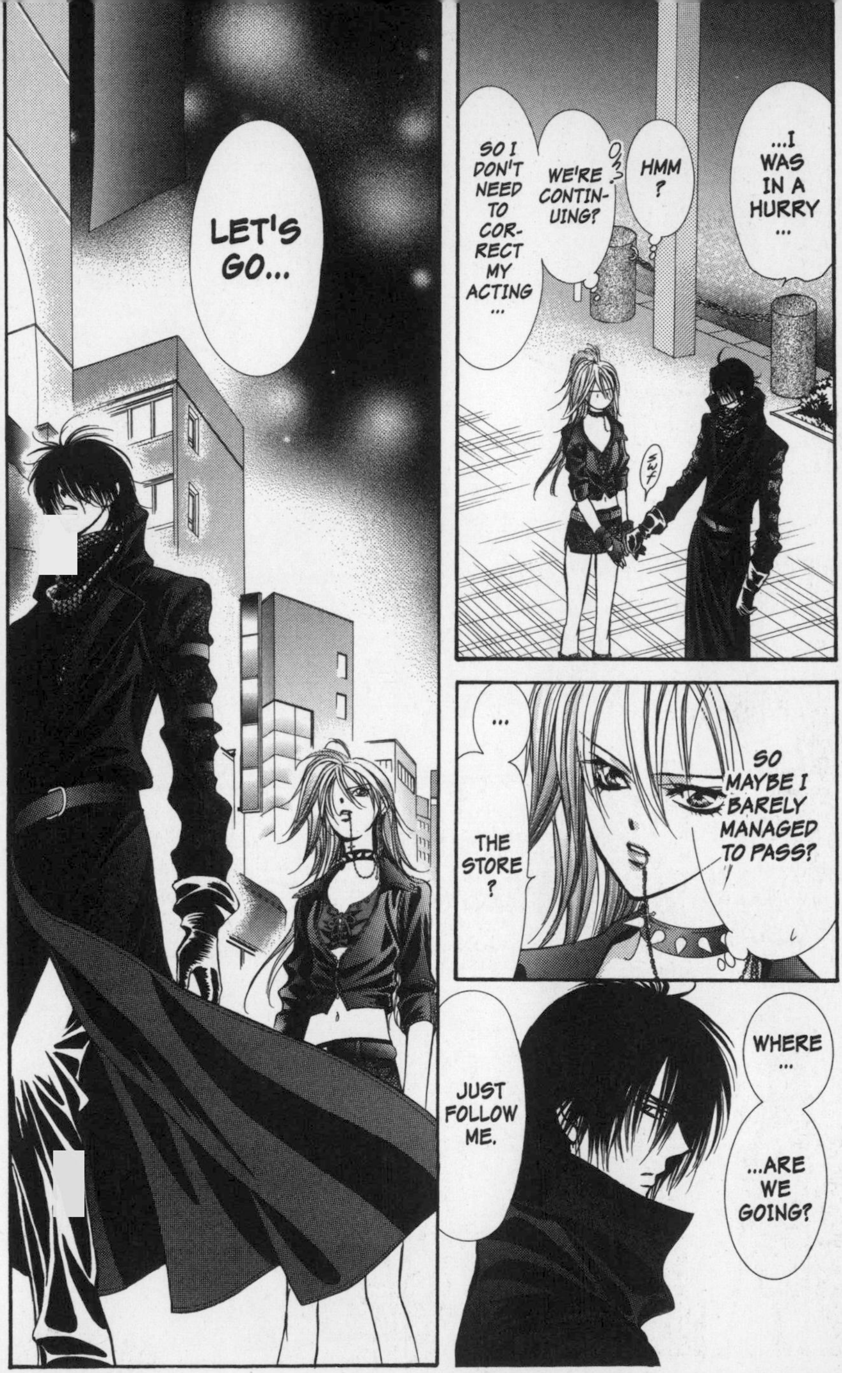
...I WAS IN A HURRY...
HMM?
WE'RE CONTINUING?
SO I DON'T NEED TO COR-RECT MY ACTING...
SO MAYBE I BARELY MANAGED TO PASS?
...
THE STORE?
WHERE...
...ARE WE GOING?
JUST FOLLOW ME.
LET'S GO...

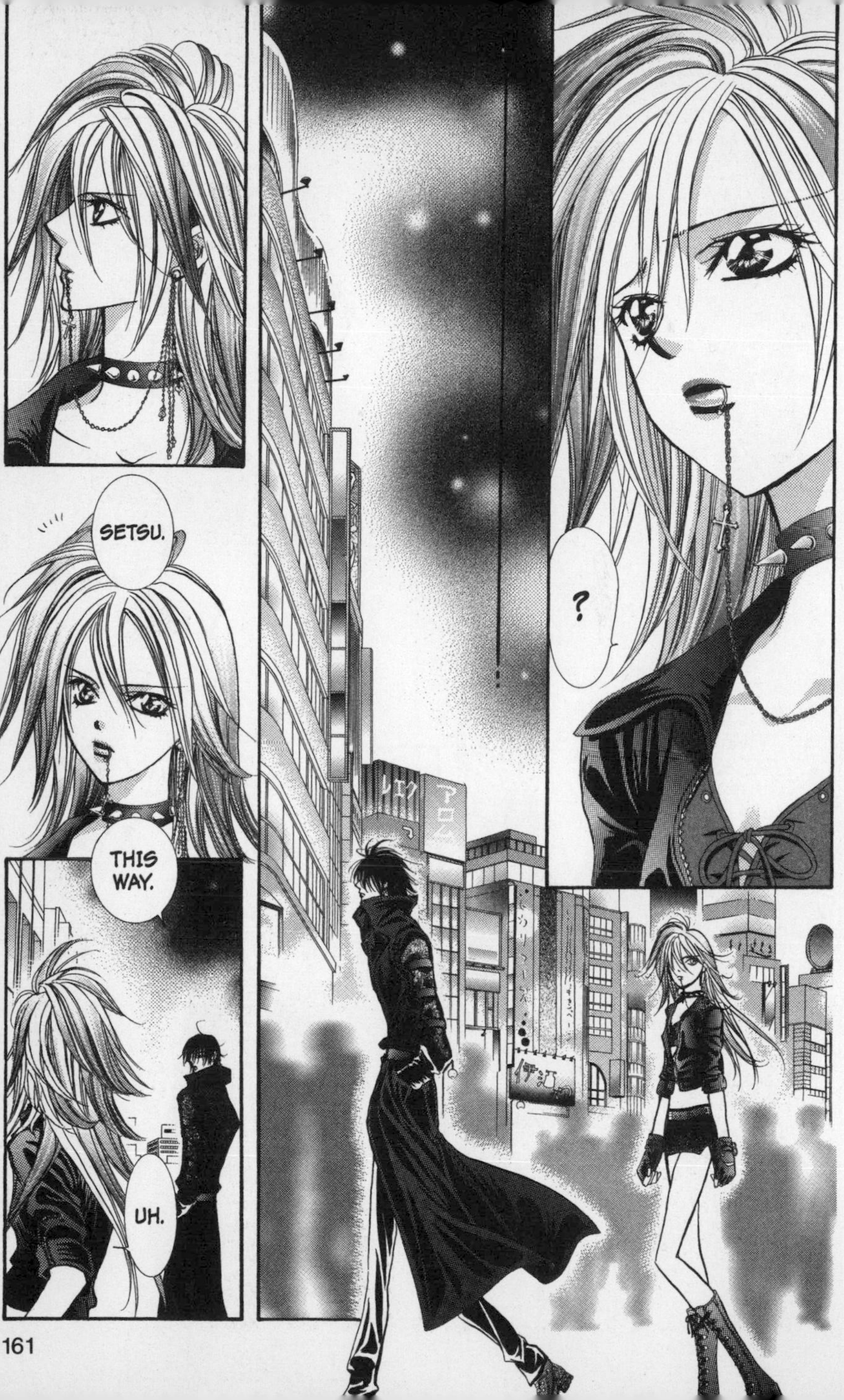
?
SETSU.
THIS WAY.
UH.

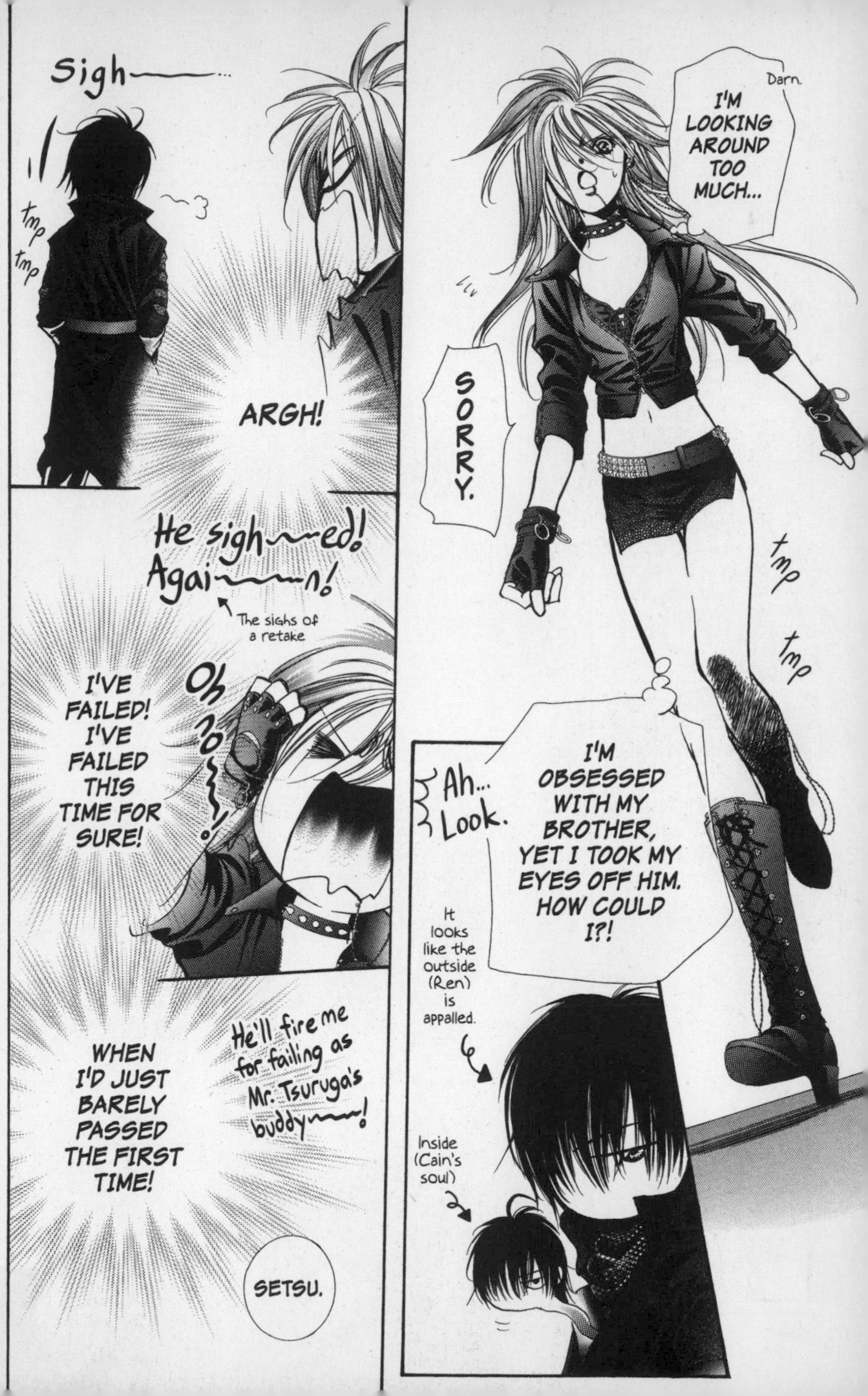
Darn.
I'M LOOKING AROUND TOO MUCH...
SORRY.
tmp
tmp
I'M OBSESSED WITH MY BROTHER, YET I TOOK MY EYES OFF HIM. HOW COULD I?!
Ah... Look.
It looks like the outside (Ren) is appalled.
Inside (Cain's soul)
ARGH!
Sigh~...
tmp
tmp
He sigh~ed! Agai~n!
The sighs of a retake
Oh no~!
I'VE FAILED! I'VE FAILED THIS TIME FOR SURE!
He'll fire me for failing as Mr. Tsuruga's buddy~!
WHEN I'D JUST BARELY PASSED THE FIRST TIME!
SETSU.

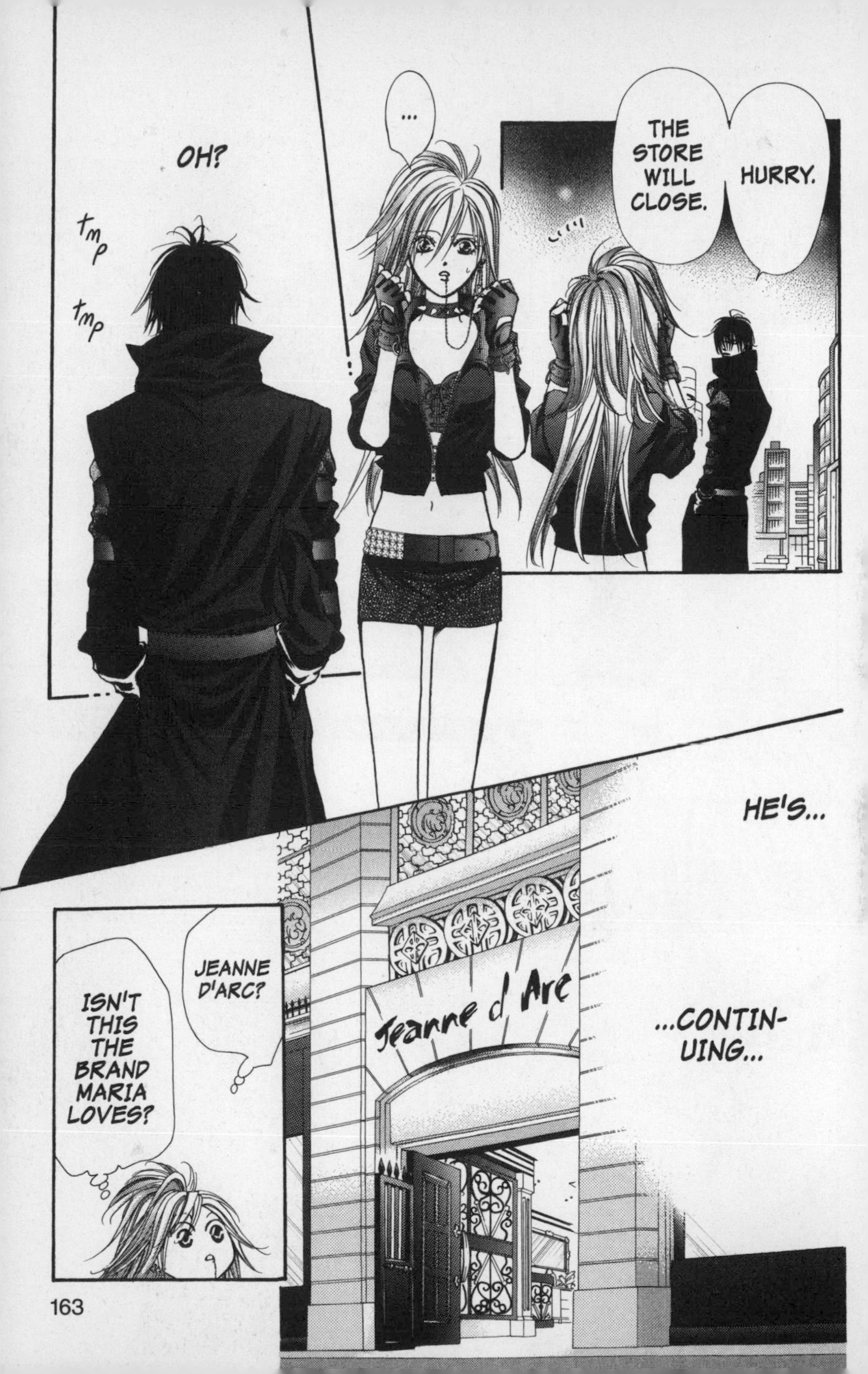
HURRY.
THE STORE WILL CLOSE.
...
OH?
tmp
tmp
HE'S...
...CONTIN-UING...
Jeanne d' Arc
JEANNE D'ARC?
ISN'T THIS THE BRAND MARIA LOVES?

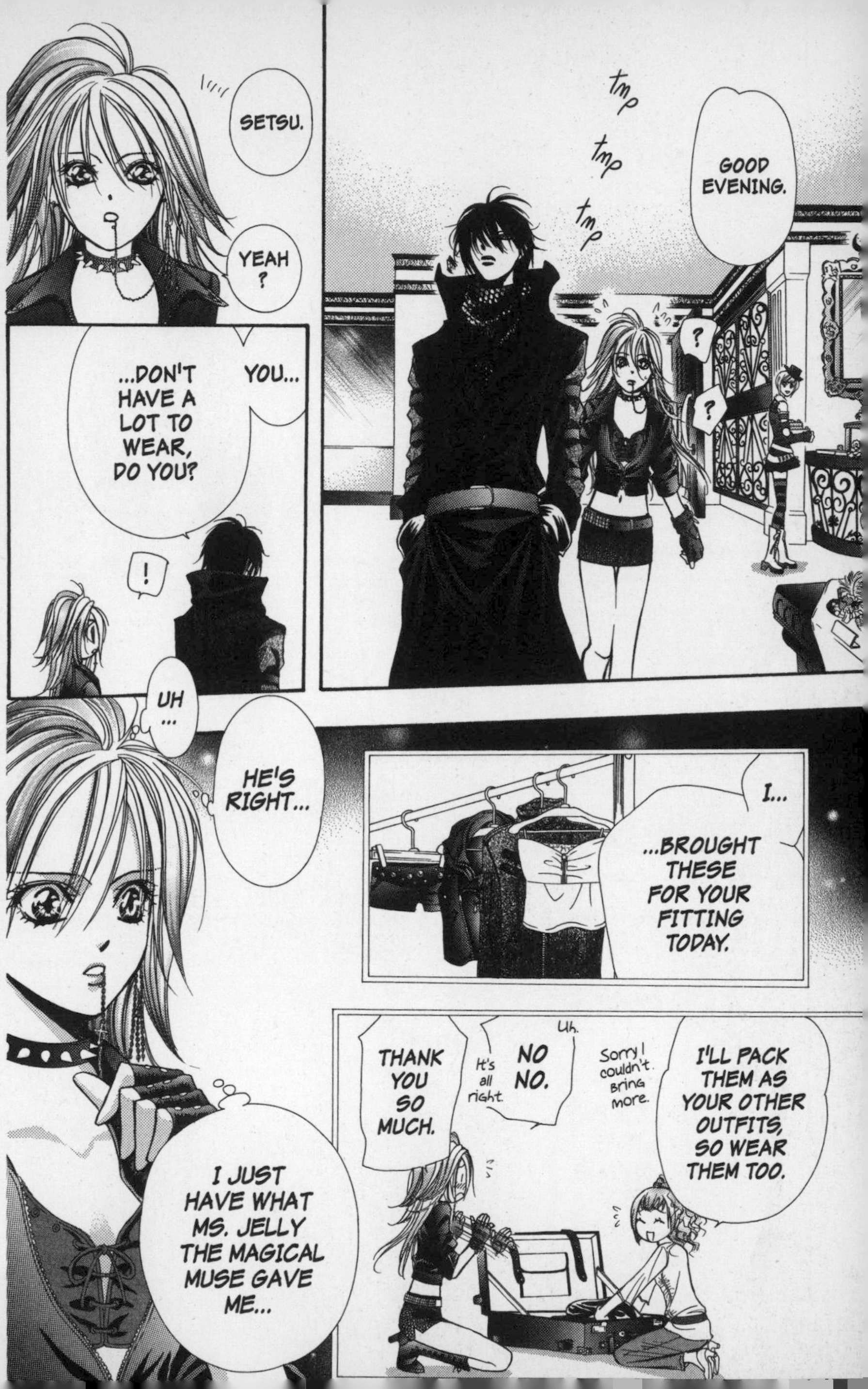
tmp
tmp
tmp
GOOD EVENING.
?
?
SETSU.
YEAH?
YOU...
...DON'T HAVE A LOT TO WEAR, DO YOU?
!
I...
...BROUGHT THESE FOR YOUR FITTING TODAY.
I'LL PACK THEM AS YOUR OTHER OUTFITS, SO WEAR THEM TOO.
Sorry I couldn't bring more.
Uh.
NO NO.
It's all right.
THANK YOU SO MUCH.
UH...
HE'S RIGHT...
I JUST HAVE WHAT MS. JELLY THE MAGICAL MUSE GAVE ME...

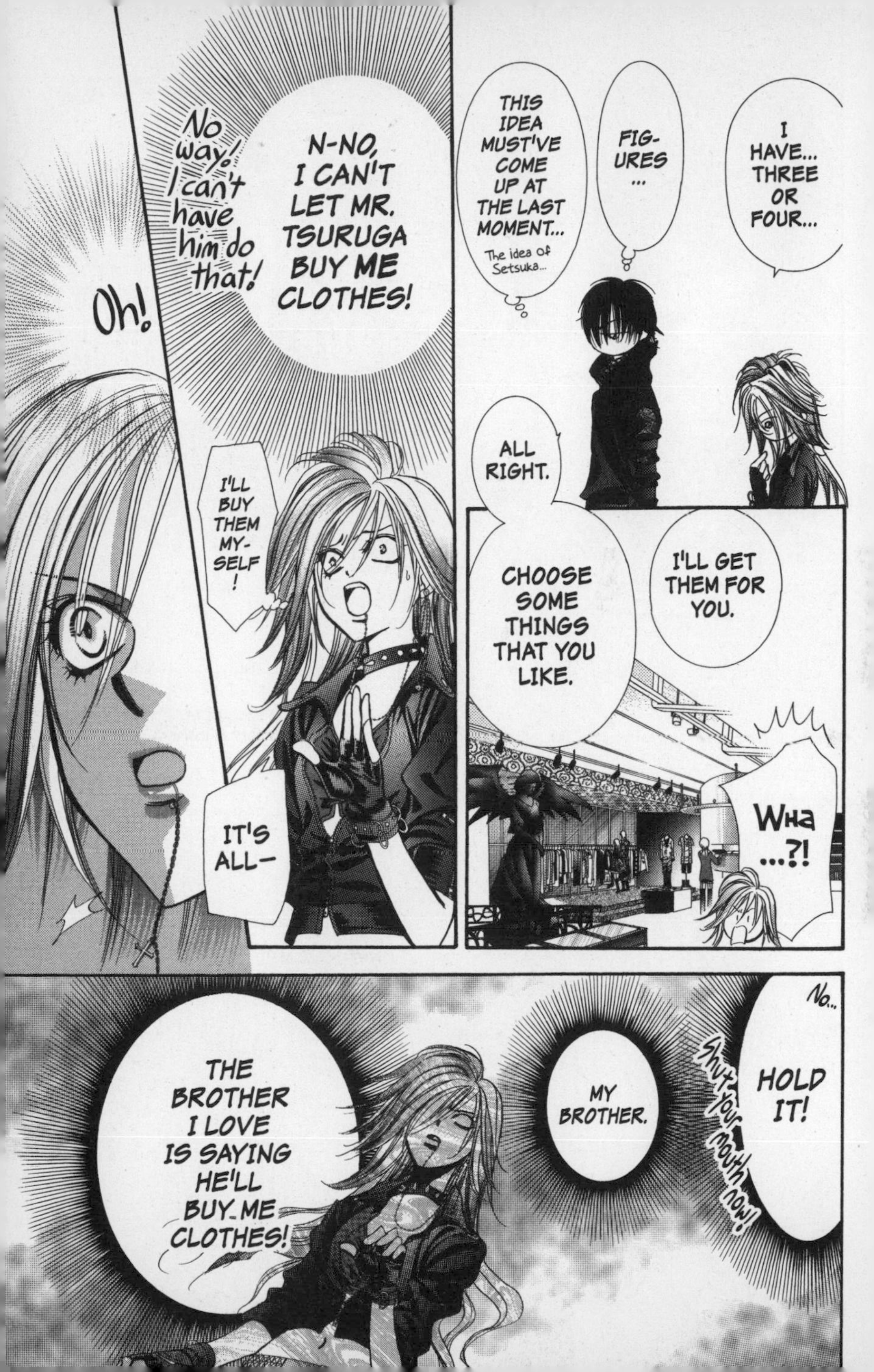
I HAVE... THREE OR FOUR...
FIG-URES ...
THIS IDEA MUST'VE COME UP AT THE LAST MOMENT...
The idea of Setsuka...
ALL RIGHT.
I'LL GET THEM FOR YOU.
CHOOSE SOME THINGS THAT YOU LIKE.
WHA ...?!
N-NO, I CAN'T LET MR. TSURUGA BUY ME CLOTHES!
No way! I can't have him do that!
Oh!
I'LL BUY THEM MY-SELF!
IT'S ALL—
HOLD IT!
No...
Shut your mouth now!
MY BROTHER.
THE BROTHER I LOVE IS SAYING HE'LL BUY ME CLOTHES!

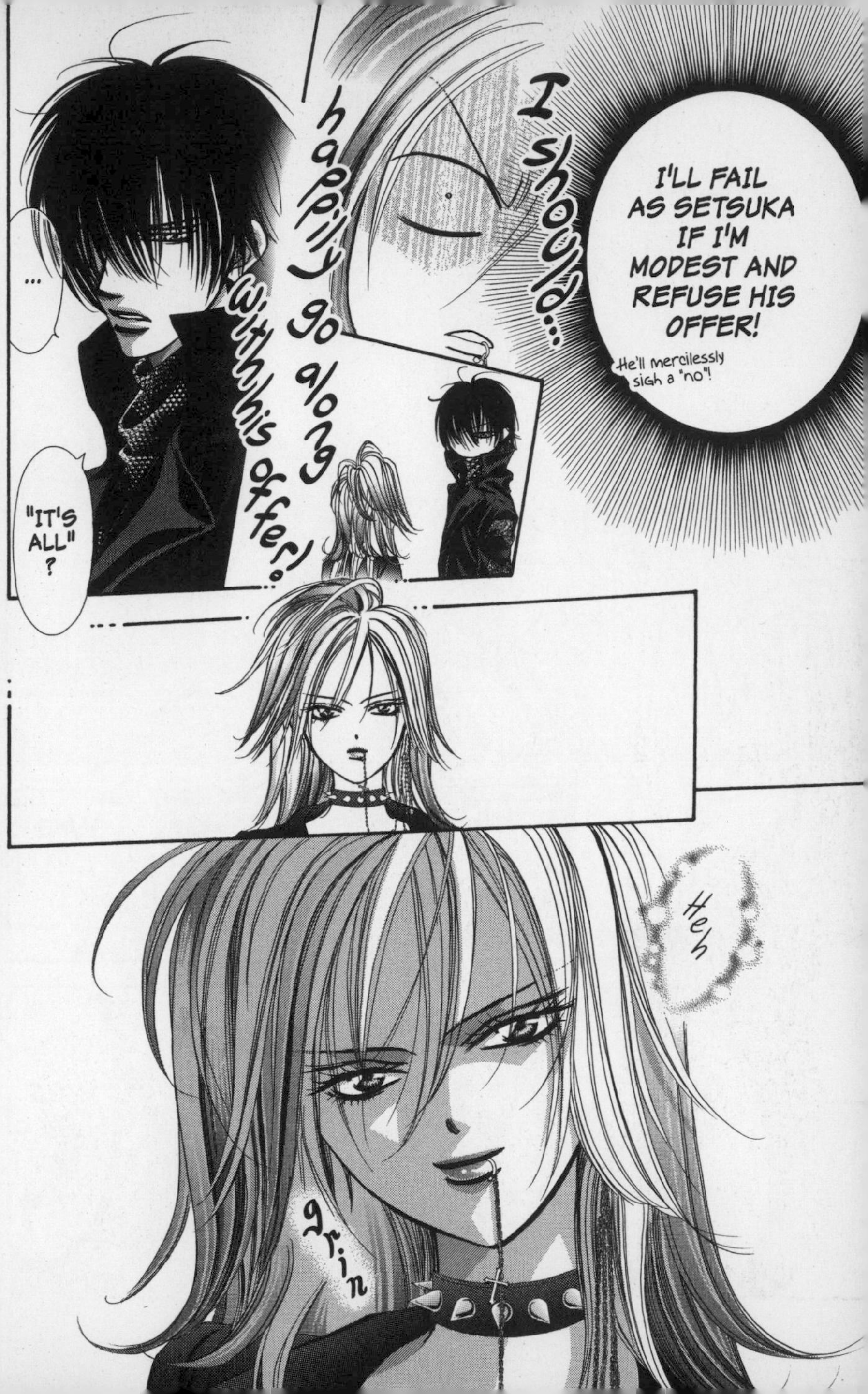

I'LL FAIL AS SETSUKA IF I'M MODEST AND REFUSE HIS OFFER!
He'll mercilessly sigh a "no"!
I should... happily go along with his offer!
...
"IT'S ALL"?
Heh
grin

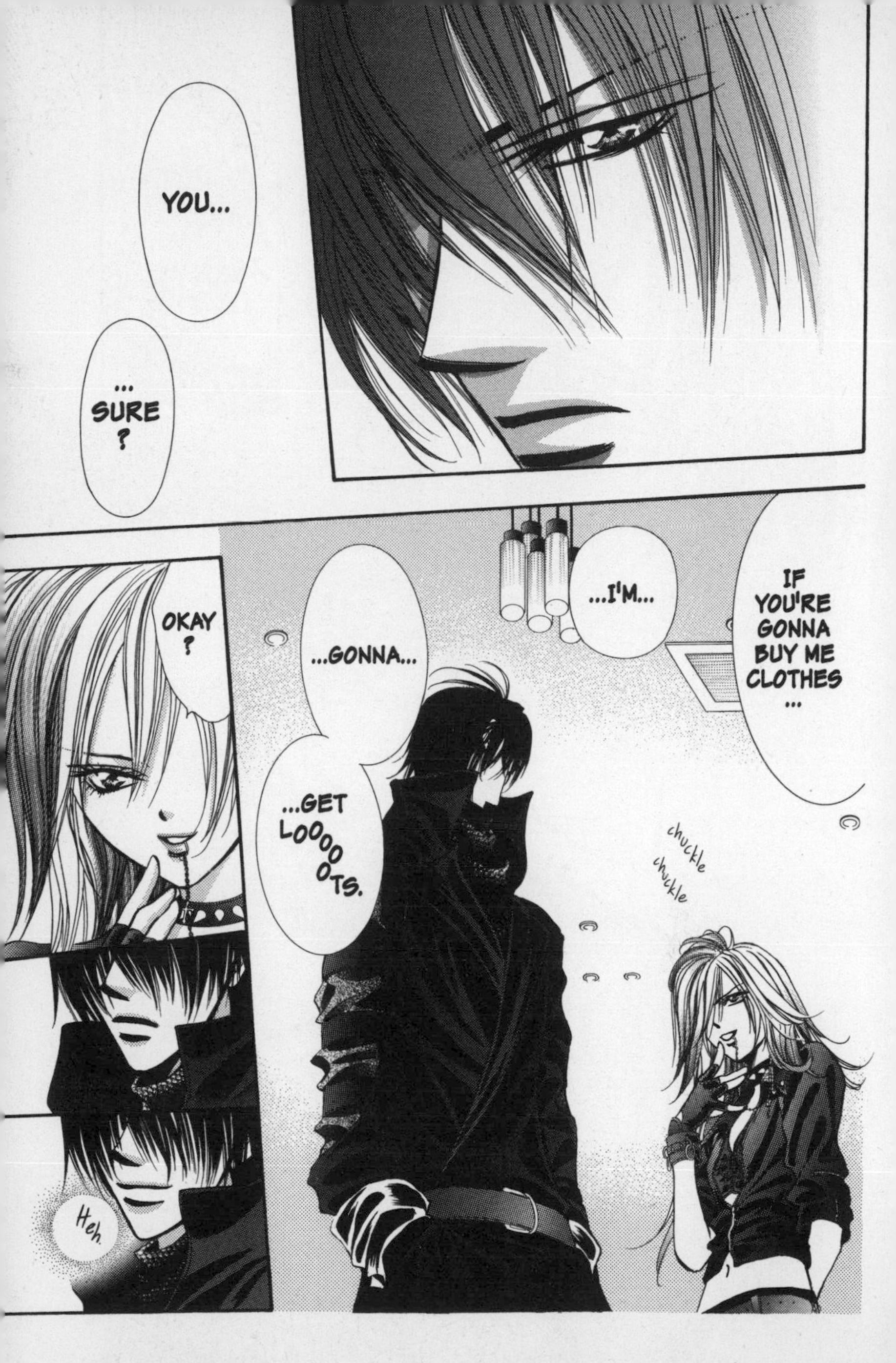
YOU...
...SURE?
IF YOU'RE GONNA BUY ME CLOTHES...
...I'M...
...GONNA...
...GET LOOOOOOTS.
chuckle chuckle
OKAY?
Heh.

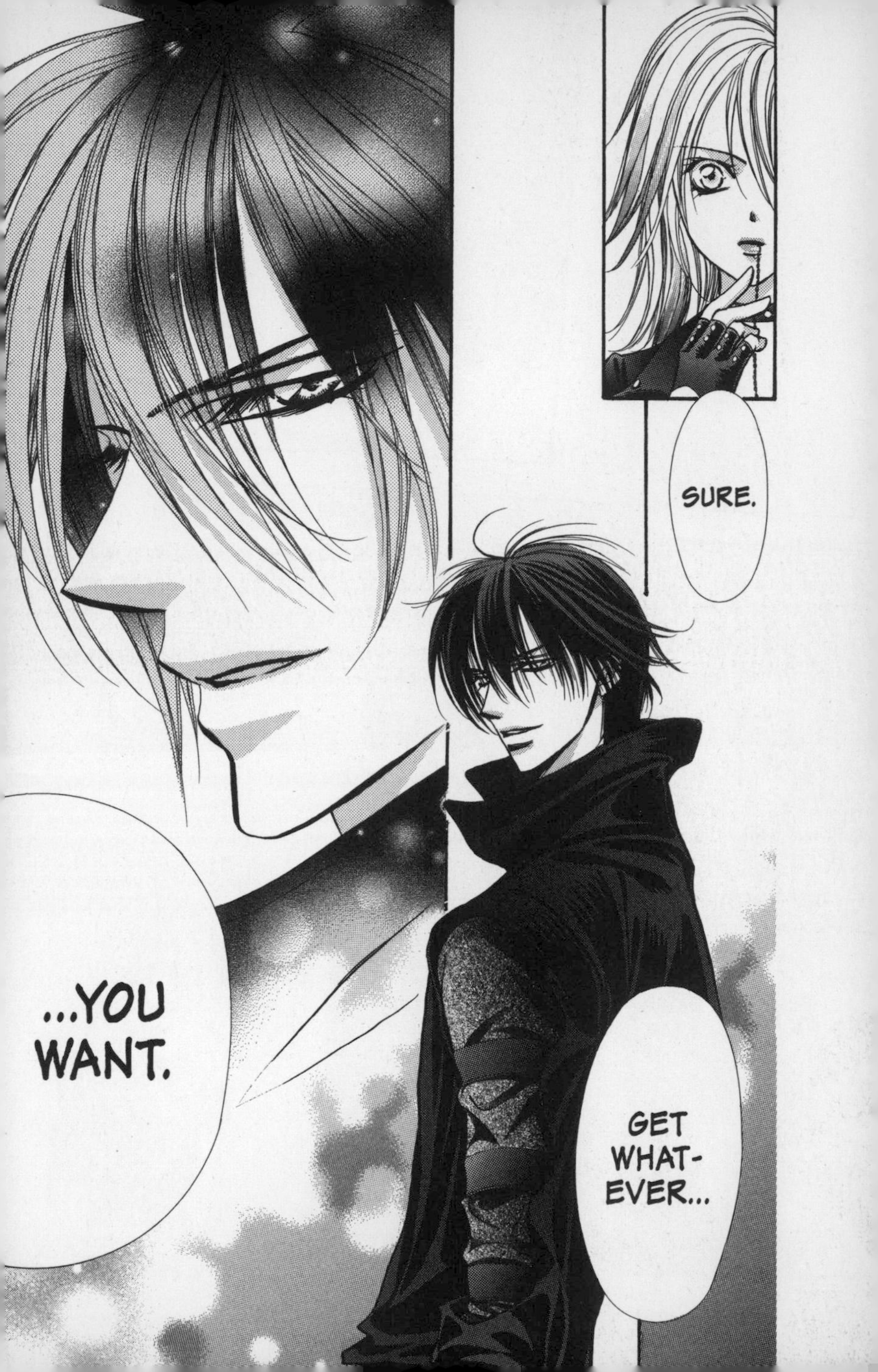
SURE.
GET WHAT-EVER...
...YOU WANT.

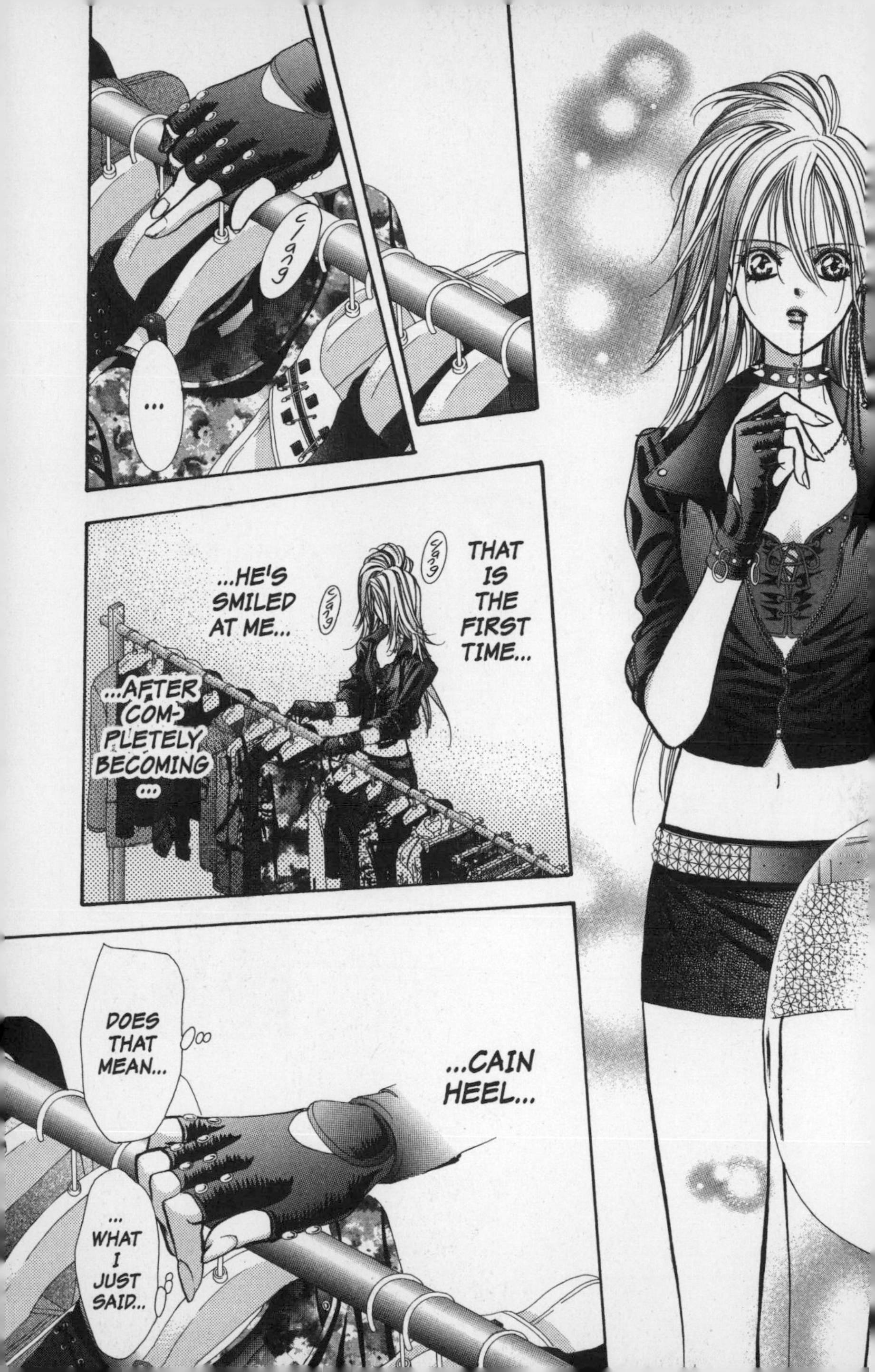
clang
...
THAT IS THE FIRST TIME...
clang
clang
...HE'S SMILED AT ME...
...AFTER COM-PLETELY BECOMING...
...CAIN HEEL...
DOES THAT MEAN...
...WHAT I JUST SAID...

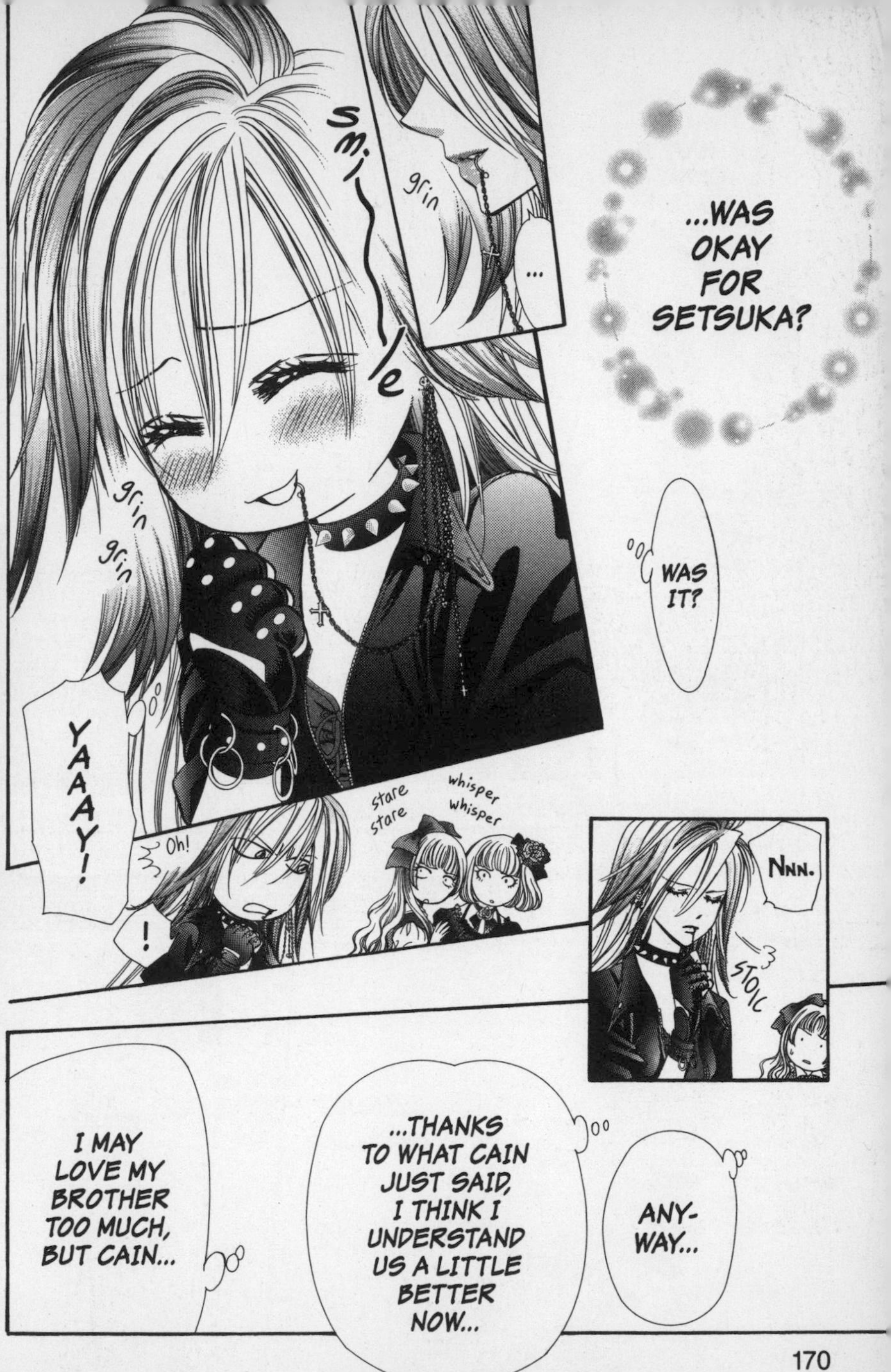
...WAS OKAY FOR SETSUKA?
WAS IT?
grin
...
smi~le
grin
grin
YAAAY!
NNN.
STOIC
Oh!
!
stare stare
whisper whisper
ANY-WAY...
...THANKS TO WHAT CAIN JUST SAID, I THINK I UNDERSTAND US A LITTLE BETTER NOW...
I MAY LOVE MY BROTHER TOO MUCH, BUT CAIN...

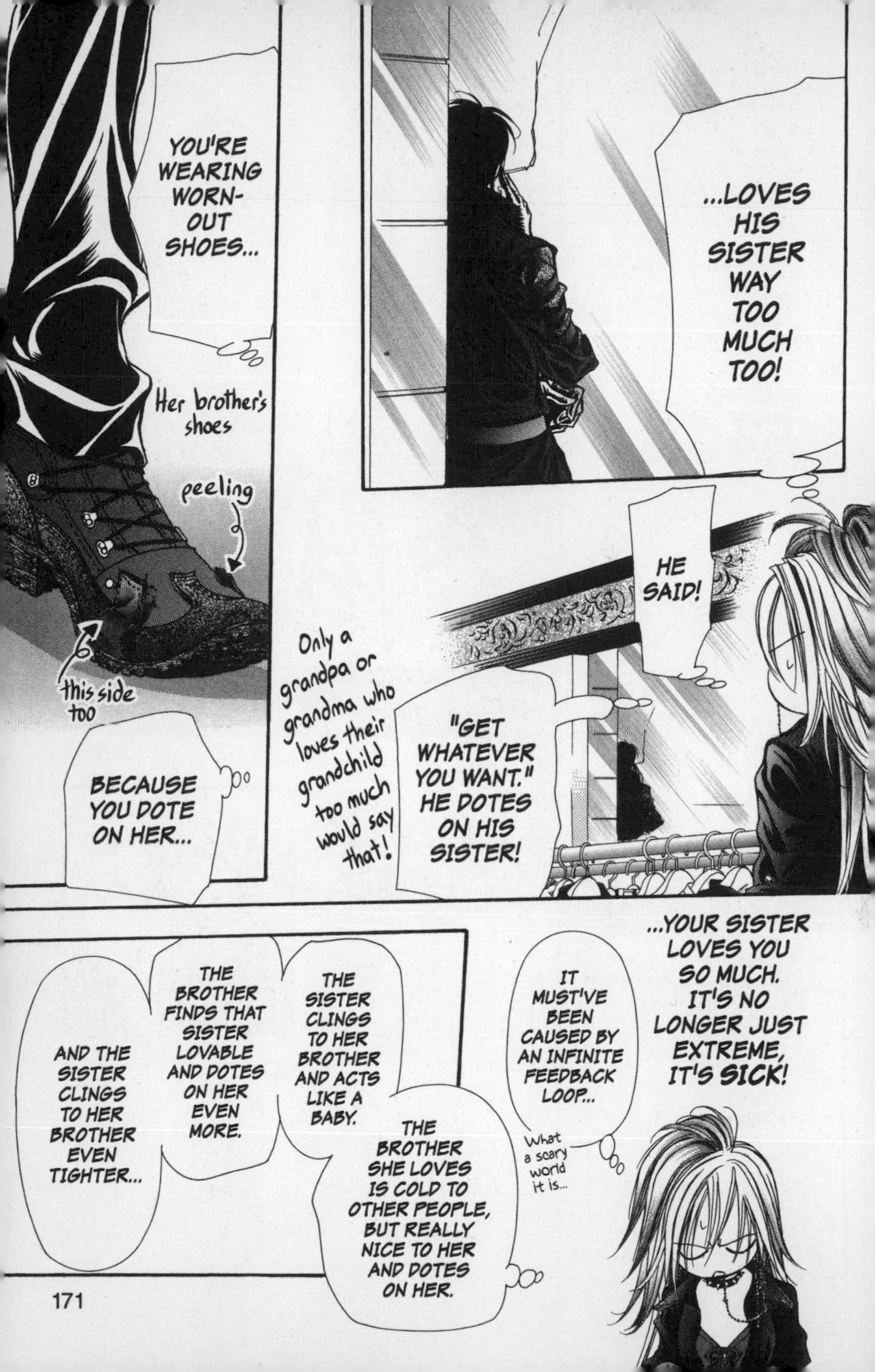

...LOVES HIS SISTER WAY TOO MUCH TOO!
HE SAID!
"GET WHATEVER YOU WANT." HE DOTES ON HIS SISTER!
Only a grandpa or grandma who loves their grandchild too much would say that!
YOU'RE WEARING WORN-OUT SHOES...
Her brother's shoes
peeling
this side too
BECAUSE YOU DOTE ON HER...
...YOUR SISTER LOVES YOU SO MUCH. IT'S NO LONGER JUST EXTREME, IT'S SICK!
IT MUST'VE BEEN CAUSED BY AN INFINITE FEEDBACK LOOP...
What a scary world it is...
THE BROTHER SHE LOVES IS COLD TO OTHER PEOPLE, BUT REALLY NICE TO HER AND DOTES ON HER.
THE SISTER CLINGS TO HER BROTHER AND ACTS LIKE A BABY.
THE BROTHER FINDS THAT SISTER LOVABLE AND DOTES ON HER EVEN MORE.
AND THE SISTER CLINGS TO HER BROTHER EVEN TIGHTER...

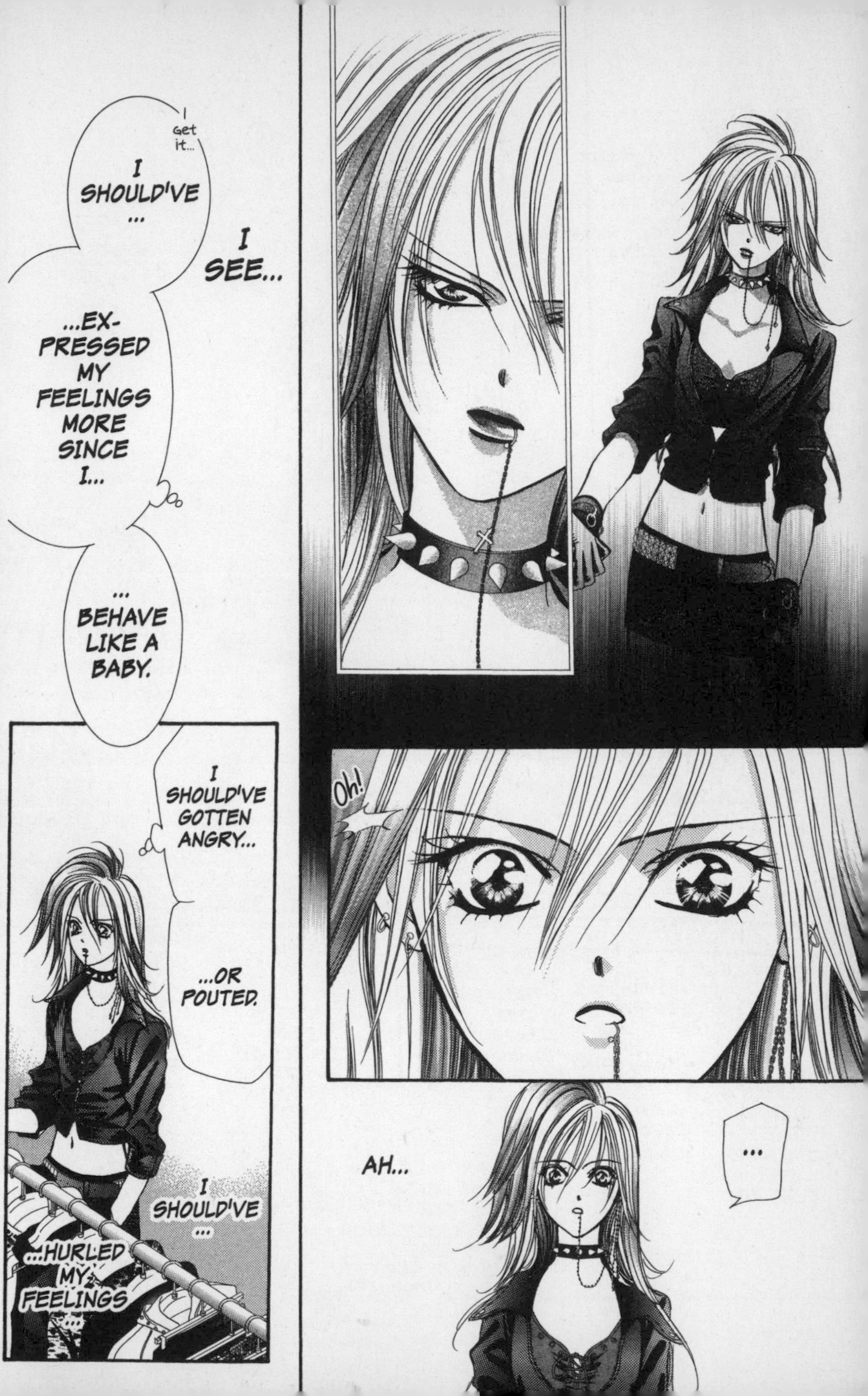
Oh!
AH...
...
I get it...
I SHOULD'VE ...
I SEE...
...EX-PRESSED MY FEELINGS MORE SINCE I...
... BEHAVE LIKE A BABY.
I SHOULD'VE GOTTEN ANGRY...
...OR POUTED.
I SHOULD'VE ...
...HURLED MY FEELINGS ...

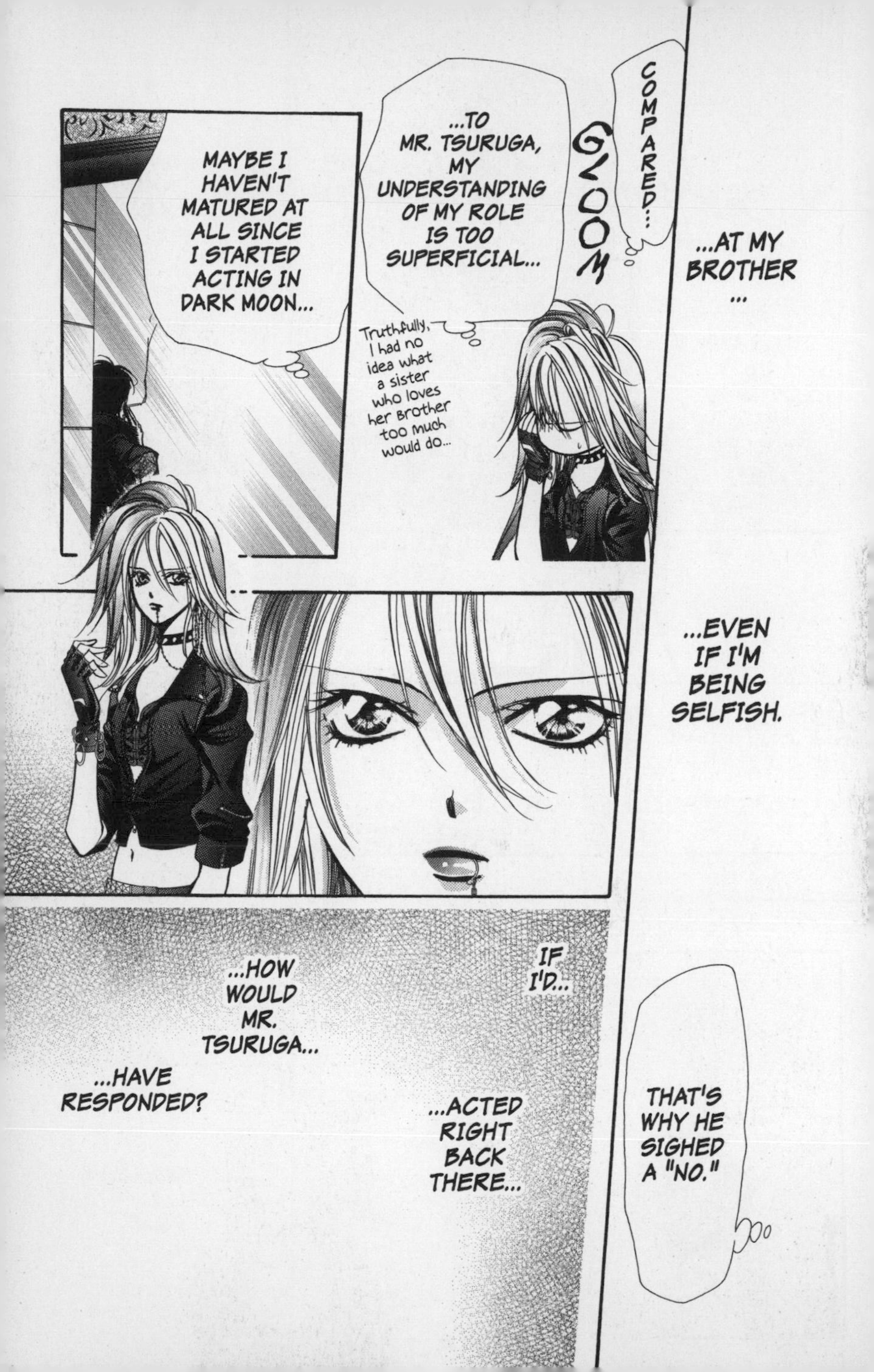
...AT MY BROTHER ...
COMPARED...
GLOOM
...TO MR. TSURUGA, MY UNDERSTANDING OF MY ROLE IS TOO SUPERFICIAL...
Truthfully, I had no idea what a sister who loves her brother too much would do...
MAYBE I HAVEN'T MATURED AT ALL SINCE I STARTED ACTING IN DARK MOON...
...EVEN IF I'M BEING SELFISH.
THAT'S WHY HE SIGHED A "NO."
IF I'D...
...ACTED RIGHT BACK THERE...
...HOW WOULD MR. TSURUGA...
...HAVE RESPONDED?

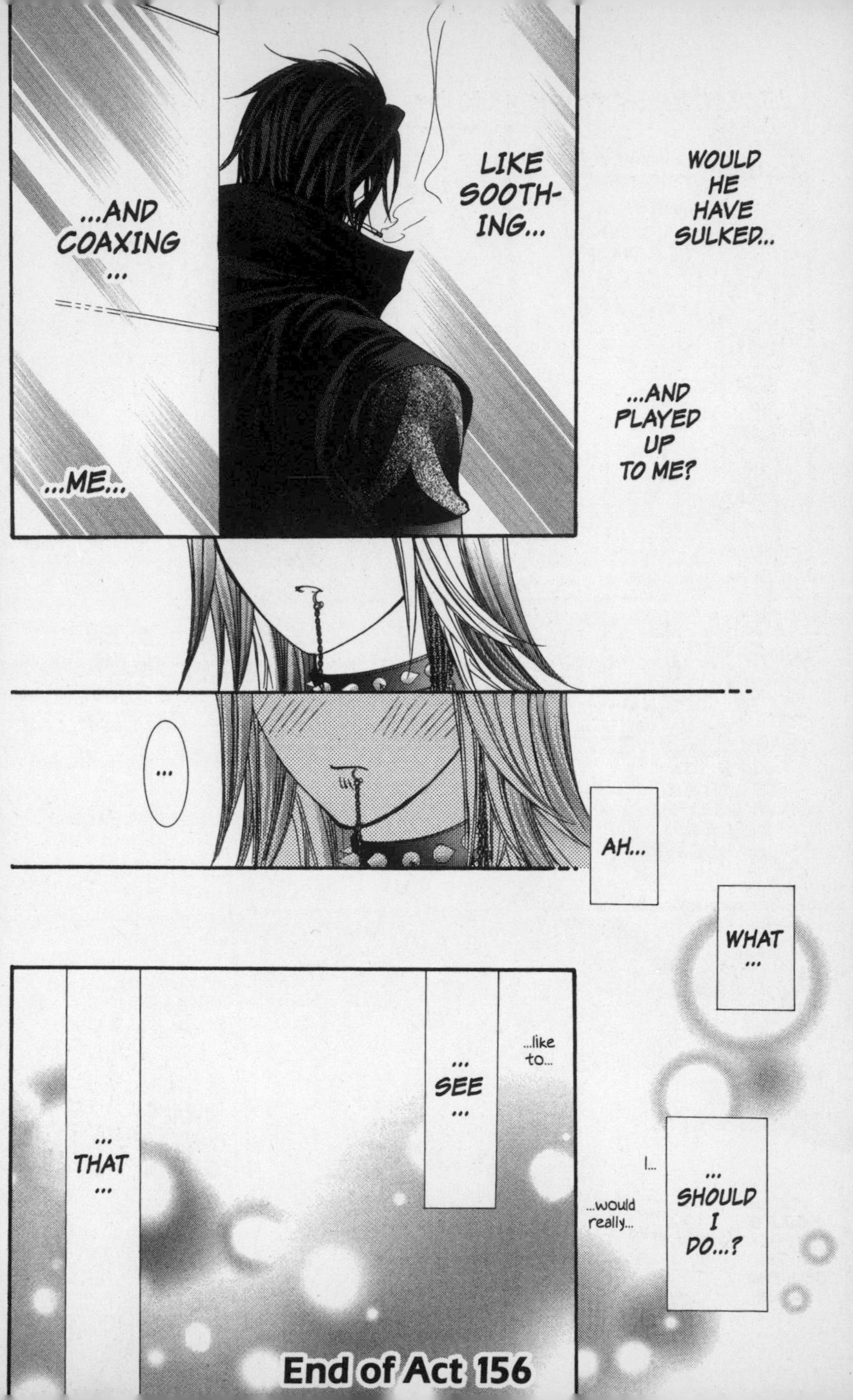
WOULD HE HAVE SULKED...
...AND PLAYED UP TO ME?
LIKE SOOTH-ING...
...AND COAXING ...
...ME...
AH...
...
WHAT ...
... SHOULD I DO...?
I...
...would really...
...like to...
... SEE ...
... THAT ...

End of Act 156

A Mysterious Valentine's Incident Part 2 *The Kyoko Mogami chapter*

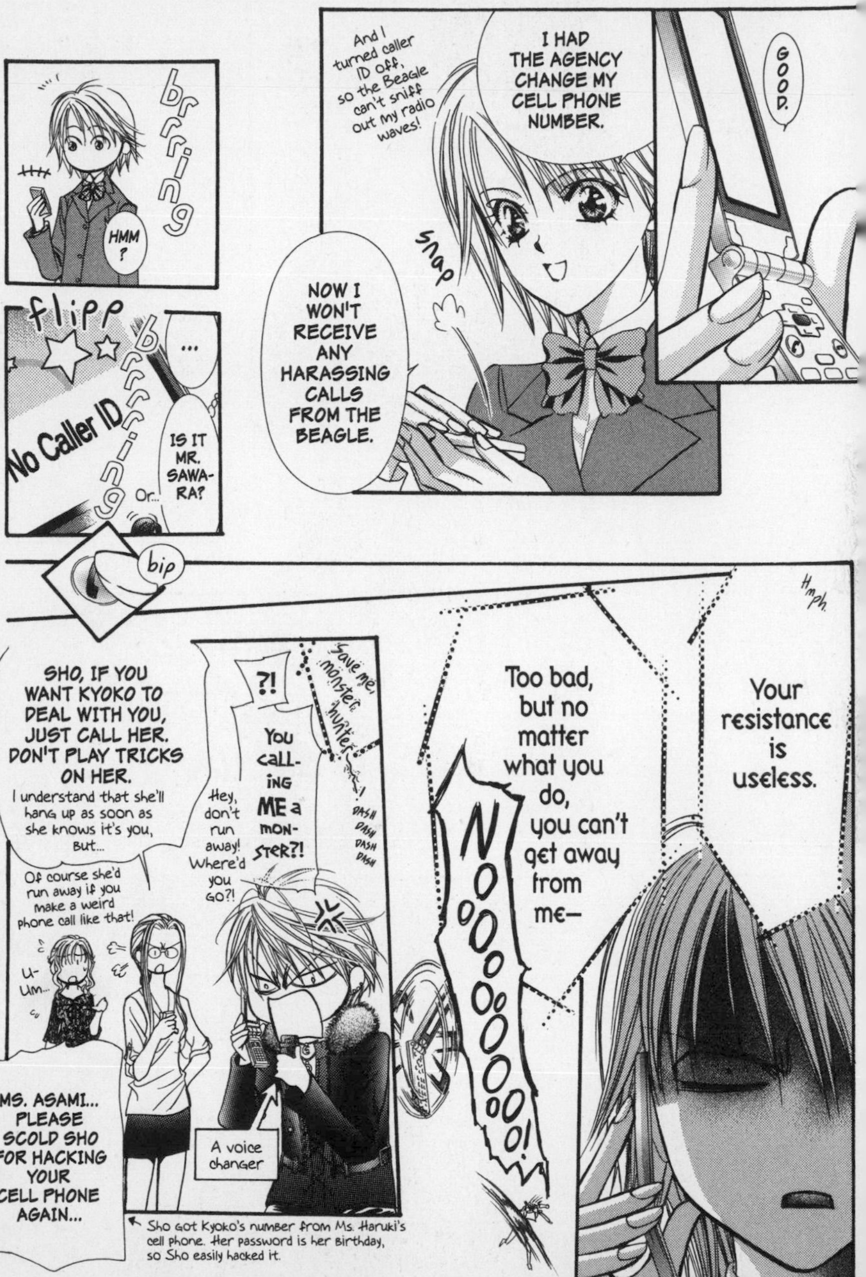
GOOD.
I HAD THE AGENCY CHANGE MY CELL PHONE NUMBER.
And I turned caller ID off, so the Beagle can't sniff out my radio waves!
snap
NOW I WON'T RECEIVE ANY HARASSING CALLS FROM THE BEAGLE.
brrring
HMM?
flipp
brrrring
No Caller ID
...
IS IT MR. SAWARA?
Or...
bip
Hmph.
Your resistance is useless.
Too bad, but no matter what you do, you can't get away from me—
NOOOOOOOOOOOOO!
Save me, monster hunter!
?!
You call-ing ME a mon-ster?!
DASH DASH DASH DASH
Hey, don't run away! Where'd you go?!
SHO, IF YOU WANT KYOKO TO DEAL WITH YOU, JUST CALL HER. DON'T PLAY TRICKS ON HER.
I understand that she'll hang up as soon as she knows it's you, but...
Of course she'd run away if you make a weird phone call like that!
U-Um...
A voice changer
MS. ASAMI... PLEASE SCOLD SHO FOR HACKING YOUR CELL PHONE AGAIN...
Sho got Kyoko's number from Ms. Haruki's cell phone. Her password is her birthday, so Sho easily hacked it.

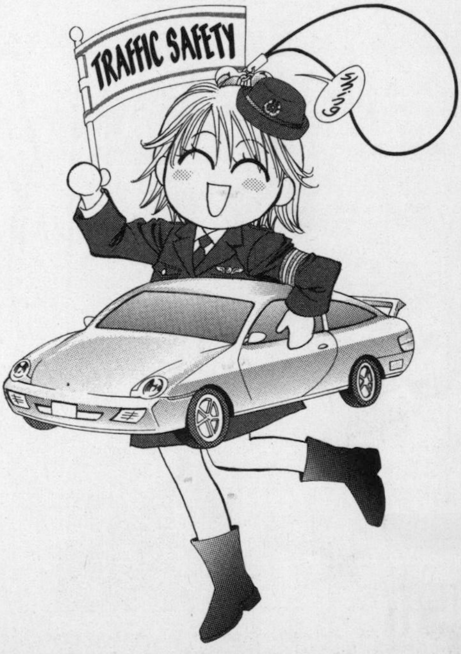
TRAFFIC SAFETY
Shing

Skip-Beat! End Notes

Everyone knows how to be a fan, but sometimes cool things from other cultures need a little help crossing the language barrier.

Page 21, panel 1: Natsuko, likes people
A pun on its name. *Hitonatsukkoi* means "likes people."

Page 46, panel 4: Hachi statue
This statue commemorates a dog that waited every day at the station for its master to get home, even after the master passed away. It is a popular place to meet.

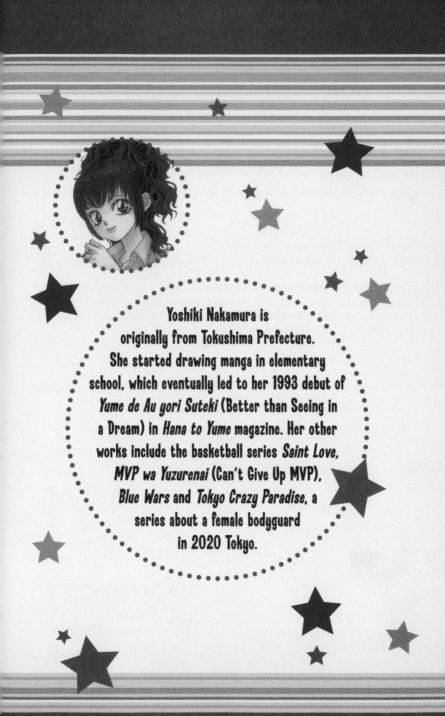

Yoshiki Nakamura is
originally from Tokushima Prefecture.
She started drawing manga in elementary
school, which eventually led to her 1993 debut of
Yume de Au yori Suteki (Better than Seeing in
a Dream) in *Hana to Yume* magazine. Her other
works include the basketball series *Saint Love,
MVP wa Yuzurenai* (Can't Give Up MVP),
Blue Wars and *Tokyo Crazy Paradise*, a
series about a female bodyguard
in 2020 Tokyo.

SKIP・BEAT!
Vol. 26
Shojo Beat Edition

STORY AND ART BY YOSHIKI NAKAMURA

English Translation & Adaptation/Tomo Kimura
Touch-up Art & Lettering/Sabrina Heep
Design/Ronnie Casson
Editor/Pancha Diaz

Skip-Beat! by Yoshiki Nakamura © Yoshiki Nakamura 2010.
All rights reserved. First published in Japan in 2010 by HAKUSENSHA, Inc., Tokyo.
English language translation rights arranged with HAKUSENSHA, Inc., Tokyo.

The stories, characters and incidents mentioned in this publication are entirely fictional.

Printed in the U.S.A.

Published by VIZ Media, LLC
P.O. Box 77010
San Francisco, CA 94107

10 9 8 7 6 5 4 3 2 1
First printing, January 2012

www.viz.com

www.shojobeat.com

 PARENTAL ADVISORY
SKIP・BEAT! is rated T for Teen and is
recommended for ages 13 and up. This
volume contains a grudge.
ratings.viz.com

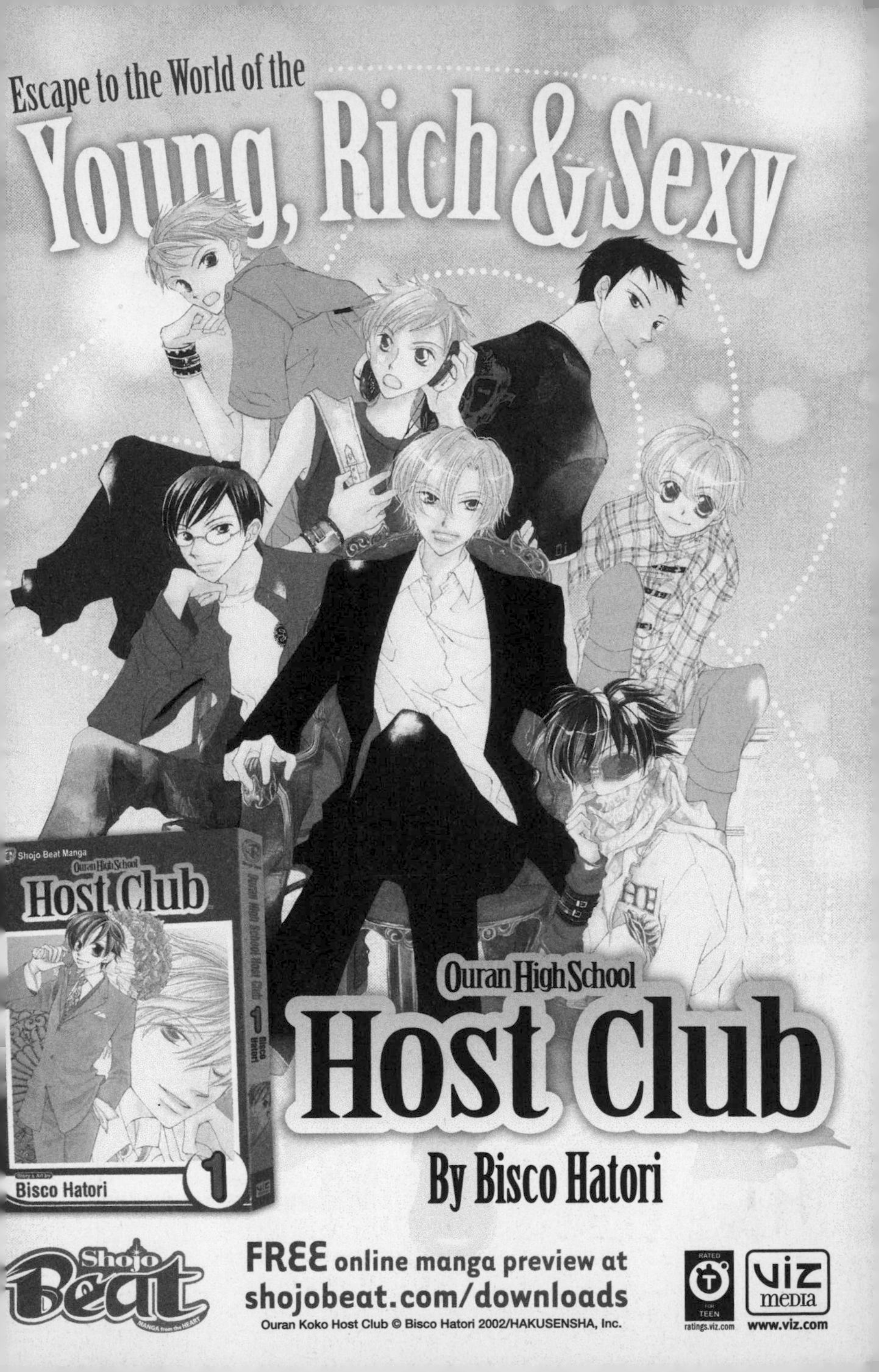
Escape to the World of the
Young, Rich & Sexy
Shojo Beat Manga
Ouran High School
Host Club
Ouran High School Host Club 1 Bisco Hatori
Story & Art by
Bisco Hatori
1
Ouran High School
Host Club
By Bisco Hatori
Shojo Beat
MANGA from the HEART
FREE online manga preview at
shojobeat.com/downloads
Ouran Koko Host Club © Bisco Hatori 2002/HAKUSENSHA, Inc.
RATED T FOR TEEN
ratings.viz.com
VIZ media
www.viz.com

Don't Hide What's *Inside*

OTOMEN

by AYA KANNO

Despite his tough jock exterior, Asuka Masamune harbors a secret love for sewing, shojo manga, and all things girly. But when he finds himself drawn to his domestically inept classmate Ryo, his carefully crafted persona is put to the test. Can Asuka ever show his true self to anyone, much less to the girl he's falling for?

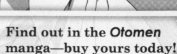

Find out in the *Otomen* manga—buy yours today!

On sale at www.shojobeat.com
Also available at your local bookstore and comic store.

OTOMEN © Aya Kanno 2006/HAKUSENSHA, Inc.